*Civilizations, Empires and Wars*

# Civilizations, Empires and Wars

*A Quantitative History of War*

*by*

William Eckhardt

*Afterword by* DAVID WILKINSON

McFarland & Company, Inc., Publishers
*Jefferson, North Carolina, and London*

355.02
E19c

**Publisher's Note:** William Eckhardt died March 17, 1992, shortly before this book went to press.

British Library Cataloguing-in-Publication data are available

Library of Congress Cataloguing-in-Publication Data

Eckhardt, William, 1918–1992.
    Civilizations, empires, and wars : a quantitative history of war /
by William Eckhardt.
      p.  cm.
    [Includes index.]
    Includes bibliographical references (p. 281).
    ISBN 0-89950-709-3 (lib. bdg. : 50# alk. paper) ∞
    1. War—Mathematical models.   2. Sociology, Military—Mathematical
models.   I. Title.
U21.7.E25   1992
355.02—dc20                     91-41450
                                    CIP

Manufactured in the United States of America

*McFarland & Company, Inc., Publishers*
  *Box 611, Jefferson, North Carolina 28640*

*To the Canadian Peace Research Institute
and the Lentz Peace Research Laboratory of St. Louis*

# Acknowledgments

Many thanks to the numerous people who helped me during the development of this book over the last ten years. Special thanks to the Canadian Peace Research Institute and the Lentz Peace Research Laboratory of St. Louis for supporting my work during the last quarter-century, and to the International Society for the Comparative Study of Civilizations, whose members helped me to relate civilizations, empires and wars. I am particularly indebted to those who criticized chapters of this book (or related articles) in their early stages: Claudio Cioffi-Revilla, Nils Petter Gleditsch, Gordon Hewes, Arthur Iberall Vytautas Kavolis, Anita Kemp, Gernot Kohler, Jack S. Levy, Matthew Melko, Raoul Naroll, Keith Otterbein, Rudolph J. Rummel, J. David Singer, Melvin Small, and many others. I am grateful to the Dunedin (Florida) public librarians for all their kind assistance in obtaining books through their inter-library loan program; without their aid I could not have accomplished much. I received invaluable help from the Pinellas IBM PC Users Group in making the most of my computer—thanks especially to Doug Gregory and George Lock. My friend and neighbor Ed Ericson helped me think through many parts of this book during our morning walks to the Dunedin waterfront.

My wife and children have been a constant source of inspiration and support during the last 50 years.

# Contents

# List of Figures

# List of Tables

*(All tables are found at the back of the book beginning on page 220.)*

# Introduction

The quantitative studies of primitive warfare reviewed in the first chapter of this book suggest very strongly that warfare was a function of development rather than instinct, because the more highly developed societies were generally more militaristic. To be sure, this was a statistical finding that established a general rule, not a universal law. There were exceptions to this rule, as to any other, but nevertheless, this was the rule.

Development influenced all forms of primitive warfare, internal and external, defensive as well as offensive, but it was particularly a factor in offensive, external warfare which, in turn, often involved territorial expansion and, consequently, the cultural survival of the most militarily fit. This sequence was succinctly expressed by Otterbein (1977): "political centralization → military sophistication → offensive external war → territorial expansion" (p. 699).

It would seem that primitive warfare was primarily a function of development. Humans biologically similar to us emerged about one hundred thousand years ago and left a large number of cave paintings, some of which depicted hunting, but none of which depicted war. Bands of gathering-hunters, numbering about 25 to 50 people each, could hardly have made much of a war. There would not have been enough people to fight, few weapons with which to fight, little to fight about, and no surplus to pay for the fighting. Then, ten thousand years ago, humans settled down to farming and herding in villages and developed a vested interest in land and the livestock, and something like a war became possible. This agricultural revolution eventually resulted in food surpluses, thus making civilization (living in cities) possible, starting about five thousand years ago. War then began to come into its own.

The anthropological evidence summarized by Textor (1967) suggested that wars started sometime after the agricultural revolution some ten thousand years ago, once the vested interest in land and cattle gave us something to fight for. It was about this time that cave paintings began to suggest something like human warfare. A few stick persons were depicted apparently shooting arrows at each other, that is, fighting with weapons—one of the basic criteria for defining a war. Whether a few armed persons constitute an army is questionable; but earlier cave paintings suggested something closer to hunting activities, not warring activities.

It was only after we humans settled down to farming and herding that the land became of some importance to us and, therefore, something worth fighting over.

Generally speaking, the anthropological evidence suggests that primitive warfare was a function of human development rather than of human instinct or nature. In any event, social development, personal frustration, war preparation, war glorification, and warfare itself (including torturing, mutilating, and killing of the enemy), all seemed to feed into one another in a vicious spiral, suggesting a dialectical evolutionary theory of development and warfare. In general, more developed societies engaged in more warfare, so far as quantitative studies of primitive warfare indicate. And these more developed societies were more authoritarian, compulsive, and egoistic in their structure.

Consequently, there seems to be some quantitative evidence to support the contention that warfare emerged prior to the urban revolution, but not before the agricultural revolution. There is also some evidence to suggest that the frequency and intensity of primitive warfare increased as the development of primitive societies progressed.

However, the evidence is overwhelming that warfare did not come into its own until the emergence of civilization some five thousand years ago. Since that time civilizations, empires and wars have tended to ebb and flow together, wars serving as both midwives and undertakers in the rise and fall of civilizations in the course of human history.

Civilizations, empires and wars all share a number of key characteristics, the most prominent of which is the desire to dominate and exploit others, in order to benefit some at the expense of those others. In all three categories, there has seemed to be an inordinate concern for the self at the expense of others. In addition, all three have seemed to be processes that obstruct their own progress. There was something about them that stopped them from going on; they got in their own way, so to speak. In short, they all have been processes of self-destruction, the inherent nature of which was hidden by a self-deception in the form of some ideology or other. This process of self-destruction, rationalized and justified by self-deception, has invariably been a violation of the golden rule of the great religions and of the categorical imperative of the great philosophies, both of which recommend the consideration of others as well as oneself.

Why have civilized peoples fought so much more than primitive peoples? A tentative answer is that they had more material things over which to fight, had metal weapons, and, above all, had some surplus wealth to pay for both the things over which they fought and the weapons with which they did so. The "savage" gatherers and hunters had little to fight over, and not much more than primitive bows and arrows to fight with. Furthermore, they had neither surplus population nor surplus wealth to support a cadre of soldiers. The "barbarian" farmers and herders had more to fight over, but nothing better to fight with, and still neither the surplus population nor wealth to support anything like an army. Civilized people have fought over land, labor, capital, and trade, all of which contributed to their expansion at another's expense, especially at the expense of primitive peoples who could not defend themselves against the armies and weapons of the civilized.

However, there seems to be something very unstable about the process of civilization so far, since civilizations which rose and expanded eventually fell and contracted in area, population, power and wealth. Civilization seems to be a process which obstructs its own progress. Too much of its energy is wasted in power struggles: (1) one civilization against another, (2) one or more civilizations against barbarians (farmers and herders) and savages (gatherers and hunters), (3) peasant and slave rebellions within civilizations and (4) struggles for power within the ruling class of a civilization.

These power struggles translated into the four types of war which have characterized every civilization that we know: (1) power wars, (2) imperial (colonial) wars, (3) class wars and (4) civil wars. Consequently, war seems to be an essential expression of a process that obstructs its own progress and thereby destroys itself. Behind this process, and moving it, seems to lie the essence of civilization itself: exploitation, which benefits some at the expense of others. Exploitation violates the categorical imperative of doing only what everyone else may also do. This may be why civilizations have failed so far. Our own civilization may also fail unless we find a way of being civilized without dominating and exploiting one another.

Clearly, exploitation can only be enforced by means of arms, so that civilization and warfare have been intrinsically linked to each other throughout human history, to the benefit of some at the expense of others in the short run, but to the detriment of all in the long run. This pattern of domination and exploitation has repeated itself over and over in the course of human history. A more comprehensive pattern of conquest, domination, exploitation and subsequent revolt has occurred throughout the world over the ages. Not only did civilization bring war in its wake, but the more civilized people became, the more warlike they became.

Yet it would seem that warfare and concomitant slavery tend to weaken civilizations in less than a millennium, making them vulnerable to other predators, civilized or barbarian. If the main force behind this combination of civilization, empire, slavery and war is the desire to dominate others to benefit oneself, in violation of the categorical imperative, it may be hypothesized that this basic violence is responsible for most other human violence. If that is the case our own civilization can be saved only if we are able somehow to make the categorical imperative central to human motivation.

Later civilizations have been more militaristic than earlier civilizations, regardless of population. Nomadic, or offensive, militarism, like general militarism, has also functioned positively with civilizational development. If the civilization gave birth to war and war eventually destroyed its creator (as the monster destroyed Dr. Frankenstein), then civilization was self-destructive, a process that obstructed its own progress. This association between civilization and its war replicated the findings of a similar association between primitive development and primitive war.

The destructiveness of modern warfare, like civilized and primitive warfare before it, was generally related to the higher level of development of modern civilizations and their technologies, and to the growth in size of modern empires. Many of the precise mechanisms by which increasing civilization led to increasing intensity of war seem obvious, but many remain to be established by further research.

The dialectical evolutionary theory proposed in this book suggests that expanding civilization increased inequalities that, brought about by armed violence, require armed violence to be maintained against revolutionary and rival forces. Opposing forces feed each other, and spiral alternately up and down with the rise and fall of empires. The theory also maintains that more civilized peoples had more to fight for, more to fight with, and more surplus to pay for the fighting, all of which increased their warlikeness.

Although warfare may perhaps be traced back to the agricultural revolution ten thousand years ago, and although it certainly began by the time of civilization five thousand years ago, there is very little evidence of battles and wars prior to 1500 B.C., and not much evidence up to 600 B.C. when the Medes and the Persians developed civilizations, empires and warfare into arts based on a hierarchical delegation of power such as the world had not known before. The next great leap came with the Muslims in the seventh century A.D., another with the Mongols in the thirteenth century and yet another with the Europeans in the sixteenth century. The Europeans reached predominance in the nineteenth century and, with the Americans, in the twentieth, but they may have peaked, at least in terms of present surplus wealth. However, the Europeans have had their ups and downs before, like other civilizations, so a putative present decline hardly precludes another rise unless, of course, the decline takes the whole world with it.

While the level of civilization, population and productivity of the whole world tended to spiral upward, as a general rule, during the last five thousand years, regional areas had their ups and downs. Consequently, the general pattern suggested by the analyses in this book was that of an evolutionary trend in one direction at the global level, but composed of cyclical processes at regional levels. At both the global and regional levels, civilizations, empires and wars were significantly related to one another, tending to rise and fall together.

At the regional levels, the rises were associated with the establishment of centralized control by a strong leader whose income, in the process, exceeded his expenditures. When his and his followers' expenditures exceeded their incomes, then came the falls, characterized by decentralization and or foreign conquest. In all cases, the rise not only involved an increase in the *quantity* of civilization, empire and war, but also a change in the social *structure* to one of greater inequality, indicated by slavery, caste systems and class and social stratification. This inequality affected the relations between civilizations as well as within them. It would be desirable to develop more precise measures of these inequalities in the process of further research. So far, the evidence is largely qualitative and needs to be made more quantitative.

According to the dialectical evolutionary theory proposed in this book, all three of these social inventions—civilizations, empires and wars—started about the same time, about 3000 B.C. The theory should be understood as proposing some very general rules at best, not as proposing universal laws. In short, the dialectical evolutionary theory is a theory of probability, not one of certainty, although the probabilities of accuracy are fairly high, as suggested by the correlations among the three variables—civilizations, empires and wars—at both the global and regional levels of analysis, and by the generalization of these correlations through factor analysis.

Extrapolating into the future, the linear trends of civilization, empire and war at the global level, it looks as if we are determined to become more civilized and more warlike in the future, although it would also seem that we have reached an imperial limit, since today virtually all the earth is under various degrees of political control. Consequently, imperial territory is subject to changes of rulers in the future, but is not capable of further increase (short of the colonization of outer space). Obviously, this limit does not prevent civilizations from fighting over the possession of existing empires.

Extrapolating these same linear trends back into the past takes us to a virtual zero in civilization, empire and war at about 3000 B.C., according to most estimates. Notwithstanding the roughness of these data, they nevertheless suggest that anything similar to the wars of civilized times seldom, if ever, occurred before those times. And even civilized wars during the first half of human history from 3000 to 600 B.C. probably did not amount to much. Civilizational activities and imperial sizes were also modest until about 600 B.C. The data that exist indicate that early civilizations and empires were not warlike, and that primitive tribes and villages were relatively peaceful; there was some feuding and raiding, but these activities fell well short of war.

The extrapolations into the future seem to bode ill, but extrapolations predict, not determine events. They can be taken into account by human beings and used in such a way as to falsify their predictions. In other words, an extrapolation can be used to frustrate itself, given the contrary nature of human beings when they are told they have little or nothing to say about their future.

On the other hand, the extrapolations into the past seem to deny that theory of human nature which holds it to be inherently warlike. Humans may very well be naturally aggressive at the interpersonal level, and even prone to feuds and raids, but we hardly seem to be innately disposed to war, judging from the evidence at hand. For several million years, we roamed this earth without leaving any trace of anything like a war, nor any trace of anything like a territorial imperative. It was only after we became civilized, that is, dependent upon land, labor, capital and trade for making a living, that anything approaching imperialism and militarism began to make any sense.

Unless we have an instinct for exploitation (which is doubtful)—that is, a desire to benefit ourselves at the direct expense of others—it would seem that we have no need for war. Human nature is pretty much the product of human beings making choices. The dialectical evolutionary theory proposed in this book suggests that we gradually developed a pattern of domination and exploitation over a very long period of time that virtually made war inevitable. If this is true, then we can change the structure of the civilization we have created by changing our choices, which means changing our values, which hardly means changing human nature, whatever it may be.

What values need to be changed in order to have a civilization without domination and exploitation and, therefore, without war? One clue would seem to lie in the basic difference between primitive and civilized societies. Primitive societies seem to be more free and equal in their human relations than the civilized societies that we have created so far. If we created more free and equal human relations, we might be able to create a civilization without war. But we have much to learn before we can achieve this happy ending.

Did civilizations, empires and wars foster one another? The answer would seem to be an unequivocal yes. The three grow together among primitive peoples, early civilized peoples, and modern peoples. Empirical findings confirmed those theories that hold that war and civilization were motivated by a sense of superiority and self-righteousness, which served to rationalize and justify destructive behavior.

What was not always clearly recognized was just how destructive such behaviors were, since the structural damage caused by armed violence in the form of imperialism tended to be invisible from the imperial point of view. Furthermore, the self-destructiveness of this behavior was completely concealed by the self-deception that resulted from the self-centeredness and self-righteousness characteristic of civilized peoples, who tend to believe in their innate superiority to others, especially primitive peoples.

Finally, the ultimate destruction possible with nuclear warfare was never foreseen in our worst nightmares. However, even the possibility of total destruction has not yet led us to make an ethical response to its challenge. Without this ethical response we may be doomed to self-destruct, guided by the will to power instead of the categorical imperative.

Can we have civilization without war? The answer would again seem to be an unequivocal yes. The empirical and statistical evidence presented in this book makes it clear that the *way* we developed civilization so far is the problem, which can be solved by changing the *direction* of civilization or by changing its *structure*. Toynbee, Sorokin and Wright have all pointed to the authoritarian, egoistic and compulsive nature of civilization as its war-making component. All called for an ethical solution to the problem of self-destruction. Simply put, we can prevent war by restructuring civilization so that human relations are more egalitarian, altruistic and compassionate. Whether we shall need a world government is problematic. If we can make these structural changes, we may not need a world government, although such changes would make one more possible. If we cannot make these structural changes, a world government will either be impossible to achieve or, if achieved, is likely to become part of the problem instead of part of the solution.

# Chapter 1
# Primitive Warfare

## *Primitive People*

The "primitive" people discussed in this chapter are defined as primarily non-literate people, that is, people in whose lives neither reading nor writing played any real role. This distinguishes them from "civilized" people, some of whom learned to read and write about five thousand years ago.

Service (1962) divided primitive people into four types of political community: (1) small bands of gathering-hunters, where leaders have little authority; (2) tribes made up of several bands speaking the same language — confederations involving central authority; (3) chiefdoms, where the leader has some authority to redistribute any surplus, but no authority to invoke the use of force; and (4) states with a governing authority that can use force within the limits of the law. Service (1968) combined bands and tribes into uncentralized "egalitarian societies" (p. 76), and chiefdoms and states into centralized "hierarchical societies."

The average population of 123 Australian tribes was about 700 (Krzywicki 1934, p. 63). That of 503 North American tribes was about 1500 (p. 71). That of 98 South American tribes was about 3000 (p. 75). The population of the hill peoples of North Africa, southern Asia, and southern Europe ranged from several thousand to more than ten thousand (p. 77). These figures show that tribes were relatively small societies compared with modern nations, whose populations number in the millions.

Bands, of course, were much smaller, a handful of families amounting to 25 to 50 people, and could hardly engage in a war, given our definition of a war, to be discussed shortly.

Most authors distinguished between external and internal warfare — internal warfare was defined as occurring between members of the same language group, and external warfare, as occurring between members of different language groups. Ember (1978) suggested that tribes smaller than 21,000 people were not likely to fight internally. Since just as many tribes fought internally as externally (Otterbein, 1970), either the estimates of tribal sizes given in the previous paragraph were on the low side, or Ember's analysis was faulty.

## Definition of Primitive War

Warfare has generally been defined as armed combat between organized groups. Not only is the combat *between* groups, but it is also sanctioned *by* groups, so that it excludes individual violence whether or not armed. In the next chapter civilized warfare will be defined as armed conflict between organized groups, including governments (and perhaps especially governments and would-be governments [Glossop 1983, 1987, p. 7]), with deadly consequences to the extent of at least one thousand deaths per year. The emphasis on governments in this definition, and the criterion of one thousand deaths per year, make this definition inapplicable to most if not all violence that might otherwise qualify as primitive warfare, in the sense of armed conflict between organized groups, regardless of whether governments are involved, and regardless of the number of deaths, if any. Some minimal number of deaths would seem to be necessary in order to set some lower limit for group violence to qualify as a war. However, it would also seem that this lower limit should be at least somewhat proportional to the number of people in the groups concerned. It would seem that feuds, raids and tournaments should not be classified as wars. Feuds and raids were individual or family affairs for the most part. Tournaments fulfilled the "group" nature of war, but usually no more than one person was killed, at which time the tournament was ended. Small bands undoubtedly engaged in some violence, but unless this violence resulted in more than one death we should not call it a war. For tribes, more than one hundred deaths might be required. Consequently, primitive warfare might be defined as armed combat between organized groups with more than one death at the band level and more than one hundred deaths at the tribal level.

## War Among the "Simpler Peoples"

A pioneering study of "simpler peoples" was conducted by Hobhouse, Wheeler and Ginsberg (1930, but originally published in 1915). The authors gathered anthropological data on more than six hundred of these peoples, whom they arranged in the order of their economic development from the Lower Hunters (nomadic gatherers and collectors) through the Higher Hunters (fishers and hunters) to the Highest Agriculturalists and Pastoralists (farmers and herders, with ploughs, cattle and metal). Development was associated with higher incidences of government (coercive authority) and law, paternalism, slaves and human sacrifice, but with lower incidences of cannibalism, feuds and infanticide. The authors were able to classify almost half of these peoples as engaging in feuds or wars. War was defined as "an operation conducted in the name of the community as a whole" (p. 228). Wars, as distinguished from feuds, were associated with economic development: "Economic causes again are associated with the development of organized warfare.... On all sides social and economic differentiation replace the comparative equality of the hunting peoples. The extension of order is also, upon the whole, an extension of subordination" (p. 254).

Wars were not so prevalent among these "simpler peoples" as the authors had expected: "There is, in fact, no doubt that to speak of a state of war as normal is in general a gross exaggeration.... As distinguished from a feud, war implies a certain development of social organization, and is probably not so common at the lowest stages as it becomes higher up.... At most it may be said that organized war develops with the advance of industry and of social organization in general" (p. 228).

This pioneering study was very crude in its methodology, all of its measures being merely a matter of incidence. No tests of statistical significance were conducted on these incidences, so that some of the differences between them could have been due to chance. All of its data had been gathered prior to the First World War, when anthropology itself, as well as quantitative methodology, was not so sophisticated as it became later in the twentieth century. The authors were well aware of the difference in size between the "lower" societies and the "highest" societies, but they failed to include size as a variable in their studies, so that we have no way of telling whether primitive warfare was a function of development, as they claimed, or merely a function of size.

## A Study of War

A monumental study of war was conducted by Wright (1965, but originally published in 1942) on the basis of 16 years of research by some 60 researchers at the University of Chicago. In the chapter on primitive warfare, Wright used the data of Hobhouse et al. (1915) plus some additional anthropological data gathered between the two world wars. Defining a primitive society as a self-determining community without writing (p. 55), and defining war as "the *legal condition* which *equally* permits two or more *hostile groups* to carry on a *conflict* by *armed* force" (p. 8), Wright was able to code 590 primitive societies for their warlikeness. Going beyond mere incidence, Wright was able to distinguish between four levels of warlikeness: (1) defensive warfare only, which Wright considered to be "unwarlike" (p. 560); (2) social warfare for purposes of prestige or revenge, as well as defense: more warlike than defense only, but less warlike than the following; (3) economic warfare for the purpose of acquiring slaves, women, cattle, land, etc., with greater casualties in proportion to population than occurred in social warfare; and (4) political warfare in order to "maintain a ruling class in power and to expand the area of empire or political control.... [M]ost warlike of all ... they receive and inflict the greatest losses of population from war of any primitive people" (p. 561).

These four levels constituted a Guttman scale, in the sense that social warriors were also defensive warriors; economic warriors were also social and defensive warriors; political warriors were also economic, social, and defensive warriors. Wright acknowledged some ambiguity about the ordering of (2) and (3), which some authors placed in the reverse order. But there would presumably be considerable agreement that (2) and (3) were more warlike than (1) and less warlike than (4).

Applying this scale of warlikeness to these 590 societies, Wright obtained mean scores of warlikeness, which he related to 11 other variables, including continent, temperature, habitat, climate, race, culture (which Hobhouse et al. [1915] had called economic development), political organization (clan, village, tribe or state), social organization (division of labor) and intercultural contacts. Size was not quantified, but presumably the differences between clan, village, tribe and state, would reflect differences in size from smaller to larger populations.

According to Wright's mean scores, more warlikeness was associated with the African continent, hot and temperate temperatures, grassland habitats, medium climatic energy, white race followed by some black races with other black races lowest of all, farmers and herders more than hunters, states followed by tribes followed by villages followed by clans (confounding political centralization with size), caste and professional division of labor and close contacts. Like Hobhouse et al. Wright performed no tests of statistical significance, so that the reliability of these associations remained in some doubt.

On the basis of these findings, Wright's most general conclusion was that "War among primitive peoples is related more closely to the complexity of culture, political organization, and extra-group contacts than to race or physical environment.... Thus, the more primitive the people, the less warlike it tends to be" (p. 68). But, the more primitive the people, the smaller the size of their group. So, we are left with a question: Is it their primitiveness or their smallness that made them less warlike? Can bands or clans really engage in any group violence that is likely to get registered or reported as a war? Apparently they can, because some of their violence has been so registered and reported.

Wright's 590 societies were composed of 5 percent engaging in defensive war only, 59 percent in social war, 29 percent in economic war, and 7 percent in political war (p. 551). Thirty-seven percent were hunters, while 63 percent were farmers and herders (p. 556). Nineteen percent lived in clans, 48 percent in tribes, 25 percent in villages, and 8 percent in states (p. 557). Forty-five percent divided the labor along age and sex lines only, while 55 percent also divided the labor along caste and professional lines (p. 558). Forty-five percent were isolated from other societies, 36 percent had moderate contacts, and 19 percent had close contacts (p. 559).

Broch and Galtung (1966) constructed a seven-point scale of civilization versus primitivity, which was based on four of Wright's variables. When this scale was compared with Wright's warlikeness scale, the percentage of cultures engaging in economic and political warfare increased in an almost monotonous manner with increasing levels of civilization (p. 37), thus confirming Wright's conclusion that more primitive people were less warlike. They also found that Wright's findings about the relations between warlikeness and ten other variables were essentially the same when only those primitive peoples were analyzed whose warlike activities were most like modern warfare, that is, where economic and political motives predominated (p. 34). This reanalysis of Wright's data provided some measure of reliability for Wright's conclusions, even as Wright's reanalysis of the Hobhouse et al. data (plus some additional data) provided some measure of reliability for their conclusions.

As a further test of reliability, I selected a random sample of 90 of Wright's 590 societies. Since Wright presented his 12 variables by continent, with the societies within the six continents arranged alphabetically (pp. 528–44), I simply selected the first 15 societies on each continent where the data were complete for all 12 variables. This completeness of data enabled me to obtain correlations which could then be factor-analyzed. (Correlations are simply measures of similarity, and factor analysis is simply a statistical method of generalization which places similar variables on the same factor. See Appendix A.) The mean scores obtained for 11 of these variables were not significantly different from the mean scores obtained from Wright's data for all of his societies (pp. 551–59), suggesting that my smaller sample was quite representative of Wright's larger sample.

When these data were correlated and factor-analyzed, the first general factor was characterized as follows, with the factor coefficients in parentheses: African continent (.79), division of labor by caste (.74), higher subculture (.68), living in states and tribes (.66), engaging in political and economic warfare (.63), making a living by farming and herding (.62), close contacts with other cultures (.55), and grasslands habitat (.51). Climatic energy, race, and temperature were loaded less than .30 on this factor. This general factor was clearly consistent with both Wright's and Broch and Galtung's findings and conclusions. Higher development was associated with more destructive warfare.

Although the data, findings and conclusions, so far, seem to be reliable enough (in the sense that different authors, using different samples of the same data, have arrived at similar findings and conclusions), the question of validity has not been answered. In fact, it has not even been raised. Validity has been taken for granted. It has been assumed that different authors classifying the warlikeness of societies would arrive at the same measures. This may indeed be the case, but it would be desirable to establish this empirically.

## Military Deterrence and Territorial Change

Naroll (1964, 1966) used an entirely different set of anthropological data to test some basic theories about war and peace: (1) cultural exchange makes war less likely; (2) warfare promotes human evolution by weeding out the weakest societies; (3) arms and arms races make wars more likely; (4) military preparations make peace more likely by increasing the cost of war and thereby deterring would-be aggressors.

Naroll defined war succinctly as "armed, licit, lethal public combat" (1964, p. 6). He carefully selected 48 primitive societies so that they would be "truly representative of all human societies" (1966, p. 16) and so that the effect of cultural borrowing on correlations would be minimized. Following Wright, Naroll was able to identify the military expectations (which Wright had called the objects of war and had labeled "warlikeness") of his primitive societies. However, unlike Wright, Naroll found that social expectations of prestige were more "warlike" (in Wright's terminology) than economic expectations of booty such as livestock, women, slaves and lands. Consequently, Naroll reversed the order of (2) and (3) on Wright's Guttman scale. "But," Naroll (like Wright) emphasized, "the evidence is not conclusive" (1964, p. 21). There was, of course, no disagreement on the order of (1) and (4).

Using this scale of military expectations plus eight other measures of "warlike traits" (1966, p. 17), Naroll correlated these variables with a crude measure of war frequency, finding that "very few of the measures of military orientations seem to have any impact, one way or the other, on the frequency of war.... The only significant correlations—*multiple expectations, military readiness, forts, and hostility*—are positive, and seem to indicate that these military orientations are positively associated with frequent wars. The strongest relationship that shows up is the positive correlation between *war frequency and military expectations*" (1966, p. 18). In fact, all Naroll's correlations were positive, but low, and hardly significant except for the correlation of .55 between military expectations and war frequency. However, military preparations in the form of forts and readiness were significantly related to military expectations (1966, p. 19), suggesting the following causal sequence: military readiness → military expectations → war frequency. Naroll concluded that "these data offer a kind of mild and tentative support for the arms race hypothesis" (1966, p. 19), that is, that military readiness contributes to war more than it deters war. *"This study gives no support at all to the deterrence theory"* (1966, p. 18).

In order to test the hypothesis about the military selection of cultural survival, Naroll obtained two measures of territorial change, one in the direction of growth and the other in both directions. The assumption was that territorial growth was an operational definition of cultural survival, while territorial loss was an operational definition of cultural extinction. If the measures of military orientation were positively correlated with growth, this would support the hypothesis of military selection. But, if the same measures were positively correlated with change of territory, regardless of direction, this would suggest that military orientation was just as likely to lose territiory as to gain it, and so not necessarily contributive to cultural survival.

Territorial growth was significantly correlated with the importation of Western technology, especially guns but also tools, and, to a lesser extent, with military readiness, suggesting that "military preparedness tends to make for territorial expansion" (1966, p. 20). But, "the correlations also show a strong tie between territorial instability [losses as well as gains] and military expectations"

(1966, p. 20), and also, to a lesser extent, between military readiness and war frequency. Naroll admitted that "the results here are equivocal," but he nevertheless concluded that "they do demonstrate that warfare is an agent of cultural selectivity, and that the notion that we can best preserve our way of life by throwing away our arms is dangerously naive" (1966, p. 20). Naroll seemed to depart from his data with this conclusion. He should have stopped with the admission that the results were equivocal, because they showed that military preparedness was associated with both territorial growth and territorial instability, so that it might be difficult to say whether military preparations led to either growth or diminution. The historical record would suggest that, so far, all past civilizations have *not* survived in spite of vast military preparations. In spite of these reservations about Naroll's conclusion, his basic finding can hardly be disputed: "Of the twenty-nine [cultures] that did have changes in territory, only three experienced the change peacefully...." (One of these was a questionable case.) Consequently, territorial "changes are almost always the result of warfare" (1966, p. 19).

In order to test the hypothesis about cultural exchanges making war less likely, Naroll included several measures of such exchanges including subsidies, trade and the exchange of women. "Our comparisons, regrettably, show no significant relationships at all between the frequency of war and these three measures of peaceful intercourse" (1966, p. 20). But subsidies were significantly correlated with military expectations and territorial growth. Trade was significantly correlated with the importation of Western technology, including guns and tools. And the exchange of women was significantly correlated with trade, wide distribution of firearms, number of foes, and importation of guns from the West. Although not significantly correlated with the frequency of war, cultural exchanges were significantly correlated with military expectations and the importation of guns from the West, so that these cultural exchanges leaned in the military direction.

Naroll included a measure of hostility among his war orientations, assuming that repressed hostility might be associated with war if Freud was correct that repressed hostility was turned outward in the form of aggression against others. As it turned out, neither expressed nor repressed hostility was significantly associated with military orientations, including expectations and preparations, nor with territorial changes, nor with the frequency of war. This finding would suggest that hostility, as such, had little or nothing to do with primitive warfare. The relation between hostility and war will be discussed further in a later section of this chapter.

Although Naroll was not concerned with any hypotheses about the relations between language and war, he made an observation that questions the hypothesis that a common language would make war less likely: "War is most frequently fought between people who have a common culture; the people one fights are often the very people one seeks a wife from!" (1964, p. 30). This observation is highly suggestive, but a more systematic study would be necessary before accepting it as final.

Naroll shared his latest thinking on primitive war in some personal correspondence shortly before his death in 1985: "Hardly any of the simplest societies fight wars for any other reason than to defend their territory against invasion or trespass or to avenge a private killing—that is, blood revenge or feuding. Feuding is extremely widespread.... Among the smallest-scale societies, warfare is fought only for defense and blood revenge, not for wealth, for prestige, or for political control.... Among a large proportion, perhaps a majority, of the smallest scale societies—those consisting merely of small foraging bands—warfare is mild and gentle. That is to say, it is fought only to defend territory against trespassers or to avenge a private killing and it does comparatively little harm to the people at war. It is only one degree more dangerous and deadly than American football or prizefighting; a few people get killed in it, but not very many. It is mostly bluff, show and noise—ceremonial combat. As societies increase in scale, warfare tends to grow progressively larger in scope and more deadly. But remember, this is a statistical average; in *some* small-scale societies like the Ona it is quite lethal. Among the largest scale societies—the higher civilizations—warfare is typically broadest in scope and deadliness" (1983a, pp. 2–3).

Naroll also described tournaments as being very widespread among many of the smallest scale societies: "Fights between hostile groups are prearranged; begin with an exchange of epithets; proceed to a shower of missiles (spears, arrows); and *end when the first man is killed*" (1983a, p. 2).

When I reanalyzed Naroll's 1964 data, I included a new variable of military expectations, which merely reversed the scores of his social prestige and economic plunder ratings, thus making this scale of military expectations similar to Wright's scale of warlikeness. In the case of his other variables, missing data were completed by inserting the mean score in their place. The two scales of military expectations were significantly correlated, at .72, with each other. Their correlations with other scales were also similar to each other and to Naroll's correlations. These results would suggest that the order of the middle two levels of warlikeness (economic plunder and social prestige) may be irrelevant for the purpose of statistical analyses. However, this order may be important for the purpose of case studies.

## The Evolution of War

Otterbein (1970) followed up Naroll's work with a different sample of cultures and some different variables. Warfare was defined as "armed combat between political communities" (p. 3). Following Naroll, a political community was defined as a "group of people whose membership is defined in terms of occupancy of a common territory and who have an official with the special function of announcing group decisions—a function exercised at least once a year" (p. 3). The goals of war (which Naroll called military expectations and Wright called warlikeness) included "subjugation and tribute, land, plunder, trophies and honors, defense, and revenge" (pp. 4–5). These six goals were reduced to a Guttman scale of four "causes of war" (pp. 66–67), that were arranged according to the order of Naroll's military expectations: defense, plunder, prestige and control.

Following Naroll, Otterbein made a very careful selection of his societies so as to cover the world adequately and so as to minimize the effect of cultural borrowing on his correlations. His 50 societies were sorted in 8 bands, 24 tribes, 8 chiefdoms, and 10 states, using Service's (1962, 1968) taxonomy as a measure of political centralization. Economic development was measured by sorting societies into 10 gathering-hunters, 9 herders, 14 shifting farmers, and 17 intensive farmers. Feuding was distinguished from war, and wars were divided into internal and external, the latter of which was divided into defensive and offensive. Eleven variables of military organization were used to develop a scale of military sophistication, which was the percent of these variables exhibited by each of his 50 societies. Success was measured by expanding boundaries. A crude measure of war deaths was also utilized: more than one-third of combatants, or less.

Otterbein found that political centralization was significantly associated with the number of reasons for going to war (p. 68) and with the degree of military sophistication (p. 75), but not with military success (p. 97). Military sophistication, in turn, was significantly associated with war deaths (p. 82), offensive warfare (p. 88), and military success (p. 94), but not with internal warfare (p. 85), nor with defensive warfare (p. 90)—this latter result suggesting that "the deterrence hypothesis is not confirmed" (p. 90).

Otterbein concluded from this study that "neither internal war nor defensive external war are related to the degree of military sophistication of a society. On the other hand, military sophistication and offensive external war are correlated. Thus societies with high military sophistication scores are no more likely to be characterized by frequent internal war than are societies with low scores, but they are likely to attack other societies frequently. Furthermore, it has been shown that the possession of an efficient military organization does not deter the attacks of other societies" (pp. 91–92). He further stated that "this chapter has demonstrated that the political communities of a cultural unit which wage war in a sophisticated manner are likely to have high casualty rates, to frequently attack the political communities of neighboring cultural units, and to be militarily successful, even though the possession of an efficient military organization does not deter the attacks of political communities of neighboring cultural units" (p. 102).

Otterbein felt that his findings clearly indicated the importance of military sophistication for military success in the form of expanding territories. "The evidence appears conclusive: it is the military ability of a cultural unit's political communities, not simply the level of their political centralization, that determines military success.... An increase in political centralization is not a necessity in order for a political community to develop a sophisticated military system and to become militarily successful. Moreover, the development of an efficient military organization appears to be a necessary condition for a political community to remain viable in intersocietal conflicts" (pp. 107–8). Otterbein (1977) later summarized his conclusions very succinctly as follows: "political centralization → military sophistication → offensive warfare → territorial expansion" (p. 699).

I completed Otterbein's missing data in his final code sheet (pp. 148–49) with mean scores. I included his military sophistication percents (p. 74) and his Guttman causes of war (pp. 66–67). I also reversed points two and three (plunder and prestige) in his four-point Guttman scale (in order to make this scale more like Wright's warlikeness), and I reversed points two and four (land and trophies) in his six-point scale of reasons for going to war (in order to make this scale more like his Guttman causes of war).

When I correlated and factor-analyzed all of these variables, the first factor was loaded as follows, with the factor coefficients shown in parentheses: military sophistication (.90), military subordination (.81), political control when the causes of war were reversed (.79), war deaths (.75), political control when the reasons for going to war were reversed (.75), political control as a cause of war (.75), both shock and projectile weapons (.74), professional military organization (.74), political control as a reason for going to war (.73), both shields and body armor (.67), political centralization in a state (.63), political communities prior to the twentieth century, such as ancient Egyptians and medieval Japanese and Javanese (.60), cavalry (.48), surprise attacks (.48), field fortifications (.47), intensive agriculture (.46), official initiation of war (.46), offensive external war (.41) and military success in the form of expanding boundaries (.31).

This general factor of military sophistication, political control as a cause of or reason for war, political centralization, intensive agriculture (as opposed to gathering-hunting), offensive external war and military success was quite consistent with Otterbein's correlations and conclusions. This factor would also suggest that military sophistication increased with political centralization and economic development in the form of intensive agriculture. Both causes of war and reasons for war in their original form and in their reversed form were all highly correlated (.73 to .79) with this factor, suggesting that the ordering of the economic and social steps on these scales was irrelevant for the statistical purposes of obtaining mean scores, correlations and factors, so that Naroll's, Otterbein's, and Wright's findings and conclusions were all equally valid. All four of these causes, expectations, reasons and warlikeness scales were significantly correlated with one another, the correlations ranging from .54 to .77.

It is worth noting that variables were *not* significantly correlated with this general factor of military, economic, and political development, offensive war and territorial expansion, such as the area of the world in which these cultures were located, their surrounding terrain (forests, mountains, deserts, savannas), defensive war, internal war and feuds.

Feuds were not significantly correlated with any other variable in this matrix, suggesting that they were randomly distributed in relation to these other variables. Defensive warfare was most associated with offensive warfare (.62), and to a lesser extent with war deaths (.42), political control as a reason for going to war (.36) and military sophistication (.33). Internal warfare was associated with political control (.30 to .37), village fortification (.35) and ambush (.31). Internal warfare was also associated with fraternal interest groups in another study reported by Otterbein (pp. 85, 87). Consequently, political control as a cause of war, in the sense of its being a goal of war or a reason for going to war, contributed to defensive and internal warfare, as well as offensive warfare, but not nearly to the same extent.

## A Cross-Cultural Summary

Textor (1967) published the correlation (phi) coefficients among some five hundred anthropological variables across some four hundred primitive cultures. Four of these variables were concerned with warfare: (1) prevalence of war (N = 43 cultures), (2) emphasis on military glory (N = 86 cultures), (3) bellicosity, or war preparations (N = 87 cultures) and (4) emphasis on killing, torturing or mutilating the enemy (N = 84 cultures). Most of Textor's data were gathered and coded after the Second World War, making it quite different from the data of Hobhouse et al. (1915) and Wright (1942). The four hundred cultures were taken from the six continents in roughly equal amounts. These four hundred cultures were recommended as a "representative sample of the world's known cultures" (Tatje, Naroll and Textor 1970, p. 649).

Stewart (1971) factor-analyzed the correlations among 488 of these variables across a random stratified sample of 98 of these cultures, and generalized these variables to 13 factors. One of these factors, which he called Aggressive Achievement Behavior, is of special interest here because it contained three of the four variables pertaining to primitive warfare: attitudes, preparations and prevalence. A factor, as mentioned previously, is simply a set of variables more closely related to one another than to any other variables in a correlation matrix. In other words, factor analysis is simply a statistical technique for sorting variables into categories (factors) on the basis of their similarity to one another (See Appendix A).

The variables correlated with the Aggressive Achievement factor were the following, with their factor coefficients shown after the variable name: narcissism or egoism .61; bellicosity or war preparations .56; military glory or favorable attitudes toward militarism .56; boastfulness .52; achievement training in childhood .48, self-reliance training in childhood .48; prevalence of warfare .42; incidence of crime .42; and full-time entrepreneurs .41.

Since Textor had included personality as well as culture among his variables (which other authors had not gone so far, except for Naroll's hostility variable), Stewart was able to show that narcissistic or self-centered behavior, including boastfulness and sensitivity to insult, was closely related to several warfare variables: attitudes, preparations and prevalence. Stewart was also able to show some relation between primitive warfare and childhood training in achievement and self-reliance. Warfare cultures tended to be those cultures where the crime rate was high and where private entrepreneurs flourished. Stewart's labeling of this factor as "Aggressive Achievement" was somewhat misleading, since there was nothing necessarily "aggressive" about this factor at the personal level of analysis, unless crime, enterprise and warfare are undifferentiatedly defined as aggressive. "Egoistic Achievement" would seem to be a more descriptive label for this factor, since narcissistic variables were heavily loaded on this factor.

Russell (1972) used all four hundred of Textor's cultures, but only 78 of his variables. Russell chose primarily those variables which were significantly correlated with the four measures of war. When these 78 variables were factor analyzed, the first factor was characterized by military glory .62, metal work .62, theft .62, games of skill −.62, games of strategy .59, social hierarchies .59, punishment of extramarital affairs .58, political integration at the state level .55, prevalence of war .54, war preparations .53, torture .53, narcissism .48, sexual and social anxieties .34 to .61, boastfulness .35 to .66, mother-son sleeping together more than one year .34 to .45, sensitivity to insult .45, child indulgence. −.45, African location .43, size of community more than 50 people .43, punishment of premarital affairs .43, social conflicts .35 to .47, pressure for achievement and self-reliance .32 to .45, affection shown to infants −.41, sexual satisfaction −.41, display of wealth .41, slavery .41, classes .40, gathering-hunters −.38, agriculture .37, entrepreneurs .36, crime .36 (pp. 283–85).

When Russell rotated his factors, his general factor was divided into two factors of culture and personality. Culture included social complexity, technology, and kinship systems. Personality included narcissism .77, warfare measures .50 to .71, crime .58, and theft .39. Since the general factor and the personality factor included all forms of "aggression" among these 78 variables, such as warfare, crime, theft and punitiveness in general, Russell concluded that these factors constituted a measure of aggression in general, and remarked that "since aggression in one form is positively related to aggression in another form, one form, such as external aggression, does not act as a 'safety valve' or cathartic for aggression in general. . . . Such channeling of aggression into war does not appear to be of great importance in reducing the level of crime and theft within a culture. . . . There is thus not a constant amount of aggression in all cultures which simply takes alternate forms of release. . . . Here is evidence that cultural factors themselves produce the level of hostility within a society" (p. 291).

Russell, like Stewart, has labeled this factor as "aggression" or "hostility," thus begging the question as to whether or not activities such as crime, punishment, private enterprise, strategic games, war, etc., are motivated by hostility. "Aggression" and "hostility" may refer to an emotion such as "anger," but there were no measures of "anger" loaded on this factor. As in the case of

Stewart's factor, Russell's factor was primarily characterized by anxiety and ego-ism or self-centeredness at the personal level of analysis. Consequently, Russell might well argue that anxiety and egoism were culturally determined on the basis of his evidence, and that one form of these does not act as a safety valve or cathartic for another form.

While Russell's general factor included both culture and personality, the rotated factor of personality was characterized by narcissism (boastfulness, sen-sitivity to insult, and invidious display of wealth), aggression (warfare, crime, theft, and punitiveness), achievement and entrepreneurial activities and many forms of anxiety: "Thus, it is possible that high levels of hostility represent as much attempts to compensate or defend against feelings of insecurity and anx-iety as an expression of intrinsic aggression. . . . In any case, this factor indicates that members of a warlike culture are not only more hostile but also more nar-cissistic and insecure than members of a peaceful society" (p. 295). This factor was also characterized by frustration and punishment of extramarital and pre-marital relations. He summarized that "hostility may appear in the form of bellicosity, personal crime, theft, or emphasis on achievement, wealth, and en-trepreneurial activities. In regard to dynamics, the level of hostility is positively related to the amount of restrictiveness or punitiveness that the culture places on its members at all age levels. . . . The result of this punitiveness is evident not only in cultural hostility but also in a deep sense of anxiety and insecurity, which appears in narcissistic attitudes, such as boasting and sensitivity to insult or an exhibitionistic display of wealth. . . . Taken together, these indicate that the warlike, repressive cultures are narcissistic and hostile and contain a general underlying element of anxiety and insecurity" (p. 297). And he concluded that "the general dynamic implied here is that warfare, crime, and anxiety are pro-duced by punitiveness and restrictiveness in regard to more basic needs at all periods of an individual's life, from infancy to adulthood" (p. 304). The evi-dence seems to support Russell's emphasis on anxiety and narcissism, but his emphasis on aggression and hostility may be questioned.

It is worth noting here that matrilineal and patrilineal variables were not at all related to warfare. Russell held that "at this level of analysis, female line-age apparently does not ensure peacefulness of the society's males" (p. 300). We shall return to this point in the next section of this chapter.

Russell's conclusion about the primacy of personality in warfare and his dismissal of culture as an important contributor to warfare is quite consistent with Stewart's factor of Aggressive Achievement (which was also a rotated fac-tor and entirely personal in its nature, including the behaviors of war, crime and private enterprise), but quite inconsistent with the findings of Hobhouse et al., Wright, Broch and Galtung, Naroll and Otterbein that warfare was re-lated to military, political and socioeconomic development.

This discrepancy can be resolved by looking at the relation between general and rotated factors. A general factor takes into consideration all of the relations among all of the variables in a correlation matrix, and proceeds to ac-count as much as possible for the variance that they all have in common. When this and other factors are rotated, this process is deliberately designed to analyze the general factor into component parts, each of which exhibits a simple structure lacking in the general complex factor. However, if the primary factors are rotated obliquely and then correlated and analyzed at the second-order level of factor analysis, the variables which have been separated at the primary level of analysis come back together again at the second-order level of analysis.

There is, of course, nothing wrong with Russell's and Stewart's rotated factors as far as they go, but it is wrong to assume that the primary level of analysis is the last word on the subject. Analysis should go on until there are no more significant correlations left among the factors. Simple structure is quite adequate and most desirable for the construction of simple scales. But simple structure ignores the complexity of any data set, which is better captured by the first general factor, or higher-order oblique factors.

In order to make sure that nothing of value had been missed by Russell's and Stewart's factor analyses, I had another look at Textor's correlation coefficients (Eckhardt, 1975). The four warfare variables — attitudes, preparations, prevalence, and intensity — were all significantly correlated with one another from .35 to .72, so that they constituted a single type of primitive militarism, whose principal member was the attitude of military glory, defined in terms of high values placed on military virtues and warfare itself. This attitudinal variable of militarism was correlated .72 with bellicosity or war preparations, .69 with the actual prevalence of warfare and .54 with sadism (the extent of killing, torturing or mutilating the enemy). This military type consisting of both attitudinal and behavioral variables, and both preparations and actualizations, suggested that primitive people prepared for war in order to make war, and that they glorified war in order to make it socially acceptable when it occurred. The following causal sequence would be suggested: military glory → war preparations → prevalence of war → extent of killing, etc.

Textor had divided his variables into 42 general categories, 15 of which were not at all related to his category of Aggression and Warfare. These 15 unrelated categories included latitude, linguistic affiliation, predominant natural environment, predominant diet, predominant writing system, jurisprudence and medicine, type of kinship group, inheritance of property, marriage between cousins customs, extent of family organization, source of authority within the family, divorce rate, status of women, fertility level and degree of contact with other cultures. These findings would suggest that primitive militarism had little or nothing to do with temperature, environment, food supply and hunting, size and type of family organization and source of authority within the family.

I combined the other 27 of Textor's categories into five larger classes in order to simplify the presentation of the positive findings of this study: (1) geographical region, (2) socio-economic-political development, (3) frustrating childhood discipline, (4) sexual repression at all ages and (5) narcissism or self-centeredness.

Geographically, Africa was more correlated with primitive militarism than any other continent. This correlation presumably reflected higher development among primitive peoples in Africa, since neither climate nor race was associated with primitive militarism.

Warfare was more prevalent where settlements were fixed and less prevalent among nomadic tribes. Technological development (especially in metal work) was related to all four military variables. Social and political development, including the presence of cities, classes, and slavery, were related to most of the military variables. Development in general was most related to the prevalence of warfare and least related to sadism.

Frustrating childhood disciplines, on the other hand, were most related to sadism and least related to the prevalence of warfare. Sexual repression in infancy, adolescence, and adulthood was related to all aspects of primitive militarism, as was narcissism, boastfulness, sensitivity to insult and games of chance and strategy as opposed to games of skill.

This study suggested that both personal and cultural variables contributed to primitive militarism, with developmental variables contributing more toward its prevalence, and disciplinary variables contributing more toward its intensity.

These findings suggested that human warfare was not so much "instinctive" as it was a function of people settling in certain territories and developing a vested interest in the land and other natural resources. This territorial imperative could hardly be considered "instinctive" either, since it was not a salient factor among the more primitive food-gathering nomadic peoples, but only became salient at the agricultural and pastoral stages of development. Development followed *after* settlement, so that social stratification, master-slave relations, and dominance-submission relations in general (including male-female relations), were all functions of cultural development rather than "instinctive" functions.

Frustrating childhood disciplines — including pressures for early socialization, achievement, obedience, responsibility, self-reliance and their associated anxieties — were related to all military variables, but especially to military glory and sadism. Crime rate and severity of punishment were also related to all military variables, but especially to military glory, the attitudinal variable.

Cultures where exclusive mother-son sleeping arrangements lasted one year or longer, where fathers avoided their sons' wives and where husbands avoided their mothers-in-law, were more likely to glorify war and prepare for it. This combination of anthropological variables constituted an operational example of the Freudian Oedipus complex (mother-son sleeping arrangements) and its repression (avoidance of sons' wives and of mothers-in-law), so that the existence of a relationship between this psychosexual complex and primitive militarism received some confirmation from these findings. Postpartum sex taboos were related to actual warfare and its glorification, and severe punishment for abortion was related to sadism. Sexual repression in infancy, adolescence and adulthood (including castration anxiety and sexual segregation) was related to all aspects of primitive militarism. These findings suggested that where sex was most frustrated or repressed, primitive warfare was most likely to be intense and prevalent. These findings further suggested that Freud's (1920) early theory of aggression as a function of frustrated and repressed libido received more confirmation from anthropological evidence than did his later theory of aggression as a "death instinct" (Freud, 1922). But, as already noted, these anthropological findings may have nothing at all to do with aggression, in the sense of hostility.

Although some of the highest correlations reported by Textor were between primitive militarism and development, the most consistent or reliable correlations were between primitive militarism and narcissism, or self-centeredness. These findings suggested that the entrepreneurial activities associated with crime, theft and primitive warfare were more of an egoistic nature than they were of an altruistic nature.

This study showed that primitive peoples who prepared the most for war were most likely to go to war and to glorify war in the process. The anthropological evidence in general showed that to prepare for war was more likely to provoke war than to prevent it. The same evidence showed that primitive warfare was an effective method for acquiring land and other natural resources at the expense of others. This study strongly suggested that primitive militarism was a function of more authoritarian and egoistic cultures, while the more democratic and altruistic cultures were more peaceful. Unfortunately, the more authoritarian and egoistic cultures won more wars, acquired more slaves and territories and survived in the struggle for cultural existence, which was decided by military selection. Or did they only survive as agents for the transmission of the more democratic and altruistic slaves in their midst? A fascinating question for further research.

## Men and Women in Anger and War

We have already noted in passing that Russell (1972) found no significant relation between lineage (whether descent was traced through the mother or the father) and primitive warfare, and that Textor (1967) recorded no significant relation between primitive warfare and authority within the family, the divorce rate or the status of women.

Although men have generally predominated both as hunters and warriors throughout human history and prehistory, hunting and warring have been the prerogative of upper-class men until recently, so that there has been a distinction by class as well as by sex so far as war is concerned. There has also been a distinction by age since younger people have generally been favored over older people as warriors. In spite of these distinctions, women have participated in war to some small extent, perhaps constituting up to 10 percent of all warriors (Naroll 1983b, p. 372). And they have participated even more as cheerleaders and victory celebrators. Turney-High (1949, 1971), for example, has noted that American Indian women had an equal role with men in victory dances (p. 156).

There has nevertheless persisted a belief that war is associated with men because men are more aggressive than women. This belief obviously assumes that war is a function of aggression. Here the term aggression can be misleading, as already noted, depending upon the meaning ascribed to it. If by aggression we are referring to consequences, especially in the sense of someone being killed, then war is surely aggressive by definition. By definition, no deaths mean no war. But, if by aggression we are referring to motives—especially in the sense of anger or hostility, that is, wanting to kill somebody as an emotional response rather than for some practical or rational purpose—then no anthropological data so far discussed can show definitively any relation between such anger and war. This is not to say that anger may not be related to war, but only that, so far, there is no definite evidence to this effect. At the personal level of analysis war has been shown to be related to anxiety and self-centeredness, but not to hostility.

The association of war with aggression (in the motivational sense) is connected with the idea of aggression as an instinct. So far as war is generally associated with men, the implication would be that men are innately more aggressive than women. But the available anthropological evidence does not support this implication. Naroll (1983b) has concluded after looking at the anthropological evidence that "In most societies the sexes do *not* differ in aggressiveness" (p. 307). Furthermore, Rohner has presented evidence that there were no significant differences in aggressiveness between boys and girls, men and women, adults and children, and males and females in 14 cultures (Table in Naroll 1983b, p. 306). The difference in levels of aggressiveness between cultures was eight times greater than the difference between the sexes. Consequently, if war was a function of human aggressiveness, these findings suggest that virtually as many woman as men would have engaged in it.

Adams (1985) has conducted a motivational analysis of the role of anger in war and peace in a case study of the Mae Enga, where wars were generally functions of disputes over land and the theft of pigs. This analysis showed that anger did not play a critical or even necessary role in their warfare, which was generally carefully planned and rationally executed. Adams also found that women were generally as aggressive as men, that "maternal aggression" matched the territorial aggression of males, and that competitive fighting may have been more common in females than in males.

Why, then, if women were as aggressive as men, were women not so prevalent as men in primitive warfare? In addition to the obvious reason that "the biological demands upon the human mother during pregnancy and nurturance of the young preclude her active role in hunting and war" (Adams 1983, p. 12), there was another reason. Internal wars most often involved a conflict with the society from which wives had been obtained. That means that these wars were fought by men against the brothers and fathers of their wives. By precluding wives from engaging in such wars, the wives were prevented from being caught between divided loyalties. In cultures characterized by patrilocal exogamy (wherein a wife taken from a different community lived with her husband's family), women were not allowed to be warriors (Adams, 1984). On the other hand, if marriages were endogamous (where the husband and wife were from the same community, so that there could be no divided loyalties in wartime), women *did* fight as warriors at some time or another in about 25 percent of such communities.

This brief review, which needs to be augmented by further studies, would suggest that war is not instinctive. Furthermore, war does not seem to be motivated by aggression, nor do the sexes seem to differ significantly in their aggressiveness, so that war would not seem to be emotional or masculine behavior, as such. Warring and hunting seem to have fallen to the lot of men simply and primarily because women, especially primitive women, were occupied with pregnancy, childbirth, breast-feeding and other nurturing which could often go on for several years. Hunting and warring fell to men primarily by default. It was not so much that they were especially suited to these tasks, but rather that they were not needed for the bearing and nursing of children. The men made a virtue out of necessity by claiming male superiority in the hunt and the war, thus offsetting the female's superiority in childbearing and nurturing.

## Summary and Conclusions

The quantitative studies of primitive warfare reviewed in this chapter were generally in agreement that warfare was a function of development rather than instinct. Warfare itself was generally defined as a group effort sanctioned by the group: "armed, licit, lethal public combat" (Naroll 1964, p. 6). Some minimum number of deaths was presumably required, but this minimum was seldom if ever made explicit. Development was defined socially in terms of the division of labor based on professional and caste lines. Economic development proceeded from gathering-hunting at the lowest level to farming and herding at the highest level. Political development proceeded from the band to the tribe to the chiefdom to the state. All forms of development in these studies were positively correlated with one another, so that there was a single type of development, any form of which could serve as an indicator of development in general.

Warfare was measured in a variety of ways in these studies: incidence, frequency, prevalence, intensity, preparations, attitudes and goals (warlikeness, expectations, causes, purposes and reasons). These various measures were always significantly correlated with one another, so that there was a single type of primitive militarism, any form of which could serve as an indicator of primitive militarism in general. The positive correlations between war preparations and the frequency and intensity of war convinced all authors that preparations provoked wars more than they deterred them, thus confirming the arms race theory of war rather than the deterrence theory.

Most forms of development were significantly correlated with most forms of militarism. The more highly developed societies were generally the more militaristic: "The more primitive the people, the less warlike it appears to be" (Wright, 1965, p. 68). To be sure, this was a statistical finding that established a general rule, not a universal law. There were exceptions to this general rule, but the rule usually obtained.

Although development contributed to all forms of primitive warfare, internal as well as external, and defensive as well as offensive, it contributed most of all to offensive external warfare which, in turn, contributed to territorial expansion and, consequently, to the cultural survival of the most militarily fit. This sequence has been most succinctly expressed by Otterbein: "political centralization → military sophistication → offensive external war → territorial expansion" (1977, p. 699).

Warfare was also associated with crime and its punishment, games of chance and strategy, full-time entrepreneurs, social stratification and slavery, suggesting that these other activities were also functions of development. (Slavery, in particular, was clearly a result of warfare.)

Where personality variables were available, warfare was associated with anxiety, frustrating childhood disciplines, narcissism and sexual repression at all ages (including the Oedipal stage). Whether warfare was a function of these personality variables, or vice versa, is an open question. Both might be more strictly explained as functions of development. In summary, primitive warfare seemed to be a function of an authoritarian culture and an anxious, frustrated, egoistic personality which, itself, may also be a function of an authoritarian culture.

Hunting and warring were primarily male activities in primitive societies, a tendency that has often been ascribed to masculine aggressiveness. However, there seems to be no significant difference in aggressiveness between the sexes. And primitive warfare seems not to be motivated by aggression, but rather a carefully planned and rationally executed activity, designed to accomplish certain purposes such as defense, acquisition of plunder, revenge, enhanced prestige, and the land and power. While warriors (and hunters) have mostly been men, women have cheered on these activities and celebrated the victories. Had they not been occupied by childbearing, child-nursing and child-rearing activities, there would probably have been just as many women warriors and hunters as men.

It would seem then that primitive warfare was a function of development. For several million years, when humans survived by gathering and scavenging, there was presumably no warfare at all; there were no tools, let alone weapons, until about two million years ago, when our forebears began to hunt. Humans biologically similar to ourselves emerged about one hundred thousand years ago and later left a large number of cave paintings, some of which depict hunting, but none of which depict war. Bands of gathering-hunters, numbering about 25 to 50 people each, could not have made war. There would not have been enough people to fight, nor arms with which to fight, and little to fight about. Then, ten thousand years ago, we settled down to farming and keeping livestock and living in villages. We developed a vested interest in our land and cattle, and something like a war became possible. This agricultural revolution eventually resulted in food surpluses, making civilization (living in cities) possible about five thousand years ago. Then war began to come into its own, as we shall see.

However, before moving it is important to remember all the things that were *not* associated with primitive warfare: race, climate and temperature, cultural exchanges (although these could tend toward warfare), hostility, language, area of the world, terrain, feuds, diet, kin type, property inheritance, lineage, cousin marriage, family organization, authority within the family, divorce rate, status of women and fertility level.

## Chapter 2

# Archaic and Ancient Wars, 3000 to 500 B.C.

*Emergence of Civilized Warfare*

The ancient period of history often includes the time from 3000 B.C. to A.D. 500, including the Egyptian, Mesopotamian, Greek and Roman civilizations. As a matter of convenience, this period will be divided into three periods throughout this book: (1) an archaic period from 300 to 1500 B.C. (using very round figures), (2) an ancient period from 1500 to 500 B.C. and (3) a classic period from 500 B.C. to A.D. 500. The reason for making these distinctions is simply that there is very little quantitative data available concerning periods earlier than 500 B.C.

Since there are so little quantitative data for the periods of archaic and ancient history, this chapter includes a brief introduction to history in general, a brief survey of these periods of history in particular, and a preliminary discussion of Quincy Wright's quantitative data on Arnold Toynbee's 26 civilizations.

In spite of the lack of quantitative data, there is no lack of agreement concerning the emergence of warfare at the beginning of history in Mesopotamia and Egypt. Military historians are generally agreed on this point: "The dawn of history and the beginning of organized warfare went hand in hand.... The record is almost entirely devoted to migrations, wars, and conquests" (Dupuy and Dupuy 1986, p. 1). We should not confuse migrations, or even conquests, with wars. Neither migrations nor even conquests necessarily implied any deaths, but wars generally did. "War may actually have been a child of Civilization" (Toynbee 1950, p. viii). "War ... began with civilization" (Wright 1965, p. 39). "The earliest cities [one sign of civilization] were nearly always at war with one another and in internal turmoil" (Bram 1979, vol. 1, p. 52).

This agreement was not merely a matter of opinion, since it was based upon empirical evidence which showed no signs of warfare in primitive art, but many signs of warfare in civilized art, monuments and written records. This is not to suggest that warfare sprang, full-blown, from the head of civilization. No doubt, there was some war during the five thousand years of agriculture preceding the emergence of civilizations about 3000 B.C. and probably increasing warfare as primitive peoples became more developed. Granting that warfare developed as human society developed, its full flowering came with the emergence of civilization, which was the beginning of history, the beginning of written records—the basic objects of historical studies.

## Civilization and History

Gatherers and hunters before the agricultural revolution about ten thousand years ago, and farmers and herders thereafter, left no written records of their lives and times because their ways of surviving required none. But with the onset of civilization those who added commerce and trade to farming and herding as ways of making a living did need written records. So the beginning of history coincided with certain economic needs associated with commerce and trade.

Toynbee suggested that there might have been 38 civilizations during the course of history, four of which were questionable and six of which were abortive, leaving 28 "full-blown" civilizations (Toynbee and Caplan 1972, p. 72). The four earliest civilizations were Sumer (3300 B.C.), Egypt (3100 B.C.), Aegea (2800 B.C.), and Indus (2600 B.C.). Sumer contributed to other civilizations—Syria (1300 B.C.) and Turkey (2000 B.C.) to its west, and Persia (1100 B.C.) to its east. Aegea influenced Hellenic civilization (1300 B.C.), and Indus contributed to Indic civilization (1400 B.C.). Chinese civilization emerged about 1200 B.C. and contributed to several other Asian civilizations. Western (A.D. 300), Orthodox (A.D. 300) and Islamic (A.D. 700) civilizations were influenced by Hellenic and Syriac civilizations. This enumerates most of Toynbee's major civilizations, except for those of East and West Africa and Central and South America.

## Civilization and War

Why did civilized peoples fight more than primitive peoples? A preliminary answer might be that the former had more material things over which to fight, had metal weapons with which to fight, and, above all, had surplus wealth to finance the endeavor. Wars take time away from more productive pursuits. The "savage" gatherers and hunters had little to fight over and only primitive bows and arrows and spears to fight with. Furthermore, they had neither surplus population nor surplus wealth. The "barbarian" farmers and herders had more to fight over, but nothing better to fight with, and still no surplus population or wealth. (The word "barbarian," as used in this book, has no connotation of inferiority; it merely refers to the farming and herding stage of human development, just as the word "savage" refers to the gathering and hunting stage of human development.) Civilized people fought over land, labor, capital and trade. They tended to expand at one another's expense, and at the expense of primitive peoples who could not defend themselves against civilized armies and weapons. "The history of civilized societies is a history of expansion" (McNeill 1982, p. 4).

However, there seems to be something very unstable about the process of civilization so far, since civilizations which rose or expanded eventually fell or contracted in area, population, power and wealth. Civilization seems to be a process which gets in its own way and obstructs its own progress. A lot of its energy seems to be wasted in four kinds of power struggles: (1) one civilization against another; (2) civilizations against barbarians (farmers and herders) and savages (gatherers and hunters); (3) peasant and slave rebellions within civilizations; and (4) power struggles within the ruling class of a civilization.

These four kinds of power struggles translate into four types of war that have characterized every civilization we know: (1) power wars; (2) imperial (and colonial) wars; (3) class wars; and (4) civil wars. Consequently, war seems to be an essential expression of a process that obstructs or even destroys its own progress. Behind this process, and moving it, seems to lie the essence of civilization itself: exploitation, which benefits some at the expense of others. Exploitation violates the categorical imperative of doing only what everyone else can do and keep on doing; it also violates the golden rule of the world's great religions. It may be that this is why civilizations have failed so far, and why the great religions emerged in the first place, in order to reform civilizations. Our own civilization may also fail unless we can find a way of being civilized without exploiting one another.

## Cameo Case Studies

This factor of exploitation in the Roman Empire was explicated in a cameo case study. "Both the mobilization of the Italian peasantry and the subjugation of the barbarians and the Orientals were now being exploited heartlessly for the pecuniary profit of the Roman governing class. The provinces were being drained of their inanimate wealth and their human inhabitants in order to provide lucrative contracts for Roman business men and cheap man-power for Roman senators' cattle-ranches and plantations; and the land which was being stocked with this alien slave-labour in order to multiply the fortunes of a small class of already rich men was Italian land which was being placed at the disposition of these capitalists by the impoverishment and eviction of the former peasant proprietors" (Toynbee 1950, pp. 106–7). The Romans were quite typical of all civilizations before and after them in regard to this exploitation between classes and between nations.

Clearly, such exploitation could only be enforced by means of arms, so that civilization and warfare have been inextricably linked to each other throughout human history, to the benefit of some at the expense of others in the short run, but to the detriment of everyone in the long run. "War has proved to have been the proximate cause of the breakdown of every civilization. . . .

The whole tragedy of militarism . . . has been acted over and over again . . . down to our own militarists in the Western World of today. . . . Militarism has been by far the commonest cause of the breakdown of civilizations during the four or five millennia which have witnessed the score or so of breakdowns that are on record up to the present date" (Toynbee 1950, pp. vii, 101, 130).

This pattern of domination and exploitation repeated itself over and over again in archaic and ancient times, as reported in all of the histories, including Dupuy and Dupuy (1986), Toynbee and Caplan (1972), Garraty and Gay (1972) and the historical books of the Old Testament. The Semitic Hyksos ("foreign kings") invaded and completely overran Egypt from 1800 B.C. to 1600 B.C. Then Thebes revolted, and the Hyksos were driven into Palestine. The Egyptians expanded as far as Libya to the west and Mesopotamia to the east. The Syrian King of Kadesh revolted against Egypt, but was severely defeated in the first recorded battle of history, the Battle of Megiddo (Armageddon) in 1479 B.C. And so the story continued for another thousand years, with occasional changes of characters, but little change of scenery, and no change in the plot until Egypt was conquered by Persia in 525 B.C., after which Egypt lived under foreign rule for more than 24 centuries.

According to an ancient Egyptian source, the Canaanites were waiting for the Egyptians at Megiddo with millions of men and hundreds of thousands of charioteers but, according to modern historians, the famous battle was nothing but a rout, with 83 deaths and 340 prisoners taken (Time-Life 1988b, p. 39). This seems to be a typical case of archaic and ancient exaggerations about battles and wars. The only other modern estimates of archaic and ancient war deaths I have been able to find came from the same source. A Sumerian king claimed to kill 3600 enemies and to bury "twenty heaps" of his own about 2450 B.C. (Time-Life 1988a, p. 32). I have no idea how many of his own occupied those 20 heaps, but presumably they were fewer than the enemy dead, which itself may have been an exaggeration. The Hyksos took Egypt by force about 1650 B.C. but, according to an Egyptian priest, they took it easily "without a single battle" (Time-Life 1988a, p. 86), suggesting few or no deaths. An Assyrian king of the ninth century B.C. claimed to kill three thousand soldiers and to take many prisoners (Time-Life 1988b, p. 24). It would seem, on the basis of the sparse data available that archaic and ancient wars might count their victims in the thousands, but not much more than that. Consequently, although the existence of archaic and ancient battles and wars can hardly be doubted, archaic and ancient accounts of them were highly exaggerated more often than not, presumably for the propaganda value of such exaggerations.

The same pattern repeated itself in Mesopotamia where Sargon of Akkad conquered Sumer in 2325 B.C., founding the first known empire in human history. This empire was dominated by Babylon for several centuries, and then by the Hittites for several more centuries until they were taken over by the Kassites.

The Assyrians became the "most warlike people of the Middle East" (Dupuy and Dupuy 1986, p. 8) from 2000 B.C. to 1200 B.C. and then became the leading power in the region for some 500 years after conquering Syria, Palestine and Babylon. Assyria was "the most efficient military, financial, and administrative system the world had yet seen. The army was its heart.... The principal business of the nation became war.... This was the first truly military society of history.... It was not unusual for them to kill every man, woman, and child in captured cities. Sometimes they would carry away entire populations into captivity" (Dupuy and Dupuy 1986, pp. 8–9). They conquered Egypt, put down revolts in the conquered territories, subdued the Arabs, crushed the Elamites and then disintegrated like all other civilizations before and after them. The Chaldeans and Medes conquered them in 612 B.C. and divided the spoils between themselves.

The Jews and Arabs fought over Palestine for almost five hundred years from 1200 B.C. to 750 B.C. The Jews repelled the Arabs in 1100 B.C., but the Philistines invaded Israel during the rest of that century, killing Saul in the process. Then David conquered all of Palestine and some of Syria. The peace and prosperity under Solomon was too much for any civilization to bear, and after Solomon's death the Jews and Syrians fought each other for two centuries, until they were both conquered by Assyria in 750 B.C., after which Palestine and Syria were under foreign control for 27 centuries.

After getting out from under Assyrian control in 625 B.C., the Medes expanded to Lydia on the west and Indus on the east: "This was the largest empire the world had yet seen, but it lacked the administrative machinery of Assyria, Egypt, and Chaldea" (Dupuy and Dupuy 1986, p. 11).

Toynbee described this general process in terms of disunity leading to unity by conquest, which sooner or later led to disunity by rebellion, and so around the sorry-go-round of conquest and revolt, alternating in periods ranging from one hundred to one thousand years.

This pattern of conquest, domination, exploitation and revolt was repeated not only throughout the Middle East, but throughout the Far East and South Asia as well, and later in Greece and Rome, although the Asians and Europeans lagged behind the Middle East in military technologies, as in most other things.

Although warfare was widespread during these archaic and ancient periods of history, "these wars were not very destructive.... Killing, like everything else, had to be done by hand; therefore mortality was usually low.... With military expansion went an enormous expansion of wealth" (Garraty and Gay 1972, pp. 145, 153).

Even more obvious than the expansion of wealth brought by military expansion was the expansion of territory, which may be the most reliable indicator available concerning the military activities of archaic and ancient civilizations.

After all, the acquisition of territory has always been one of the chief goals of war, including its contents of natural resources, population, and trade. However, as we have already noted, territory may be taken by migration or relatively nonviolent conquest as well as by war.

## Imperial Sizes

Taagepera (1978a) has provided a measure of size for the largest empires throughout history, defining an empire as "any large sovereign political entity whose components are not sovereign" (p. 113). This measure shows that Persia achieved the largest empire during the period from 3000 B.C. to 500 B.C. at 5.5 square megameters (500 B.C.), Media 3.0 (600 B.C.), Assyria 1.4 (660 B.C.), Shang 1.1 (1150 B.C.), and Egypt 1.0 (1450 and 1300 B.C.), with the rest being less than one square megameter (386,000 square miles) during this time period. These measures of territorial size would suggest that Persia was the most warlike of all civilizations or empires in this archaic-ancient period of history, followed by the Medes, assuming that territorial size was a function of military conquest and nothing else, which has to be empirically determined.

Whether or not this is the case, it is of great interest to note how imperial territories became larger and larger over time: the largest empire from 3000 B.C. to 2500 B.C. was Egypt with 0.4 square megameters in 2500 B.C.; Akkad was largest from 2400 B.C. to 2000 B.C. with 0.6 square megameters in 2300 B.C.; Egypt and the Hyksos were the largest from 1900 B.C. to 1500 B.C. with 0.65 for the Hyksos in 1600 B.C. and the same for Egypt in 1500 B.C.; Shang was the largest from 1450 B.C. to 1000 B.C. with 1.1 square megameters in 1150 B.C.; and Persia was the largest from 950 B.C. to 500 B.C. with 5.5 square megameters in 500 B.C.

These measures would suggest that civilizations or empires became more warlike with the passage of time, assuming that increasing sizes were a function of military activities. Further assuming that the passage of time made people more civilized, on the average, then these figures would suggest that not only did civilization bring war in its wake, but the more civilized people became, the more warlike they became.

Taagepera recommended caution in equating territorial size and imperial power: "In general . . . area reflects the power of an empire to some extent: A large but powerless empire would soon cease to be large" (1978a, p. 111). "Areas reflect political power only indirectly. . . . The geographical size is often but not always correlated with the extent of political or military power. It may have no relation at all with cultural, spiritual, or even commercial power" (1979, pp. 116, 119). "Changes in power often tend to bring territorial changes" (1981, p. 2). "Neither [population nor size] reflects fully the power relations" (1986, p. 11).

## War and Class

It would seem that in these archaic-ancient civilizations war and slavery tended to deplete the civilization in less than a millennium, making it fair game for other predators, civilized or barbarian. (Savages never conquered civilizations, because they never had the wherewithal.) The main motive behind this combination of civilization, empire, slavery and war was the desire to dominate others to benefit oneself, which violated the categorical imperative. It might be hypothesized that this basic violence is responsible for most other human violence, in which case our own civilization may be saveable only if we can somehow make the categorical imperative central to human motivation.

Toynbee expressed this combination of war and slavery as follows: "War and Class have always been with us ever since the first civilizations emerged.... Of the 20 or so civilizations known to modern Western historians [the known number increased by 1972], all except our own appear to be dead or moribund, and ... we invariably find that the cause of death has been either War or Class. To date, these two plagues have been deadly enough, in partnership, to kill off 19 out of 20 representatives of this recently evolved species of human society.... Greco-Roman civilization finally died of the twin diseases of War and Class in the course of the fifth, sixth and seventh centuries of the Christian era" (1948, pp. 23–24).

## Civilized Warfare

Wright (1965) made a splendid effort to quantify 26 of Toynbee's civilizations, including their warlikeness and other military characteristics, military techniques, frequencies of four different kinds of battles (imperialistic, interstate, civil and defensive), and general characteristics, including political organization and bloodthirstiness (Wright 1965, pp. 571–72). Although this was a noble effort, its reliability may be questionable. How can 26 civilizations, lasting for almost two thousand years on the average, be reliably rated on a four-point scale for 27 variables? It is true that such crude scales were also used on primitive peoples, but these were smaller groups observed over a relatively short period of time, and they were observed at first hand. Wright's ratings of civilizations were made not on living peoples available to current observation, but had to be made on the basis of artistic, monumental and written records, and these records extended over some two thousand years on the average. The ratings were made more manageable by limiting them to the universal state of each civilization, which lasted for only about 260 years on the average. This universal state, which occurred at the height of the civilization, was a time of stability, when records were likely to be most reliable. But the task of rating even these universal states on 27 variables would seem to be very difficult.

At the very least, it would seem to be desirable and necessary for two or three people, preferably historians, to rate these variables independently for these 26 civilizations. Then these ratings could be correlated to provide a measure of reliability. It would be most desirable if a few historians could take on this task, so that we should at least have some measure of the reliability of Wright's ratings. Unless and until this is done, Wright's ratings remain uncertain. Perhaps no one has the historical expertise for this task. At least, no one has tackled it so far since Wright's monumental book was first published in

1942. In the meantime, since no other such quantitative data exists for these civilizations in archaic and ancient times, we shall have to make do with them.

Wright's rating of warlikeness was simply the sum of five other ratings: (1) the degree of absolutism in political organization; (2) bloodthirstiness — defined as habituation to human bloodshed in the form of religious sacrifices, sports and spectacles, executions, feuds and private wars; (3) the frequency of imperialistic battles; (4) the frequency of interstate battles; and (5) the degree of discipline and enthusiasm of the population participating in war (Wright 1965, p. 574). The summing of unreliable ratings can increase the reliability of the sum somewhat, but such ratings as these are more questionable the further back we go in time, when the data get very sparse indeed, such as during this archaic-ancient period of history.

Until the reliability of Wright's ratings has been established, we can at least correlate Taagepera's (1978a) careful measurements of imperial sizes with Wright's five-point ratings of populations — probably one of the most reliable of Wright's ratings. We should expect there to be at least a significant correlation between these two measures, since more people generally occupy more land. For example, Gernot Kohler (1986) found a correlation of .55 (significant at the .01 level of confidence) between the area and population of 142 nations in 1980. When I correlated Taagepera's sizes (logged to correct for skewness) with Wright's populations for 26 civilizations, the correlation was .66 (significant at the .01 level of confidence). So far as it goes, this significant correlation would suggest some reliability for Wright's ratings of population. This is helpful, but it is hardly enough to assume reliability for Wright's other ratings, which would have been harder to estimate than population.

In the meantime Taagepera's measurements of imperial size should be useful as a rough indicator of warlikeness, since both historical and primitive warfare were associated with territorial expansion. However, Wright's warlikeness ratings were not significantly correlated with his population ratings, nor were they significantly correlated with Taagepera's size measurements. If Wright's warlikeness ratings were reliable, then warlikeness has nothing to do with power as indicated by population and size. It is possible that Wright's "warlikeness" indicates the intensity of military activities, while Taagepera's size indicates their extent. Some combination of the two may prove to be a more accurate indicator of military activity. We should remember that, although Taagepera's size measurements may be more reliable than Wright's ratings, they are hardly perfect: "In our study, a 10 percent error on all areas reported should be expected" (Taagepera 1978a, p. 111).

According to Taagepera's size measurements, and my assumption that there is some relationship between imperial size and military activity, archaic-ancient civilizations became more warlike as they became more civilized from 3000 B.C. to 500 B.C. Consequently, the tendency for warfare to increase with primitive development, especially from the gathering-hunting stage of development to the farming-herding stage, as demonstrated in the first chapter of this book, has continued into this archaic-ancient period of history. Consequently, war is a function of historical and prehistoric development, and not a function of human nature as such. In the next chapter we shall see whether this tendency continues into the classic period of ancient history, 500 B.C. to A.D. 500. At least we shall find a little more quantitative data for this later time period.

Before proceeding to this next historical period, however, let us look at Wright's quantitative data in more detail, and at some other quantitative data involving archaic-ancient civilizations, empires and wars, in order to provide ourselves with a bird's-eye view of archaic-ancient history. A brief review of Wright's study of war can be found in Eckhardt (1981c).

## Analysis of Wright's Data

In spite of the possible lack of reliability of Wright's ratings of civilizations, based on Toynbee's historical descriptions, it is nevertheless desirable to analyze these data statistically. Wright never did this analysis, in spite of the tremendous expenditure of time, talent and effort that went into his ratings. Computer facilities were not quite so readily available before the Second World War. Wright and his colleagues and students at the University of Chicago performed the research that went into his monumental book, with some 60 scholars working from 1926 to 1942. The lack of computers was probably the reason why no statistical analyses were undertaken on the 27 variables rated for 26 civilizations.

We should note here that Wright was limited to the 26 civilizations that Toynbee described in the first six volumes of his monumental *Study of History*, which were published 1934–39. Toynbee later published six more volumes, 1954–61, and a one-volume edition in 1972, by which time his 26 civilizations had been changed to some extent. Eight were now regarded as part of larger civilizations, so that these eight were no longer considered independent civilizations: Babylonia, Germany, Ireland, Scandinavia, Nestoria, later China (as distinct from early China), Maya and Yucatan. Their place was taken by ten other civilizations, either newly discovered or separated from larger civilizations: East Africa, West Africa, Southeast Asia, Tibet, Vietnam, Korea, North Andes, South Andes, Mississippi and Southwest America. These changes remind us that there is nothing final about the listing of civilizations. Not only do different authors list different civilizations—and different numbers of civilizations—but the same author (as in this case) may present different lists at different times. Nevertheless, 18 of the 26 civilizations in his early list remained in his later list of 28 civilizations.

Wright's ratings are shown on pp. 571–72 of the 1965 revised edition of his book. The definitions of the 27 variables are given on pp. 573–74. Further information on the dates, durations, stages and survival of these 26 civilizations will be found on pp. 461–63. I used this information to develop five additional variables: region, from east to west (1. China and Japan, 2. India, 3. Middle East, 4. Mediterranean, 5. Europe, 6. America); total number of battles (sum of imperialistic, interstate, civil and defensive battles); living civilizations (p. 461); duration (p. 463); and average year of civilization's existence (mean of beginning and ending year as given on p. 463). These additional variables can be classified as measures of geographical space and historical time. Wright classified the other 27 variables as general characteristics (population, period, geography, agriculture, commerce, contacts, heterogeneity, politics and bloodthirstiness), battle frequency (imperialistic, interstate, civil and defensive battles), military techniques (public morale, professionalization, infantry, cavalry, navy, archery, hand weapons, body armor, fortification and siegecraft) and military characteristics (attack efficiency, defense efficiency, superiority of defense, and warlikeness [ political absolutism, bloodthirstiness, imperialistic battles, interstate battles and public morale]).

I correlated these 32 variables with one another. In order to generalize the 496 independent correlations obtained in this manner, the correlation matrix was analyzed into seven factors. A factor is simply a set of variables in the correlation matrix. In short, a factor contains variables that are related to one another on the basis of structural similarity. Whatever causal relations there may be among them has to be determined outside of the statistical analysis. Further information on correlations and factors will be found in Appendix A.

The first factor included the following variables, with the factor coefficients shown in parentheses. The higher this number the more closely the variable was related to the factor: defense efficiency (.93), infantry (.87), hand weapons (.85), siegecraft (.81), defense superiority (.77), total battle frequency (.75), body armor (.75) attack efficiency (.73), military professionalization (.71), population (.69), morale (.67), heterogeneity (.63), contacts (.59), civil battle frequency (.59), warlikeness (.58), cavalry (.54), navy (.52), fortification (.51), defensive battle frequency (.49), living civilizations (.48), commerce (.48), archery (.47), imperialistic battle frequency (.44), interstate battle frequency (.42), bloodthirstiness (.37), Eastern civilizations (.35), later historical period (.30).

All of these variables were significantly related to this general factor, which might be called a factor of general militarism, since it included all of the military characteristics, all of the military techniques, and all of the battle frequencies. In addition to the militarism variables, this factor was also related to larger populations (.69), heterogeneous populations (.63), intercivilization contacts (.59), living civilizations (.48), commerce (.48), bloodthirstiness (.37), Eastern civilizations (.35) and later historical period (.30). These general characteristics were mildly to moderately correlated with the military factor. This militarism factor was more related to later civilizations than to earlier ones, including those with larger and more heterogeneous populations to whom commerce was important. Neither agriculture (grazing versus irrigation) nor geography (plateaus and steppes versus maritime and rivers) was significantly related to this factor of general militarism. This general factor, as crude as it is and as far as it goes, supports the theory that later civilizations were more warlike.

The second factor was characterized by plateau and steppe geography (.73), imperialistic battle frequency (.68), bloodthirstiness (.68), grazing versus irrigation (.67), warlikeness (.62), lack of commerce (.57), lack of fortification (.56), political absolutism (.54), defensive battle frequency (−.45), archery (.44), Western civilizations (.42), population (−.42), later historical period (.41), attack superiority (.36), and lack of navy (.33).

This factor might well be called offensive militarism, with its emphasis on attack rather than defense. Compared to the general militarism factor, this factor was characterized by more bloodthirstiness, herding versus farming, less commerce, political absolutism, more western than eastern, less population and later historical period. This factor, with its emphasis on herding versus farming and commerce, and with its lesser population, would seem to fit more nomadic civilizations, so that this factor might also be called nomadic militarism.

Both of these factors of militarism supported the notion that later civilizations were more militaristic than earlier civilizations. They also suggested that general militarism was more civilized than nomadic militarism and, therefore, more warlike.

Factor scores were generated for the 26 civilizations on these two factors. The factor scores were standardized so that their mean score was 50 with a standard deviation of 10. Those civilizations with a high score of 60 or more on general militarism were the following: Western Christianity (69), classical Greece and Rome (67), Syria (66), Babylonia (63), Orthodox Christianity (61) and Persia (60), while those civilizations with a low score of 40 or less were: Nestoria (30), Maya (37), Egypt (39) and Minoa (39). All the others were average in general militarism, with scores ranging from 41 to 59. The Mesopotamian *region* was highest (57) in general militarism, and the American *region* was lowest (43). Table 2.1 in Appendix B shows general, offensive and total militarism scores for all 26 civilizations. (All the tables in this book have been placed in an Appendix for those who are interested in more details. These tables may be skipped by the more casual reader.)

High scores on offensive militarism were: Tartars (69), Arabs (67), Mexico (64) and Andes (62). Low scores were: Han China (30), Mesopotamia (37), classical India (37), Egypt (39), Manchu China (40) and Minoa (40). The American *region* obtained the highest score (58) on offensive militarism, while the Far Eastern *region* obtained the lowest score (41).

Since these factor scores were independent of each other, they were added together, and then divided by two, to form a total militarism score. Table 2.1 shows that Syria obtained the highest total score (60), followed by Arabia (60), Persia (60), Tartars (60), Greece/Rome (57), Japan (57), Babylonia (56), Western Christianity (56) and Mexico (55). Lowest total scores were obtained by Han China (39), Egypt (39), Minoa (40), Mesopotamia (41), Nestoria (41), classic India (43), Maya (44), Ireland (46) and Manchu China (46).

Table 2.1 also includes Wright's warlikeness ratings and my assignment of Taagepera's imperial sizes to Wright's (Toynbee's) civilizations. These assignments were very crude indeed. Almost half of the 26 civilizations were not included among Taagepera's three largest empires throughout history (3000 B.C. to A.D. 1975), but Taagepera kindly provided additional data for smaller empires, although he could not identify five of Wright's (Toynbee's) civilizations as single empires, to wit, Syria, Nestoria, Scandinavia, Western and Orthodox Christianity. I estimated the size of these as well as I could with the help of maps published by Toynbee and Caplan (1972). In all cases the size was taken at the time of the civilization's universal state, maturity, or time of stability, so that it would be at the same approximate time as the rest of Wright's ratings.

When the variables in Table 2.1 were correlated with one another, general militarism, offensive militarism, total militarism and warlikeness were all highly correlated with one another (.58 to .85), but territorial size (logged to correct for skewness) was not significantly related to any of these military variables. Consequently, we are left with the choice between Wright's ratings and Taagepera's size estimates as the most reliable indicators of militarism or warlikeness among civilizations. In either case, both indicators suggest that military activities increased over historical time. They could both be indicating the same thing, but from different points of view. They are not contradicting each other, even though they are not correlated with each other. Since they are independent of each other, they could be standardized and added together as a more complete indicator of warlikeness, which has been done in the last column of Table 2.1. It is possible that Wright's ratings, so far as they turn out to be reliable, may be indicating the intensity of militarism, while Taagepera's size estimates may be showing its extent. Adding the two together may result in a more comprehensive measure of militarism than either one taken alone. The validation of this measure remains to be determined.

## Archaic and Ancient Civilizations, Empires and Wars

Table 2.2 in Appendix B shows an assortment of data on archaic-ancient civilizations, empires and wars. These data have been listed by centuries from 3000 B.C. to 500 B.C., which constitutes the first half of human history.

It can be seen that these figures were all increasing over these 25 centuries, some more gradually (like population and pages of history), and the rest more exponentially. It can also be seen from the percentage figures in the last row of Table 2.2 that civilized activities (such as statesmanship, philosophy, religion, literature, painting, sculpture, science, music, business, etc.), imperial sizes, battles and wars were a relatively small percent of the total over five thousand years, ranging from less than 1 percent to less than 7 percent for the first half of human history.

When I correlated the seven variables in Table 2.2 (including the centuries themselves as a measure of time), all of these variables were so highly correlated with one another that they constituted a single factor: population (.96),

# Figure 2.1 Civilizations, Empires and Wars, 3000 to 500 B.C.

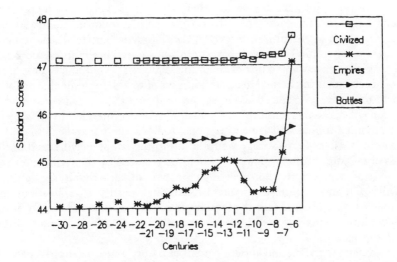

Notes to Figure 2.1: Some of the points in the early centuries had to be omitted because there were too many points for my program to handle. All of the points will be found in Table 2.2. The same reason accounts for any missing points in the other graphs in this book. Civilized = Number of historical persons mentioned in the ninth edition of the *Encyclopaedia Britannica*, weighted by their influence as indicated by the number of lines devoted to them. These "historical persons" were collected by John V. Boldyreff for a doctoral dissertation, but the most readily accessible source for them is Sorokin (1937, vol. 4, pp. 328–29). Their activities included religion, state, literature, scholarship, science, philosophy, business, miscellany, fine arts and music. The arithmetic averages of these ten groups of activities were used in Table 2.2, which was used as the data for this graph. These activities were assumed to provide a rough measure of civilization. Empires = The sum of imperial sizes in square megameters per century, based on Taagepera (1978a). Wars = The number of battles in Dupuy and Dupuy (1986). All three measures were standardized to a mean of 50 and a standard deviation of 10 over the 50 centuries from 3000 B.C. to A.D. 2000, in order to make them comparable to one another. It can be seen that all three measures during the first half of human history were less than the average standard score of 50 for all 50 centuries, ranging from 44 to almost 48.

---

century (.95), pages (.89), battles (.89), wars (.89), imperial sizes (.89), civilized activites (.84). Battles, wars, imperial sizes and civilized acts were logged prior to analysis in order to correct for their skewed distributions.

This factor clearly shows that all of these variables were growing together over these 25 centuries. Since population, as such, has already been shown to be unnecessary for the increase in warlikeness in the two factors generated from Wright's coding of Toynbee's civilizations, we cannot explain these increases by the increase in population alone. Population is further ruled out by the data in Table 2.2 because its gradual increase cannot explain the exponential increase in battles and wars. These considerations would suggest that civilizations, empires and wars all grew together in a dialectical evolutionary progression, so that they fed back and forth into one another, following upon a similar tendency seen at the primitive level of development. The relations between civilizations, empires and wars have been shown graphically in Figure 2.1.

Without assuming a first cause in this dialectical evolutionary process, it would seem that war helped to create a surplus of wealth for some that enabled them to engage in civilized activities and to spread these activities to others, by force if necessary, resulting in empires. This process tended to grow by its own momentum, as well as by its response to both internal and external challengers. A successful challenge would result in the fall of a civilization or the loss of an empire which, however, would be replaced by the civilization and empire of the victor, to whom would go the spoils of war — that is, the defeated civilization and empire. Consequently, although particular civilizations and empires would rise and fall, the total process of civilization and empire at the global level of analysis would continue to rise, as shown by the data in Table 2.2 and Figure 2.1.

When the archaic and ancient periods of history were considered separately (3000–1500 B.C. and 1500–500 B.C.), the mean scores on all the variables in Table 2.2 were significantly higher for the ancient period than they were for the archaic period. The correlations among these variables for each period taken separately were very similar to those obtained for the whole 2500 years. There seems to be no doubt that civilizations, empires and wars were increasing together during these archaic and ancient periods of history, even as primitive warfare had increased with primitive development, as shown in the first chapter of this book.

We will now turn to a consideration of classic wars, that is, those wars that occurred from about 500 B.C. to about A.D. 500.

# Chapter 3
# Classic Wars,
# 500 B.C. to A.D. 500

## Introduction

In order to distinguish this period from the previous one, which was called Archaic-Ancient, I have called this period Classic History, although both periods have often been grouped together as Ancient History. The distinction is useful in order to call attention to the relative lack of quantitative data concerning the wars of the archaic-ancient period, and the increased availability of some quantitative data for the wars in this classic period. I shall use the term "classic" throughout this book only to refer to the time period of 500 B.C. to A.D. 500.

Not only was the archaic-ancient period lacking in quantitative data, but it was generally lacking in data of any kind. As expressed by some military historians, the period from 600–400 B.C. constituted a "transition from semilegendary chronicles to serious, reliable histories" (Dupuy and Dupuy 1986, p. 16).

## Archaic, Ancient and Classic History

An overview of the similarities and differences between the two periods will be presented in this section, the most obvious difference being the difference in imperial sizes. Using Taagepera's (1978a) size estimates, I added the size of all these empires century by century, and found that the average sum of the archaic empires was 0.6 square megameters; ancient empires, 2.6 square megameters; and classic empires, 13.6 square megameters, as shown in Table 3.1 (Appendix B). In short, the average empire in the classic period was more than five times larger than that in the ancient period, and more than 22 times larger than that in the archaic period. Not only was more territory being brought under political control, but the average empire was becoming larger as time went on.

The rest of the variables in Table 3.1 also increased significantly from period to period, as determined by analyses of variance. Most of the variables

41

in this table (except centuries, pages and population) were logged for the purpose of this test, in order to correct for the skewness of their distributions. (Skewed variables will almost always be logged throughout this book, except as otherwise noted, for the purpose of statistical analyses.)

Table 3.2 (Appendix B) shows the same data in terms of percentages, which facilitate comparisons among variables as well as between periods. The average percent of all six variables near the bottom of the table shows that only about 1 percent of these variables of civilization, empire and war occurred during the 15 centuries of the archaic period, while 3 percent of them occurred during the 10 centuries of the ancient period, and 12 percent of them occurred during the 10 centuries of the classic period. Altogether about 16 percent of these variables occurred during the first 35 centuries (70 percent) of human history.

As the last row of this table shows, these 35 centuries of human history were characterized by far fewer activities than the number of centuries might lead us to expect. The archaic period contained only about 4 percent of the amount of activity that might have been expected in 15 centuries, if these activities were evenly distributed across all 50 centuries from 3000 B.C. to A.D. 2000. The ancient period contained only about 15.5 percent of what might have been expected. The classic period came closer to what might have been predicted, evidencing about 60 percent of its expected civilized, imperial and warlike activities. The first 35 centuries of human history showed less than one-quarter of what would be expected for that length of time if such activities were distributed equally over all 50 centuries. The data upon which Tables 3.1 and 3.2 were based is found in Table 2.2 for the archaic and ancient periods and in Table 3.3 for the classic period (Appendix B).

There was, of course, some continuity between these periods. The relatively large empires of Egypt, Mesopotamia and Turkey all came to an end about 550 B.C. (with Egypt and Mesopotamia never to return as large empires, but with Turkey to return in the medieval and modern periods). India, China and Persia continued to maintain large empires during the classic period. Persia, to be sure, was a latecomer, achieving empire status after 700 B.C. In fact, Persia conquered Turkey in 546 B.C., Mesopotamia in 539 B.C., and Egypt in 525 B.C. These three did not really wane; they simply were conquered by Persia and remained under Persian rule into the classic period. Central Asia produced a newcomer in the classic period, the Hsiung-Nu Huns, whose empire was the largest yet (5.7 square megameters in 150 B.C.). Another newcomer was European; Rome ruled 4.4 square megameters from A.D. 100 to 350. Although Egypt and Mesopotamia expired early as independent empires, they nevertheless were longer-lived than any others, except China. China has endured some 3900 years; Egypt and Mesopotamia each lasted about 2500 years.

Although there were sufficient changes to distinguish one period from the next, the pattern of events show a remarkable similarity in the rise and fall of empires. Egypt rose and fell four times (at least), thus giving rise to historians' demarcations of the Old, Middle, New and Late empires. Mesopotamia rose and fell some five times, its incarnations being Akkad, Sumer, Babylon, Mitanni and Assyria. India rose and fell perhaps three times (Harappa?, Maghada/ Maurya and Kushan). China rose and fell at least four times (Hsia, Shang, Han and Chin); Turkey, several times (Hyksos, Hittites and Phrygia/Lydia); Persia, five times (Media, Achaemenia, Alexander, Parthia and Sassania); and Rome, once. Our Eurocentered history books may have been unduly influenced by the Roman example, thus giving us the impression that civilizations rise and fall only once. The general pattern seems to be one of several rises and falls. In fact, if we count the Roman Empire as early Europe, then Europe itself has risen twice and fallen once, so far.

What can account for this pattern of rising and falling? Spengler (1926–28) made an analogy to individuals' living and dying, an extension of some sort of biological necessity. Toynbee (Toynbee and Caplan 1972) suggested a more conscious response to special challenges faced by civilizations, challenges often coming from dissatisfied parties within and without the civilizations—the proletariat within and the barbarian without. Toynbee's suggestion holds more hope than Spengler's for human control over the fate of civilization. I submit that the most general challenge facing all civilizations was (and is) the prophetic challenge to do justice and to love mercy, to follow the golden rule and the categorical imperative. The problem can be solved if it is possible to satisfy everyone to some reasonable extent. As we trace the rise and fall of civilizations, however sketchily, in this and succeeding chapters, we shall look for further clues to confirm or deny Toynbee's suggestion.

Although I agree with Toynbee on the general nature of the rise and fall of civilizations, I should like to disagree with his postulation of 26 or more civilizations. Toynbee himself emphasized the need to study "civilizations" rather than smaller units such as nations or states. I think we should carry his reasoning one step further and suggest that civilizations can be generalized to their geographical locations such as Egypt, Mesopotamia, India, China, Turkey, Persia, central Asia, Europe, Africa and America. We can also take advantage of Taagepera's emphasis on size, and suggest that only relatively large empires be considered as subjects of civilizational and or imperial studies. These suggestions are made primarily for the sake of convenience and feasibility. They constitute an arbitrary way of making the historical task more manageable by generalizing it to certain geographical regions and by limiting it to certain territorial sizes. Without unlimited resources, one cannot study everything. These suggestions provide one way of limiting what we study in the hope of making the most efficient use of our limited resources. In any event, whatever we study, the size factor should be taken into consideration and clearly specified as one important dimension in the field of study.

Although it was never much larger than it is today, archaic Egypt was the largest empire in the world for two-thirds of the archaic period of history, but for only one-fifth of the ancient period, and for none of the following periods. So, while Egypt was declining in its relative imperial size, the world as a whole was rising, as shown in Table 3.4 (Appendix B).

Mesopotamia was the largest empire for only one-fifth of the archaic period and three-tenths of the ancient period. India was the largest empire only once during the archaic period, and tied for the largest once later. China was the largest empire twice during the ancient period, but not at all during the archaic period. In the classic period China had the largest empire in 40 percent of the 10 centuries, followed by Persia with 30 percent, and Europe with 20 percent.

## Western History

History in the West began with the classic period. In fact, it might be fairly accurate to say that history as we know it was a Greek invention. Herodotus, who chronicled the Persian Wars, was called (by us, to be sure) the father of history; and Thucydides, who chronicled the Peloponnesian War, was called (again, by us) the first historian. Note that Western history was first and foremost a history of war.

Shortly before Herodotus and Thucydides were recording the Greek wars in the last half of the fifth century B.C., Sun Tzu had written the first known military treatise on *The Art of War* in China about 500 B.C. Modern military historians had this to say about classic wars: "By 400 B.C. war had assumed the major characteristics which it retained at least into the dawn of the nuclear age. Weapons themselves were essentially unchanged . . . for nearly 2,000 more years" (Dupuy and Dupuy 1986, p. 16). "Save for the wars of Alexander, Hannibal, and the offensive-minded Romans, pitched battles were relatively infrequent. The opposing generals concentrated on raiding one another's resources while at the same time blockading towns and fortresses" (p. 37). This blockading of towns and fortresses served the purpose of starving the enemy to death, since "walled cities or fortresses were impervious to everything but starvation" (p. 18).

The blockade and siege of cities was not something new since it can be traced back to the ancient period in places such as Troy, to use an example with which we are familiar. Such procedures were not uncommon and remind us that war was seldom limited to the soldiers involved, but extended to any civilians that got in the way, so that from the beginning civilians as well as soldiers were killed in wars. My own impression is that just as many civilians were killed as were soldiers, but we shall return to this point later.

The active army size seemed to range from about 10,000 to about 40,000, at least in classic Europe. And, in fact, armies of 100,000 or more were uncommon prior to the Napoleonic wars, according to figures presented by Zook and Higham (1966). Presumably, army sizes in the earlier periods were smaller than these. Sargon, one of the most powerful Sumerian kings, had 5400 professional warriors about 2600 B.C. (Time-Life 1988a, p. 32). There were 20,000 Egyptians at the Battle of Megiddo in 1479 B.C., and 20,000 Egyptians confronted 17,000 Hittites at Kadesh in 1285 B.C. (Time-Life 1988b, pp. 15–16,

41). In the eighth century B.C. the Greek city-states had armies of about 1600 men (Time-Life 1988b, p. 97). The Shang armies numbered up to 13,000 from the eighteenth to the twelfth centuries B.C. (Time-Life 1988b, p. 144).

## China

The Han empire from about 200 B.C. to about A.D. 200 reached its peak size of 6.5 square megameters about A.D. 100, by which time it had exceeded the Hsiung-Nu size of 5.7, making it the largest empire thus far, the largest imperial size achieved during the classic period. Han exceeded both Persia (5.5 square megameters in 500 B.C.) and Rome (4.4 square megameters, in A.D. 100–350).

The classic period in China was ushered in by an era of warring states, which had developed out of the disintegration of the previous Chou empire. This era of warring states was a "challenge," in Toynbee's terms, to which Confucius and Lao-Tzu responded in the sixth century B.C. Both of these philosophies were reactionary, in the sense that they called for going back to a previous time: back to the early Chou, in the case of Confucius, when rulers ruled by personal example; back to nature, in the case of Lao-Tzu, when primitive agricultural communities followed the laws of nature. These ethical responses may have been the salvation of China, enabling it to survive while other empires in Egypt, Mesopotamia and Turkey did not.

The disintegration within was accompanied by invasions from without by the Hsiung-Nu Huns. These outside challenges were successfully handled by building the Great Wall from about 228–204 B.C. The Han dynasty emerged about this time and established Confucianism as the official ideology, appointing administrators on the basis of merit rather than birth. Slavery was abolished about the turn of the millennium. But, during the late Han dynasty, incompetence crept back into government, demoralizing it and leading to Taoist rebellions, and to the establishment of private armies by large landowners who fought one another for dominance. Disintegration within was again accompanied by barbarian invasions from without, so that China at the end of the classic period was following the same pattern it had at the period's beginning. The ethical response had failed for the time being, but, even if China did not survive, it did revive itself later.

## Ethical Response to the Challenges of Civilization

The end of the ancient period and the beginning of the classic period was characterized by a number of ethical responses occasioned by the challenges of civilization. We have mentioned Confucius and Lao-Tzu in sixth century China. The Hebrew prophets were the earliest of the lot, with Amos, Hosea, Micah and the first Isaiah emerging 750–700 B.C., followed by the prophetic book of Deuteronomy in 686 B.C., then Jeremiah and Ezekiel in 626–570 B.C., and finally the restoration prophets, including the second Isaiah, in 550–450 B.C. Surely the survival of Israel benefitted greatly from their predictions that if Israel did justice and loved mercy it would live, but otherwise would die. Ethics, religious or otherwise, were presented as a matter of life and death: "I have put life and death before you, the blessing and the curse; therefore choose life" (Deuteronomy 30:19).

Zoroaster came in Persia in 630–541 B.C., followed by Mahavira and Buddha in sixth century B.C. India, and finally Socrates in fifth century B.C. Greece. The ethical responses of all of these philosophical and religious leaders boiled down to a golden rule: "Cease to do evil, learn to do good; seek justice, restrain the oppressor; uphold the rights of the orphan, defend the cause of the widow!" (Isaiah 1:17). "They shall not build, and another inhabit; they shall not plant, and another eat" (Isaiah 65:22). "Do justice and righteousness; deliver the despoiled from the hand of the oppressor" (Jeremiah 22:3). "Let justice roll down like waters, and righteousness like a perennial stream" (Amos 5:24). "You have been told ... what is good ... : Only to do justice, and to love kindness" (Micah 6:8).

In short, "Love thy neighbor as thyself." Or, as Confucius said: "What you do not want done to yourself, do not do to others." Or, in Taoism: "Regard your neighbor's gain as your own gain, and regard your neighbor's loss as your own loss." And, according to Buddha, "To him in whom love dwells, the whole world is but one family.... Minister to others ... by treating them as you treat yourself." And Hinduism: "Treat other as they themselves wish to be treated."

In Plato's *Lysis*, Socrates defined friendship in terms of loving one's enemies. But this was treason. While waiting for his execution, as recorded in Plato's *Crito*, he said to a friend: "We must injure no one at all.... We ought not to retaliate or render evil for evil to any one." Socrates believed that "doing injustice is the greatest of evils.... [T]o do injustice is more to be avoided than to suffer injustice" (Plato's *Gorgias*).

Jesus agreed with Socrates and all the others: "Insofar as you did it to the least of these, you did it to me.... Do unto others as you would have them do unto you.... [L]ove your enemies." He was also tried for treason. And Islam: "No one of you is a believer until he loves for his brother what he loves for himself."

This Golden Rule of Reciprocity was a response to the self-centeredness of civilization. It was addressed to the rulers especially, but also to the people. It was seldom heeded. The golden calf was more attractive than the Golden Rule. It was not preached until near the end of the ancient period, 750–400 B.C., and the peoples of Egypt, Mesopotamia and Turkey did not have the advantage of hearing it.

The classic civilizations all heard the message, but not many paid attention. As we shall see, these civilizations also violated the Golden Rule, and paid the penalty by the end of the classic period.

# Greece

Greece was a creator of civilization but not of empire. The Greek city-states never did manage to sufficiently unify politically to develop an empire. They never amounted to more than city-states, the way Sumer began about 3000 B.C. Greece was simply a loose confederation of independent city-states, such as Athens, Corinth, Sparta and Thebes. They sometimes acted together in the face of a common enemy, as when Persia attacked them about 490–479 B.C. in retaliation for revolts against Darius I by some Greek colonies in Ionia, on the western coast of Asia Minor (Turkey). Their defenses at Marathon and Salamis were quite successful, in spite of their defeat at Thermopylae.

At the end of the Persian Wars Athens was in a dominant position among the other city-states. This was the Golden Age of Athens under the rule of Pericles. It was indeed a golden age of art and science. But the other city-states were chafing under Athenian dominance, and their dissatisfaction culminated in the Peloponnesian War (431–404 B.C.) between Athens and Sparta. Sparta won, and the other city-states breathed a sigh of relief to be freed from the pre-eminence of democratic Athens: "Her rule had ended in tyranny abroad and demagoguery at home.... When the Spartans took the city, survivors and exiles joined in pulling down the long walls to the sound of flutes, 'believing that day was the beginning of freedom for Greece'" (Garraty and Gay 1972, p. 176).

So Athens failed to survive in spite of its culture and wealth, and in spite of its democracy. But the other city-states were no happier with aristocratic and militaristic Sparta dominating them than they had been with democratic Athens. So, Athens and Thebes combined against Sparta in 371 B.C., leading to Theban dominance. This, in turn, led to an alliance between Athens and Sparta in 369 B.C. The triangular pattern of two-against-one seemed to prevail during the fourth century B.C. Finally, Philip of Macedon developed what some military historians have called "the first scientifically organized military force of history" (Dupuy and Dupuy 1986, p. 38), which he used to annex Greek colonies in 359 B.C. Philip reigned supreme over the Greek city-states by 338 B.C., and declared war against Persia in 337 B.C., but died before he could put this declaration into action.

# Persia

Persia emerged from the ancient period as a large empire, having conquered the Medes in 558 B.C., Lydia in 546 B.C., Babylon in 539 B.C. and Egypt in 525 B.C. This resulted in a larger empire than ever before existed (5.5 square megameters). But, in spite of its size, Persia was stopped by the Greeks at Marathon and Salamis in 490–479 B.C., after which the Persian empire began to decline. The final blow was struck by Alexander, the Macedonian, who executed his father's plan to make war on Persia. He defeated Persian troops in a series of battles from 334–331 B.C. Alexander's empire was hardly a creation, but rather a hostile takeover of territory that Persia had itself taken from others. At his death in 323 B.C., Alexander's empire was 5.2 square megameters, somewhat smaller than the Persian empire had been.

Alexander's generals contended for the Persian throne after his death. Seleucus won this struggle, and Persia remained subordinate to the Seleucid empire until it was overthrown by the Parthians who, in turn, were finally overthrown by the Persians in A.D. 226. The Persians then invaded India, conquered Armenia, and engaged in some seven wars with Rome from about 240 to 420. Near the end of the fifth century the "White Huns" attacked Persia, defeating it and exacting heavy tribute for years thereafter. So another empire succumbed to barbarians from without. Since they had violated the rights of others, it should have come as no surprise that their rights were violated in return. They set the example for others to follow. Should we be surprised when others follow our example?

## Rome

From its beginning Rome was characterized by class wars between the rich and the poor, the patricians and the plebs, the aristocrats and the populace. In spite of this internal discord, Rome conquered most of Italy between 510 and 264 B.C., and then proceeded to conquer the Mediterranean world between 264 and 133 B.C., starting with the Punic wars against Carthage and the Macedonian wars against Greece. Carthage was defeated in 202 B.C. and Macedonia and Corinth in 146 B.C. Internal conflicts arose from 133 to 27 B.C. between the rich and the poor, during which time Caesar was assassinated in 44 B.C.

The Roman Republic became the Roman Empire in 27 B.C., after Octavius defeated Antony, his former ally, and Cleopatra in 31 B.C. By act of the senate Octavius was renamed Augustus, and became the first Roman emperor. Although more peaceful than the Republic, the Empire was also plagued by internal wars and barbarian invasions. After Constantine overcame all his rivals by the sword, he made Christianity the official religion (much as Asoka made Buddhism the official religion of India after he had been successful in uniting India by the sword in the third century B.C.). Rome was sacked by the Visigoths in A.D. 410. The Vandals conquered Roman Africa. The Huns seized Gaul and Italy. Teutonic tribes rebelled against Rome in 476, and that date marks the end of the (Western) Roman Empire: "The barbarian tribes which normally numbered about 20,000 fighting men ... dominated a population of about ten million. The Roman empire in the west fell only because most of its subjects would not fight to preserve it" (Garraty and Gay 1972, p. 241). "Ultimately Rome's dependence on slavery contributed significantly to her downfall" (Bram 1979, vol. 21, p. 409). "Greco-Roman civilization finally died of the twin diseases of War and Class" (Toynbee 1948, p. 24).

It is worth recalling Toynbee's brief description of class in the Roman empire: "Both the mobilization of the Italian peasantry and the subjugation of the barbarians and the Orientals were now being exploited heartlessly for the pecuniary profit of the Roman governing class. The provinces were being drained of their inanimate wealth and their human inhabitants in order to provide lucrative contracts for Roman businessmen and cheap man-power for Roman senators' cattle-ranches and plantations; and the land which was being stocked with this alien slave-labour in order to multiply the fortunes of a small class of already rich men was Italian land which was being placed at the disposition of these capitalists by the impoverishment and eviction of the former peasant proprietors" (1950, pp. 106–7).

Wright also emphasized the relation between war and class in the process of civilization: "The rise of wider aggregation and division of labor, division of ruler and ruled, created conditions favorable for the development of war in the interests of the ruling class" (1965, p. 99). Is it possible that wars are always fought in the interests of the ruling class? If so, the abolition of war might depend upon the elimination of classes. However, we have already noted that class wars constitute only one of several kinds of war, which include civil wars, colonial wars, imperial wars and international wars, not all of which (nor even all of any category), could be subsumed under class wars.

In comparing Roman treatment of the Jews to that by Babylon, Greece and Persia between 586 B.C. to A.D. 70, an Israeli statesman and scholar found that "Rome was the harshest and cruelest of them all" (Eban 1984, p. 90).

## India

The Hindus invaded Ceylon in 500–400 B.C. The Maurya empire, like most other empires, was established by the sword over the period 325 to 200 B.C., reaching its peak size of 3.5 square megameters in 250 B.C. When Asoka saw the suffering caused by his military conquests, he renounced war and made Buddhism the official religion. After his death in 232 B.C., the empire declined. The Gupta empire from A.D. 320 to 480 was relatively peaceful. The "White Huns" of Central Asia broke up this empire toward the close of the fifth century. The Huns always seemed to be waiting in the wings to take over empires who have taken over others. The Huns may have been history's response to those civilizations who had ignored the ethical response, which seem to be most if not all civilizations to date. Or, since the Gupta empire was relatively peaceful, maybe the Huns were ready to take over whether one's response was ethical or not. What kind of a choice is this?

## Analysis of Sorokin's Data

During the 1930s, when Wright (1965) was working on his monumental study of war, Sorokin (1957) was working on his monumental study of social and cultural dynamics, which was originally published 1937–41 in four volumes, the third volume of which was devoted to wars and revolutions. (All quotations in this section refer to the one-volume edition published in 1957, unless otherwise noted.) Sorokin's studies were largely limited to the western world, and his quantitative data were entirely limited to the western world from 600 B.C. to A.D. 1925. Consequently his studies included the classic, medieval and modern periods in Europe. With the help of some colleagues, Sorokin gathered and quantified data on cultural characteristics, wars and revolutions for 12 European nations: Greece and Rome in the classic period; Russia, Austria-Hungary, France and England in the Middle Ages; and then, in addition to those last four nations, Poland, Spain, Italy, Netherlands and Germany in modern times. Internal disturbances were also collected and quantified for Byzantium in the Middle Ages.

Measures of war included frequency, duration and military casualties (both killed and wounded, and both absolute and relative to population). Measures of internal disturbances included area, duration, population and intensity, all of which were combined into a single geometric average used to indicate the magnitude of these disturbances. A list of all 967 wars was given in 1937 (vol. 3, pp. 543–77). A list of all 1622 internal disturbances was given in 1937 (vol. 3, pp. 578–620). There were actually fewer than 967 wars, since Sorokin counted each nation-war as one war, so that World War I, for example, which involved six of Sorokin's major European nations, was counted as six wars. When such duplications are removed, there remain 656 wars, 96 of which occurred in the classic period, 500 B.C. to A.D. 500.

Sorokin recorded 24 Greek wars from 500 to 146 B.C., when Greece was conquered by Rome, and 81 Roman wars from 390 B.C. to A.D. 476, when Rome fell to the German barbarians. In both these civilizations wars were more frequent, longer-lasting and more deadly in the earlier centuries than in the later centuries. This was true of internal disturbances as well as wars. In fourth century B.C. Greece, wars destroyed rich markets, causing economic crises and generating revolutions and counterrevolutions. These conditions were made worse by more wars, which disrupted trade and ruined farms. Wars that were designed to promote commerce and trade ended up destroying commerce and trade. This was surely a self-destructive process.

Sorokin classified cultures (and minds) into two basic types: Sensate and Ideational. These were divided into several subclasses, and there was also another mixed type called "Idealistic," which was "a balanced synthesis of both pure types" (p. 25). The Sensate type was primarily secular, as exemplified by 129 European czars and kings from A.D. 938 to 1922, while the Ideational type was primarily religious, as exemplified by 256 Roman Catholic popes from A.D. 42 to 1932. Western civilization was primarily Ideational during the Middle Ages from A.D. 500 to 1500, and primarily Sensate in classic times up to A.D. 500 and in modern times since 1500.

Sorokin gathered together a vast amount and a wide variety of data to measure these ideal types, including forms of art, systems of truth and reality, first principles of knowledge, ethical and legal standards, social relations, wars and revolutions, culture and personality and theories of social change. Readers who are interested in more details on these matters are referred to Sorokin (1957) or to a brief review of his work (Eckhardt 1983a). Sorokin claimed to find a remarkable correlation among these variables, but these "correlations" must have been found by inspection, because Sorokin (like Wright) seldom reported any statistical analyses of his quantitative data.

Sorokin found neither linear nor cyclical trends in his data, only irregular ✳ fluctuations. There was, however, a regular and steady movement from Ideational faith through Idealistic reason to Sensate evidence, then back to the Ideational. Sorokin found this movement once for Greece and Rome, and again for Europe, from 600 B.C. to A.D. 1925. He also found "somewhat similar rhythms in seveal other cultures, like the Hindu, the Chinese, the Arabian, and a few others" (p. 676). No quantitative evidence, nor any other kind of evidence, was presented on these other cultures in this work. Again without offering much evidence, Sorokin claimed that civilizational crises had often been ended by religious revivals, as in Egypt several times (at the end of the Old Kingdom, the Middle Empire and the New Empire), in Babylon in 1200 B.C., with Taoism and Confucianism in China in the sixth century B.C., with the prophets of Israel from the ninth to the third centuries B.C., and with Christianity in Greece and Rome (p. 702). These religious revivals marked the transition from dying Sensate cultures to new Ideational cultures.

Sorokin studied 967 nation-wars, including civil and colonial wars, and 1622 internal disturbances. He found that these important conflicts ("important" because they were mentioned by historians) were determined by transitional periods between major culture types: *The periods of transition from the Ideational to the Sensate, or from the Sensate to the Ideational phase of culture are the periods of notable increase of war activities and war magnitude....* All in all, the movement of war by century periods agrees well with the hypothesis. In a modified form, it is also warranted by the movement of internal disturbances.... It seems to be entitled to claim a validity perhaps greater than any other hypothesis in the field" (p. 570).

Unfortunately, Sorokin provided eight different sets of these transitional centuries in several different books (1937, vol. 3, pp. 377–79, 501–3; 1941, pp. 215–16, 220–21; 1947, pp. 511–13; 1957, pp. 596, 677). In all cases, one of the lists was for wars and the other for revolutions, since "the war curve lags by decades, sometimes even a century or so" (1947, p. 511). Using the chi-square technique on fourfold contingency tables, I found no significant relation between wars, revolutions and transitional centuries, neither for Greece, nor Rome, nor Europe, nor for all of them combined, except once for European revolutions (Eckhardt, 1983a, pp. 160–61, 164–66). These findings suggest that there is little or no relation between wars, revolutions and transitional periods between major cultural types. In fact, when six of Sorokin's lists were combined, 19 out of the 26 centuries were "transitional" according to one list (or more), while only 7 centuries were stable: the first, second, sixth, seventh and ninth through eleventh. I replicated these chi-square analyses with factor analyses and analyses of variance, with similar results (Eckhardt, 1988, 1989a).

As in all of his data, Sorokin found neither linear trends nor periodic cycles in his wars and revolutions: "All that we can say is that the war-peace curve fluctuates, but in its fluctuations . . . no regular periodicity or uniform rhythm is noticeable. . . . The curve just fluctuates, and that is all" (pp. 561, 564). Likewise for revolutions: "No continuous trend, no regular periodicity, and no uniformity in the amplitude of ups and downs by quarter centuries, nor by century periods are noticeable. . . . The curve fluctuates, that is all one can say" (pp. 583–84, 593). We should remember that the absence of trends and cycles was determined by inspection only, and not by any statistical analysis that was reported.

Sorokin made some other observations about the fluctuations of wars and revolutions. "In the life history of nations, the magnitude of war, absolute and relative, tends to grow in the periods of expansion — political, social, cultural and territorial — of the nation at least as frequently as in the periods of decline. In such periods of blossoming the war activities tend to reach the highest points, probably more frequently than in the periods of decay, and vice versa. Such seems to be one of the relatively valid but limited generalizations" (p. 565). This was true for the glory that was Greece and the grandeur that was Rome. "In the life history of a nation, in its occupied areas, most of the periods of its political, social, economic, moral and mental effervescence, the most brilliant periods in its history, the period of the climax of its grandeur, power, magnificence, and genius are usually also the periods of its high militarism and warfare" (p. 568). The same was said of the magnitude of revolutions in Greece. "In the history of Greece the most turbulent centuries and periods were, like those periods of the maximum of war activities, not the periods of decline but of resplendence, when Greek culture reached its peak" (p. 583). Something similar was seen in Rome (p. 589). Again, these observations, like all of Sorokin's observations, were based only on inspection of quantitative data.

When I correlated 25 of Sorokin's cultural characteristics across 26 centuries, they were for the most part correlated with one another as he had predicted. Most of these characteristics were significantly correlated with a general factor that confirmed Sorokin's sensate versus ideational types of culture; only particular things are real (.94); everything exists in time (.93); truth is determined by the senses (.90); happiness is the purpose of life (.90); everything is relative (.89); universals are real ( −.88); reality is ideal ( −.86); universals are concepts (.85); universals are words (.83); love is the purpose of life ( −.79); truth is determined by faith ( −.78); reality is material (.77); number of scientific discoveries (.77); indeterminism or free will ( −.75); determinism (.72); reality is eternal ( −.68); mysticism ( −.62); number of technological inventions (.61); ideational percent of art ( −.61).

Although Sorokin's pure types of "Sensation" and Ideation" were confirmed by factor analysis, the same cannot be said of his "Idealistic mix," which was supposed to be "a balanced synthesis of both pure types" (p. 25). This

# Figure 3.1    Sensate Factor, 600 B.C. to A.D. 1925 (Based on Sorokin, 1937, vol. 2; 1957)

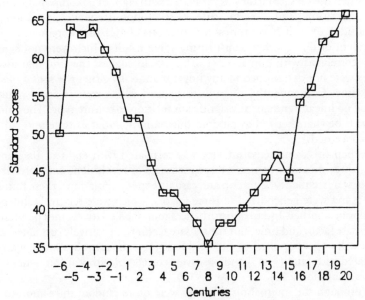

Notes to Figure 3.1: These factor scores were generated from nine of Sorokin's variables: singularism .94, senses .92, temporalism .92, happiness .90, nominalism .86, determinism .82, scientific discoveries .79, materialism .77, and technological inventions .65. The factor scores have been standardized to a mean of 50 and a standard deviation of 10, so that, theoretically, approximately two-thirds of the scores should range between 40 and 60.

---

cultural and mental type of reason (versus faith and evidence) leaned more toward the sensate pole of the general factor, suggesting that it was, at best, an unbalanced synthesis with the senses predominating over faith.

Sensate factor scores were obtained for the 26 centuries and standardized to a mean of 50 and standard deviation of 10. The six centuries B.C. obtained an average score of 62, making them sensate or materialistic; first five centuries A.D., 48 (so that the Roman Empire was more ideational or religious than both the Greek city-states and the Roman Republic); the Middle Ages, 40 (most religious); modern times, 58 (materialistic to almost the same extent as the first six centuries B.C.). The historical curve of this dimension from ideation to sensateness has been graphed in Figure 3.1.

Greece and Rome were not significantly different from each other in their mean scores on a number of Sorokin's variables, as shown in Table 3.5 in Appendix B.

The correlations between wars and revolutions with time for Greece and Rome are shown in Table 3.6 (Appendix B).

When the sensate factor was correlated with eight of its components, three measures of time, and three measures of revolution (frequency, duration and magnitude), over all 26 centuries, the three sets of measures were relatively independent of one another, constituting three factors which were not significantly correlated with one another. This would suggest that internal disturbances were not determined in any linear manner by either the sensate factor or by time. Consequently, these disturbances, which were relatively minor, showed no linear trend nor any significant relation to culture type. They might very well be characterized as random fluctuations, so far as time and culture were concerned.

When this same sensate factor was correlated with eight of its components, three measures of time, three measures of revolution, *and* three measures of war (frequency, duration and casualties per population), these four sets of measures were generalized to three factors, which were relatively independent of one another. Internal disturbances remained relatively independent of the sensate factor and time, but the sensate factor was positively correlated with war casualties per population (.68), and time (over the centuries) was negatively correlated with faith ( −.65) and positively correlated with war frequency (.88) and war duration (.70).

Although the internal disturbances were quite random in relation to the sensate factor and to time, the wars (including civil and colonial wars) were explained to some extent by their relation to the sensate factor and to time, to the extent that 46 percent of the variance in casualties per population was explained by their positive relation to the sensate factor, 77 percent of the variance in war frequencies was explained by their positive relation to time, and 49 percent of the variance in war durations was explained by their positive relation to time. Consequently, it can be seen that wars were not so random in their occurrence as internal disturbances. Their frequencies and durations did increase over time, and their relative casualties did increase with cultural sensateness or materialism (and decrease with cultural ideation or Christianity).

Was this relation between war casualties and the sensate factor a functional relation, or a spurious relation contingent upon particular historical circumstances? If Europe regressed in civilization after the fall of the Roman Empire, as is suggested by the term "Dark Ages," then both the increase in ideation and the decrease in war casualties could have been functions of this regression. Europe became more peaceful because it became less civilized. This interpretation would be consistent with the general theory that war is a function of civilization.

It might be noted here that sensate may be taken to mean scientific for most practical and theoretical purposes; idealistic, philosophical; and ideational, religious. None of the centuries turned out to be purely idealistic or philosophical, since philosophy tended to support science rather than religion. There was no significant relation between religion and internal disturbances in

# Figure 3.2 Civilizations, Empires and Wars, 1500 B.C. to A.D. 500

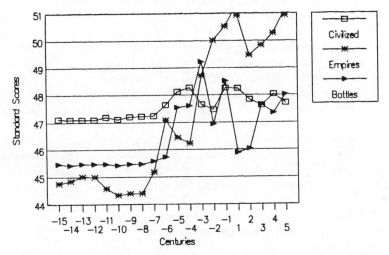

Notes to Figure 3.2: See the Notes to Figure 2.1. Most of the classic scores remained below the average standard score of 50, except for the sum of imperial sizes, which did not get much above average. This graph provides a ready means for comparing classic times (500 B.C. to A.D. 500) with ancient times (1500 to 500 B.C.). It can be seen that, for most centuries, all classic scores were higher than all ancient scores. The data in this graph were based on those in Tables 2.2 and 3.3.

Greece and Rome from 600 B.C. to A.D. 500. When the war measures were correlated with the religious scores century by century, the correlation was negative but not significant for Greece or for Rome.

Sorokin was careful to note the problem of missing data, especially in classic times, and the unreliability of existing data (p. 536). Wright also noted that "the historic record is, except for the most recent time, extremely fragmentary" (1965, p. 102). However, according to Wright, Sorokin's figures for war casualties and internal disturbances in Greece and Rome were "roughly similar" to those of Harbottle (p. 596), suggesting some reliability on that score.

Finally, we note that Wright also suggested that Sorokin's "Ideation" might be interpreted as religion: "His periods of 'ideational' and 'sensate' domination may correspond to periods of predominantly religious and economic interest, while the 'mixed' and 'idealistic' periods may be predominantly political or artistic" (p. 449). As we have found, sensate and idealistic variables combined with each other in opposition to ideational variables on a general factor, which has been interpreted as science/philosophy versus religion.

## Classic Civilizations, Empires and Wars

When the seven variables in Table 3.1 (Appendix B) were correlated with one another across the ten classic centuries and factor-analyzed, the result was quite different from that obtained for the previous periods. Two factors emerged; where battles and wars were negatively related to population, century, historical pages and imperial sizes on the first factor; where battles were negatively related to civilized activities on the second factor.

This classic period, unlike previous periods, did not show consistently positive correlations among the variables of civilization, empire and war. Although population, pages of history and imperial sizes increased over these classic centuries, wars decreased, and battles and civilized activities decreased slightly but not significantly. It will require further research to sort out these anomalies that, so far, appear only in this classic period of history, the latter (imperial) half of which was apparently less civilized and less warlike than the earlier (republic) half.

When compared with the archaic-ancient periods, however, the classic period continued to increase in civilized activities, imperial sizes, and battles, as shown in Figure 3.2.

# Chapter 4
# Medieval Wars,
# A.D. 500 to 1500

## Constancy and Change

Like Taagepera (1978a), Naroll also defined empires as "large states" (1967, p. 86). Using this definition, Naroll found that only one out of 28 empires had been established by voluntary association (p. 83), and this one — the Great League of Ancient China — had lasted for only a few years. Naroll noted that foot soldiers had established and maintained empires until the 1500s. It took about six months to march across the Roman Empire at 32 kilometers per day, and cavalry units were not much faster than foot soldiers (p. 84). Consequently, the increasing size of empires, as observed up to and including the period discussed in this chapter, was not a function of increased speed of communication and transportation, both of which remained relatively constant during human history until large sailing ships after 1500 enabled Europeans to reach any seaport in the world in six months. Consequently, until modern times, increases in the sizes of empires could not be explained by improvements in communication or transportation.

Military techniques also remained relatively constant over this same time period, being dependent on weapons that were effective, for the most part, only at close range: bows and arrows, spears and swords. Catapults and early cannons were not accurate at a distance. What, then, made empires keep on getting bigger with the passage of civilized time? To recapitulate this increase briefly, the average size of empires was 0.6 square megameters from 3000 to 1500 B.C., 2.6 square megameters from 1500 to 500 B.C., 13.6 square megameters from 500 B.C. to A.D. 500, and 20.9 square megameters from A.D. 500 to 1500. It seems as if imperial size grew on human beings, like some sort of addiction. The bigger we got, the bigger we wanted to be.

## Classic and Medieval Comparisons

Some comparisons between the classic and medieval periods might help to provide a framework for further discussion in this chapter. The territory of

India did not change at all, on average, from one period to the next. The territory of China increased somewhat, from 3.5 to 4.0 square megameters, while the territory of Persia decreased somewhat, from 3.1 to 2.8 square megameters. The grandeur that was Rome (4.4 square megameters) was reduced to 2.3 for Byzantium in 600, to 1.5 for Kiev in 900, and to 1.8 for Russia in 1500. European empires did not thrive in the Middle Ages; none achieved a greater size than India during the same period. Thus, while the global trend was ever upward and onward, regional areas continued to suffer the effects of the rises and falls of their civilizations, as shown in Table 3.4 (Appendix B).

Imperial sizes increased with the passage of time, but the same cannot be said of duration. "No detectable change in empire duration has taken place over the last 5,000 years" (Taagepera, 1986, p. 2). Larger empires lasted no longer or shorter, on average, than did smaller empires. Although size may be taken as an indicator of power, it is apparently no indicator of longevity. In fact, Wright's (1965, p. 463) measures of duration of Toynbee's 26 civilizations showed a decrease in imperial longevity as history progressed. When I correlated Wright's measures of duration with the average year of each civilization's existence, the correlation was −.62, which was significant at the .01 level of confidence. This negative correlation might suggest that smaller (older) empires lasted longer, but it seems more likely that older empires lasted longer simply because they had a head start. In any event, duration was not positively correlated with imperial size in Wright's sample of 26 civilizations. Consequently, power would seem to be a transient thing, having no bearing on longevity.

The medieval increase in territorial sizes was largely produced by two new players in the game. The Arabs dominated the scene in the first half of this period, creating the largest empire yet. It averaged 7.6 square megameters and reached its zenith of 11 in 750, after which it has steadily waned. The Mongols dominated the last half of the period, surpassing the Arabs with an average 21 square megameters. They reached their maximum of 24 in 1300. This Mongolian empire was not surpassed in size by any other until the British empire in the twentieth century.

These two medieval empires both ranked higher in offensive militarism than in general militarism. These were the only two "offensive" empires in the Middle East and Asia. Most of Europe and all of America at this time were "offensive" (or nomadic) in the same sense, but while the Arabs and the Mongols acquired tremendous territory through their offensiveness, the Americans and Europeans generated relatively small empires.

The rejuvenated Seljuk Turks' empire had an average size of 3.5 square megameters. Tibet achieved an average size of 3.0 square megameters, the Incas, 2.0 square megameters and the Africans, 1.7.

In the course of the archaic and ancient periods of history the world population approximately doubled. It doubled again during the classic period, and doubled yet again during the medieval period. The world population may have been about 50 million in 3000 B.C., 100 million in 500 B.C., 200 million in A.D. 500, and 400 million in 1500. These population increases were virtually negligible compared to what happened during the modern period from 1500 to 2000, during which the population increased about 15 times in only 500 years. Although population and imperial sizes increased together, their increases were not proportional. While population was doubling from archaic to classic to medieval periods, imperial sizes increased almost 23 times from the archaic to the classic period, but increased only 1.5 times from the classic to the medieval period. Consequently, population as such was neither a (proportional) cause nor effect of imperial sizes.

In spite of malaria and tuberculosis during the so-called Dark Ages, in spite of the Crusades in the twelfth and thirteenth centuries and in spite of Black Death (bubonic plague) of the fourteenth century, European population also doubled from 500 to 1500. Presumably, these European catastrophes were matched by similar catastrophes in other parts of the world, so far as their effect upon population is concerned. Consequently, these catastrophes cannot account for the European "darkness" during the Middle Ages.

## Muslim Empire

The Muslim Empire dominated the Middle East form 750 to 1258, inspired by the religion revealed by Muhammad early in the seventh century. This religion was spread by force and persuasion to Persia, Syria, Armenia, Egypt, Libya and Algeria by the end of the seventh century, and to Morocco and Spain early in the eighth century. However, Arabian history hardly began with Muhammad, since the southern Arabs had been civilized, or urbanized, by 1000 B.C., later claiming the Biblical Ishmael as their ancestor (Garraty and Gay, pp. 253, 273). But this Arabian civilization regressed to nomadism for several centuries prior to the advent of Muhammad, so that the renaissance of Arabian civilization directly attributed to the rise of the Muslim religion, whereas the rise of Christianity was associated with the "darkening" of Europe. However, religion was hardly the only motive for Arab expansion. Booty was also an inspiration. Without profits from plunder to pay the way, expansion would have been impossible. So, although Islam may have pointed the way, providing direction and inspiration, the way had to be paved by booty (p. 263). God and Mammon were seldom opposed to each other in world affairs; on the contrary, they complemented each other most of the time. Military adventures have always had to be paid for by booty, directly or indirectly. An army must eat, to say the least, and somebody has to provide the food. Combatants have other things to do.

Islam conquered nearly half the civilized world between 600 and 800, building up the "most formidable offensive force in the world at the close of this period" (Dupuy and Dupuy 1986, p. 200).

It is of some interest to note that some of the glory that was Greece began to be recaptured during the last half of the Middle Ages. Averroes, a twelfth century Spanish Arab, synthesized Aristotle with Islam, Maimonides a twelfth century Jew, did the same for Judaism, and Aquinas, a thirteenth century Christian, did the same for Christianity. In this manner, Greek philosophy influenced all of these Middle Eastern religions, and perhaps there was a reciprocal effect on Greek philosophy.

## Mongolian Empire

Christian Europe stopped the expansion of the Arabs at Tours in 732; the Seljuk Turks began to conquer the Muslim Empire about 1000; the Christians began to retake Spain by 1100. But it was the Mongols that wreaked the most widespread havoc and devastation, plundering and destroying everything in their path, including the Muslim Empire. The result was a Mongolian Empire that lasted for three centuries, an empire that became more than twice as large as the Muslim Empire, an indication that it may have been twice as warlike.

The Mongolian empire began with the ascendency of Genghis Khan in the early thirteenth century. Although illiterate, Genghis is considered to be one of the greatest military geniuses of all time (Dupuy and Dupuy 1986, p. 330), Genghis meaning "great warrior" and Khan meaning "lord." His "hordes" were usually no more than 150,000 men, but they were very efficient. He began by uniting all the Mongol tribes, and then proceeded to conquer other Central Asian states, much of China, Korea, Persia, Mesopotamia, Armenia and Georgia. Baghdad was captured in 1258, bringing the Muslim Empire to an end. Then the Golden Horde surged toward Europe led by one of Genghis' grandsons, who sacked Kiev and Moscow, continued through Eastern Europe, and was preparing to invade Western Europe when a death in his family obliged him to turn homeward in order to take part in matters of succession. The Mongolian Empire dominated the Far East, the Middle East and Russia for about a century.

## The Divine Right of Might

What drove these great Khans to conquer most of the civilized world at the time? Genghis claimed some sort of divine right, yet the only superior authority which he acknowledged was a code of law which he had drawn up. In short, he was responsible to no one but himself. *He* was the superior authority that he acknowledged. His was the divine right. If this is what drove Genghis — and his grandsons after him — it would seem that the same drive motivated Muhammad and his followers, and that this drive might account for the two largest empires of the Middle Ages. It might also account for the abortive attempt to establish a Holy Roman Empire, which never coalesced. Either the Popes could not muster enough righteousness, or they could not muster enough strength, or both. It apparently takes both might and right to build a large empire. And, if this was true of the Middle Ages, it was probably just as true of the archaic, ancient and classic periods of history.

Rulers have generally tended to identify themselves and their laws with gods and lords throughout history. The Egyptian pharaohs were considered to be divine and supreme rulers, guided by the Egyptian religion and advised by powerful priests and nobles (landlords). God and Mammon worked together even at the very beginning of civilization and history. The earliest code of laws known in its entirety was made by the Babylonian king Hammurabi in the eighteenth century B.C. The king was depicted in a bas-relief as receiving the code from the sun god (Funk and Wagnalls 1979, vol. 12, p. 167), even as Moses later received the tablets of the law from his lord Yahweh. Prior to Hammurabi, Sumerian laws were associated with Sumerian deities (Funk and Wagnalls 1979, vol. 22, p. 311), and the king impersonating a shepherd-god married a priestess impersonating the goddess of love, procreation and war, in an annual ceremony (p. 312).

Earthly rulers represented gods and goddesses from the beginning of history. The gods and their earthly representatives worked together to rule the world, so that the church and state were intertwined. Chinese rulers were associated with the Mandate of Heaven (Funk and Wagnalls 1979, vol. 6, p. 66). Early Persian rulers worshipped Ahura Mazda (Wise Lord) as revealed by Zoroaster (Funk and Wagnalls 1979, vol. 25, p. 473). About 324 B.C., Alexander the Great "ordered that he be considered a god" (Kohn 1987, p. 8). So, government and religion were closely tied together in most civilizations, and sometimes the priest and the ruler were the same person.

Later civilized religion seemed to be like a two-edged sword, or a two-faced person, designed to criticize and to support the government at the same time, whereas there seems to have been little or no criticism prior to that of some (but not all) of the Hebrew prophets. The first two thousand years of civilized religion was primarily supportive of the government, including its civilizing and imperial efforts. This supportive function placed religion in the service of power, while the critical function placed religion in the service of truth. The supportive function has generally predominated throughout human history, perhaps simply because religious persons have to make a living the same as every one else.

It would seem that some sort of righteous motive has been involved in most of the conquests in human history, whether this motive was associated with religion, or associated with a single ruler or a group or a nation that believed in its own righteousness and superiority—to the extent that it had not only the right but even the duty to impose its law and rule upon others, perhaps under the self-serving assumption that this would benefit the others as well. It is more likely, however, that the belief of superiority involved the assumption of the inferiority of the others, so that their benefit was not part of the equation. The superior ones perhaps felt justified in sacrificing the inferior ones to benefit themselves, or, at most, that inferior ones were only entitled to inferior benefits. Civilization and fascism may be brothers under the skin.

Consequently, instead of being guided by the simple notion that "might makes right," it seems that conquerors have used might to impose their righteousness. In their minds, the righteousness could have come first, followed by the use of might to bring the benefits of their righteousness to others, according to their merit. In short, the superiority of right may have preceded the superiority of might: right justified using might to benefit all, at least in a hierarchical manner—rewarding those who recognized the right more than those who did not (some of whom might have to be sacrificed for the greater good).

## The Holy Roman Empire

It has been said that the Holy Roman Empire was neither holy, Roman nor an empire, and that seems to be a fairly accurate description. In its attempts to be an empire, it was hardly holy. Far from being Roman, it was ruled first by German emperors and later by Austrian emperors. And, finally, it never succeeded in effectively ruling central Europe. But it was as close as Europe came to an empire in the Middle Ages. To be sure, Byzantium achieved dominion over an area of two square megameters from 500 to 600, Kiev over one and one-half square megameters in 900, and Russia over somewhat less than two square megameters in 1500, but that was the extent of European political coherence during the Middle Ages. The French and the Germans never controlled more than one square megameter, and England's empire lay well in the future. The Romans and the Germans had amalgamated by 800, resulting in a less advanced civilization than had existed in Europe during the classic period. The Pope crowned Charlemagne "Emperor of the West" in 800, thus beginning the myth of a Holy Roman Empire. Although Europe had lost touch with its Hellenic heritage, there was still a highly developed culture during the Middle Ages. But it was not nearly as developed as that of the Arabs during the same period, which probably accounts for the Arabs being more warlike than the medieval Europeans.

Medieval wars in Europe, like so many wars, were often fought over land and religion, might and right, mammon and God. They were fought by feudal lords versus other landlords, Christians versus other Christians and Christians versus Muslims. Financed and directed by the Pope, Christians (primarily French Christians, but also those of England and Austro-Hungary) crusaded during the twelfth and thirteenth centuries against the Muslims (especially Turkish Muslims) and also against the Byzantine Christians. These crusades also served the purpose of persecuting heretics and Jews along the way. Not many European soldiers were killed or wounded in these crusades. No crusade resulted in one thousand European battle casualties, according to figures estimated by Sorokin (1937, Vol. 3), In fact, all of them together resulted in fewer than five thousand European battle casualties, although there were many additional deaths due to starvation and disease. Nothing much was accomplished, except possibly to sow enough discord in Byzantium so as to help make it vulnerable to Turkish conquest in the fifteenth century. This gave the Turks an entry into the Balkans, which they conquered by the end of the century. So the Muslims, driven out of Spain at the west end of Europe, came back into the Balkans at the east end of Europe, via Constantinople. Something ventured, nothing gained: the story of civilization.

The Norman Conquest of England in 1066 brought nothing but trouble between England and France for the rest of the Middle Ages and beyond, including the Hundred Years' War, plus hundreds of years of other wars. But medieval wars were waged with relatively small forces, so that much of the population was untouched by war. War was indeed the sport of kings and nobles, blessed by priests and characterized more by sound, fury and incense than anything else.

Byzantium was said to have the "most efficient military body in the world in its day" (Dupuy and Dupuy 1986, p. 214), with 200,000 deaths claimed in its war against Persia in the early seventh century, and another 200,000 in its war against the Arabs during the last half of that century. Death estimates were very rare for the Middle Ages, except for those developed by Sorokin (1957), to which we now turn.

## Analysis of Sorokin's Data

Although others (Harbottle, 1904; Eggenberger, 1967; Dupuy and Dupuy, 1986; Kohn, 1987) have provided lists of battles and wars for archaic, ancient, classic and medieval times, Sorokin (1937, vol. 3) was the only one who provided a systematic estimate of casualties for these wars. His casualty estimates were limited to military casualties for major European nations during classic, medieval and modern times, starting with Greece in 500 B.C., and Rome in 400 B.C. Casualties included losses due to wounds as well as battle deaths, but losses due to disease and epidemics were excluded. Casualties need to be clearly distinguished from fatalities, which include losses due to battle deaths only.

A summary of some of Sorokin's data in Table 4.1 (Appendix B) enables us to compare these data for classic and medieval times. The figures in the body of this table are mean scores per nation per century, the medieval means being based on four European nations: Austria-Hungary (central Europe), England, France and Russia.

There were no significant differences in war frequencies or durations among Greece, Rome and medieval Europe, as shown in the top half of Table 4.1, but there were significant differences in the levels of military casualties in classic and medieval times. These casualties, proportional to population and to army size, were significantly lower in medieval times compared to classic times, suggesting that classic Europe, especially Rome, was more warlike than medieval Europe. This conclusion is consistent with my averaging of Wright's warlike ratings of six medieval European civilizations, and my comparison of these with Wright's warlike ratings of classic civilization (1965, pp. 463, 467, 572).

Classic civilization was twice as warlike, twice as populous and rated twice as high in imperialistic battles, when compared with medieval Europe. These differences seem consistent with the difference between the number of city-states (in the case of Greece) and the average of the number of nations not yet states (in the case of medieval Europe); or, between an empire (as in the case of Rome) and the average of a number of nations not yet states, let alone empires (in the case of medieval Europe). In short, these differences in war casualties reflected the difference between a higher and a lower level of civilization. The more civilized classic period was more warlike than the less civilized medieval period.

But how do these conclusions fit the finding that medieval imperial sizes continued to increase unlike those in the classic period? Here we must distinguish between Europe and the world, in spite of our Eurocentric tendency to equate the two. Europe's imperial sizes definitely decreased between these two periods. Rome's imperial size of 4.4 square megameters — being almost twice the size of Byzantium's 2.3 in the sixth century (and Byzantium was not included among Sorokin's nations so far as wars were concerned) — shrank to less than 1.5 in 900 and to less than 1.0 in 1300. As already noted, the increased imperial sizes in the Middle Ages were largely due to the Muslim and Mongolian Empires, which more than made up for the fall of Rome, so far as imperial sizes are concerned.

The first half of medieval Europe was "dark" enough so that Sorokin (1937, vol. 3) was unable to quantify the wars of this period, but he was able to quantify internal disturbances, however crudely, for Austria-Hungary (central Europe), Byzantium, England, France and Russia. It was only during the latter half of the Middle Ages that Sorokin was able to quantify the wars within and between four of these nations: Austria-Hungary, England, France and Russia. These wars were relatively small wars, since they were primarily the business of kings and knights, as already noted.

According to Sorokin, medieval European wars rarely involved more than 20,000 fighters (p. 281), who were mainly nobles, their minions and professionals (mercenaries).

England and France had about 40 percent of their medieval wars with each other, while Poland and Russia had about 30 percent of their medieval wars with each other, and Austria-Hungary had about one-third of its medieval wars with Italy and Turkey.

These very crude figures reflect a general historical tendency for many wars to be quarrels between neighbors (if not simply family quarrels), over who was going to rule whom.

As shown in the bottom half of Table 4.1, there were no significant differences in internal disturbances between Greece, Rome and medieval Europe.

## Wars and World Views

The last row of Table 4.1 shows the ideation scores which I developed from Sorokin's (1937, vol. 2) data by means of factor analysis of eight of his measures of philosophy, religion and science. Sorokin's measures in these regards were made by expert counts (and percentages) of various philosophies expressed by a sample of writings throughout these 26 centuries since 600 B.C. I based the factor scores on eight of these measures which were statistically independent of one another: ontological idealism (spirit versus matter as the nature of reality), unchanging nature of reality, existence of universals (Platonic ideas), societies more real than individuals, free will versus determinism, ethics of love versus happiness and principles (including, but not exclusively, love), faith versus sense and reason as sources of knowledge and truth, and ideational versus sensate personalities as described in the *Encyclopaedia Britannica*.

These eight measures were loaded on the ideation factor as follows: universalism (.94), idealism (.91), societies more real than individuals (.89), love (.84), free will (.81), faith (.74), reality unchanging (.67) and ideational personalities (.61). Consequently, the ideation scores reflected these eight measures in proportion to their loadings on this factor.

Sorokin (1937, Vol. 2) reported a few correlations among some of these variables (pp. 631–32), but he felt that they added nothing to his intuitive sense of their relationships. However, without a careful statistical analysis, his intuition cannot be totally relied on. Sometimes his intuition turned out to be right, but sometimes it was wrong, as we have seen.

First, however, we should acknowledge that the statistical results of factor analysis showed that most of Sorokin's measures of ideation versus sensation were closely enough related to constitute a single general factor, with a few minor exceptions. But his expectation that reason would constitute a relatively independent factor was not confirmed, nor was his expectation that reason would ally itself with faith more than with the senses. On the contrary, reason (as measured by Sorokin and his colleagues) allied itself with the senses, as opposed to faith, and it did not emerge as an independent factor. Consequently, there were no centuries where reason prevailed, such as Sorokin expected of the fifth and fourth centuries B.C., the twelfth and fourteenth centuries and the seventeenth century (1957, p. 241).

The centuries varied only along the factor of faith versus sense and reason, as shown at the bottom of Table 4.1. These factor scores were of course, limited to Europe, so they tell us nothing about the rest of the world along this dimension. It would be desirable if someone could develop this dimension in other parts of the world. In the meantime, Table 4.1 shows us that Europe was relatively low in faith before the time of Christ, and relatively high thereafter, peaking in the eighth century with a standard score of 66 on the ideation factor composed of eight of Sorokin's variables. (The factor scores were standardized to a mean of 50 and a standard deviation of 10, so that two-thirds of the scores ranged from 40 to 60.)

As Christianity spread, most measures of European war casualties decreased, indicating a negative correlation between these two measures of war and religion. When war casualties were correlated with the ideation factor over these centuries, the war casualties were, indeed, negatively correlated with this factor. This finding suggests that either the Christian religion diminished war, or that both the decrease in war and the spread of Christianity were functions of the regression from Greco-Roman civilization to the fragmented feudalism of the Middle Ages.

Table 4.2 (Appendix B) shows that ideation was on the decrease, but not significantly so, during the Greek civilization; on the increase during the Roman civilization; and on the decrease again in the course of the Middle Ages, reaching its peak in the eighth century.

Table 4.3 (Appendix B) shows that all measures of war went down from the time of the Roman Republic to that of the Roman Empire, and then down further until the Middle Ages, and most of these latter decreases were statistically significant. While these measures of war were getting lower, the measure of faith was rising significantly. There seems to be little doubt that, according to Sorokin's measures, there is an inverse relationship between war and faith. Sorokin did not make anything out of this relationship, emphasizing instead that, as a general rule, the type of culture (ideational or sensate) determined the *kind* of wars but not their quantity. Ideational cultures were said to cause religion wars, while sensate cultures were said to cause economic wars; neither culture seemed to be more warlike than the other. "A well-ordered and crystallized Ideational society may be as peaceful or as militant as the well-ordered Sensate" (1957, p. 570). Sorokin's data would seem to warrant a more positive assertion concerning the relationship between culture and war, if we can assume the reliability and validity of Sorokin's data. An attempt to support this assumption will be made later in this chapter, but at present we turn to a theory of war and revolution that Sorokin made quite explicit.

## Transitional Theory of War and Revolution

Sorokin believed that wars and revolutions were primarily caused by transition from one culture type to another: "*The periods of transition from the Ideational to the Sensate, or from the Sensate to the Ideational phases of culture are the periods of notable increase of war activities and war magnitude....* All in all, the movement of war by century periods agrees well with the hypothesis. In a modified form, it is also warranted by the movement of internal disturbances.... It seems to be entitled to claim a validity perhaps greater than any other hypothesis in the field" (1957, p. 570).

Sorokin identified a set of transitional centuries for wars and another set for revolutions, since he believed that internal disturbances reacted more immediately to culture changes, while wars lagged by a century or two. He provided similar sets in 1937 (vol. 3), 1941, 1947 and 1957, but all these sets were somewhat different from one another. When I combined them all, 19 of the 26 centuries were "transitional" according to one or another list, and only 7 centuries were stable: the first, second, sixth, seventh and ninth to eleventh. When I compared those centuries which were higher than average in wars and revolutions with those which were supposed to be "transitional," using the chi-square technique of analyzing the differences among frequencies, I found little support for Sorokin's transitional theory of wars and revolutions (Eckhardt, 1983a). Wars were simply not related to Sorokin's transitional centuries for either Greece, Rome or Europe (whether taken separately or together); nor were revolutions related to transitional centuries for Greece or Rome (taken separately or together), but there was a significant relation for Europe taken alone.

More recently (Eckhardt, 1988, 1989a), I correlated Sorokin's transitional centuries (eight sets from 1937, 1941, 1947 and 1957) with his war casualties per population and per army size (logged to normalize skewness in the raw scores), his revolutionary magnitudes and my factor scores of his ideational variables. Since Greece and Rome overlapped for several centuries, the data for Rome (only) and Europe were used in these analyses. The correlations were factor-analyzed for the 25 centuries (500 B.C. to A.D. 2000) for which there were complete data for internal disturbances, and for the 20 centuries (400 B.C. to A.D. 500 and 900 to 2000) for which there were complete data for wars. The results of these analyses for revolutions are shown in Table 4.4 (Appendix B), which shows that revolutionary magnitudes increased over 25 centuries for Rome and Europe from the fifth century B.C. to the twentieth century A.D. The transitional centuries in factor 2 were unrelated to the revolutionary magnitudes in factor 1. The two factors were independent of each other.

Table 4.5 (Appendix B) shows the results when wars as well as revolutions were included in the analysis. Fewer centuries were available (N = 20), since Sorokin provided no Roman war data for the fifth century B.C. nor European data for the sixth through ninth centuries A.D., presumably because of lack of reliable data. Factor 1 shows that relative war casualties were negatively related to ideational (religious) centuries. Ideational scores were above average (50) during the third through fifteenth centuries, a period including the late Roman Empire and the whole of the Middle Ages. They were above 60 from the seventh through tenth centuries only and they were below 40 during the five centuries B.C. and the eighteenth through twentieth centuries A.D. Factor 2 shows revolutionary magnitudes increasing over these 20 centuries, just as they increased over the 25 centuries in Table 4.4. They were also moderately related to the ideational centuries, just as they were in Table 4.4. The transitional centuries for both wars and revolutions were related to each other in factor 3, but neither set of transitional centuries was related to either war casualties nor revolutionary magnitudes. This finding clearly contradicted Sorokin's transitional theory of wars and revolutions. Relative war casualties and revolutionary magnitudes were not related to each other, which confirmed Sorokin's finding in this regard.

The analysis of variance in Table 4.6 (Appendix B) simply confirmed the previous results by another method of analysis. This table compared the mean scores obtained by the stable and transitional centuries on the war, revolution and related variables. The results showed no significant differences in century, ideation, revolutionary magnitude or relative war casualties. These results made it quite clear that whether a century was stable or transitional made no significant difference to its relative war casualties nor to its revolutionary magnitudes.

We can only conclude from these analyses that either Sorokin's measurements were faulty or his transitional theory was false. Evaluation of the reliability of some of Sorokin's measurements will be presented after examining some of his other theories of wars and revolutions.

## Other Theories of Wars and Revolutions

Sorokin's theories of wars and revolutions went through a number of transitions. He first developed a frustration theory of revolution in 1925, at which time he offered no theory of war. The transitional theory, just discussed, followed in 1937. After the Second World War, in 1947, Sorokin proposed a dominance theory that emphasized the lust for power and the striving for superiority as the basic causes of violent conflicts. By 1954 he was emphasizing egoism and hostility at the group level as basic causes of wars and revolutions. Finally, in 1959, he held that wars and revolutions were caused by governments themselves, simultaneously causing a disintegration of values. Governments and other ruling groups, corrupted by too much power, were found at fault.

Clearly, power is at stake in every war and is obviously associated with egoism or tribal selfishness. If the lust for power and the striving for superiority are frustrated, this can generate hostility toward the frustrating party, which can lead to war. Sorokin provided no operational definitions of these concepts, so that these other theories do not lend themselves to testing as readily as the transitional theory, but they are worth further research. The problem lies in measuring concepts such as egoism, selfishness, lust for power and striving for superiority at the national level of analysis.

## Reliability and Validity of Sorokin's Data

Sorokin claimed some reliability for his data on the ground that "the results [of Wright's study] confirm the main movements of the curves and indicators here" (1957, p. 539). However, Wright's (1965) list of wars did not begin until 1482 and did not include death estimates until after the Second World War. Consequently, if there was some concurrence between the two lists since 1482, that would establish some reliability for Sorokin's frequencies and durations of modern wars, but not for classic and medieval wars.

Harbottle's (1904) battles included classic and medieval battles, but no wars, as such, were listed, so no direct comparisons between Harbottle and Sorokin can be made. It might be possible to reconstruct a list of wars based on Harbottle's battles, but this has not been done, and even if it had, such a reconstructed list would provide a measurement of frequency, but not of duration or casualties.

Dupuy and Dupuy (1986) compiled records of a large number of wars throughout human history, and these provide a way of comparing frequencies and durations, but not casualties, concerning which little was recorded prior to modern times, as Sorokin carefully noted (1957, p. 272). Before Dupuy and Dupuy could be used, however, their lengthy descriptions would have to be reduced to a few essential details, such as name of war, location, dates, participants, type of war, causes, etc. Then this list could be compared with that of Sorokin. I used the Dupuys' (1986) Index of Wars (pp. 1516–24) to develop a list of 1266 wars over the centuries after 3000 B.C. Sorokin's casualties correlated .54** with the frequency of the Dupuys' European wars over the 21 centuries for which data were available for both lists.

Fairly recently, a *Dictionary of Wars* (Kohn, 1987) was published. In it a war was defined as "an overt, armed conflict carried on between nations or states (international war) or between parties, factions, or people in the same state (civil war)" (p. v). Since Kohn included wars since 2000 B.C., classic, medieval and modern wars are available here for comparison with Sorokin's wars. However, Sorokin's European war casualties again correlated — .54** with Kohn's European war frequencies. These two correlations would suggest that war frequencies over these centuries could be used as a rough measure of war intensities for those centuries where no casualty nor death estimates are available.

## Comparison of Sorokin's and Kohn's Medieval Data

Compared with Sorokin's 217 wars in the tenth through fifteenth centuries, Kohn listed 387. Kohn's frequency was greater because Sorokin focused on four European nations in the Middle Ages, while Kohn used the whole world — a difference that suggests that Europe was responsible for more than one-half of the wars during these centuries. When only those wars that involved one or more of Sorokin's four nations were selected from Kohn's list, then Kohn's frequency became 165, closer to Sorokin's 217. When I counted participants in each set of wars, they averaged approximately two per war for Sorokin, two and one-half for Kohn. Great Powers averaged 0.6 per war for Sorokin and 0.67 for Kohn. The starters of wars won 53 percent of the wars in Sorokin and 48 percent in Kohn. The relative frequencies of several causes and types of wars were also very similar. On the whole, then, there were similarities between Sorokin's and Kohn's lists of wars for these major countries of Europe. There was one outstanding difference, however, and that was in the duration of these wars. Sorokin's medieval wars lasted two and two-thirds years on the average, while Kohn's medieval wars lasted eight and one-half years on the average. This difference in duration requires further study.

It might be noted here that only 38 percent of Sorokin's medieval wars involved one thousand or more casualties per year, so that 62 percent of these wars would not meet the requirement of one thousand deaths per year that I have set for modern wars. Richardson (1960) set a minimum of 317 deaths per war for his list of deadly quarrels, while Singer and Small (1982) set a minimum of one thousand battle deaths per war for interstate wars and one thousand battle deaths per year for civil, colonial and imperial wars. Sorokin's list of wars would seem to be more like Richardson's list than that of Singer and Small, so far as casualties are concerned. On the other hand, Richardson estimated fatalities rather than casualties, and his fatalities included civilian as well as military deaths. Since Kohn included mutinies and revolutions as wars, his list goes beyond Sorokin's list of wars, but may nevertheless be quite comparable as far as casualties are concerned. In any event, we shall use it, bearing in mind its limitations.

## Comparison of the Dark Ages and the Later Middle Ages

Although Sorokin collected data on internal disturbances throughout the 26 centuries from the sixth B.C. to the A.D. twentieth, he collected data on wars only from the fifth century B.C. for Greece and from the fourth century B.C. for Rome, to the fifth century A.D., and then skipped to the tenth through the twentieth centuries, presumably because of the lack of data for the sixth through ninth centuries. If we consider the Dark Ages to be the period from the sixth through the tenth centuries, then we have war data for only the tenth century, and even that century provides data or estimates for only Russia (the whole century), Austria-Hungary (the last quarter), and France (the last decade). Data or estimates for England begin to appear in the second half of the eleventh century, after the Norman Conquest in 1066.

I assume that the data for the tenth century could be used to represent the Dark Ages to some extent. Presumably, the centuries prior to the tenth were even "darker" than the tenth itself. However, with Kohn's data available, we can compare his data for the Dark Ages with his data for the later Middle Ages, and then assume that the ratio between these two sets of data might also hold between Sorokin's data for the same tie periods *if* Sorokin had provided data for both periods.

As previously noted, Kohn provided very few death estimates, so the only variables that can be used to compare these two five-hundred-year periods are war frequencies and durations. There were almost three times as many European wars during the later Middle Ages than in the Dark Ages, but the wars during the Dark Ages were twice as long in duration, on average. As Sorokin noted in his own data, the longer wars of earlier centuries were characterized by a few battles of one day each, with lengthy periods between them, so that the First World War was much longer in actual combat time than the Hundred Years' War. Assuming, then, that the longer wars of the Dark Ages suffered no more casualties than the shorter wars of the later Middle Ages, then the greater frequency of the later wars would suggest more casualties. This ratio of 3/1 would imply more casualties even after taking into account the possible twofold increase in population from one period to the other.

Let us assume, for the time being, that the relative casualty ratio between the two periods was at least 3/2, using Kohn's data and taking population doubling into account. But, using Sorokin's own figures, as shown in Table 4.3, the ratio would be 5/1 (with population increase already taken into account). In either event, the relative war casualties were less during the Dark Ages than during the later Middle Ages.

In summary, it seems that Sorokin's estimates have some reliability, so far as there is some agreement between Sorokin's frequencies and those of Kohn for the later Middle Ages. Both lists suggest greater casualties during the later Middle Ages compared to the earlier Dark Ages. Since the duration of earlier wars has been exaggerated, because of the long periods of inactivity between battles (as Sorokin carefully noted), and since Sorokin estimated casualties by their typical percent of army strength multiplied by the duration of the war (1962, p. 282), this means that the casualties of earlier wars have been greatly exaggerated by treating long periods of inactivity between battles as if they were periods of active warfare. Consequently, earlier wars, especially longer wars, were less violent than Sorokin's casualty estimates would lead us to believe. Some way of taking this into account must be found eventually. In the meantime, this consideration means that classic wars by durations probably have to be weighed less than Sorokin weighed them in relation to medieval wars by durations (which he himself noted were exaggerations). By the same token, medieval wars have to be weighed less than modern wars; earlier medieval wars in the Dark Ages have to be weighed less than those in the later Middle Ages; and earlier modern wars have to be weighed less than later modern wars, especially those in the twentieth century.

## Medieval Civilizations, Empires and Wars

The data for civilizations, empires and wars for the Middle Ages are shown in Table 4.7 in Appendix B.

When these variables were correlated and factor-analyzed, most of these variables appeared on the first factor, which accounted for 76 percent of the variance: population (.98), century (.96), Kohn's wars (.96), civilized activities (.94), Dupuys' battles (.92), historical pages (.89), and imperial sizes (.18, which was not significant). Imperial sizes then appeared on the second factor by itself, so that imperial sizes were independent of the other six variables in this time period. It can be seen in Table 4.7 that, while all of the other variables

# Figure 4.1  Civilizations, Empires and Wars, 500 B.C. to A.D. 1500

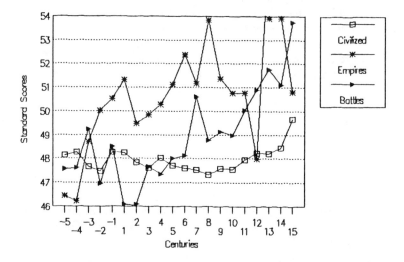

Notes to Figure 4.1: See the Notes to Figure 2.1. Medieval centuries were generally higher than classic centuries in civilized activities, imperial sizes and battle frequencies, but civilized activities were lower than average throughout the historical periods shown in this graph, while battle frequencies and imperial sizes were generally above average during the Middle Ages, 500–1500.

increased significantly over these ten centuries, imperial sizes did not. They were correlated only .22 with centuries, which was not significant. So, while civilizations and wars increased during the Middle Ages, imperial sizes remained fairly constant. The relations between these three variables have been shown graphically in Figure 4.1.

Table 4.8 (Appendix B) compares mean scores for civilization, empire and war among the four historical periods so far discussed in this and the previous two chapters. Table 4.8 shows that most of these variables have increased significantly from period to period, but the number of historical pages per century did not increase significantly from the archaic to the ancient period, and the number of civilized activities did not increase significantly from the classic to the medieval period.

Table 4.9 (Appendix B) shows the same data in the form of percentages of the grand total of all 50 centuries from 3000 B.C. to A.D. 2000. On average the medieval period was almost twice as active as the classic period in military and imperial activities, although civilized activities did not increase significantly. On the average, medieval activities were not much more than would have been expected on the basis of its number of centuries. The four periods, constituting 90 percent of all 50 centuries, accounted for less than 40 percent of all activities as measured by these six variables. Accordingly, we can expect the modern period to account for six times as much activity in relation to its percentage (10) of all 50 centuries.

*Chapter 5*

# Modern War: An Overview

## Introduction

The work of some half-dozen authors of quantitative studies of modern warfare will be reviewed in the next several chapters, including Richardson, Sorokin and Wright, the pioneers of these studies. Richardson and Sorokin started in 1917, and Wright started in 1926. Others followed later: Harbottle (1904, revised and updated by Bruce, 1971, 1981), Eggenberger (1967, 1985), Dupuy and Dupuy (1971, 1977, 1986), Singer and Small (1972), Bouthoul and Carrere (1976, 1978, 1979), Eckhardt (1980 to 1990), Small and Singer (1982), Westing (1982), Levy (1983), Kaye et al. (1985) and Kohn (1987). Some others provided lists and analyses, starting with wars and other disputes in 1945, such as Kende (1971, 1979), Butterworth with Scranton (1976, 1979), Eckhardt and Azar (1978, 1979) including the 11 lists summarized by SIPRI (1969), and the 56 lists surveyed by Leitenberg (1977), which also included a survey of 13 lists of successful and 9 lists of unsuccessful military coups. Cioffi-Revilla (1990) has reviewed and compared several of these data sets on modern wars.

I shall not spend much time on those studies limited to wars since 1945. Most of the attention will be given to Richardson, Sorokin and Wright because (1) they were pioneers, and (2) although they spent a considerable amount of time on the collection and organization of quantitative data, they spent little time on the statistical analysis of their data, Richardson being an exception to this general statement. The reason for this is not hard to find: they had *no* computers at their disposal, which made statistical analyses so time-consuming as to be downright prohibitive. Rummel (1967) and Wilkinson (1980) have done some statistical analyses of Richardson's data, in addition to those analyses done by Richardson himself, but no one has done such analyses of Sorokin's or Wright's data. No analyses were provided by Harbottle, nor by Bruce, nor by Bouthoul and Carrere, nor by Westing, nor by Kohn. In most of these cases I shall present some statistical analyses of these various lists, along with some comparisons among them as a check on their reliability. Singer and Small (1972), Small and Singer (1982), Levy (1983) and Levy and Morgan (1984) have provided the most in the way of statistical analyses of their data. Singer and Small (1972) have also provided some comparisons between their own data and those of Richardson, Sorokin and Wright.

Before getting into these quantitative details and statistical analyses in the following chapters, the rest of this chapter will provide a more general overview of modern history and modern warfare.

## Modern History

Modern history began about 1500, but it was ushered in by some notable (or notorious) events, developments and inventions in the latter half of the fifteenth century: the printing press (the beginning of mass communication at a distance), the gun (the beginning of death at a distance greater than that achievable by spears and arrows), the Inquisition, the Renaissance, the confiscation of Jewish property (which helped to finance foreign expeditions), and the expulsion of Jews from England, France, Portugal and Spain. Modern history was primarily the story of the expansion of Western civilization into much of the rest of the world by means of military conquest, Christian missions and capitalist trade, including the Atlantic slave trade. Trade and war have been interrelated in modern civilization, as in previous civilizations.

Modern wars were generally not much different from civilized wars, but they were more deadly in technology and more global in scope, involving world domination on a scale not before possible. If there was more than a touch of fascism at the beginning of world civilization, there was a blaze of it later on, and quite a bit of it throughout.

## Toynbee's Analysis of Modern Civilization

Toynbee (1948) put civilization on trial after the Second World War. On the basis of his monumental 12-volume study of history (1934–61), revised and abridged by Toynbee and Caplan (1972), he concluded that wars and class distinctions had wiped out all the previous civilizations that he had studied. These comprised 20 civilizations in 1948, increased to 26 by 1961, and increased to 38 (including four questionable and six abortive civilizations) by 1972. "Western 'know-how' [atom bomb] has ... inflamed the institutions of War and Class, which are the two congenital diseases of civilization, into utterly fatal maladies.... War and Class have always been with us ever since the first civilizations emerged.... Of the 20 or so civilizations known to modern Western historians, all except our own appear to be dead or moribund, and ... we invariably find that the cause of death has been either War or Class. To date, these two plagues have been deadly enough, in partnership, to kill off 19 out of 20 representatives of this recently evolved species of human society.... Greco-Roman civilization finally died of the twin diseases of War and Class in the course of the fifth, sixth and seventh centuries of the Christian era.... We have to abolish War and Class.... We are aware that the atom bomb and our many other new lethal weapons are capable, in another war, of wiping out not merely the belligerents but the whole of the human race" (1948, pp. 23–25).

The trouble with modern civilization, as with all previous civilizations, was arrogance, pride and the myth of superiority. "Every one of them was convinced that it was the only civilized society in the world, and that the rest of mankind were barbarians, untouchables or infidels" (p. 71). This myth of superiority might well be a central feature of all those ideologies that rationalize self-destructive behavior both at the individual and at the social level of analysis. Clearly, if one were so vastly superior to others, this might seem to justify imposing one's values on others by whatever means necessary: It would be for their own good. The end of civilizing others and elevating their standard of living would justify almost any means that might be required to bring about such noble ends.

This motive presumably moved modern civilization much more than previous civilizations, since we have felt obliged not merely to civilize some parts of the world, as had happened in the past, but rather to civilize or dominate the whole wide world. "Western civilization is aiming at nothing less than the incorporation of all mankind in a single great society" (p. 186).

Toynbee (1950) found a close relationship between war and civilization, and that, in fact, "war has proved to be the proximate cause of the breakdown of every civilization. . . . Indeed War may actually have been a child of Civilization" (pp. vii, viii). If this was the case, then war was a child who killed its own parent, time after time. "The whole tragedy of militarism . . . has been acted over and over again . . . [in] twenty different civilizations down to our own militarists in the Western World of today. . . . Militarism has been by far the commonest cause of the breakdowns of civilizations during the four or five millennia which have witnessed the score or so of breakdowns that are on record up to the present date" (pp. 101, 130).

Toynbee had not changed his mind on this score in 1975, the year of his death at age 86: "I conclude that war is no older than civilization and that, since the two are coeval, war is one of the congenital diseases of civilization" (Toynbee and Ikeda 1976, p. 202). And what is the other congenital disease of civilization? "The two congenital social maladies of civilizations have been war and social injustice" (p. 288).

According to Toynbee, in brief summary, civilizations fell from the sheer weight of their own immorality. Ideologically, their immorality took the form of the myth of superiority. Operationally, their immorality took the forms of class injustice and warfare. Civilizations have died primarily by their own hands. They committed suicide. And modern civilization seems determined to go down that same old path, blinded by that same old myth of superiority, and aided by the same old authoritarianism and militarism.

Somehow or other, it would seem, the immorality of self-righteousness, the myth of superiority, or the divine right of might worked very well in helping civilizations to rise, that is, to expand the range of their power over others. But there always came a time when what once succeeded began to fail, and to

contribute to the fall of what had risen. This process that obstructs its own progress seems to be some function of power itself, or reaction to power, such that
the inequality of power gives rise to social forces that try to equalize power,
thus depriving the holder of power of whatever power it once had. In addition
to the will for power, which may help to explain the rise of civilizations, there
seems to be a will for equality, which may help to explain their fall. We need
to find out more about processes that obstruct their own progress. Whatever
power is, it is expressed by an ideology that works on the way up, but which
turns against itself on the way down. On the way up, the ideology is confirmed
by the success of strength. The ideology has nothing to hide because nothing
succeeds like success. As long as you are winning, nothing has to be explained
except your superiority, which is simply asserted without explanation. But, on
the way down, the ideology has to justify and rationalize the diminution of
strength. What makes successes fail? That is the difficult question that has to
be answered to arrest the fall. The will to equality may explain the pattern.
A dual theory of evolution and entropy may be required to account for the rise
and fall of civilizations.

## Wright's Analysis of Modern Civilization

The process of world civilization was associated with the rise of capitalism
from its early commercial period, 1250–1750, through high industrial capitalism, 1750–1914, to finance capitalism since 1914 (Wright 1965, p. 206, pp.
1160–61). Wright classified modern wars into the same four types that he
classified civilized wars: (1) imperial wars of expanding modern civilization at
the expense of other cultures, (2) defensive wars against aggression by other
cultures, (3) balance-of-power wars between states of modern civilization and
(4) civil wars within states (p. 638).

Wright's description of modern wars has not been equaled by any other
author: "The expansion of the culture and institutions of modern civilization
from its centers in Europe was made possible by imperialistic war. . . . It is true
missionaries and traders had their share in the work of expanding world civilization, but always with the support, immediate or in the background, of armies and navies" (pp. 251–52).

Gunpowder was essential to Western empire-building: "The European
states built great empires through the use of gunpowder against small states
and overseas peoples not so equipped" (p. 1520). The imperial process was a
forceful and violent process, as it had always been — the will for power at work.
"Beginning after the age of discoveries with attacks by European states on
America and Asia, this type of [imperial] war increased until in the 19th century it absorbed as much, if not more, military energy than balance-of-power
wars" (p. 640). "European trade with American Indians in the 17th century,
with East Indians in the 18th century and with China and Japan in the 19th
century were initiated by armed force" (p. 858). "World-empire is built by

conquest and maintained by force" (p. 965). "Empires are primarily organizations of violence" (p. 969).

It seems that empires, as a rule, are analogous, on a large scale, to the Mafia. They provide protection at a price, but there is an element of coercion in the bargains that they strike; they make offers that cannot be refused without paying a price more dear than most humans can afford or endure.

This modern imperial process did not differ essentially from the imperial process in archaic, ancient, classic and medieval times, where always and everywhere it has been a process of benefitting some at the expense of others, a process of exploitation that violated Kant's categorical imperative and the golden rule of all the great religions. Although imperial wars were always a part of this process, they were not the whole process, which was often executed in an ostensibly "peaceable" manner. Balance-of-power wars were seldom independent of the imperial process, since they were usually fought between imperial rivals over imperial spoils, like gang wars, but far more deadly in their consequences.

These balance-of-power wars were one expression of the will for equality, at least among superiors, a demand that imperial spoils be shared among imperial powers. Civil and class wars within states were simply analogues of balance-of-power and imperial wars between states. From this point of view, most wars were imperial wars at several levels of analysis. However, the parties differed in that both antagonists were dominating parties in balance-of-power and civil wars, while only one of the parties was dominating in imperial and class wars, the other party being dominated or repressed. Wright put it briefly: "This fact [dominance] is probably the most important single element in the causation of major modern wars" (p. 815), and it also "figured prominently in the causation of civilized war" (p. 139). Dominance, we might add, is the chief characteristic of the Mafia, whose own beginnings were a reaction to domination. The uprising of the dominated, or the return of the repressed, was a clear expression of the will for equality, analogous to the second law of thermodynamic entropy.

Modern civilization was simply the expansion of Western civilization to the rest of the world, accomplished by world domination. "In the 18th and 19th centuries war was less intense in Europe but the European states by means of war or threats of war extended their dynamic civilization at the expense of the traditional cultures of America, Africa and the Pacific and injected the virus of their civilization into the ancient civilizations of China, Japan and India" (p. 271). Civilization might very well be called a "virus" since it has always had a deadly effect upon the peoples infected by it.

Civilization has been an unequalizing process par excellence. "The struggle for empire has greatly increased the disparity between states with respect to the political control of resources, since there can never be enough imperial territory to provide for all.... Imperialism has, therefore, required vast armaments for defense of empire by the states immediately successful in the struggle and vast armaments for acquisition of empire by the states which have been unsuccessful in the first round.... Imperial rivalries ... were in the 17th and 18th centuries important causes of war and in the 19th century important causes of armament" (pp. 1190–91).

Both world wars of this century were imperial wars in the sense of resolving the conflicts between imperial rivals. Wright pointed out that "the struggle for colonies, markets and raw materials, precipitated in the 1870s, contributed to national rivalries, which, in accord with balance-of-power principles, organized the world into two great hostile groups and culminated in World War I" (p. 1107). Wright felt that World War II was simply a continuation of World War I (pp. 227, 241), and that the two taken together might become known to future historians as the Second Thirty Years War (pp. 253, 362).

If Wright's description of modern civilization was accurate, then it is safe to say that modern civilization, like all previous civilizations, was motivated by imperialism and its associated militarism. Together they spell exploitation, the taking from some for the benefit of others. Nobody submits to exploitation unless they have no choice in the matter. Civilization has to be forced on some by others. Civilization *is* exploitation. Civilization violates the golden rule, which is why, I assume, the great religious prophets railed against it. This rule has become a keystone of modern ethical philosophy—a form of Kant's categorical imperative of doing what every one can do—and a keystone in the modern politics of democracy with its emphasis on equality.

## Sorokin's Analysis of Modern Civilization

Like Wright, Sorokin (1957) spent a great deal of time and effort in quantifying his list of wars and revolutions of classic, medieval and modern European civilization between 600 B.C. and A.D. 1925. Also like Wright, Sorokin generally analyzed his data by inspection only. Neither Sorokin nor Wright can be faulted on this account, since both did the bulk of their research prior to the Second World War, a time when computers were not yet available. (The sheer mass of their data precluded the feasibility of hand calculation.)

According to Sorokin's (1957) study of art, philosophy, religion, science and technology, modern civilization was materialistic and scientific in its basic orientation to life. In this respect it was more like classic Greece and Rome than medieval Europe.

The materialism of modern civilization made its wars more secular than religious in nature. "They are wars of economic, imperialistic, utilitarian and other Sensate colors mainly: wars for 'a place in the sun,' for 'white man's domination,' for maintenance of high standards of living, for exploitation of the rich natural resources unexploited by the native savages, for political independence, and so on and so forth" (1957, p. 570).

If we think of imperialism as being somewhat undemocratic, we probably should not do so, according to Sorokin, because "the so-called democracies of the past and the present have been fully as imperialistic as the autocracies...."

Almost all such democracies . . . have been based upon the severest exploitation of colonies" (1947, p. 520).

Sorokin reserved his greatest contempt and criticism for the modern world: "During the past few centuries the most belligerent, the most aggressive, the most rapacious, the most power-drunk section of humanity has been precisely the Christian Western world. During these centuries Western Christendom has invaded all the other continents; its armies, followed by its priests and merchants, have subjugated, enslaved, robbed, pillaged and exterminated most of the non–Christian peoples, beginning with the pre-literate tribes and ending with the non–Christian nations. . . . Somewhat similar has been the conduct of Christians toward one another during these centuries" (1954, p. 179).

The twentieth century was the worst of all, since "the 20th century, so far [1937], has been the bloodiest and the most turbulent period – and therefore one of the cruelest and least humanitarian – in the history of Western civilization and perhaps in the chronicles of mankind in general" (1957, pp. 594–95). This was written 50 years ago, before World War II, Korea and Vietnam.

Both Sorokin's and Wright's analyses of modern civilization would seem to be very pessimistic indeed. However, that did not stop either one from spending his life seeking ways of preventing war and saving civilization from itself. Their recommendations will be saved for later, since this chapter is primarily an overview of the problem, not an attempt at its solution.

The problem seems to be that modern civilization, like previous civilizations, is motivated and structured to benefit some at the expense of others, a process that seems to be doomed to obstruct its own progress. It would further seem that such self-contradictory, self-destructive behavior can occur only with the aid of self-deception, without which one would have to intentionally contradict and destroy oneself. Mindful self-destruction appears to be absurd, and this appearance would soon put an end to such behavior.

What can it be that disguises the true nature of self-destruction, so as to permit us to destroy ourselves without knowing it? At the individual level, rationalization enables us to destroy ourselves without recognizing what we are doing, as the psychoanalysts of the twentieth century have suggested.

At the social level of analysis, ideology performs the function of rationalization, as the Marxists have suggested. Like rationalization at the individual level, ideology rationalizes the absurd at the social level – it makes the absurd appear rational.

In this manner ideology makes self-destruction possible by self-deception or, more properly perhaps, it makes social destruction possible by social deception. According to my hypothesis we would all recognize the rationality of the categorical imperative, or the golden rule, or the will for equality, if we were not blinded by an ideology that devalues the golden rule and transvalues its opposite into appearing rational, as Nietzsche (1956) did so successfully with his vision of the "Superman," and as Rand (1964) did so successfully with her virtue of "Selfishness."

## *Richardson's Analysis of Modern Civilization*

Richardson openly declared that "science ought to be subordinate to morals" (1960b, p. 278), but in his study of war, he made no moral judgments. Before the Second World War, he believed that all arms on both sides of any conflict were for defensive purposes only. Consequently, he was never able to identify an "aggressor" nor to recognize any "injustice" being done.

After the disclosures at the Nuremberg trials, he was obliged to admit that "Hitler and his associates planned the war deliberately" (1960b, p. 231), but when he developed his list of 315 wars from 1820 to 1952, he was still unable to determine "which side was the aggressor, or which was morally or legally wrong.... In arranging the following list [of 315 wars] the author has been unable to name the aggressor" (1960a, pp. 14, 18).

Richardson's desire to be "scientific" led him to suppose that the social sciences (in dealing with human phenomena such as war) had to be like the natural sciences which treat their subject matter "objectively." Since physical objects are morally neutral in their relations to one another — for example, an earthquake presumably does not have an intent to destroy, so that it is "scientific" to treat an earthquake without any moral judgment being brought to bear upon its consequences — Richardson, like many social scientists, assumed that he had to treat human beings as if they were morally neutral objects. He seemed to assume that moral judgments were "unscientific." However, human beings, especially civilized human beings do behave immorally — with the intention, conscious or otherwise, of doing harm. To be morally neutral in the face of such behavior can hardly be the "scientific" thing to do. While it is "unscientific" to treat physical objects as if they were human (anthropomorphism), it is just as "unscientific" to treat human subjects as if they were physical objects (social physics). Such a philosophy of science may itself be a part of an ideology that justifies treating some human beings as means to the ends of others, thus violating the categorical imperative.

As a social physicist, Richardson had nothing to say about modern civilization. Perhaps this was in part because he limited his list of wars to 1820–1952, which did not give him the broad view of history that Sorokin and Wright acquired looking at wars over a much longer period — including animal and primitive hostilities in the case of Wright. In addition, Richardson's background was mathematical and meteorological, so he lacked the background in the social sciences that both Sorokin and Wright brought to their studies. Finally, and perhaps most importantly, Richardson was a Quaker and a pacifist; his religion may have made it difficult for him to pass judgment upon human behavior. He may have taken the injunction "judge not, that ye be not judged" literally. However, the sources of his philosophy of science only influenced his interpretation and evaluation of facts. They may have been a positive influence on his collection of facts, which he did very comprehensively and conscientiously. I shall make full use of his facts, no matter how much I may disagree with his metaphysics or epistemology.

Singer and Small (1972) and Small and Singer (1982) were great admirers and followers of Richardson, Sorokin and Wright, but found their lists of wars lacking in precision and rigor. Like Richardson, they limited their list to 1816–1980, which also meant that they did not have the broader vision of history provided by Sorokin and Wright. Like Sorokin and Wright, however, Singer and Small were both social scientists—a political scientist and a historian, respectively. Yet, in spite of their backgrounds, they also hesitated to make moral judgments—presumably because these would have violated their philosophy of science—and they also failed to provide a comprehensive historical background beyond the time period they covered. Their list, however, is generally acknowledged to be the most reliable and carefully researched list of wars for the time period involved. They had little to say about modern civilization, although they provided a mass of reliable data for 1816–1980 to facilitate its study. Like Richardson, they were politically concerned citizens but, also like Richardson, they tried to keep their scientific work value-free.

## Compassion

This may be as good a place as any to make my own philosophy of science explicit. I believe that natural scientists dealing with physical objects should be value-free and should not treat physical objects as if they were human subjects (anthropomorphism); I also believe that social scientists should not treat human subjects as if they were physical objects (social physics). In short, social physics is just as unscientific in the social sciences as anthropomorphism is in the natural sciences. If sticks and stones should be treated as the unconscious objects they are, then human beings should be treated as the conscious subjects they are.

I believe that the social sciences are primarily sciences of value, and that values can and should be studied both descriptively and normatively. Eventually, if we ever get started, we shall be able to develop a science of value as well as a science of fact. Until we do, my own values—which have necessarily colored the way this book has been written (and how the facts have been selected, interpreted and evaluated)—are as follows: I believe that human beings are essentially equal and deserving of freedom, and that actualization of this belief is to be valued more highly than anything else. We should, both as citizens *and* as scientists, be working toward it as much as possible. I have spelled out this philosophy of science in more detail elsewhere (Eckhardt, 1972, 1978, 1980, 1981a).

This set of beliefs has been called a philosophy of compassion, one guided by the principle of coherence and its standards of judging the authenticity of values according to their universality, eternity, unity, honesty and freedom. "Compassion" comprised a radical faith in human nature, altruistic morality, cognitive creativity, justice (defined as equality), behavior aimed at actualizing all these values and a social structure compatible with and conducive to their actualization. Something is authentic to the extent that it reflects a determination to value for others what we value for ourselves. In short, authenticity is simply another form of the categorical imperative, the golden rule or the will to equality, according to one's philosophical or religious preferences. Compassion is believed to be the truth that will set us free from the compulsion to destroy ourselves, especially from any ideology that rationalizes this self-destructive compulsion.

The standards for judging authenticity are all characterized by equality, the cornerstone of compassion: (1) universality requires that what is good for one should be good for all; (2) eternity, that what is good in the short run be good in the long run; (3) unity, that an authentic value should be consistent with other authentic values, or at least not contradict them; (4) honesty, that what is worth talking about be worth doing, and; (5) freedom, that authentic values are freely chosen rather than coerced.

Some argue that a value-laden philosophy must make scientific work unscientific. I argue that, if human relations are value-laden, it is unscientific in my field to leave such values out of our equations. Value-free equations would leave out what is most instructive in the study of human behavior. If human relations were merely a function of factual matters, it would be proper to limit these scientific studies to the facts. But since human relations cannot be understood without taking values into account, I hold that our studies cannot be scientific if we disregard that which is most essentially human—human values.

## Imperial Sizes in Modern Civilization

If levels of warfare relate to the size of empires, we must assume that warfare in modern times was much more prevalent than ever before in human history. The average size of the three largest empires, as measured by Taagepera (1978a), was 13.5 square megameters in modern times (1550 to 1975), compared to 4.1 in medieval times (550 to 1500), 3.1 in classic times (450 B.C. to A.D. 500), 0.6 in ancient times (1450 to 500 B.C.) and 0.2 in archaic times (3000 to 1500 B.C.). The average sum of the sizes of all empires per century was 75.25 square megameters in modern times, 20.9 in medieval times, 13.6 in classic times, 2.6 in ancient times and 0.6 in archaic times, as shown in Table 5.1 in Appendix B.

According to these figures, admittedly not precise, modern empires, on average, were more than 67 times larger than archaic empires and, at times, more than 125 times larger. We have come a long way indeed during the last five thousand years, as far as imperial sizes are concerned. These figures suggest that, so far as empires have been created by wars, modern civilization has been far more warlike than previous civilizations. This conclusion would be consistent with Sorokin's, Toynbee's and Wright's descriptions of modern civilization and warfare.

We shall test this conclusion in more detail in the following chapters. But first we shall briefly summarize what has happened to empires over the course of human history, using Taagepera's (1978a) data as our guide. Empires first arose in Egypt and Mesopotamia about 3000 B.C. Egypt rose and fell in imperial size through the Old, Middle, New and Late Kingdoms from 3000 to 550 B.C. (archaic and ancient times), after which it vanished from the ranks of the three largest empires. Between 1450 and 1300 B.C. the New Kingdom achieved Egypt's greatest imperial size of one square megameter, the largest size that any empire had achieved up to that time.

Mesopotamia also had gains and losses during the same period. Mesopotamia was not an empire in 3000 B.C., but thereafter was the site of a large number and variety of civilizations over the next 2500 years; these included Akkad, Babylon, Mitanni and Assyria, the latter achieving, about 650 B.C., the greatest imperial size of the four—one square megameter.

Turkey's empires date from about 1600 B.C. with the Hyksos at about 0.65 square megameters. They were followed by the Hittites, Phrygia and Lydia, none of which managed to achieve an imperial size of 0.5 square megameters, but all of which were, nevertheless, among the three largest empires between 1600 and 500 B.C.

Persia was a latecomer, but an overachiever, starting about 700 B.C. with less than 0.5 square megameters, but achieving about 5.5 square megameters by 500 B.C. with the Achaeminds. According to these figures, and assuming that imperial sizes were functions of military activity, Persia was by far the most militaristic civilization of archaic and ancient history, followed by Media, Assyria, China (Shang) and Egypt (New).

Moving east, we find that India achieved status among the top three empires from 2400 to 1800 B.C., but never grew larger than 0.3 megameters, and its imperial status was questioned by Taagepera (1978a); he questioned its political cohesion.

China flourished from about 1900 B.C., reaching a peak of 1.1 square megameters on 1150 B.C., but usually achieved less than 0.5 throughout archaic and ancient history. A paragon among empires, China has maintained imperial status to the present day, the only region in the world to achieve this feat. China ranked among the three largest empires twice as frequently as its closest rivals in this respect: Mesopotamia, Persia, Egypt and Central Asia. If all the European empires from classic Rome to modern times are treated as one, that entity would be among the three largest empires only two-thirds as frequently as China.

It is remarkable to note that while no empire was larger than 1.1 square megameters up to 660 B.C., there are 26 such empires or states of that size in the world today (Sivard, 1990), with two others (Mauritania and Egypt) at 1.0. Since Egypt today, because of advances in technology, must be far more powerful than archaic Egypt, that would suggest that the archaic empires of Egypt, China and Mesopotamia were also far less powerful than Egypt today. Furthermore, the maximum achievement of 1.0 square megameters did not occur until ancient times, when imperial sizes, on the average, were about three times archaic imperial sizes, as shown in the "Average" row of Table 5.1. This comparison would suggest that wars between archaic empires caused no more deaths, on average, than were caused by the wars between the Arabs and the Israelis since 1945, which, in turn, constituted less than 1 percent of all war-related deaths from 1945 to 1990 (Sivard, 1990). The latter include five wars that were waged over a total of about 11 years.

This is probably a liberal estimate of the war-related deaths in ancient times, since the average imperial size was less than 1.0, as shown in Table 5.1. The estimate is probably much too high for archaic times, since there were only two empires (Egypt and Sumer) in existence from 3000 to 2500 B.C. and, considering the questionability of the Indian empire, possibly only two up to 1800 B.C.

Furthermore, populations were smaller, weapons were less deadly and wars were of greater duration and less concentration.

Consequently, I tentatively suggest that war-related deaths in ancient times were probably no more than 1 percent of those occurring since 1945, while those in archaic times were about one-quarter of 1 percent of those occurring since 1945 (since the average sum of archaic imperial sizes was about one-quarter of that sum for ancient times, as shown in Table 5.1).

If one were simply to take the imperial size ratios between archaic and ancient times, respectively, and modern times as a measure by which to compare the war-related deaths of these two pairs of times, then the archaic/modern ratio would be 0.8 percent and the ancient/modern ratio would be 3.5 percent. These ratios would mean that archaic war deaths were less than 1 percent of modern war deaths, and that ancient war deaths were 3.5 percent of modern war deaths.

Having established some validity for these imperial ratios—but not enough; more research is required—I shall use them as a rough estimate of the relative war deaths of the various historical periods as a percentage of modern war deaths. This gives the following percentages: Archaic = 0.8 percent, Ancient = 3.5 percent, Classic B.C. = 15 percent, Classic A.D. = 21 percent, Early Medieval = 26 percent and Late Medieval = 29 percent.

There isn't a great deal of difference in these ratios from A.D. 1 to 1500, that is, from late Classic to late Medieval times. The most noticeable increases are from archaic to ancient, from ancient to classic B.C., from classic B.C. to classic A.D. and from late medieval to modern. I shall try to develop more detailed estimates of war-related deaths throughout history in Chapter 13. In the meantime these crude estimates suggest that war-related deaths have increased considerably from the beginning of history to modern times.

Returning to Table 5.1, we can see that Turkey (Hyksos in Egypt) was the outstanding empire in archaic times, Persia in ancient times, Central Asia (Hsiung-Nu Huns) in classic B.C. times, Rome and China in classic A.D. times, Muslims in early medieval times, Central Asia (Mongols) in later medieval times and England in modern times.

# Figure 5.1   Civilizations, Empires
# and Wars, A.D. 1 to 2000

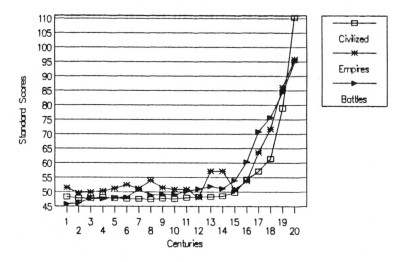

Notes to Figure 5.1: See the Notes to Figure 2.1. Modern times (1500–2000) were much higher than all previous historical periods in civilized activities, imperial sizes and battle frequencies.

---

Dividing the imperial world into three large regions at the foot of Table 5.1, enables us to see that the Middle East and Asia monopolized archaic times, with an average imperial size of much less than 1.0. The Middle East prospered until the early Middle Ages, after which it declined. Asia prospered into modern times, with a slight drop in the early Middle Ages. Europe was a late starter, but compared favorably with Asia and the Middle East during classic times, declined considerably during the Middle Ages, and then rose with a vengeance, becoming king of the hill in modern times.

## Modern Civilizations, Empires and Wars

Table 5.2 (Appendix B) shows the data for modern civilizations, empires and wars that constituted, on average, well over half the activities represented by the six variables in this table.

When these variables were correlated and factor-analyzed, the results were similar to those obtained in most of the historical periods previously analyzed. A single factor emerged: civilized activities (.98), imperial sizes (.98), battle frequencies (.97), centuries (.97), population (.96), historical pages (.96) and war frequencies (.92). The relations between civilizations, empires and wars during the last two thousand years are shown graphically in Figure 5.1.

Table 5.3 (Appendix B) presents these same data in percentage form over all historical periods to facilitate comparisons. The modern period contained almost 3 times as many activities per century as did the medieval period, 5 times more than the classic period, 20 times more than the ancient period, and almost 50 times more than the archaic period.

Table 5.4 (Appendix B) provides another way of comparing the modern period of history with the previous periods in the form of activity ratios. The modern period's activity level was generally equal to or greater than all other periods taken together.

Table 5.5 (Appendix B) provides percentages within the modern period, so that these centuries can be compared with one another. The twentieth century contained almost 40 percent of all modern activities, exceeding each one of the previous centuries.

# Chapter 6

# Wright's List of Modern Wars, 1480–1964

## Introduction

In this and the following chapters several lists of modern wars will be discussed and analyzed, beginning with those covering the entire period, such as Wright's list in this chapter, then Levy's list (limited, however, to wars of the Great Powers) in the next, then Sorokin's and then mine. Chapter 10 will compare Sorokin's list with that of the Dupuys and Kohn over the entire historical period. Chapter 11 will discuss and analyze those lists focusing on later time periods, such as Kaye et al. (1985) for 1720–1985, Bouthoul and Carrere (1978) for 1740–1978, Dunnigan and Martel (1987) for 1786–1986, Richardson (1960a) for 1820–1952 and Small and Singer (1982) for 1816–1980. Chapter 12 will review three lists of battles by Harbottle (1904; Bruce 1981), Eggenberger (1967, 1985), and Dupuy and Dupuy (1986). Chapter 13 will present an estimate of war-related deaths since 3000 B.C. Chapter 14 will present a dialectical evolutionary theory of the relations between civilizations, empires and wars. In a concluding chapter the various lists throughout the book (see Appendix C), the conclusions derived from them, and the solutions to the problem of war suggested by them will be compared and contrasted.

## Wright's Studies of Previous Wars

Before proceeding to Wright's modern wars, his work on previous wars will be briefly reviewed. All quotations from (and references to) Wright in this chapter are from his *A Study of War,* 1965, (2nd edition) unless otherwise noted.

Starting with animals, and using a very broad definition of war to include all *"violent contact* of *distinct* but *similar* entities" (p. 8), Wright concluded that "on the whole, war does not exist among animals other than man" (p. 38).

In discussing primitive warfare, Wright introduced his definition of war that was used to cover all human warfare: "the *legal condition* which *equally* permits two or more *hostile groups* to carry on a *conflict* by *armed* force"

(p. 8). Wright defined primitive people as "human beings that live in self-determining communities which do not use writing" (p. 55), and studied some six hundred such groups. He concluded that "the more primitive the people, the less warlike it tends to be" (p. 68). As primitive people became more developed, they became more warlike, as measured by the simple addition of five ranked variables: political absolutism; exposure to human bloodshed in the form of religious sacrifices, sports and spectacles, executions, feuds, etc.; frequency of imperialistic battles; frequency of interstate battles; and degree of discipline and enthusiasm of the population participating in war.

With regard to civilized warfare, Wright distinguished it from primitive warfare as follows: "The presence of an ideological conflict, a struggle for values ... has distinguished civilized war from animal and primitive war and from other forms of civilized violence. . . . The later civilizations have emphasized the ideological conflict more than have earlier civilizations" (pp. 160–61). According to these observations, the more civilized we became, the more ideological war became in its nature. In relating civilization to his definition of war, Wright virtually identified war with civilized activity. "War in the sense of a legal situation equally permitting groups to expand wealth and power by violence began with civilization. . . . Only among civilized peoples has war been an instrument serving political and economic interests of the community" (p. 39).

However, these statements, suggesting that war sprang full-blown from the head of civilization, were modified by other statements suggesting an evolutionary development of war alongside an evolutionary development of society from primitive to civilized forms: "Primitive warfare was an important factor in developing civilization. . . . Civilization was both an effect and a cause of warlikeness. . . . Out of the warlike peoples arose civilization, while the peaceful collectors and hunters were driven to the ends of the earth, where they are gradually being exterminated or absorbed" (pp. 98–100). According to these observations, war and civilization developed together, feeding each other's development. I have labeled this a "dialectical evolutionary" process.

War was not nonexistent among primitive peoples—Wright's study of primitive times showed the existence of warfare among the more developed primitive peoples, where it served the same economic and political purposes that emerged more fully among civilized peoples. In other words, instead of a sharp division between primitive and civilized peoples, he found a gradual, evolutionary development from one to the other, the agricultural and pastoral stages of development providing links between the two: "Slavery, social classes, empires and minorities are phenomena of civilization and the most highly developed of the primitive peoples" (p. 78).

In short, civilized warfare merely evinced more clearly the elements of Wright's definition of war that had already appeared among the more developed primitive peoples—the "right" to use "might" to conquer and dominate others to benefit oneself. According to Wright's definition of war, "might" was a "legal right" even though it was not a "divine right."

What made might legal, let alone divine? Might itself, which declared itself preeminent and challenged others to usurp its position.

These were the historical beginnings of the rise and fall of civilizations during the last five thousand years, a pattern characterized by the dominance of some over others, until those others mustered enough might to satisfy their need for independence, which "like dominance, is a drive peculiarly characteristic of civilization" (p. 142). Without exception up to the present time, civilizations that began by conquering others, ended being conquered themselves. The paradox of power is that it cannot sustain itself. It obstructs its own progress. It gets in its own way. It destroys itself.

Civilized warfare was traced through Toynbee's 26 civilizations until, about 1500, modern civilizations began to emerge, eventually covering the globe. This brings us to Wright's study of modern warfare.

## Modern Warfare, 1480–1964

Wright divided modern history into several periods: "Renaissance, Reformation, and Discovery," 1480–1520; "Wars of Religion," 1520–1648; "Political Absolutism and Dynastic Wars," 1648–1789; "Democracy, Industrialism, and Nationalistic Wars," 1789–1914; "World Wars," 1914–45; and the "Atomic Age," 1945–64 (pp. 196, 294, 1505).

Modern wars were classified into the same four types as civilized warfare: imperial wars to expand modern civilization at the expense of other cultures; defensive wars against the expansion of others; balance-of-power wars between states of modern civilization; civil wars within modern states (p. 638).

There were 278 wars from 1480 to 1941, plus 30 "hostilities" from 1945 to 1964. "Hostilities" was defined as armed conflicts between human groups "in which more than 317 persons were killed" (p. 1544), following Richardson (1960a). For periods before 1941, a "war" was defined by its legal recognition as such, or by the involvement of more than 50,000 troops, or by its important legal results (p. 636). There were 2,659 battles from 1480 to 1941, a "battle" being defined by total casualties of more than one thousand in land engagements, or more than five hundred total casualties in sea engagements (p. 625). The average battle lasted about one day, the average campaign lasted about six to eight months and the average war lasted four or five years (p. 227).

Wright attributed a great (and increasing) number of deaths to modern warfare: "Probably at least 10 percent of deaths in modern civilization can be attributed directly or indirectly to war. . . . The trend of war has been toward greater cost, both absolutely and relative to population. . . . [There has been an] increasing intensity of war as modern civilization has progressed" (pp. 246–47, 639). Wright suggested that the intensity of war might be measured by the frequency and duration of battles (p. 237), and noted that "for this purpose intensity must be measured by units of military activity occupying as limited a time and place as possible. The frequency of battles seems to conform more closely to this requirement than any other of the readily available indices" (p. 220).

## Correlational Analyses of Wright's Modern Wars

From 1480 to 1964 there were about 64 wars per century, but the eighteenth century was significantly lower than average with 38 wars, and the nineteenth and twentieth centuries were significantly higher than average with 89 wars and 84 wars, respectively (p. 651). Fifteen important states (12 of which were European) participated in 37 wars each on the average, but England (78), France (71), Spain (64), Russia (61) and Austria (52) were significantly higher than average, while the Netherlands (23), Germany, (23), Denmark (20), the United States (13), China (11) and Japan (9) were significantly lower than average (p. 650). While Wright provided all of the basic statistics for this chapter, he conducted no statistical analyses. Such analyses were conducted by the present author unless otherwise noted.

Sixty-seven percent of all wars were fought mainly in Europe, but this percentage was much higher for the sixteenth (94 percent), seventeenth (89 percent) and eighteenth (82 percent) centuries, and much lower for the nineteenth (33 percent) and twentieth (46 percent) centuries (p. 651). The high frequency of wars in the nineteenth century and the high percentage of wars fought outside Europe in this century reflected the high frequency of imperial wars of conquest during the period. The frequency of wars in general was significantly lower than average in the eighteenth century and significantly higher than average for the nineteenth and twentieth centuries—the twentieth century being prorated—as shown in Table 6.1 (Appendix B).

Wright provided no death estimates for modern wars up to 1941, but did provide the number of important battles for almost one-half (45 percent) of his wars. When I correlated Wright's battles with Levy's (1983) deaths for the 74 wars where data were available from both sources, the correlation was .69, indicating that the number of battles might be used as a rough measure of the intensity of wars, as Wright had suggested.

The number of important battles over ten 50-year periods from 1480 to 1941 was correlated with these time periods at .93, suggesting that the intensity of wars increased significantly over this time, a confirmation of Wright's impression. The average number of important battles per war also increased significantly over this time by .82, indicating an increase not only in the absolute intensity of wars during modern times, but also in the intensity of each war, on average. Assuming that we were becoming more civilized during this time, this finding further confirmed the general theory that the more civilized we became, the more warlike we became, so far as "warlikeness" was measured by the intensity of war in general or by the average intensity of each war. When I repeated this operation for Wright's battles per war and Sorokin's (1937, vol. 3) casualties per war, the correlation was .79 over 65 wars.

The total number of states participating in wars, as well as the average number of involved states per war, also increased significantly over this time period, the correlations being .86 and .74, respectively. This can be taken as another measure of the increasing intensity of war over this period.

While the frequency of wars over these ten of 50-year periods did not increase significantly, the intensity of wars did increase significantly, and the average duration of wars decreased significantly ( −.66). This negative correlation reflects the fact that earlier wars were longer (presumably because of longer inactive periods between battles) but not so deadly as later wars.

Finally, Wright's data at the bottom of his p. 651 show that balance-of-power wars constituted almost one-half (49 percent) of all wars, civil wars, more than one-quarter (28 percent), imperial wars, 16 percent and defensive wars, 8 percent. When we consider that defensive wars were imperial wars on the part of non–European empires (especially the Ottoman Empire during this time period), then imperial wars constituted almost one-quarter (24 percent) of all wars. And when we further consider that balance-of-power wars were fought primarily between imperial powers, fighting over the spoils of imperialism, then imperial wars are seen to constitute almost three-quarters (72 percent) of all wars. In short, most modern wars, up to and including the Second World War were fought to achieve or maintain dominance on the international scene to the advantage of one nation, alliance or empire, at the expense of others. The civil wars were also attempts to achieve or maintain dominance, albeit within nations, to the advantage of one group at the expense of others. On the other end of the see-saw, of course, were those nations and groups fighting to free themselves from domination. And this destructive see-saw has not simply been going up and down at a constant rate; its tempo increased over this period of time.

## Factor Analyses of Wright's Modern Wars

Wright's data (pp. 641–46b) were summed together over 20-year periods. I added a few variables, such as the number of Great Powers (using Levy's 1983 list), the duration of each war (obtained by subtracting the starting year from the ending year provided by Wright) and the percentage of wars won by those who started them. When these variables were correlated and factor-analyzed over these 24 time periods, three factors emerged, as shown in Table 6.2 (Appendix B).

It can be seen that all measures of intensity were correlated with the first factor along with the sixteenth to the twentieth centuries. Thus, these results are consistent with the theory that wars became more intense as we became more civilized during the last five centuries (assuming, of course, that we *did* become more civilized during that time period—a reasonable assumption, based on the lists of civilized activities provided by Sorokin, 1941, vol. 4 and Kroeber, 1944, among others).

The second factor shows that the frequency of wars also increased over this same time period, but frequency was independent of intensity, and negatively correlated with the duration of wars. Although wars were becoming more frequent and more intense during the last five hundred years, they were also becoming shorter.

The third factor shows that the percentage of starters who won these wars was not significantly associated with their frequency, duration or intensity, although there was some tendency for starters to win longer wars. Since longer wars occurred earlier in time, this last finding probably reflects starters winning earlier wars more than later ones.

While Table 6.2 shows the results of factor-analyzing the correlations among variables across time (measured by centuries), Table 6.3 (in Appendix B) shows the results of factor-analyzing the same variables across space (as measured by eight geographical regions: Europe, the Far East, Latin America, the Middle East, North America, northern and South Africa, south Asia and sub-Saharan Africa). Intensity variables were associated with one another across space as they were across time, as shown in Table 6.3.

Battles, Great Powers and war frequency were associated with Europe and North America, earlier centuries, and a lower percentage of starters winning wars they started. The intensity factor was relatively independent of the duration factor and the participation factor, as shown in Table 6.3, although there was some tendency for both duration and participation to be associated with intensity across geographical regions, as shown by their factor coefficients of .50 and .40, respectively, on the intensity factor. This factor clearly reflected those wars in which the European Great Powers participated, especially in the earlier centuries of the modern period.

## Analyses of Variance of Wright's Modern Wars

The same variables were subjected to analyses of variance in order to detect any deviations from linearity, which would have been missed by the factor analyses. Table 6.4 in Appendix B shows that almost one-third of Wright's modern wars occurred in the nineteenth century, while the eighteenth century was significantly low in this respect. The years-per-war figures were significantly higher in the earlier centuries than in the last two centuries.

There were no significant differences in the Start/Win percentages from century to century, so that the average of 49 percent was fairly representative of all these centuries. This percentage would suggest that the odds of winning a modern war that you started were about even. Half the time you won, and half the time you lost. This finding raises a question as to how many lives should be risked in the face of these odds? (The question assumes that what is gained from any war is worth any lives at all.) It hardly seems worthwhile to start a war if you have to pay for two wars in order to win one.

(What is gained from war? Power. But we have found that power destroys itself, so, what does it mean to gain something that is self-destructive? It means gaining nothing at all, since that which destroys itself ends up as nothing. Consequently, even the winners of wars gain nothing, at a cost of lives, property, resources, etc. Was there ever any human activity so senseless as war? And how it has to be rationalized or ideologized in order to cover up its absurdity!)

While war duration decreased over these centuries, war participation increased, as did intensity (as measured by battles per war), especially in the twentieth century. The participation of Great Powers reached its peak of almost two per war in the eighteenth century and thereafter returned to is previous average of about one Great Power per war.

Table 6.5 in Appendix B shows that during this time period significantly more wars occurred in Europe than occurred outside Europe. European wars lasted significantly longer than non–European wars. Starters of European wars won only 44 percent of them, but this was not significantly less than those winning non–European wars, unless a one-tailed test is warranted. This would be the case if a convincing argument could be made that Europeans found it more difficult to win wars against other well-armed Europeans than against less well-armed non–European countries. But this argument requires more research before it can be taken seriously.

There were more participants per war in European wars, but this difference was not significant, thus it could have occurred by chance. There were significantly more Great Powers participating in European wars, which simply reflected the fact that Europe was where the Great Powers were during most of this time period. There were also more battles per war, but this difference was not significant because of the great variability of battles per war within both regions. Finally, the European wars occurred earlier during this time period than did non–European wars, as noted at the bottom of Table 6.1. It would seem that European nations were first fighting among themselves over Europe itself, although they were interested in the Americas and Afro-Asia from the beginning of the modern period. However, their colonial interests increased over time.

Finally, Table 6.6 in Appendix B shows how these same variables were distributed across different types of war, as these wars were typed by Wright. Balance-of-power wars constituted almost half of Wright's modern wars. These were wars fought between European powers for the most part, in their efforts to control more of Europe than their competitors, that is, in order to become more powerful than their neighbors. These efforts expanded beyond Europe rather early: Portugal and Spain quarreled over South America, then England and the Netherlands over the East Indies and then England and France over most of the rest of the world.

Defensive wars, fought primarily against encroachment by the Ottoman Empire on European territory, were the longest wars, lasting 7.5 years on average, while imperial wars of European nations against other cultures were the shortest, lasting 2.5 years on average; this suggests that it was harder for the Ottoman Empire to invade the Balkans than it was for Europeans to invade the

Americas and Afro-Asia, and further suggests that Europe was much better prepared for war than the rest of the world. Yet defensive wars, presumably started by the Ottoman Empire, were eventually won by the Ottoman Empire 80 percent of the time, while balance-of-power wars between European nations and civil wars within them were won only 50 percent and 40 percent of the time, respectively, by their starters.

Balance-of-power wars attracted the most participants. Great Powers were also often involved in these wars, but no more often than they were in defensive wars. Balance-of-power wars had the most battles per war, but this difference was insignificant unless a one-tailed test could be justified. It might be argued, as was previously argued in the case of the large number of battles per war regarding European wars, that balance-of-power wars were more intense because they engaged well-armed European powers, including Great Powers.

Finally, defensive wars against the Ottoman Empire came early in this time period, while imperial wars of European nations against the rest of the world came later. These facts hardly contribute anything new to our knowledge but, like some of the other facts established by these analyses, they establish the reliability of the analyses themselves, making us more confident of other results not so self-evident.

## Summary and Conclusions

In general, wars, battles and participants increased over these five centuries of modern history, according to Wright's list of modern wars. Although war frequency and intensity increased over this time period, the average duration of wars decreased. This was probably due to the fact that earlier wars were often characterized by brief battles separated by long periods between battles, whereas later wars were characterized by more continuous fighting.

The evidence concerning the participation of Great Powers is more ambiguous. While their participation was associated with increasing intensity of war over 20-year periods, this was not the case over 100-year periods, their participation having peaked in the eighteenth century. This ambiguity needs to be clarified by further research.

About 50 percent of starters won the wars they started, and there was no significant linear or curvilinear trend in this percentage over this time period. What can be asserted about Wright's list of wars is simply that starters won half of them and lost half of them, raising a question about the rationality or sensibility of starting war.

Region-wise, Europe was the location of most of these modern wars, two-thirds of which occurred primarily in Europe. Two-thirds of their participants were also European nations. Also, the vast majority (87 percent) of important battles, which presumably killed most people, occurred in Europe. This tendency for wars to center on Europe was especially true during the sixteenth through the eighteenth centuries, and less true during the nineteenth and twentieth centuries, when Europe spread its wars more widely throughout the world. Europe was not only high in frequency and intensity of wars, but also in duration of wars. Great Powers, which were largely European nations, also participated more in European wars.

Type-wise, balance-of-power wars were most frequent, had the most participants, including Great Powers, and had the most battles per war. Thus, these wars between European powers were among the most intense in terms of their frequency, participation and destructiveness. They were average in duration and average in their Start/Win percentage, i.e. starters won half and lost half. Presumably, the gains and losses canceled each other out, leaving everyone back at the starting line, as if they had never fought at all, except that they lost a lot of lives, a lot of money and a lot of property in the process of achieving or balancing power.

Civil wars within European powers were average in frequency, duration and intensity. They were lower than average in the percentage of starters winning them, in the number of participants and in the number of Great Powers participating. The odds of starting and winning a civil war were less than even.

Defensive wars against the Ottoman Empire was very low in frequency — largely occurring in the earlier centuries of the modern period — frequently won (80 percent of the time) by the Ottoman Empire against the less developed Balkan nations, involved a large number of Great Powers, were long-lasting but not very intense, and were average in number of participants.

Finally, imperial wars of Europe against others were significantly low in frequency, duration, participation (including Great Power participation) and intensity. These imperial wars came later in the time period. The aggressor won more often than not (60 percent of the time), but hardly enough to warrant the risks involved and the consequences that ensued. While not involving a great deal of armed violence, these imperial wars did a great deal of structural violence, as a result of domination and exploitation of others. This structural violence killed more people through hunger and disease than did the combat of all the wars in modern times added together. In the twentieth century alone, noted for the intensity of its armed violence, 15 to 20 times as many people died from structural violence as died from combat in all of the twentieth century wars and revolutions taken together (Eckhardt and Kohler, 1980; Eckhardt, 1983b).

## Chapter 7
# Levy's List of Great Power Wars, 1495–1975

*Great Powers*

Since several authors have found that the Great Powers or strong nations engaged in the most wars, the longest wars and the most deadly wars, Levy (1983) decided to concentrate his studies on wars involving Great Powers in the modern period of history, which he defined as starting with the French invasion of Italy in 1494–95. Not only did Great Powers engage in many wars after becoming "great," but they became "great" in the first place through success in war, so that the relation between great powers and war in modern times was very much like that between civilizations and war throughout human history: Great Powers make war, which makes powers great. Conversely, when Great Powers start losing wars, or stop going to war, they start losing their greatness. Levy emphasized the economic control over resources, such as territory and population, that led to great power status, including more military capability, which led to more wars.

Unless otherwise indicated all quotations and references in this chapter are to Levy's *War in the Modern Great Power System, 1495–1975*, 1983.

Great Powers were defined by Levy by their self-sufficiency in security, secondary invulnerability, and power projection (1983, p. 14). According to this definition, there were 13 great powers during this time period, but only five to eight during any one century. England and France maintained their great power status during all five centuries; Austria, over the first four centuries; Spain, for the first three centuries; Turkey, the first two centuries; the Netherlands and Sweden, the seventeenth century only; Russia and Prussia/Germany, the last two centuries; Italy, the last half of the nineteenth century and the first half of the twentieth; the United States, the twentieth century; Japan, the first half of the twentieth century; and China, the last half of the twentieth century.

There were five Great Powers in the sixteenth century, seven in the seventeenth, six in the eighteenth and nineteenth, and eight in the twentieth (but only six as of 1975: England, France, the USSR, West Germany, the United States and China. Notice that ten of the Great Powers were European nations during this time period, and that all were European nations until the twentieth century. Consequently, Levy's list of wars was very Eurocentric, 88 percent of them occurring largely in Europe.

## Definition of War

Levy defined a war as "a substantial armed conflict between the organized military forces of independent political units" (1983, p. 51). He excluded international wars without a Great Power, civil wars unless they were internationalized, and imperial and colonial wars without intervention. Levy and Morgan (1984) included imperial and colonial wars involving Great Powers, but provided no death estimates for these wars, so they will not be discussed in this chapter, except to note that there were 89 such wars, which increased the frequency of the original list considerably, but whose battle deaths were assumed to be marginal, at least for the Great Powers. Of these 89 colonial / imperial wars, 50 occurred in the nineteenth century, and 17 occurred in the twentieth century up to 1975 (Levy and Morgan 1984, p. 741).

The question remained of defining the meaning of "substantial." What made an armed conflict substantial? Wright (1942) had suggested 50,000 troops. Richardson (1960a) had suggested 317 deaths, which is what Wright (1965) used after the Second World War. Bodart (1916) had suggested two thousand military casualties (deaths and injuries). Singer and Small (1972) had suggested one thousand military battle deaths. Levy decided to include all of Singer and Small's interstate wars since 1816, involving a Great Power (with some modifications), and any earlier war listed in at least two of Sorokin (1937, vol. 3), Wright (1965) and Woods and Baltzly (1915) (p. 58). This combination resulted in the same wars that were included in Singer and Small for 1816–1915, suggesting some reliability for this procedure.

## Death Estimates

Levy obtained his estimates of deaths after 1816 from Singer and Small (1972), and from Sorokin (1937, vol. 3), Bodart (1916), Dumas and Vedel-Peterson (1923) and Harbottle (1904; Bruce 1981) for deaths prior to 1817. These death estimates were limited to military deaths in battle. Since Bodart and Sorokin provided casualty (dead and wounded) estimates, there is some question concerning how comparable these were to the death estimates of the other authors. However, prior to the nineteenth century, many of the wounded probably died, so casualties prior to 1816 and deaths thereafter might be fairly comparable.

These definitions and procedures produced 119 wars involving 263 Great Powers from 1495 to 1975, so that there were 2.2 Great Powers per war in Levy's list. These wars lasted 4.4 years on average, and killed about 280,000 Great

Power soldiers in battle on the average. Levy assumed a 25 percent error in his fatality estimates and fatality-based indicators (p. 86). More than half of these wars (N = 64) involved at least one Great Power on both sides of the conflict. These latter wars lasted one year longer on the average, and killed twice as many soldiers on the average (p. 96). Levy used the phrase "Great Power Wars" to indicate these latter wars, in order to distinguish them from wars involving Great Power(s) on one side only. I shall use the same phrase to indicate both kinds of wars, distinguishing between them by making clear whether Great Powers were involved on one side only or on both sides of any armed conflict.

The deaths in these 119 wars were significantly correlated from .46 to .92 with deaths/population, nation-years of war, deaths/nation-years, duration of war, and number of Great Powers involved. These correlations suggested that "human losses in warfare have generally increased as rapidly as population" (p. 105). The same pattern of correlations was found for the 64 wars with Great Powers on both sides. A similar pattern was found when correlations were obtained over time (p. 107).

## Historical Trends

Singer and Small (1972, Ch. 8) found no historical trends from 1816 to 1965 in international war frequency, nation-years, deaths or deaths/population. Richardson (1960a, Ch. 4) found frequency going down slightly from 1820 to 1952. Although more deadly wars were becoming more frequent, there was no upward trend in deaths/population. Using Richardson's data, Denton found frequency relatively constant, but a combination of other measures increasing (Levy 1983, p. 113). Woods and Baltzly (1915, Ch. 2) found duration declining for 11 European nations from 1450 to 1914. Sorokin (1937, vol. 3) found army size increasing for nine major European nations during the last millennium, and casualties increasing even faster except during the nineteenth century. Wright found the frequency of European wars declining since 1480, but the human and economic costs of war increasing "both absolutely and relative to population" (Wright 1965, p. 303), and war becoming more concentrated in time and more extended in space.

After providing this survey with its ambiguous results, Levy analyzed his own data for historical trends, finding that the frequency of wars involving Great Powers (119) was declining (p. 116), particularly where those wars (64) involved a Great Power on both sides (p. 117). Wars were getting shorter, as were the nation-years of war (p. 123). There was little change in the number of Great Powers participating in these wars. Deaths were increasing by a small amount, as were deaths/war, but neither of these changes was significant (p. 124), nor was the declining deaths/population (p. 125). Deaths/nation-year were increasing significantly, however. In summary, analyses of these 119 wars showed little change over this time period, except for decreasing duration and increasing deaths/nation-year.

On the other hand, analyses of the 64 wars with Great Powers on both sides showed significant changes, except perhaps in duration and nation-years. The number of Great Powers involved was increasing; and "Great Power wars have also become increasingly destructive" (p. 128). This last finding remained true whether or not the world wars were included in the analysis (p. 129). In spite of this finding, Levy concluded that "in general there has been no significant increase in the total losses of human life from wars involving the great powers or from Great Power wars" (p. 135), but he added that the "bloodiest years are getting bloodier" (p. 135), which seemed to be a more accurate descripton of his statistical results. The following statement also seemed to describe more accurately the results concerning wars with Great Powers on both sides: "In contrast to the general decline of war in most respects, Great Power wars [those with great powers on both sides] are becoming much less frequent, but those that do occur are much greater in extent [number of great powers involved], severity [deaths], intensity [deaths/population] and concentration [deaths/nation-years], somewhat greater in magnitude [nation-years], and unchanged in duration" (p. 136).

The number of war measures and or indicators used by Levy in his attempt to capture the complexity of the phenomenon can be overwhelming. When he ranked 12 of them and obtained the average rank for each century, he found the nineteenth century the most peaceful, followed by the twentieth, sixteenth, eighteenth and seventeenth, in that order (p. 139). When he did the same for his 64 Great Power wars, the nineteenth century was still the most peaceful, followed by the sixteenth, eighteenth, twentieth and seventeenth, in that order: "By almost any indicator the 19th century was unquestionably the most peaceful of the modern period. The 20th century, though characterized by a high severity [deaths] and concentration [deaths/nation-years] and low frequency of Great Power [on both sides] war, is generally comparable to the earlier centuries in most other respects. . . . During the last 500 years Great Power wars have been rapidly diminishing in frequency but increasing in extent [number of great powers involved], severity [deaths], intensity [deaths/population], concentration [deaths/nation-years] and (to a certain degree) magnitude [nation-years]" (pp. 144–45).

If we are primarily interested in war deaths, then many of Levy's measures are not crucial to our central concern. Adding them together and averaging them is of questionable value. What makes war abominable is not its frequency, nor its duration, but rather the number of people killed in the process. This brings us back to the meaning of "substantial" in Levy's definition of war as "a substantial armed conflict between the organized military forces of independent political units" (p. 51). Levy never defined "substantial," but he illustrated it by Wright's requirement of 50,000 troops, Richardson's requirement of 317 deaths, Bodart's requirement of two thousand casualties, and Singer and Small's requirement of one thousand battle deaths, with all of which Levy is in basic agreement. Clearly, premature death is a defining characteristic of war; if absent, wars could be as frequent or as enduring as they pleased without anyone objecting. Following Richardson, Singer and Small expressed this point most clearly: "We strongly share Richardson's implied view that the single most valid and sensitive indicator of the 'amount of war' experienced by the system is that of battle deaths, or severity" (1972, p. 130). Levy and Morgan expressed the same point remarking that "the best and most widely used indicator of the seriousness of war is its 'severity' in terms of battle deaths" (1984, p. 740) and that "the severity of war for each great power is measured in battle deaths and is the best indicator of the human cost of war" (1986, p. 34).

I strongly agree with that point of view but, like Richardson, I extend it beyond the battle deaths alone of soldiers and include military deaths due to famine, disease, or any other war-related cause, and I include war-related civilian deaths (Richardson, 1960a, pp. 6, 8). Singer and Small had good reasons for omitting these other deaths, because of the unreliability, and sometimes the unavailability, of estimates, but they did include civilian battle deaths in civil wars (Small and Singer, 1982). These unreliabilities and unavailabilities made Levy's estimates for periods prior to 1800 even harder to make. In any event, by this criterion Levy's battle deaths increased significantly during these five hundred years—from 941,000 in the sixteenth century to 4 million in the seventeenth, 3.8 million in the eighteenth, 2.6 million in the nineteenth and 23.3 million (prorated) in the twentieth century. The trend was generally upward, except during the nineteenth century. Levy's death estimates for these centuries correlated .88 with Wright's battle frequencies during the same five centuries. Not only was the general trend upward, but in the twentieth century deaths were significantly higher than in the other four centuries added together—which was also the case with Wright's battles, as noted in the previous chapter. Deaths/population and battles/population followed a similar pattern.

Levy attributed the increasing destructiveness of war to weapons technology, transportation, communication, industry, "mechanization of war at the beginning of the 20th century," war as an instrument of policy, political centralization, "commercialization of war," popularization of war, professionalization of military power and social-political factors (pp. 147–48). The rationalization and centralization of force were particularly effective starting in the seventeenth century. Levy gave Clausewitz' dictum a new twist: "Commerce was a continuation of war . . . and war was a continuation of commerce" (p. 148). This new perspective, it seems to me, contributes considerably to our understanding of war. War is a means to expand commerce, and commerce in turn expands the economic foundations of military power.

## War Weariness and War Contagion

Levy found no sign that wars gave rise to either more or less war in the future, thus disproving both the war weariness and war contagion hypotheses—

at least so far as wars between Great Powers were concerned. "Likelihood of war does not increase during the period immediately following the termination of a previous war" (p. 158). This finding concerning contagion held for wars involving Great Powers on either one or both sides of an armed conflict (p. 160), and likewise for war-weariness: "There is no empirical evidence that periods following wars are more peaceful than other periods, nor is there any evidence that periods following the more serious wars are any more peaceful than those following less serious wars" (p. 161). These findings held for durations and deaths as well as frequencies: "The results are remarkably consistent" (p. 164). Levy and Morgan (1986) replicated these results at the national level of analysis.

Whatever provokes or prevents wars seem not to be wars themselves, which neither facilitate nor inhibit further wars when Great Powers are involved. These findings suggest that war is neither a habit nor an addiction, as has sometimes been claimed.

## War Cycles

Levy found no cyclical patterns in any of his measures of war. "It is consistently found that the outbreak of war is random rather than contagious, regardless of whether we look at short-term contagion or long-term periodicity. . . . There are no hints of cyclical patterns in either the occurrence of war or in any of its other dimensions [which] appear to be scattered at random" (pp. 136–37). This finding was based on visual inspection of the evidence rather than statistical analysis, but Goldstein (1988) found ten war cycles by inspection in Levy's data, and these ten cycles corresponded with long wave peaks (p. 239).

Sorokin also found no cycles (1937, 3, pp. 352–60), but Wright found a 50-year cycle (1965, p. 78), which Goldstein (1988) confirmed. Using Wright's data, Denton and Phillips found a 20-year cycle before 1680 and a 30-year cycle since that time (Levy 1983, p. 137), but Richardson (1960a, pp. 128–31) found no cycles in Wright's data. Singer and Small found no cycles in the outbreak of international war (1972, pp. 205–7), but did find the suggestion of a 20-year cycle in wars underway, more pronounced for European wars, but noted that "the evidence is far from conclusive" (1972, pp. 215–16).

The evidence of war cycles is ambiguous at best.

## Further Analyses of Levy's Great Power Wars

Levy was careful to note that the highly skewed distributions of most of his war measurements did not satisfy "many of the assumptions underlying most tests of statistical significance . . . and caution must be exercised in the use and interpretation of significance tests" (p. 97). As a result, Levy limited the analysis of his data to some basic statistics, such as the mean, median, minimum, maximum, standard deviation (pp. 96, 99, 101), rank-order correlations (pp. 105–11) and regression analyses (pp. 116–32). These statistical analyses and their results were summarized in preceding chapters. Levy's caution is well taken, but Lindquist (1953) has shown that statistical distributions can deviate to a great extent from normal assumptions without distorting the results of statistical analyses of variance. I assume that his conclusions can be generalized to other parametric procedures as well. In doubtful cases nonparametric procedures can be used, of course, just as Levy used rank-order correlations in his regression analyses. However, in view of Lindquist's findings, it seems that final conclusions need not depend entirely upon conformity to statistical assumptions.

In this section I applied factor analysis as a method of generalizing and summarizing correlational results, and analysis of variance as a way of comparing and contrasting mean scores among centuries, regions and Great Power participation.

Skewed distributions have been logged in order to make them more normal, statistically speaking, so that logged results may be compared with the results obtained from raw scores.

## Factor Analysis

All of the death measurements (logged) were highly loaded on the first factor, as shown in Table 7.1 in Appendix B, along with the number of Great Powers involved on one or both sides, and along with the number of years that the war lasted.

The second factor was characterized by time, as measured by beginning date, ending date and century, along with the number of deaths per nation-year (or concentration).

Duration in years was also significantly loaded on the third factor by itself. The results clearly suggested that the death figures were influenced more by the number of Great Powers participating in these wars and by their duration, than by the date of their occurrence, although the latter was just as influential on deaths/nation-year and, to a lesser extent, on deaths/year. Furthermore, Great Power participation was more influential than duration, judging by the relative size of the factor loadings.

When none of the variables was logged, all the death measures were loaded on the first factor with time, as shown in Table 7.2 in Appendix B because the two (presumably) deadliest wars of all time occurred in the twentieth century. The number of Great Powers was also significantly loaded on this factor.

The results were more consistent with the fact that battle deaths did increase over these centuries, and with the fact that these wars involved Great Powers on both sides more frequently in the earlier centuries when wars were also longer. The analyses of variance to follow also support this factor analysis.

## Analyses of Variance

BETWEEN CENTURIES.    The perfect alignment between beginning and ending dates from century to century, as shown in the first two rows of Table 7.3 in Appendix B, is neither surprising nor significantly substantive. It merely reflects the fact that dates were highly correlated with other dates, which provides us with no empirical knowledge at all, but does provide some evidence about the validity of this procedure.

The duration of wars, as measured by years in the third row of Table 7.3, was significantly higher (about six years on average) in the first three centuries than it was during the last two centuries (about two years on average). Before the nineteenth century, wars were characterized by battles with long periods of inactivity between them. Nation-Years in the fourth row followed a pattern similar to that of Years, since they were influenced more by the number of years than by the number of nations (Great Powers), which did not differ significantly from the average of about two Great Powers per war over these five centuries, as shown in the fifth row of this table.

Although the number of Great Powers per war did not vary much, the percentage of wars with Great Powers on both sides was significantly higher in the sixteenth century than it was during the last three centuries, as shown in the sixth row. About 70 percent of the wars during the first two centuries had Great Powers on both sides, while only 30 percent of these wars had Great Powers on both sides during the last three centuries. Great Powers on both sides, years of duration, and nation-years were clearly negatively related to time as measured by centuries, which was the case in the second factor of Table 7.2 (raw scores), but which was not significantly the case in the second factor of Table 7.1 (log scores). As far as it goes, this finding confirms the raw factor analysis more than the log factor analysis.

All of the death measurements in rows 7 through 10 were significantly higher in the twentieth century than in the other centuries, which did not significantly differ from one another—except for the Deaths/Year, where the sixteenth century was significantly lower than the nineteenth and twentieth centuries. The variable of deaths/year was not included in Levy's original data. I added this variable in order to determine how many of Levy's wars had a minimum of one thousand Great Power deaths per year. All but three of them met this criterion, the exceptions being the Bavarian Succession of 1778, the Franco-Spanish War of 1823 and the Sinai War of 1956.

When the skewed variables (death measures, years, nation-years and number of Great Powers) were logged, the results remained the same or very similar, except for Total Deaths and Deaths/Population, which did not differ significantly across these five centuries. For twentieth century deaths to lose their significantly high position as a result of logging makes the procedure of logging dubious in this case, where the raw scores more closely approximated the reality of the situation than the logged scores. (Both tables have been provided so that readers may make their own choices.)

The raw factor scores near the bottom of Table 7.3 are preferred over the log factor scores at the bottom of this table. The logged analyses have been provided here and elsewhere for those who find them more meaningful. The raw factor scores of death and time (Factor 1 in Table 7.2) were significantly higher in the twentieth century than they were in the other four centuries. The raw factor scores of both-sided Great Power wars over time periods were significantly higher in the sixteenth century than they were in the nineteenth and twentieth centuries. These raw factor analyses of variance provided a general summary of the other analyses in this table.

BETWEEN REGIONS.    Table 7.4 in Appendix B repeated the analyses in Table 7.3, but by geographical regions rather than by centuries. This table shows how the variables were distributed in space rather than in time. Most of the Great Power wars occurred in Europe during this period: 105/119 or 88 percent. Consequently, the rest of the world was aggregated into one group labeled Others, which still constituted a small sample of only 14 wars.

The first three rows in this table containing the time variables simply show that Great Power wars outside Europe began more than two centuries later than those within Europe, on average. The next three rows show no significant differences in duration, nation-years, or in the number of Great Powers involved in wars occurring both inside and outside Europe. (Logging, however, did make Europe significantly higher in nation-years and number of Great Powers involved, as noted at the foot of this table.) Great Powers on both sides were significantly higher inside Europe than outside; that is, 58 percent of the Great Power wars in Europe were both-sided, while only 21 percent outside Europe were both-sided. Although all death measurements were higher for wars within Europe, these differences were not significant, except for deaths/population when logged.

In summary of this table, the raw factor scores of death and time were not significantly different between Europe and Others, but Europe was significantly higher than Others with regard to earlier both-sided Great Power wars.

BETWEEN ONE-SIDED AND BOTH-SIDED GREAT POWER WARS.    One-sided wars occurred later in time than both-sided wars by almost a century, as shown in the first three rows of Table 7.5 in Appendix B. This finding was consistent with the raw factor analysis in Table 7.2 and with the analysis of variance in Table 7.3.

The next three rows show that both-sided wars were significantly higher in duration, nation-years and number of Great Powers than one-sided wars.

All of the death measures were higher for both-sided wars, but deaths/nation-year was not significantly different and total deaths were significant at the .10 level of confidence only (but this latter measure became more significant when logged, as noted at the bottom of this table).

In summary of this table, the raw factor scores of death and time and both-sided wars in the earlier centuries were both significantly higher for both-sided wars than for one-sided wars.

## Summary of Factor and Variance Analyses

Factor analysis of the raw scores, as shown in Table 7.2, seemed to be meaningful, both in the sense of describing the known facts accurately and in the sense of coinciding with the analyses of variance. The first factor showed that all the death measurements were associated with the number of Great Powers involved, with later centuries and, to a lesser extent, with nation-years. The second general factor showed that all the time measurements were associated with one-sided and shorter wars.

Time, then, was split by these two factors, partly associating itself with deaths and number of Great Powers, and partly associating itself with one-sided and shorter wars. Over time, then, some Great Power wars were becoming more deadly, especially in the twentieth century, and a greater number of Great Powers were becoming involved in them. At the same time, but unrelated to this first factor, some other Great Power wars were becoming more one-sided, taking up fewer nation-years and, to a lesser extent, less time in general. What we have here, judging from this analysis, are two types of Great Power wars, one type becoming more deadly, and the other type becoming more one-sided, shorter and involving fewer nations.

Twelve of these wars obtained scores greater than one standard deviation above the mean on Factor 1 (Deaths and Time): World War II, World War I, the Napoleonic Wars, the Korean War, the Spanish Succession, the Seven Years' War, the French Revolutionary Wars, the Russo-Finnish War, the Swedish-French phase of the Thirty Years War, the Franco-Prussian War, the Austro-Prussian War and the Russo-Turkish War. Ten of these twelve wars were both-sided. They began in 1837 on average and lasted 5.84 years on the average. They killed almost 28 million soldiers in battle, which is 84 percent of all the battle deaths in the 119 Great Power wars. Each of these 12 wars killed 2.33 million soldiers on average.

There were 25 wars which obtained scores greater than one standard deviation above the mean on Factor 2 (one-sided and short, when the signs were reversed), but only the first 12 of them will be mentioned and discussed here, for the purpose of comparison with the 12 wars in the previous paragraph: the Sino-Indian, Russo-Hungarian, Italo-Ethiopian, Sinai, Manchurian, Russo-Finnish (same as above), Italo-Turkish, Russo-Japanese, Sino-Japanese, Vietnam, Sino-French and Anglo-Persian wars. None of these wars was both-sided (in fact, only one of the top 25 was both-sided). These 12 began in 1928 on average, the earliest beginning in 1856. They lasted 1.59 years on average. They killed 431,000 soldiers in battle, which is 1.3 percent of all the battle deaths in the 119 Great Power wars. Each of these 12 wars killed 36,000 soldiers on the average, or 1.55 percent of those killed in the top 12 wars on Factor 1.

So, we have these two types of war increasing over time: (1) one with increasing deaths and increasing number of Great Powers, but relatively indifferent to both-sidedness and duration; and (2) the other with increasing one-sidedness of Great Power participation, decreasing nation-years and decreasing duration, but relatively indifferent to deaths and the number of Great Powers involved.

The mean scores of the top 12 wars on these two factors are compared and contrasted in Table 7.6 in Appendix B, which shows that those 12 wars with the highest scores on Factor 1 were more both-sided in Great Power participation, started earlier on the average, lasted longer and involved more deaths. So far as deaths are concerned, those wars with the highest scores on Factor 1 are clearly more relevant to our concern than those wars with the highest scores on Factor 2.

## Comparison of Levy's and Wright's Wars

Table 7.7 in Appendix B provides a summary of some comparisons between Levy's and Wright's lists of wars.

Their time period and number of years covered were about the same, but Levy's wars occurred about one-half century earlier than did Wright's wars, on average. We should keep in mind throughout this comparison that Wright listed all the important wars according to his criteria of legal recognition, legal results, or the use of 50,000 troops, while Levy limited himself to those wars involving Great Powers and causing at least one thousand military battle deaths to these Great Powers. This is why Wright's list contains almost three times as many wars as Levy's. Keeping this in mind, Levy's wars occurred earlier, on average, than did Wright's simply because Great Powers were involved in more wars in earlier centuries than in later ones. For the same reason, Levy's wars involved almost twice as many Great Powers, on average, as Wright's. These findings suggest the possibility that the Great Powers may be losing some of their power, either because they are losing more wars or because they have stopped making wars.

Years per war averaged somewhat more than four for both Levy and Wright, so there was no significant difference in durations. Although Levy found no cycles, and Wright found a 50-year cycle, Denton and Phillips found a 20-year cycle in Wright's data prior to 1680, while Richardson found no cycles in Wright's data. Singer and Small's statement summarizes our knowledge about cycles of war very well: "the evidence is far from conclusive" (1972, p. 215).

When Europe was compared with other world regions in the two sets of data, both found most of the wars occurring in Europe, almost 90 percent of Levy's and almost two-thirds of Wright's. An even larger percentage of Levy's deaths and Wright's battles occurred in Europe. The average years/war, number of Great Powers per war, and deaths (or battles) per war were higher in Europe than outside Europe, but these differences were not significant for Levy, nor were Wright's battles/war. The average century of war was about two centuries earlier in Europe than outside for both Levy and Wright. It would seem that Europe's wars were more like family quarrels in the first part of the modern period, and then extended beyond the European family to the whole world in the latter part.

So far as historical trends were concerned, as determined by the correlations of variables over the five centuries, the pattern was generally the same for Levy's Great Power wars and for Wright's wars with and without Great Powers: total deaths (or battles) and deaths (or battles) per war were both increasing at about the same rate, and years per war were decreasing at about the same rate. In other words, according to both lists of wars, the intensity of war was increasing over these five centuries, while its duration was decreasing (but not significantly), so that deaths (or battles) per years of war would certainly have increased. The number of Great Powers per war did not change significantly over these five centuries, but the frequency of Levy's Great Powers wars decreased, while Wright's war frequency tended to increase, but not significantly.

The general wars, which involved most of the Great Powers at any time, accounted for most of Levy's deaths and for two-thirds of Wright's battles. These deaths and battles were highly correlated: .90 for Levy's 10 general wars and for Wright's 15 general wars. These correlations approached 1.00 when taken over the five centuries for all deaths and battles and for deaths and battles per war, so that the number of battles may well be used as a measure of intensity when the number of deaths is not available. The number of Great Powers per war was also correlated more than .90 with each other. Although not so high as this, years per war were also correlated .80 between both lists of wars. Frequency was not at all correlated between Levy and Wright, since Wright's frequencies were significantly lower than Levy's in the eighteenth century, and significantly higher than Levy's in the nineteenth and twentieth centuries. This pattern reflected the fact that Great Power wars were more frequent in the earlier centuries and less frequent in the later centuries of the modern period.

Although Levy's and Wright's frequencies were not correlated over the five centuries, they were highly and significantly correlated more than .90 over the 13 Great Powers. Those Great Powers with more wars in one list were also the ones with more wars in the other list, and conversely. Combining both lists, France engaged in the most wars in the modern period, followed in descending order by England, Spain, Austria, Russia, Turkey, Sweden, the Netherlands, Germany, Italy, the United States, Japan and China. However, this order of war frequency has to be corrected for the number of years any nation was a Great Power, which varied from 480 years for England and France down to 26 years for China and 40 years for Japan. When a rank-order correlation was obtained between the war frequencies and the number of years as a Great Power, the correlation was .95 (significant at the .01 level of confidence), which would suggest that no one of these nations was significantly different from any other in war frequency when their years as a Great Power was considered.

In other words, war frequency can be more readily explained by the fact of a nation being a Great Power (and vice versa) than by any other national characteristic, none of which seem to have any explanatory power. To be sure,

Germany engaged in fewer wars than expected from its years as a Great Power, and Sweden engaged in more wars than expected from its years as a Great Power, but these differences were hardly significant in the overall picture which showed Great Powers engaged in more wars, no matter which nation that power happened to be. England and France were usually at the top of any such list, simply because they were Great Powers more than twice as long as any other nation in the modern period, except for Austria, Spain and (just barely) Russia. Those which have engaged in the fewest wars (China, Japan, the United States and Italy) were all Great Powers for the shortest times, less than one hundred years.

Finally, factor analyses of correlations over all wars sometimes showed deaths (or battles) significantly loaded on the same factor with centuries, but sometimes centuries were negatively associated with duration on a second factor. Over time, however, deaths (or battles) were always significantly loaded on a factor with centuries (or half centuries). Both over-wars and over time, deaths were always significantly associated with the number of Great Powers involved in wars. These analyses clearly related deaths to Great Powers and, to a lesser extent, to time itself during these last five centuries.

In spite of their different definitions of war, Levy's and Wright's lists demonstrated more similarities than differences. The most outstanding differences were generally functions of the fact that Levy's wars were limited to the Great Powers, while Wright cast his net more widely. Levy's list was more Eurocentric than Wright's, simply because European powers were the Great Powers of the modern period for the most part, although the Far East and the United States came into the picture during the twentieth century. As we look at other lists of wars in succeeding chapters, we shall look for similarities and differences in relation to Levy's and Wright's lists. This will provide one way of determining the reliabilities of various findings.

# Chapter 8

# Sorokin's List of Modern Wars, 1500–1925

*The Classic Period*

Since Sorokin, like Wright, covered more than the modern period, his findings for previous periods will be briefly reviewed here for comparative purposes. (Unless otherwise indicated references are to Sorokins' *Social and Cultural Dynamics*, 4 vols. 1937–41.) Unlike Wright, Sorokin limited his quantitative studies of war to Western Civilization, beginning with Greece in 500 B.C. and Rome in 400 B.C., so far as his list of 967 wars was concerned. Greek wars were primarily with Persia and among the Greek city-states. The first Greek war with Rome was in 215 B.C., according to Sorokin, and the last Greek war with Rome was in 146 B.C., when Rome conquered Greece, putting an end to its independent existence and making it the first province of the embryonic Roman Empire.

Although the Roman civilization was preceded by that of Greece, Rome established an empire, which the Greeks did not, unless we count Alexander's conquest of Persia as an empire, which indeed it was, but rather short-lived and Macedonian, not Greek. Rome conquered a substantial amount of the world, but not so much as had been conquered by the Persian Achaemenid Empire in the fifth century B.C., nor by the Central Asian Hsiung-Nu Empire in 150 B.C., nor by the Chinese Han Empire from 50 B.C. to A.D. 200. Rome was eventually conquered by German barbarians by A.D. 476, an event that ushered in the so-called "Dark Ages," a period for which Sorokin was unable to find any reliable data on wars in Europe. Consequently, he recorded no wars from the sixth to the ninth centuries, inclusive.

Sorokin was aided in his collection of wars by two Russian generals (1937, vol. 3: p. 259), which contributed at least somewhat to the reliability of his list. His wars included civil wars, but not, as a general rule, lesser internal disturbances such as riots, revolts, coups, etc., which were recorded separately. His procedure for estimating military casualties (dead and wounded soldiers, excluding civilians) was as follows: (1) estimate army strength per war by using the typical size of armies at the time and multiplying this typical size by the number of years that any war lasted; (2) estimate casualties by using their typical percentage of army strength per war multiplied by the number of years of any war (1937, 3: p. 284). For example, typical casualties of Greek and Roman wars were estimated to be 5 percent of army strength, so this percentage was used for any war for which no specific estimates were available, usually the case prior to the seventeenth century. The casualty percentage was reduced to about 2 percent from the tenth to the fourteenth centuries, and increased to about 5 percent from the fifteenth to the nineteenth centuries, but the Holy Roman Empire figure was always about twice as high as that for England, France and Russia, and the twentieth century was much higher than previous centuries (3: p. 292). Sorokin estimated that the casualty percentage of army strength increased from the twelfth to the twentieth centuries (3: p. 339). Included in these casualty estimates was Sorokin's assumption (based on estimates for the eighteenth to the twentieth centuries) that there was one death for every three to four wounded (3: p. 291). Medieval armies were rarely, if ever, more than 20,000 soldiers up to the fifteenth century (3: p. 281). Greek armies (and their adversaries) rarely exceeded 25,000 to 30,000 soldiers (3: p. 291), and Roman armies never exceeded 250,000 soldiers (3: p. 299). Sorokin was aware of the limitations of these procedures, but he felt that these estimates would be reliable enough for comparative purposes (3: p. 543), that is, for comparing the frequencies, durations and intensities of war over this time period.

## The Medieval Period

The classic period of history lasted from 500 B.C. to A.D. 476, according to Sorokin's list of wars, during which time 96 wars occurred. The next war recorded by Sorokin was in Russia, A.D. 906, which may be taken as the beginning of the Middle Ages, so far as Sorokin's data on wars were concerned. However, Sorokin found very few wars in Europe during the tenth century: five involving Russia, three involving Austria-Hungary (Holy Roman Empire) and one involving France. From the beginning of the tenth century to the end of the fifteenth century, there were 217 wars involving primarily four of the major nations in Europe, which included England after 1066, plus a few others starting much later: Poland and Lithuania, 1392, and Spain, 1476. While there were 9.6 wars during the average classic century, there were 36.17 wars during the average medieval century (from the tenth to the fifteenth centuries). So far as the frequency of war was concerned, the medieval centuries were significantly more warlike than the classic centuries. Since there were primarily four major European nations (Austria-Hungary, England, France and Russia) during the medieval period, but only two such "nations" (Greece and Rome) during the classic period, this difference would suggest that the medieval period could have had twice as many wars simply by chance, that is, simply by virtue of there being more "nations" able to make more wars either externally or internally. However, even if we take this difference into account the relative frequency of medieval wars would still be over twice that of classic wars.

## Mean Scores for Wars

Although Sorokin listed 967 nation-wars, these were reduced to 656 wars when the duplication of nations was removed. For example, six of Sorokin's nations participated in World War I, which was then counted as six wars by Sorokin, one for each nation involved. For these 656 wars, I obtained the mean scores on a number of variables for each 500-year period from the fifth century B.C. to the twentieth century A.D. Naroll (1967) suggested the awkward term "pentacossy" for such 500-year periods, which I shall use for lack of a better term. The analyses of variance (difference) between these mean scores is shown in Table 8.1 in Appendix B. More than half of these wars (N = 343) occurred in the last pentacossy from 1500 to 1925, even before prorating the twentieth century frequency.

The first pentacossy, with its Greek and Roman Republic wars, contained the longest wars of 6.5 years on the average. This length was largely due to these conflicts: the Greco-Persian War, which lasted 52 years; the Peloponnesian War, which lasted 28 years; the Wars of the Diadochi (Alexander's successors), which lasted 23 years; and the Holy War against the Phocians, which lasted 14 years. All of these wars occurred in Greece. Without these exceptional wars, whose lengths were probably exaggerated (as Sorokin noted), it seems quite likely that this period might not have had any longer wars on average than any other period. In an example taken from a later period Sorokin noted "the duration of real fighting in the Hundred Years' War was in fact many times shorter than in the World War" (3: p. 339). This tendency to exaggerate the length of earlier wars may be due to the convenience of aggregating a series of related wars separated by inactive periods, or truces, into a single war. If so, this would also account for the lower frequency of earlier wars. Although there was a significant difference among the pentacossies in the duration of wars, this difference accounted for less than 3 percent of the variance, which was negligible. Our best guess at this point is that the average length of European wars did not vary much from one pentacossy to another since 500 B.C.

The percentage of starters who won wars they started was 45 percent, according to my identification of starters and winners in Sorokin's wars. The second pentacossy was highest in the percentage of starters who won wars they started, and the last pentacossy had the lowest percentage. These percentage differences, like those between average durations, were negligible, since they accounted for less than 2 percent of the variance between pentacossies. It would seem that starters generally won less than half the wars they started, which makes one wonder why nations and other groups ever started wars at all, especially in the modern period. The odds of winning were never better than chance. They might as well have determined the winner by flipping a coin. That would have saved time, trouble, expense and lives that could have been used in more constructive purposes.

Army size, casualties (dead and wounded soldiers), and casualties per year (according to my calculations based on Sorokin's data) showed no significant differences in their raw form because of the extreme skewness of their distributions, but the logged scores of these variables (which corrected for extreme skewness) all followed a similar pattern: high casualties per war during the classic period, low during the Middle Ages, and high again during the modern period. This pattern suggested that the Middle Ages was significantly lower than the other periods in the average intensity of its wars. However, its total intensity was not significantly lower than that of the classic period, although both those periods were significantly lower than the modern period in intensity of war, as measured by total casualties.

Finally, the participants per war, by my count, averaged about 2.5. The modern period had more participants per war than the other periods, presumably because of the First World War. The Great Powers per war, by my count, averaged about one per war, with the early classic period and the Middle Ages being significantly low in Great Powers per war, and the late classic period (Roman Empire) and the modern period being significantly high in Great Powers per war. I determined Great Powers for the classic and medieval periods on the basis of Taagepera's (1978a) imperial sizes. Nations whose political organization extended over at least one square megameter (or 386,000 square miles, the size of present-day Egypt) were classified as Great Powers. For the modern period I used Levy's classification of Great Powers, which were listed in the previous chapter.

Classic Great Powers included Persia (550 B.C. to A.D. 500), China (500 B.C. to A.D. 500), India (450 B.C. to 200 B.C., A.D. 50 to 250, and 450), Egypt (300 B.C. to 250 B.C.), Hsiung-Nu in Central Asia (150 B.C. to 100 B.C.), Rome (100 B.C. to A.D. 476), Byzantium (400 to 500), and Attila's Huns (450 to 500). However, not all of these Great Powers were involved in wars with Greece and Rome during this period. Those that were included Persia, India and the Huns. Consequently, there were no more than four Great Powers involved in Sorokin's classic wars at any one time.

Medieval Great Powers included China throughout, Persia (500–600, 900–50, 1400–50), Byzantium (500–1050), Tu Chueh (550–600), Tibet (650–1250), Muslim (650–850), Turkey (650, 1050–1100, 1450–1500), Prati (850), Khazar (850–900), Kiev (900–1050), Bujid (950), Fatimid (950–1050), Liao (950–1150), Ghaznavid (1050), Al-mohad (1150–1250), Egypt (1250–1450), Mongolia (1250–1450), Khmer (1250), Mali (1300, 1450), Chagatai (1350), Lithuania (1450), Inca (1500) and Russia (1500). Only a few of these Great Powers were involved in European wars during this period: Byzantium (906–1043), Turkey (1061–1100, 1444–1500) and Mongolia (1224–1496). This extensive list of Great Powers would suggest that one square megameter was too small a minimum to set for entry into a list of Great Powers in the medieval period. Perhaps a minimum requirement of three, or even five, square megameters might result in a more reasonable list. Byzantium would drop from this shorter list, as would Turkey in 650 and 1450–1500, but Mongolia would remain, at least up to 1400. None of Sorokin's major European nations made this shorter list. Not many made the much longer list, which included only

Byzantium, Kiev and Lithuania in Europe. For the time being, I have kept Byzantium, Turkey and Mongolia. Following Sorokin, I also treated England since 1150, France since 1200, Poland and Lithuania from 1400 to 1500 and Russia since 1475 as European Great Powers. Except for Lithuania, this would not be justified by a minimum of one square megameter of political organization. In any event, there were no more than seven Great Powers involved in Sorokin's medieval wars.

## Mean Scores for Centuries

Table 8.2 in Appendix B shows the mean scores for centuries instead of for wars as in Table 8.1. In both tables the first pentacossy (Greece and Roman Republic) was labeled B.C.; the second (Roman Empire), A.D.; the third (Middle Ages, which was actually six hundred years instead of five hundred), Med; and the fourth, Mod.

### Sorokin's Data

The frequency of war increased over these four pentacossies, being significantly lower than average during the classic period and significantly higher than average during the modern period. Was this because wars were really more frequent as time went on? Or was it because later records were more complete than earlier records?

The number of war years per century was significantly greater during the modern period than any previous period.

All of the casualty measures (absolute and relative to number of wars, to number of nations, and to European population) were significantly higher than average during the modern period. Sorokin's casualties per European population were also higher than average during the Greek period (which was also the period of the Roman Republic). The number of participants and Great Powers were also higher than average during the modern period.

### Other Data

Some data other than Sorokin's have been analyzed at the foot of Table 8.2 for comparative purposes. BatSum is the sum of battles and sieges obtained from Dupuy and Dupuy (1986), who listed 4460 battles recorded from that of Megiddo in 1469 B.C. to guerrilla wars going on in 1984. These battles were clearly on the increase over these four pentacossies, being significantly lower in frequency during the classic period and higher in frequency during the modern period.

As in the case of Sorokin's war frequencies, the question remains concerning how much this pattern of battle frequencies reflected the intensity of wars over this time period and how much it reflected the fact that battles have been more fully documented in modern times than in classic times. A sample of these battles were sorted by geographic region, as well as by century, and then European battles were correlated with Sorokin's war casualties and frequencies, in order to see how much they were measuring the same thing, that is, the intensity of European wars. The correlation was .78. Similar patterns were found for Harbottle's (1904; Bruce 1981) battles and for both sets of battles when population was controlled.

Imperial sizes were significantly higher in the modern period than in the three previous periods, which simply showed that modern empires were significantly larger than earlier empires. When these imperial sizes were correlated with Sorokin's war casualties, both absolute and relative to nations and populations, to war frequencies and also to the battle frequencies of the Dupuys and Harbottle, all these correlations were significant and moderately high (.62 to .81). These findings were consistent with the theory that wars and empires grew up together, feeding into each other: wars creating empires, and empires making wars.

The findings in this section on other data in relation to Sorokin's data also help answer the question of whether the relative frequency of battles and wars reflected the reality of events or merely the "fading rate of history," as Taagepera (1988) has called this phenomenon. Although the frequency of battles and wars might well fade in historical memory and even over geographical distance, and although the accuracy of our data undoubtedly diminishes with geographical or historical distance, it hardly seems likely that imperial sizes diminish in human memory as we get farther away from them in space or time. Their measurement would seem to be fairly reliable, no matter how far away from them we might be. Consequently, their correlation with battles and wars, as expected by the theory that wars are some function of civilizations which, in turn, are some function of empires, leads us to believe that battle and war frequencies are entirely at the mercy of the fading rate of history.

This belief was checked by dividing the frequency of the Dupuys' battles and of Sorokin's wars by a measure of the fading rate of history which was developed by Taagepera (1988). This measure involved the counting of sentences per century in a 600-page book titled *Timetables of History* (Grun 1979), which lists events in politics, literature, religion and philosophy, figurative arts, music, science and technology and everyday life from 4000 B.C. to 1975. The classic period "receives up to three times more coverage than the average trend would lead us to expect, while the early Christian era receives undertreatment to the same degree. . . . [F]or the post–1500 period the data points are clearly and systematically above the long-range exponential pattern" (Taagepera 1988, p. 2).

When I obtained rough figures for these sentences per century by reading them off Taagepera's graphs (1988, pp. 12–13), I divided the battle and war frequencies by them in order to control for the fading rate of history. The Dupuys' battles controlled for historical fading were still significantly correlated with centuries at .56; Sorokin's wars controlled for historical fading were still significantly correlated with centuries at .57; and Harbottle's battles controlled for historical fading were still significantly correlated with centuries at .67. Further research is required, but these preliminary findings suggest that the increasing intensity of war from 500 B.C. to the twentieth century, as measured by battle and war frequencies from three different sources, remained a significant finding even after these frequencies were controlled for the fading rate of history.


## The Modern Period

In addition to the four European nations (Austria-Hungary, England, France and Russia) which Sorokin included in his medieval period, he added five other nations in his modern period: Poland and Lithuania, 1501–1794; Spain, 1501–1925; Holland, 1566–1925 (but with no wars since 1833); Italy, 1551–1925; and Germany, 1651–1925.


### Centuries of War

Table 8.3 in Appendix B shows the differences between mean scores over the five centuries from 1500 to 1925. When the twentieth century was prorated for its frequencies of war (N = 14 multipled by four = 56), the nineteenth century was significantly higher than average in its number of wars, while the eighteenth and twentieth centuries were significantly lower than average. The average frequency of wars per century was 77, when the twentieth century was prorated.

Neither the duration of wars nor the percent of starters winning wars varied significantly from century to century during the modern period.

The number of participants did increase over these centuries, as did the number of Great Powers involved in these wars, but Great Powers participation was also high in the eighteenth century.

Army strength, casualties and casualties per year were also high during the twentieth century (remembering that this century only extended to 1925 for Sorokin's data), and high during the eighteenth century when these data were logged. These measures all indicated the intensity of the average war. When the casualties were summed rather than averaged, chi-square analysis of total casualties over these five centuries showed that the prorated twentieth-century casualties were not only significantly greater than the other four centuries taken separately, but also significantly greater than all four of them taken together. In fact, it was significantly greater than all 20 of Sorokin's previous centuries (500 B.C. to A.D. 500 and 900 to 1900) taken together. There were 96.2 million prorated casualties in the twentieth century, while there were 12.8 million casualties in the sixteenth to nineteenth centuries, and 14.6 million casualties from 500 B.C. to A.D. 1900.

## Regions of War

Table 8.4 in Appendix B shows the differences between those wars that occurred primarily in Europe and those that occurred primarily outside of Europe—in Afro-Asia for the most part. Most of these wars occurred in Europe, as might have been expected, but 26 percent of them occurred outside of Europe, many more than had done so prior to the modern period. And most of these wars in Afro-Asia occurred during the last two centuries when colonial wars of independence involved some of the major European nations in Afro-Asia and Latin America.

As already noted, the wars that occurred in Afro-Asia came much later (1878 on the average) than those that occurred in Europe (1726 on the average), as shown under Century Difference in Table 8.4.

Although the wars in Europe lasted longer, this difference was not significant. Most of the other differences in Table 8.4 were not significant either, except for the percentage of winning starters, which was significantly higher in Afro-Asia, where the Europeans were better prepared for winning than colonial targets.

The raw scores of army strengths, casualties and casualties per year were not significantly different between these two regions, because of the extreme skewness in these measures within regions. However, when these measures were logged to normalize this skewness, there were significant differences. In all cases, these measures of war intensity were higher in Europe than outside, which reflected the fact that it required greater armies (and higher casualties) to fight other well-armed adversaries in Europe than it did to fight less well-armed people in less developed countries.

## Types of War

Table 8.5 in Appendix B presents the results from analyzing the variance among different types of war: civil, colonial, imperial and international. Imperial wars occurred when one nation went to war in order to dominate another nation, either inside or outside Europe. Proportionally speaking, European nations tried to dominate each other just as often as they tried to dominate nations outside Europe. Colonial wars occurred whenever a dominated nation (inside or outside of Europe) tried to free itself from foreign dominance. Proportionally speaking, this type of war occurred more often outside Europe. The modern period did not differ significantly from earlier periods in the distribution of these four types of war, but within the modern period, colonial wars of independence occurred more frequently in the nineteenth and twentieth centuries.

Imperial wars were the most frequent type of war during the modern period, while civil and international wars were the least frequent. There would be considerable agreement concerning the classification of civil and colonial wars, but I may have leaned too heavily toward the imperial classification, which might have been classified as international by others (and by myself at other times). Consequently, this difference between imperial and international wars may be greatly affected by the method used to define them.

Colonial wars occurred later in time, while civil wars occurred earlier.

Starters won more imperial wars (where they were clearly militarily superior to their targets), while the starters of civil and colonial wars (being less well armed than the well-established governments against which they fought) won fewer of these wars than might be expected by chance. International wars, where the two sides were more equally matched, did not differ significantly from the 39 percent average of starters winning wars they started. Starters of wars were not very successful during the modern period, according to my classification of Sorokin's wars. Even the starters of imperial wars won only 54 percent of the time. Why do governments and other groups start wars when the odds are so unfavorable and the costs in casualties so high? Something other than rational considerations such as these must be coming into play as determining factors, such as the will for power or the will for equality.

More Great Powers were involved in international wars (where there were often one or more on each side), while fewer of them were involved in civil wars, where there were seldom more than one involved.

There were no other significant differences among types of war for the rest of the variables in Table 8.5. War durations were not significantly different, nor were the the number of participants, nor were any of the measures of war intensity, regardless of whether the mean scores were raw or logged.

## Causes of War

I assigned six causes to Sorokin's wars, as noted at the foot of Table 8.6 in Appendix B. These causes were closely associated with the types of war previously discussed. Ethnic and political causes (including Left and Right ideologies) were largely associated with civil wars. Independence was entirely associated with colonial wars. Territory was primarily associated with imperial wars, and secondarily with international wars.

Territorial causes were the most frequent of all causes in Sorokin's list of modern wars, as shown in Table 8.6. This was true for most of the earlier periods as well, except for the Greek period.

Ethnic, leftist, and political causes occurred earlier in the modern period, while territory, independence and rightist causes occurred later in this period.

Starters won more wars when the cause was territory, 51 percent of them, but starters won none of them when the cause was rightist ideology.

Rightist ideology was also associated with more intense wars (as measured by army strength, casualties and casualties per year, when these measures were logged to correct for extreme skewness). Territory was also associated with greater army strength, but not much greater than average.

## Summary of Sorokin's Modern Wars

More than half of Sorokin's wars occurred during the modern period from 1500 to 1925. Compared to earlier periods, the modern period was further characterized by fewer starters winning wars they started and by a greater average intensity of war, as measured by the logged scores of army strength, casualties and casualties per year. All measures of casualties per century, including casualties per nation and casualties per population, were significantly higher than those of the earlier periods. In fact, total casualties in the modern period were significantly higher than all previous periods taken separately and taken together.

Within the modern period, the twentieth century was generally the highest in the number of participants and Great Powers, and in average intensity per war, although the eighteenth century was just as high when these scores were logged. But total casualties were significantly higher in the twentieth century than in the previous four centuries of the modern period taken together and even in the previous 20 centuries (500 B.C. to A.D. 500 and 900 to 1900) taken together. Wars occurring in Europe were more intense than those occurring outside. War intensity did not vary as a general rule among different types of war, nor among different causes of war.

## Comparison of Levy, Sorokin and Wright

Table 8.7 in Appendix B provides some data for comparing Sorokin's list of wars with those of Levy and Wright, which were compared with each other in Table 7.7.

Levy had fewer modern wars (N = 119) than either Sorokin (N = 343) or Wright (N = 308) simply because he limited himself to wars involving the Great Powers, starting in 1495, which included France and England for his entire period up to 1975, the Ottoman Empire until 1699, Spain until 1808, Austria until 1918, the Netherlands from 1609 until 1713, Sweden from 1617 until 1721, Italy from 1861 to 1943 and Japan from 1905 until 1945. The rest started at different times, but lasted until Levy's data ended in 1975: Russia (USSR) beginning in 1721, Prussia (Germany) beginning in 1740, the United States beginning in 1898 and China beginning in 1949. I have used Levy's list of Great Powers in my own assignment of nations to this category in the modern period. When this was done to Sorokin's and Wright's wars, 83 percent of Sorokin's wars involved one or more Great Powers on either one or both sides, while only 68 percent of Wright's wars involved Great Powers. Since most of Levy's Great Powers were European nations, and since Sorokin limited himself to nine major European nations (eight of which were Great Powers at some time or another during the modern period), it is not surprising that his wars involved more Great Powers than Wright's wars, which were more worldwide in their geographical extent.

Because of this same limitation, Levy's wars involved almost twice as many Great Powers on the average as those involved in Sorokin's and Wright's wars. The duration of wars did not differ significantly among these three authors, averaging about four years, suggesting that Great Powers did not make a significant contribution to the duration of wars during the modern period.

Levy found no cycles in his data: "It is consistently found that the outbreak of war is random rather than contagious, regardless of whether we look at short-term contagion or long-term periodicity.... There are no hints of any cyclical patterns in either the occurrence of war or in any of is other dimensions.... [which] appear to be scattered at random" (1983, pp. 136–37). Although Sorokin found fluctuations, he found neither regular cycles nor historical trends: "All that we can say is that the war-peace curve fluctuates, and that is all.... There is hardly any definite periodicity" (1957, pp. 564, 593). Wright did find a 50-year cycle, but that was all. In all of these cases the absence or presence of cycles was determined by inspection of the data (Levy inspected scattergrams of his data), which is not the most reliable procedure that can be used, but some other authors (Small and Singer 1982) used some statistical analyses which generally supported these analyses by inspection.

## Comparing Europe with the Rest of the World

Eighty-eight percent of Levy's wars occurred in Europe, while this was true of 74 percent of Sorokin's wars and 62 percent of Wright's wars, which reflected the relative Eurocentricity of the different lists. Most of the deaths (or casualties or battles) occurred in Europe, since Levy counted only the deaths of Great Powers (which were usually European) and Sorokin counted only the casualties of European nations. Although Wright's list of wars was more worldwide, his counting of battles was apparently more limited to those occurring in Europe, either because of less information concerning battles outside Europe, or because military engagements outside Europe did not meet Wright's criterion of one thousand casualties. This raises an important question concerning a "fading rate of geography," which may have to be considered as well as the fading rate of history which we have already considered. Admitting that Levy and Sorokin deliberately limited themselves to Great Powers (mostly European) and to major European nations respectively, Wright placed no such limits upon himself and aimed to include the world in his list of wars, two-thirds of which were located in Europe, where 93 percent of his battles occurred. How much of this reflects the geographical facts and how much is due to the fading rate of geography?

War durations were generally longer in Europe, but this difference was not significant except in the case of Wright's list of wars. The number of Great Powers per war was significantly higher in Europe, except in the case of Levy's list of wars, all of which involved Great Powers. When these data were logged, deaths (or casualties or battles) per war were always greater in Europe, but not significantly so, except in the case of Sorokin. The wars in Europe occurred earlier on average than elsewhere, reflecting the fact that European nations were for the most part fighting one another and the Ottoman Empire in the earlier centuries of the modern period, and not venturing so much into Afro-Asia until the later centuries, especially the nineteenth and the twentieth.

## Historical Trends

Deaths, casualties, or battles per war increased over these five centuries, as did total deaths, casualties, or battles (especially when logged to correct for skewness). Durations per war tended to decrease over these five centuries, while Great Powers per war remained relatively constant, and frequencies were somewhat mixed.

When the correlations were performed over decades rather than centuries, the results were similar for total deaths, casualties, or battles, but not for durations (except in the case of Levy). Frequencies were mixed over decades, as they were over centuries.

## Correlations Among Authors

Regardless of these trends, or lack of trends, Levy, Wright and Sorokin were in significant agreement concerning deaths, durations and frequencies over some 45 decades, suggesting some reliability in the distribution of their measures over time. This amount of agreement was rather remarkable, considering their different definitions of war, their different samples of nations, and their different purposes. Levy required one thousand deaths for an armed conflict to be listed among his wars, which were limited to Great Powers. Wright required 50,000 troops to be engaged anywhere around the world, but he also used some less stringent criteria. Sorokin required only that historians should identify an armed conflict as a war, with the further limitation that at least one of nine major European nations be involved.

This agreement among these three authors held up over five centuries, as well as 45 decades, primarily for deaths and deaths/war, less so for durations and Great Powers per war, and not at all for frequencies, as shown in Table 8.7. The distribution of deaths over these five centuries seems to be very reliable indeed, as shown in Figure 8.1.

## Factor Analyses

Factor analyses simply provide a method of analyzing correlation coefficients in order to group together those variables that are correlated more highly with one another than they are with any other variables in the same matrix. Factor loadings, or coefficients, are relative measures only, depending upon the subjects and variables in any matrix.

Centuries and Deaths constituted a single factor for Levy, Sorokin and Wright, showing a clear and reliable tendency for all three measures of war's

# Figure 8.1   Modern War Intensities, 1500 to 2000

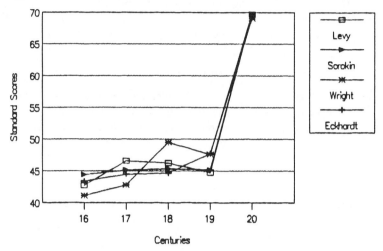

Notes to Figure 8.1: Levy = Levy's (1983) death estimates for Great Powers in wars from 1500 to 2000, the twentieth century estimates being prorated to make the twentieth century more comparable to previous centuries. More details in Chapter 7. Sorokin = Sorokin's (1937, vol. 3) casualty estimates for nine major European nations in wars from 1500 to 2000 (twentieth century prorated). More details in Chapter 8. Wright = Wright's (1965) estimate of the number of battles in worldwide wars from 1500 to 2000 (twentieth century prorated). More details in Chapter 6. Eckhardt = Eckhardt's (Sivard 1990) death estimates for civilians and soldiers in worldwide wars from 1500 to 2000 (twentieth century prorated). More details in Chapter 9. All four estimates were standardized to a mean of 50 and a standard deviation of 10 over the five centuries from A.D. 1500 to 2000, in order to make them comparable to one another. It can be seen that all four estimates during the fifteenth to the nineteenth centuries were less than the average standard score of 50 for all five centuries, ranging from 41 to almost 50, while the twentieth century estimates were all two standard deviations (20 standard scores) above average.

---

intensity—battles, casualties and deaths—to co-vary with time during these five centuries. When more variables were added to the matrix (Great Powers and Years), Sorokin's Casualties were still associated with Centuries, but Levy's Deaths and Wright's Battles were associated with Great Powers, but not with Centuries, which were negatively associated with Duration for all three authors. When 5 to 10 variables were included in the correlation matrix, then Casualties and Deaths were associated with Centuries, but Battles were not. These three analyses were performed across all of the wars in each sample.

When the analyses were done across time, the results were generally somewhat similar: Battles and Deaths were associated with time, but Casualties were not. Duration was negatively related to time for Sorokin and Wright, but not for Levy.

In general, the factor analyses showed a tendency for the intensity of war (as measured by battles, casualties and deaths) to increase over these five centuries. This tendency was not always present in all three authors, nor was it always significant, but it was generally there, as shown in Figure 8.1.

## Analyses of Variance

Analysis of variance is simply a method of determining the statistical significance (or reliability) of the differences among mean scores. In this section we are primarily concerned with the differences among the mean scores of the deaths, durations and frequencies of wars over the five centuries of the modern period. If the F-Ratio is significant, that is, if an F-Ratio is high enough that it could not have occurred by chance beyond a certain probability, then the observed differences among means are said to be significant, that is, reliable.

The last part of Table 8.7 shows that mean deaths (or casualties or battles) were always significantly higher in the twentieth century than in the earlier centuries. This finding simply means that the average war was more intense in the twentieth century, as well as the sum of all wars.

Mean years showed no such pattern. For Sorokin, there was no significant difference among the century means. For Wright, the differences were significant only if we have a hypothesis prior to analysis. The only hypothesis we might have had was that durations should have decreased over time, but Wright's mean scores showed no such pattern, the seventeenth century mean being higher than average, and the eighteenth century mean lower than average. Levy's durations were significantly different and in the expected direction, with higher durations in the sixteenth and seventeenth centuries, and lower durations in the nineteenth and twentieth centuries. These results would suggest that the decrease in war durations during the modern period held for Great Power wars, but not for wars in general, even when these wars were limited to those with European involvement.

The results for war frequencies were all significant but quite mixed, showing no one general pattern over these five centuries. Levy's frequencies were highest in the sixteenth century; Sorokin's, in the sixteenth and nineteenth centuries; and Wright's, in the nineteenth and twentieth centuries. The seventeenth century was average, and the eighteenth century was lowest for all three authors. Two out of three of them were high in the sixteenth and nineteenth centuries. So much for agreement and partial agreement, since there was no agreement at all in the twentieth century.

These analyses of variance show that the intensity of war was significantly higher in the twentieth century than in the earlier centuries of the modern period, but that the duration and frequency of war did not differ significantly from century to century. There was, however, a general tendency for wars to decrease in duration.

## *Summary*

The most reliable finding from this comparison of Levy, Sorokin and Wright is that the intensity of war increased significantly during the modern period, and especially so in the twentieth century, while the duration of war tended to decrease.

Since Sorokin provided no wars for the sixth to ninth centuries, we shall examine two lists of wars based on Kohn (1987), whose *Dictionary of Wars* claimed to include "wars in all parts of the world from 2000 B.C. to the present" (p. v), and Dupuy and Dupuy (1986) in a later chapter. I hope that these lists will fill in the gap of the "dark ages" left empty by Sorokin. They will also provide a check on the reliability of Sorokin's list throughout the classic, medieval and modern periods. First, we shall look at another list of modern wars in the next chapter.

# Chapter 9

# Eckhardt's List of Modern Wars, 1500–1990

## Definition and Background

Following Richardson, Singer and Small, and Levy, among others, I defined a war as "any armed conflict, including one or more governments, and causing the deaths of one thousand or more people per year" (1989c, p. 89). Deaths included civilian as well as military deaths, and also deaths from war-related famine and disease, as well as war-related massacres. In this respect, my definition was more like that of Richardson than like those of Singer and Small and of Levy, who limited their deaths to battle deaths of military personnel only.

My list of wars began with major world conflicts, 1945–1975 (Eckhardt and Azar 1978), which was later extended to 1978 (Eckhardt and Azar 1979). My "Wars and Interventions, 1960–1980," was published by Sivard (1980). None of these lists included death estimates, but both civilian and military death estimates were provided in "Wars and Deaths 1960–1982" (Sivard 1982), where a war was defined by one thousand or more deaths. "Wars and War-Related Deaths Since 1945" (Sivard 1983) included those wars with more than one thousand civilian and military deaths per year. "Deaths in 20th Century Wars" (Sivard 1985) included 207 wars, where a war was defined as "any conflict including one or more governments, involving the use of arms, and causing deaths of 1,000 or more people per year" (p. 9). There were 14 "Wars with Deaths of 100,000 or More" in the nineteenth century and 43 in the twentieth century (Sivard, 1986). "Wars and Deaths 1700–1987" (Sivard 1987) included 471 such wars, which had increased to 475 in 1989 (Sivard 1989).

## Wars and Related Deaths, 1700–1987

Some of the results of analyzing these lists will be found in Eckhardt (1989c), which was based on 471 wars from 1700 to 1987. There were only 50 of these wars in the eighteenth century, but more than 200 each in the nineteenth and twentieth centuries. These wars lasted 2.4 years on the average, but longer than this (3.5 years) in the eighteenth century and shorter than this (2.0

years) in the nineteenth century. There were about 6 million war-related deaths in the eighteenth century, 10 million in the nineteenth century, and 86 million in the twentieth century up to 1987, making about 116 million deaths altogether when the twentieth century was prorated.

Not only were there more war-related deaths in the twentieth century (primarily due to the two world wars), but also more deaths per war, and more deaths per sovereign nation and as a percentage of world population, so that war-related deaths could not be explained by the number of sovereign nations or by world population taken by themselves. About half of these war-related deaths were civilian deaths during these three centuries. Some instances of civilian deaths in wartime prior to the eighteenth century suggested the possiblity that civilian deaths may have always been a "normal" part of war. The starters of these wars won less than half (44 percent of them: 56 percent in the eighteenth century, 48 percent in the nineteenth century, and 39 percent in the twentieth century.

About two-thirds of war-related deaths occurred in Europe and about one-fifth in the Far East. The remaining 14 percent occurred throughout the rest of the world: in Latin America, south Asia, Africa, the Middle East and North America. Two-thirds of war-related deaths occurred in wars fought over territory (which included land, labor, capital and trade), and three-quarters of war-related deaths occurred in international wars.

In summary, this study showed that wars have increased in frequency, duration, and deaths from the eighteenth to the twentieth centuries. The increase in deaths was almost five times the increase in world population and four and one-half times the increase in sovereign nations. The civilian portion of these deaths remained at about 50 percent from century to century. In that unarmed civilians have been killed in most wars during the last three centuries, very few of these wars could be called "just." Imperial and international wars killed the most civilians. The starters of wars lost more wars than they won.

In conclusion, "Caring for one another and sharing with one another may be a prerequisite to putting an end to arms and wars" (p. 97).

## Wars and Related Deaths, 1500–1990

These earlier lists were recently backdated to 1500 and updated to 1990. This latest list will be found in Sivard (1990).

Table 9.1 in Appendix B shows the wars and deaths by century, plus the civilian percentage of all deaths, the percentage of starters who won the wars that they started, and the average number of Great Powers which participated in these wars. There were 613 wars and 145 million deaths since 1500, after prorating for the twentieth century. Fifty-six percent of these deaths were civilian, on average, and means for centuries did not differ significantly from each other, although this percentage was highest in the twentieth century. Only 44 percent of the starters of these wars won the wars they started, and this percentage was lowest in the twentieth century. Almost one Great Power participated in each war on average, and more in the earlier centuries than in the nineteenth and twentieth.

The frequency of wars was significantly higher than average in the nineteenth and twentieth centuries, but only the latter was significantly higher than average in the number of deaths. These wars averaged 2.7 years in duration. There were 2.8 nations participating in these wars on average. Battle estimates were available for 257 of these wars and they yielded an average of 16 battles per war.

When the twentieth century was analyzed by decades, the war frequency was significantly higher than average for the 1980s, as shown in the bottom half of Table 9.1. The deaths were significantly higher than average for the 1910s and the 1940s, when the two world wars occurred.

## Percentages

Thirty-eight percent of these wars occurred in the twentieth century and 36 percent in the nineteenth century, while 76 percent of war-related deaths occurred in the twentieth and 13 percent in the nineteenth century. According to these figures, the twentieth century was six times more violent than the nineteenth century, and it was three times more violent than the previous four centuries combined.

Thirty-four percent of these wars occurred in Europe, but 67 percent of war-related deaths occurred in Europe, as shown in Figure 9.1, so that overall Europe was twice as violent as the rest of the world during modern times, but the average war in Europe was four times as violent as the average war in the rest of the world.

Fifty-one percent of these wars were fought over land, labor, capital or trade, but 77 percent of the deaths occurred in these wars, so that such wars were three times more violent than those wars fought over all other causes added together: equality, freedom, power, race and religion. The average war fought over territory, etc. was three times more violent than the average war fought over these other causes.

Twenty-seven percent of these wars were international, but 73 percent of war-related deaths occurred in these wars, so that these wars were three times more violent than all other types of war combined: civil, colonial and imperial. The average international war was nine times more violent than the average war of all other types.

Although colonial and imperial wars were, relatively speaking, not very violent in their direct consequences, their indirect consequences involved a tremendous amount of structural violence, especially in the twentieth century (Eckhardt and Kohler 1980). The seeds of structural violence, however, were being planted since the beginning of modern times.

## Figure 9.1   Region % Deaths, 1500 to 1990 (N = 140 million)

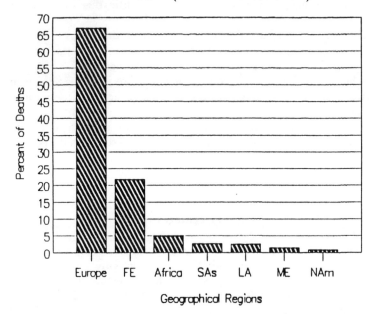

Notes to Figure 9.1: The percent of war deaths in this figure was based on my wars and related deaths in Sivard (1990). Europe = Europe, including the USSR. FE = Far East, including Southeast Asia. Africa = Sub-Saharan Africa, including South Africa. SAs = South Asia, including India and Pakistan. LA = Latin America, including the Caribbean and Central America. ME = Middle East, including North Africa. NAm = North America, including Canada and the United States.

### Factor Analysis

When these variables were analyzed over 49 decades from 1500 to 1990, there was a single factor that included all these variables except for Start % Win: parties .95, wars .94, decades .91, centuries .89, years .86, deaths .75, civilian % of deaths .75 and Great Powers per war −.52. In other words, all of these variables were increasing (or decreasing, in the case of Great Powers per War) over the 48 decades, except for Start % Win, which was, essentially, constant.

### Analysis of Variance

All of these variables were significantly higher in the twentieth century than they were in the previous centuries, but the frequency of wars and the number of Great Powers participating in wars were also significantly higher than average in the nineteenth century.

## Comparison of 1700–1987 and 1500–1990

Table 9.2 in Appendix B presents a comparison of the wars from 1700–1987 in relation to those from 1500–1990. The only outstanding differences not attributable to the greater incidence of wars over the longer period of time can be explained by the greater participation of Europe in the wars of the earlier centuries, and by the smaller percentage of twentieth century wars in relation to five centuries compared to its percentage in relation to three centuries.

The factor analyses of both sets of wars were generally similar, the only outstanding difference being the nonsignificance of Start/Win percentage in the larger and longer wars.

Otherwise, both analyses showed that wars, years, deaths, parties and percentage of civilian deaths were all increasing over these centuries, while the participation of Great Powers per war was decreasing. This latter decrease reflected the fact that European war involvement was largely confined to Europe itself in the earlier centuries, while its involvement extended to the rest of the world in the later centuries.

## Comparison of Levy, Wright, Sorokin and Eckhardt

The most reliable finding from the comparison of Levy, Sorokin, Wright and Eckhardt was that the intensity of war increased significantly during the modern period, especially in the twentieth century (as shown in Figure 8.1) while the duration of war tended to decrease.

Table 9.3 in Appendix B presents a comparison of all four lists of modern wars discussed in the last four chapters. My average century was later than that of the other three authors, showing that my list contained more wars in later years. As a result, my wars and years increased over these five centuries, as shown in the "Correlations Over Five Centuries" farther down in this table. The others' wars and years tended to decrease over these five centuries, especially those of Levy's Great Powers, followed by Sorokin's European nations, while Wright's wars and years remained relatively constant from century to century. Taking these findings along with my significantly fewer Great Powers per war would suggest that Great Powers and major nations tended to have longer wars.

More specifically, over the last five hundred years, European nations engaged in more and longer wars in the earlier centuries of modern times than they did in the later centuries. This conclusion is supported by the fact that my wars were significantly shorter in duration (2.7 years on average) than the other's (3.54 to 4.35 on average). This conclusion is also supported by the fact that Levy, who had the greatest proportion of Great Power wars (100 percent) and the largest number of Great Powers per war (2.21), also had the longest wars on the average (4.35 years), the highest portion of wars located in Europe (88 percent), and the greatest decrease in wars and years over these five centuries.

## Europe Compared with Other Geographical Regions

My percent of Great Power wars (55 percent) was lower than that of the other three authors, especially Levy, in Table 9.3, as was my percent of wars and deaths located in Europe. European wars lasted longer than those in other parts of the world, but this difference was not usually significant, except in the case of Wright. However, the fact that the difference was in the same direction for all four authors suggests some reliability. The number of Great Powers in wars was always greater in Europe than that in other regions, and usually significant.

## Historical Trends

Deaths per war were generally increasing over these five centuries, while the years per war were generally decreasing, as shown by the correlations in Table 9.3. (Positive correlations in this table indicate that the variables were increasing over time, while negative correlations indicate that the variables were going down.) Great Powers per war were generally staying constant, except that the number of Great Powers per war was decreasing in my list.

My wars, years and deaths were all increasing over these five centuries. While the others' wars and years were generally decreasing (especially Levy's), Wright's battles, Sorokin's casualties and Levy's deaths, as well as mine, were all increasing significantly. These same findings held over 45 decades (to a lesser but significant extent) as well as over five centuries, so that the conclusion that the violence caused of modern warfare was significantly increasing over these decades and centuries was very reliable. War was increasing not only in total deaths, but also in deaths per war, so that the average war was increasing in intensity as were all wars added together.

Analyses of variance confirmed the finding for battles, casualties and deaths/decade, where the twentieth century was significantly higher than all previous centuries in these measures for all four authors, as shown in Table 9.3. The same consistency was not found for wars and years per decade. Years were especially erratic and relatively insignificant, but the seventeenth century was the highest in years of war per decade. The frequencies of war per decade were also somewhat erratic but more significant. The sixteenth century was highest for Levy, the sixteenth and nineteenth centuries for Sorokin, and the nineteenth and twentieth centuries for Wright and Eckhardt.

## Reliability

The reliability of these four lists was established by correlating their frequencies, durations and deaths with one another over some 45 decades and five centuries. There was general agreement among them concerning the relative distribution of these three variables, especially deaths and deaths/war, where the similarities were significant in all cases. This agreement is rather remarkable, considering the different definitions of war, as shown in Table 9.3, the different samples of nations, and the different purposes for which these lists were constructed.

Although 30 out of 36 correlations over five centuries were positive, only 14 of these were significant, and most of these were found for deaths and deaths/war. Almost all of the correlations were positive over 45 decades, and most of these were significant, so that the similarity over these decades was greater than that over the five centuries. Both sets of correlations suggest a fair amount of agreement among these authors in the distribution of wars, years, deaths, deaths/war, years/war and Great Powers per war in modern times.

## *Summary and Conclusions*

The most reliable finding of these four studies of modern wars is the increase in war deaths and deaths per war during the last five centuries. Not only has the total violence of war increased over these centuries, but the average war has also increased in violence. This finding raises a question about the nature of twentieth century civilization in general. What does it mean to be civilized? To be violent? Is war an essential component of civilization?

My own studies reported in this chapter also showed that less than one-half of modern wars have been won by those who started them, raising a question about the rationality of war. More than one-half of war-related deaths have been unarmed civilians, raising a question about the "justness" of modern war. Two-thirds of all war-related deaths occurred in Europe, as shown in Figure 9.1, raising a question about the nature of European civilization in particular. What has made Europe more violent than all other geographical regions added together?

In the next chapter we shall look at a list of wars based on a *Dictionary of Wars* (Kohn 1987) that claimed to cover the world since 2000 B.C.

# Chapter 10
# Civilized Wars
# Throughout History

## Kohn's Wars, 2000 B.C. to A.D. 2000

The front cover page of this dictionary (Kohn's *Dictionary of Wars* 1987, to which references in this chapter will be simply by page number) claims a bit too much by saying that it is "the complete one-volume reference guide to *every* global conflict, civil war, mutiny, punitive expedition, undeclared war, rebellion, and revolution in human history" (my emphasis). This universal claim is modified somewhat on the back cover page, where it is stated that this is "the only book that concisely identifies and describes all the wars, revolutions, and other *significant* armed conflicts in mankind's history" (my emphasis). However, what makes an armed conflict "significant" is not specified, nor is the subjectivity of this concept acknowledged.

In his preface, the author is somewhat more modest in his claim that the book provides "a quick, convenient, authoritative, and comprehensive source of information on the *major* wars, revolutions, revolts, and rebellions which have for so long been a part of history. No one-volume reference work like this can possible include *every* war" (p. v, my emphases), but what makes these events "major" is not specified. However, the author has to be credited with trying to include "wars in all parts of the world from 2000 B.C." and with covering "the entire sweep of the globe in selecting entries" (p. v).

There is only one entry for about 2000 B.C., which involved the Mycenaean invasion of Greece (p. 142), after which there were no further entries until about 1700 B.C. The latest entry was the Indian siege of the Sikh Golden Temple in 1984 (p. 550). The number of wars in the twentieth century had to be divided by the last two digits of the year of the latest entry and multiplied by 100 in order to obtain a rough estimate of the total war frequency for the twentieth century, so as to make the (prorated) frequency somewhat comparable to that of the previous centuries.

The author "defined war fairly broadly, to mean an overt, armed conflict carried on between nations or states (international war) or between parties, factions, or people in the same state (civil war)" (p. v). These "wars" included rebellions, insurrections, uprisings, revolts, and revolutions, as well as "conquests, invasions, sieges, massacres, raids, and key mutinies. . . . In addition, there are separate entries for a number of exceptionally complex and significant battles. . . . Each entry gives the name(s) of the conflict, the dates it spanned, how it began, the opposing sides involved, and a concise description or summary of events, and the outcome or significance" (p. v). This is a very broad definition of war indeed. The author provided some estimates of army sizes and some death estimates, which can be used for some analyses, but not for all.

No sources were given, but the author said in private correspondence dated November 13, 1987, that he relied "quite heavily" on the *Cambridge Histories*, and that "a large number of my sources are in Dupuy and Dupuy's *The Encyclopedia of Military History*'s bibliography, but by no means did I rely on that book."

In the course of his research, the author noted some outstanding reasons for international wars, which included territorial disputes, injustice, race and prejudice, commercial and economic competition and coercion, military envy and cupidity for conquest. The reasons for civil war included rival claims for power, and struggles for liberties of some sort.

There were more than 1700 entries, which I increased to 1778 by changing some of the early wars, which were shown as lasting for several hundred years, into a larger number of shorter wars. This resulted in increasing the frequency of the earliest wars and decreasing their duration, which made them somewhat more comparable to later wars. When I prorated the twentieth century wars, the number of wars grew further to 1826. The dates before 500 B.C. were often approximate, and this was sometimes the case even after 500 B.C.

I extracted the following variables from Kohn's dictionary: starter, target, geographical region, beginning Date, ending Date, duration, description, winner, starter winning, army size, deaths, type, cause, number of participants, number of Great Powers, distance from London, intervenors and regional similarity of starter and target. The results of analyzing these variables will be presented, and then Kohn's list of wars will be compared with that of Sorokin.

## Analyses of Kohn's Wars

There were 1826 wars in Kohn's dictionary, after I increased the number of wars in the ancient period of history (by subdividing longer wars), and after I prorated his wars for the twentieth century. As noted, Kohn's first war was the Mycenaean invasion of Greece about 2000 B.C. I listed this as a separate war, although it was only one part of Kohn's listing of Dorian Invasions, the next part of which did not occur until about 1500 B.C. There were only 28 wars listed in Kohn prior to the fifth century B.C. until I increased this number to 83 by increasing 10 of these earlier wars into 65 wars by subidviding them into wars of shorter lengths. I also subdivided 36 later wars, but not by so much as these earlier wars. In any event, after these increases were made, the wars that occurred prior to 500 B.C. was 4.55 percent of the total, suggesting that less than 5 percent of recorded wars occurred in the first half of recorded history.

Recorded wars did not go back beyond 2000 B.C. (and only one of them went back beyond 1700 B.C.), so that there were virtually no wars in the archaic period of history. The Middle East was the primary and, often the only scene of action prior to 500 B.C., with Europe a distant second, as shown in Table 10.1 in Appendix B. Asian wars did not appear until the classic period, and Africa and the Americas did not come into the picture until modern times.

There was no significant difference between the European and non–European average *number* of wars per century. There was a significant correlation of .74 between the European and non–European *pattern* of wars over the 40 centuries from 2000 B.C. to A.D. 2000, suggesting no Eurocentric bias in these *patterns*.

Although the European percentage of wars increased significantly over these centuries ($r = .45**$), this was not the case with the non–European percentage ($r = .18ns$). When the total war frequencies (logged) were correlated with these 40 centuries, the correlation was .93, showing a very significant and exponential increase in wars over these centuries.

## Additional Analyses of Kohn's Wars

In addition to these basic analyses of Kohn's wars, some other variables were extracted from the Kohn dictionary, as mentioned previously. The results of analyzing some of these variables will now be described.

### Analysis of Variance

Analysis of variance is simply a statistical technique for determining whether one or more mean differences are statistically significant (reliable), or whether they could be due to chance. Neither this nor any other statistical technique can tell us anything about the causal relations concerning such differences (or similarities). Causal relations have to be determined outside of the statistical situation by empirical evidence and or logical argument. Statistics may be suggestive but never conclusive.

Although fewer than half (46 percent) of Kohn's wars occurred in Europe, Europe was involved in more than two-thirds (68 percent) of all wars. Of course, some of the wars located in Europe involved non–European forces, such as Mongols and Turks. In any event, it is clear that Europe engaged in wars all over the world in addition to those in Europe. How much does this reflect human history and how much does it reflect a Eurocentric bias? We were presumably not biased in our count of population, nor in our estimates of imperial sizes, so why should we be biased in our count of wars?

The average war in this dictionary began about 1260 and ended about 1265, lasting 5.45 years, even after I reduced the length by increasing the frequency of 46 long wars to 180 shorter wars. The wars during the first millennium of this time period were significantly longer than average (about 15 years), while the wars during the modern period were significantly shorter than average (3.6 years).

Fifty-three percent of the starters of these wars won them, suggesting that the odds of winning a war that you started were about 50-50. However, the first millennium was characterized by a very high percentage (90 percent) of starters winning, while the last millennium was characterized by a relatively low percentage (50 percent) of starters winning, as was the first five hundred years of the Christian era (47 percent), when the Roman and Han empires ruled most of the world in Europe and Asia. In general, starters won more wars in earlier centuries and when fighting occurred between nations of different geographical regions. No other variables had any significant effect on starters winning: neither arms, nor deaths, nor durations, nor participants, nor Great Powers nor distances from London.

The average war involved less than one (0.72) Great Power, defined primarily in terms of Taagepera's (1978a) imperial sizes (along with Sorokin's [1937, vol. 3] list of great European powers from 950) until the sixteenth century, after which Levy's (1983) list of Great Powers was used. This figure did not change very much over the centuries, but it was slightly more than one prior to 500 B.C. and in the first five centuries of the Christian era.

There were 2.45 participants in the average war, and this number did not change significantly over these centuries.

The average war occurred 2850 miles from London, which was used as a measure of Eurocentricity, and especially Anglocentricity, since most of these data were obtained from English-speaking (or English-writing) sources. This distance was lower than average (about 2000 miles) from 2000 B.C. to A.D. 1500, but higher than average (3582 miles) during the modern period. This might suggest some Eurocentricity during the first 3500 years of this period, which lessened during the last five hundred years. It might also reflect the fact that the world "grew smaller" in the modern period, when modern technology made it possible to communicate and travel farther and faster than previously.

Finally, 69 percent of these wars were fought by nations within the same geographical region, as determined by Sivard's (1990) assignment of nations to geographical regions, with one outstanding exception: I assigned Turkey to the Middle East (where it seemed to belong throughout most of this time period), while Sivard assigned it to Europe because of its modern association with Europe. This percentage would suggest that about twice as many wars have been fought within geographical regions as have been fought between them. This would further suggest that antagonists were generally more similar to each other (in language, religion, color and culture) than they were different. This finding contradicted Richardson's (1960a) basic hypothesis about war and peace to the effect that war is a function of differences, while peace is a function of similarities. It seems that neither a world language nor a world religion would prevent or limit war. Although fighting within the same geographical region had no significant effect upon wars' durations, or upon the number of participants or army sizes, there were significantly more deaths, significantly fewer starters winning, significantly earlier centuries, significantly fewer Great Powers and significantly shorter distances from London when the fighting occurred within the same geographical region.

This predominance of fighting within geographical regions (more than 90 percent) was especially true of the first 1500 years of ancient history, when the Middle East was just about the only active (civilized) region. The classic period, immediately following, was characterized by the most fighting (about 50 percent) between regions (primarily between Europe and the Middle East). The last 1500 years of medieval and modern history were about average in this respect, with about two-thirds of the wars fought within regions.

## Factor Analysis

Factor analysis, like analysis of variance, is very useful for establishing the significance, or reliability, of similarities or differences. Causal relations have to be determined outside the statistical situation by empirical evidence and or logical argument.

The results of factor analyses generally confirmed the findings of the variance analyses in the previous section.

When army sizes and deaths were analyzed together (N = 71), they always came out on the same factor. It was hardly surprising to find that larger armies were associated with more deaths. This same factor included a larger number of Great Powers and of participants, a longer duration and a shorter distance from London. This general factor was not associated with centuries, with starters winning or with fighting within the same geographical region. This solution was fairly, but not entirely, stable. When it was rotated, arms and deaths remained together, along with earlier centuries and shorter distances from London. Deaths were also associated with participants and Great Powers as well as longer durations. Neither arms nor deaths were associated with starters winning or with fighting within the same geographical region.

When arms were omitted from the analysis, death estimates were available for 210 of the wars. When deaths were omitted, the estimates of army sizes were available for 260 for the wars. In both cases the factor analyses were similar to that described in the previous paragraph. Arms were associated with Great Powers, participants and shorter distances from London. They were also associated with earlier centuries, longer durations and starters winning. Deaths were associated with Great Powers, participants, durations and shorter distances from London.

Over the centuries from 2000 B.C. to A.D. 2000, the frequencies of these wars increased exponentially. The general factor of war frequency was also associated with starters not winning, shorter durations, fewer Great Powers per war and longer distances from London. All of these associations taken together could have simply been a function of time.

When deaths were included, war frequencies were associated with distance from London, centuries, shorter durations and deaths (.49*). When army sizes were included, they were not significantly associated with war frequencies. When both arms and deaths were included, war frequencies were associated with deaths but not with arms over these 40 centuries.

When these analyses were conducted across nine geographical regions (instead of 40 centuries), war frequencies were associated with durations, earlier centuries, arms, fighting within the same regions, deaths, participants, shorter distances from London and Great Powers. When this solution was rotated, arms, deaths and frequencies were still associated with one another, along with durations and fighting within the same regions. Frequencies were also associated with shorter distances from London and earlier centuries on another factor.

## Summary of Additional Analyses

Although less than half of Kohn's wars were located in Europe, more than two-thirds of them involved European nations.

These wars lasted about 5.5 years on the average, ranging from less than 4 years in the modern period to 15 years in the ancient period of history. This difference in duration from ancient to modern times seemed to reflect the vagueness of the historical record in ancient times that makes it difficult to establish clearly the beginnings and endings of wars (if indeed they *were* wars in the sense of causing at least one thousand deaths per year).

Fifty-three percent of the starters of these wars won them, but this percentage was much higher (90 percent) during the first millennium, and lower (50 percent) during the last millennium.

The average war had about 2.5 participants, less than one of which was a Great Power, but the latter figure was slightly more than one prior to 500 B.C.

The average war occurred about 2000 miles from London prior to A.D. 1500, after which it occurred 3600 miles on the average in modern times. This difference may reflect a Eurocentric bias, or it may reflect the world's "getting smaller" with the aid of modern technology.

Sixty-nine percent of these wars were fought within the same geographical region, Europeans fighting Europeans, Asians fighting Asians, etc., but this percentage was much higher (90 percent) prior to 500 B.C., much lower during the classic period (50 percent) and average during the medieval and modern periods. Wars fought within the same region had more deaths, fewer starters winning, fewer great powers involved and shorter distances from London.

Arms, deaths, Great Powers, participants, durations and shorter distances from London tended to go together over these 40 centuries.

War frequencies followed a different pattern, being associated with starters losing, fewer years, fewer Great Powers and longer distances from London. War frequencies were associated with deaths, but not with army sizes.

When these variables were correlated over nine geographical regions, most of them were associated with one another as follows: war frequencies, durations, earlier centuries, army sizes, fighting within the same regions, deaths, participants, shorter distances from London and Great Powers.

## Comparison of Kohn's and Sorokin's Wars

When Kohn's European war frequencies were correlated with Sorokin's war frequencies over the 21 centuries for which these latter were available, the correlation was .56**. Kohn's years of war were correlated .44* with Sorokin's years of war. Although not high, these moderate correlations showed a significant similarity between the frequencies and durations of Kohn's and Sorokin's wars. When Kohn's war frequencies and war durations were correlated with Sorokin's war casualties (logged), the correlations were .64 and .71 respectively, both of which were significant at the .01 level of confidence and approaching a high correlation, suggesting that Kohn's frequencies (or durations) could be used as a rough measure of war intensity when casualty or death estimates were not available.

Although both Kohn's and Sorokin's war frequencies increased over the centuries from 500 B.C. to A.D. 2000 (excluding the sixth to the ninth centuries, which were not available for Sorokin's data), Kohn's frequencies increased at a much faster rate than those of Sorokin. And while Kohn's years of war increased at the same rate as Kohn's frequencies of war, Sorokin's years of war did not increase at all, presumably because of the much greater lengths of his earlier wars.

Kohn's European frequencies of war were 1.2 times Sorokin's frequencies. This difference was probably because Sorokin's definition of war (historical identification as a "war") resulted in a somewhat more restricted list than that of Kohn, which included a variety of armed conflicts generally classified as much less intense than a war, such as rebellions, insurrections, uprisings, revolts and revolutions, as well as sieges, massacres, raids and key mutinies. In spite of these differences in definition, which resulted in some difference in *levels*, the *patterns* of Kohn's and Sorokin's frequencies and, to a lesser extent, durations over the centuries were remarkably similar.

Some of the statistics for comparing Kohn's and Sorokin's wars are shown in Table 10.2 in Appendix B, which also includes statistics from another list of wars to be discussed in the next section of this chapter.

## Another List of Wars

I generated another list of wars from the "Index of Wars" in Dupuy and Dupuy (1986, pp. 1516–24), starting in 2500 B.C. According to Wright, "There is little evidence of organized military activity before 2500 B.C." (1942, p. 575). The three lists of wars that we have examined in this chapter, including the present one, would suggest that no further evidence along these lines has been developed during the 50 years since then. Since there was one war in the Index for the twenty-fifth, twenty-fourth, and twenty-second centuries B.C., I inserted one war each in the thirtieth to the twenty-sixth centuries B.C., the twenty-third century B.C., and the twenty-first to the nineteenth centuries B.C. These additions along with the prorating of the twentieth century resulted in 1266 wars from 3000 B.C. to A.D. 2000.

Table 10.2 shows some remarkable similarities among the three sets of wars, in spite of their different definitions, different frequencies, and different centuries. To be sure, their centuries differed where they mattered the least— in the first 25 centuries from 3000–500 B.C. Sorokin had half the wars that the other two had because of his limitation to wars involving major European nations. This limitation naturally increased the percentage of wars which occurred in Europe (Euro%Freq), which was twice as high as the European frequency percentages of the other two.

For both the Dupuys and Kohn, about 5 percent of their wars occurred prior to 500 B.C., even after I increased the frequency of these wars by dividing longer wars into shorter wars. Clearly, recorded wars were in short supply during the first half of human history.

The average number of years per war was almost 11 years, which was exaggerated by a 1300-year war assigned to the twenty-fifth century B.C. and a two hundred year war assigned to the seventeenth century B.C. This was much higher than the average of 3.6 years for Sorokin's wars and the average of 5.4 for Kohn's wars.

The starters won 45 percent of the wars that they started over these 50 centuries, which was close to the 53 percent of the Kohn wars over 40 centuries, and the same as the 45 percent of the Sorokin wars over 21 centuries, as shown in Table 10.2.

Seventy percent of the wars were fought within the same geographical regions, compared with 30 percent between regions. A similar percentage was found for both Kohn and Sorokin: 69 percent and 67 percent, respectively.

Both Kohn's and Sorokin's wars had about 2.5 participants per war, on average, of which more than one was a Great Power in Sorokin's wars involving major European powers, but less than one in Kohn's wars involving all nations.

The percentage of wars occurring in Europe increased as time went on in both the Dupuys' and Kohn's lists. The percentage of wars occurring outside Europe did not change significantly for Kohn, but decreased significantly for the Dupuys, as shown by the negative correlation in Table 10.2.

On the whole, European war frequencies did not differ significantly from non–European wars for either the Dupuys or for Kohn, so that wars occurring in Europe and outside Europe could have been equally frequent except by chance.

All three sets of wars increased significantly over their centuries, and this increase, which was exponential, held for European and non–European wars taken separately as well as together. All three sets of war frequencies were also

## Figure 10.1   War Frequencies, 1000 to 2000

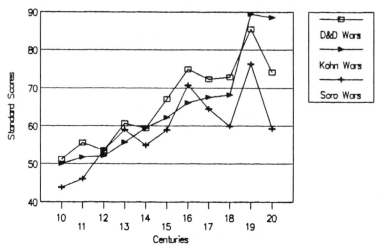

Notes to Figure 10.1: D & D Wars = The frequency of wars per century was obtained from the Index of Wars in Dupuy and Dupuy (1986, pp. 1516–24). Kohn Wars = The frequency of wars per century was obtained from Kohn (1987). Soro Wars = The frequency of wars per century was obtained from Sorokin (1937, vol. 3 pp. 543–77). All three sets of frequencies were standardized to a mean of 50 and a standard deviation of 10, in order to make them comparable to one another.

significantly correlated with Sorokin's war casualties (dead and wounded soldiers), so that war frequencies over these centuries could be used as a measure of war intensity whenever estimates of casualties or deaths are not available.

The three sets of war frequencies are shown graphically during the last millennium in Figure 10.1. They could not be compared for the sixth to ninth centuries, since Sorokin had no data for these four centuries. All three sets of frequencies were less than average from 500 B.C. to A.D. 500.

Even as the archaic and ancient war frequencies were lower than expected, so the modern war frequencies were higher than expected. The modern frequencies were at least 50 percent of all wars compared with 5 percent (at the most) for archaic and ancient wars. These figures would suggest that modern wars were altogether about 10 times as intense as archaic and ancient wars. However, the Kohn ratio was 38 for Europe, 1 for the Middle East (meaning that Middle Eastern wars were no more intense in modern times than they were in archaic and ancient times), and infinity for south Asia and for the Far East (since Kohn had no wars for them until the classic period). All of these ratios are assumed to be very conservative, because they take no account of the fact that archaic and ancient wars extended over five times as many centuries as did modern wars (25/5). Taking all the non–European wars together, their intensity increased by nine times, which was more than four times less than the European increase. The Dupuys' European wars, on the other hand, increased from the archaic and ancient periods to the modern period by eight times more than non–European wars.

Although Kohn's wars continued to increase during the modern centuries, there was no significant increase in either Sorokin's or the Dupuys' war frequency, as shown near the bottom of Table 10.2.

## Summary of Consistent Findings

About 45 percent of recorded wars were fought in Europe, which suggested that more than twice as many wars occurred in Europe than would have been expected from its share of world population (19 percent). However, there was no significant difference in frequency between wars fought inside and outside of Europe, so that this 45 percent figure could have differed from 50 percent by chance.

One-half of all recorded wars took place in the modern period of human history, 1500–2000. This was 10 to 12 times more wars than occurred in the archaic and ancient periods of history, 3000–500 B.C. Taking into account the number of centuries in these historical periods (25 in the archaic and ancient periods and 5 in the modern period), the ratio of 10 to 12 would have to be multiplied by 5 to give a ratio of 50 to 60 times more wars per century in the modern period compared with the archaic and ancient periods. If we assume that relative frequencies of war may be taken as indicators of war's intensity (in the absence of any systematic and reliable estimates of casualties or deaths for the archaic and ancient periods), then the intensity of war in the modern period has been 50 to 60 times greater than in the archaic and ancient periods.

The evidence for using war frequencies as measures of war intensity over these centuries is that all three frequencies were significantly correlated with Sorokin's estimates of war casualties over 21 of these centuries, 500 B.C. to A.D. 500 and 900 to 2000.

The increase in war frequencies over these 50 centuries has been exponential, and this increase has taken place inside and outside of Europe, taken separately as well as together.

These wars were won by about 50 percent of those who started them, suggesting that wars hardly paid as a general rule.

About two-thirds of these wars were fought between nations within the same geographical regions, suggesting that similarities in culture, history, language, religion, etc., encouraged war rather than discouraging it.

On average, 2.5 parties took part in these wars, and less than one of these parties was a Great Power.

## Burning Questions

Two of the most consistent and outstanding findings from the analyses of these three data sets were (1) that there were no records of wars before 2500 B.C., and no clear records before 1500 B.C., and (2) that Europe was the location of about half of these wars during this time.

Concerning the first finding, the burning question is: Were there earlier wars that were not recorded (or not recorded clearly), or were there simply no wars worth recording? Since historians have seldom, if ever been loath to record wars whenever there was the least bit of evidence of their occurrence, I assume that the wars prior to 2500 B.C. were not worth recording.

Wright also found that "there is little evidence of organized military activity before 2500 B.C." (1942, 1: 575), and the military historians, Dupuy and Dupuy, found that "not until about 1500 B.C., however, are we able to visualize the actual course of any of the constant wars in the Middle East, or dimly to perceive primitive military organization and methods of combat" (1986, 1).

It required less than two pages of their 1400-page text to record the military history of ancient Egypt from 3100 to 600 B.C. This included the unification of upper and lower Egypt in 3100 B.C. by Menes ("the first identifiable figure in history"), the Hyksos invasion in 1800 B.C., the revolt of Thebes in 1600 B.C., the first permanent army around 1580–1557 B.C., the Battle of Megiddo in 1469 B.C., the Battle of Kadesh in 1294 B.C., the invasions by the Aegean "Sea Peoples" in 1200 B.C., the Ethiopian conquest of Egypt in 730 B.C., Assyrian conquest of Egypt in 671–661 B.C., Egyptian revolts in 661–626 B.C., the invasion of Palestine and Syria in 609–593 B.C., the Second Battle of Megiddo in 609 B.C. and the Battle of Carchemish in 605 B.C.

Their record of Mesopotamian and Hittite military history from 4000 to 600 B.C. occupied about three pages and dealt with Sumer, Akkad, Babylonia, the Hittite Kingdom, Assyria, Palestine, Syria, Chaldea and Media. Greece and Rome from 2000 to 600 B.C. took about one page; south Asia (India) from 2000 to 600 B.C., about a half a page; and east Asia (China) from 1600 to 600 B.C., another half a page.

Add another two and one-half pages devoted to Egypt, Persia and Greece, and that brings us to about 500 B.C., so that altogether archaic and ancient military history from 3500 to 500 B.C. (some 3000 years) required less than ten pages to tell. More than one-half of the time period of military history occupied less than 1 percent of this 1400-page encyclopedia. The question remains: Was this due to the lack of relative unimportance of early events or was it simply due to their not being recorded?

Since writing was invented about 3000 B.C., and since historians love to record warlike events, I assume for the time being that military events simply did not amount to much until about 500 B.C. The relationship between various years of military history and the number of pages devoted to various time periods by Dupuy and Dupuy (1986) is shown in Table 10.3 in Appendix B.

As rough as these figures may be, they clearly show what Taagepera (1988) has called the fading rate of history, based on his analyses of seven sets of data provided by Grun (1979): history and politics, literature and theatre, religion and philosophy, visual arts, music, science and technology and daily life—all of these being recorded from 4241 B.C. to A.D. 1978. Taagepera also analyzed four other sources providing data on art, history and creativity, with similar results in the form of exponential curves from 4000 B.C. to A.D. 2000. In all cases, the most upward shift in these curves occurred about A.D. 1500, the beginning of modern times, although the classical period was somewhat above average, while the "dark ages" were slightly below average. Otherwise, the exponential curve remained steady over these six thousand years.

Taagepera raised the crucial question of whether it is the "fading of history or increased activity?" (p. 3). Taking population into consideration, he concluded that world population increased too slowly prior to A.D. 1900, and too fast since, to account for the increased activity over this time period. Neither could he account for the increasing activity on the basis of increasing creativity, "since creative fields show the slowest change" (p. 4). Taagepera concluded that "the simplest hypothesis to explain the patterns observed is collective loss of memory and interest" (p. 5). In short, activity (including military activity) has not increased; instead, we have lost information about, and interest in, ancient events, so that current and recent events seem to occur more frequently simply because we remember them better and because they are more interesting to us—not because we have become more active or creative, or because more of us have become active as the population has increased. Taagepera recognized that many problems remain and that further research has to be done.

But why should our memory (or interest) be failing more rapidly during the past five hundred years than previously? Taagepera recognized this issue and, again, called for further research. In the meantime, it seems to me that a fading of history would progress more rapidly the less recently the memory traces were laid down in whatever form: in generations of brains or in ancient libraries. Older traces should fade more rapidly. Consequently, I am inclined to interpret the "fading rate of history" as just another sign of less activity, of fewer newsworthy events, such as battles and wars, as well as other civilized activities, in older times. But I agree with Taagepera that further research needs to be done.

Before leaving this first "burning question," it is worth noting that the relative absence of wars prior to 1500 B.C., and not many to mention prior to 500 B.C., suggests the possibility that civilization and warfare may not have begun as early as conventional chronology would have us believe. Dayton (1978) found many contradictions in conventional chronology. Heinsohn (1988) has provided evidence for advancing the date of the beginning of civilization. And Wescott (1989) has argued that civilization may have begun much later than we think. The statistical evidence presented in this chapter is consistent with the arguments and evidence put forth by these authors. It is possible, then, that the "fading rate of history" is a function of the fact that there was no history there in the first place.

The second burning question is: Does the relative frequency of wars located in Europe — not to mention those involving Europe but located elsewhere — reflect the "reality" of events or does it merely reflect the Eurocentricity of European historians? This question is not unlike the first, which raised the possibility of historical (temporal) egocentricity; the second question raises the possibilty of geographical (spatial) egocentricity. Since the accounts of history most widely read during the last five hundred years were written in English or some other European language, and since Europe virtually ruled the world during that time — and probably wrote world history from its own point of view — I decided to use the distance between London and the place where a war occurred as a means to measure Eurocentricity and, especially, Anglocentricity. I assumed that if the frequency of wars was to some signifiant degree negatively correlated with the distance of their occurrence from London, this would indicate Euro-centricity and would, therefore, call into question the comparability of Euro-pean and non–European war frequencies. A great frequency of these events in Europe could simply be due to the Eurocentricity of European historians. On the other hand, if this measure of Eurocentricity was not significantly related to the frequency of wars, it would suggest no Eurocentricity in the frequency of wars. So far this test has been conducted only on Kohn's wars, since this was the only data set where I included the distance from London.

The findings were ambiguous, to say the least, and some of them were artifactual, containing no empirical information at all. Across the 40 centuries, war frequencies were significantly associated with longer distances from Lon-don; that is, later centuries, which were characterized by more wars, were also characterized by wars located farther away from London. This finding con-founded geography with history, so that it is difficult to draw any conclusion from it. On the other hand, across the nine geographical regions, the frequency of wars was significantly associated with shorter distances from London. This was simply because Europe was the region with the most wars, and Europe was closer to London than any other region simply by geographical definition.

Fortunately, there is another way to test this proposition about Eurocen-tricity, which has already been mentioned. If our historians were unduly Euro-centric, we might expect them to find more European wars in archaic and an-cient times. On the contrary, they found quite the opposite prior to 500 B.C. On average, there were more than nine times as many Middle Eastern wars as there were European wars in the archaic and ancient periods. This ratio held almost as well for involvement as it did for location: in only one case — the siege of Troy — was a European entity — Greece — involved in a Middle Eastern war prior to 500 B.C. These findings argue very strongly against Eurocentricity in this set of wars, especially in archaic and ancient times when one might expect the Eurocentric temptation to be the strongest, in order to establish European priority in the origin and progress of civilization. Clearly, if any such tempta-tion was at work, it was successfully resisted.

## Summary and Conclusions

In summary of these two points, my tentative conclusion is that wars did not amount to much, relatively speaking, prior to 500 B.C., and those that did occurred in the Middle East with no outside involvement except in the single case of Troy in the twelfth century B.C.

Other points worth mentioning by way of summary of this chapter were the following: European and non–European war frequencies over these centuries followed a remarkably similar pattern, and this pattern was one of exponential increase. This pattern of increasing frequency may be taken as a pattern of increasing intensity, since these frequencies were significantly correlated with Sorokin's estimates of war casualties from 500 B.C. to A.D. 500 and from 900 to 2000. Kohn's war frequencies were also signifiantly associated with his own estimates of war deaths, and Sorokin's war frequencies were also significantly associated with his own estimates of war casualties. Consequently, three sets of war frequencies were significantly correlated with Sorokin's estimates of war casualties, suggesting that war frequencies might be used as measures of war intensities in the absence of casualty and death estimates.

In spite of getting off to a late start, Europe was the location of about one-half of the wars since 2000 B.C., and Europe was involved in two-thirds of them. If these findings are reliable, and if they are not due to Eurocentricity, they raise at least two crucial questions for further research: What is it about Europe and or Europeans that has made Europe the location of so many wars? And what is it about Europeans that have made them the most warlike group of people in human history?

The average war lasted about 5.5 years. About one-half of the starters of wars won them, suggesting that starting a war can result in no more than breaking even, on average, which further suggests that war is basically a losing proposition for all concerned, since the gains of one war won can hardly compensate for the cost of two wars fought, in the long run. This argument applies only to the material economics of war. When the loss of life, limb, brain, family members (both civilian and military, old and young, male and female), etc., are included, there is no possible compensation: these are 100 percent losses with no gains at all, neither for individuals nor for societies.

About two-thirds of all wars were fought between parties of the same geographical region, where the fighting groups were presumably more like each other in culture, language, race, religion, etc., suggesting that neither a universal language nor a universal religion would be likely to put an end to war. This finding would further suggest that neither cultural nor physical differences are basic causes of war.

## Chapter 11
# Wars Since the Eighteenth Century

*Five Lists of Wars*

This chapter contains a brief review of five lists of wars that have occurred since the eighteenth century. These lists are worth reviewing since their data during the last several centuries are probably most reliable, being most recent.

1. Kaye, Grant and Emond (1985) listed 654 conflicts over a period of 265 years from 1720 to 1985, where a "major armed conflict" was originally defined as "an event where one or more nations or actors used armed force against another nation or actor. The violent actions must result in significant casualties" (p. 13). The first requirement was tightened up so that "at least one nation must be involved" (p. 14). The second requirement was loosened up because "some conflicts with virtually no casualties have had a significant effect on the history of the nation or nations involved and, therefore, merit inclusion" (p. 14). Consequently, "Major armed conflicts may include: international wars, civil wars, guerrilla wars, limited wars, nuclear wars, colonial wars, revolutions, occupation by force, massacres (if committed for or against a government), violent civil disorders with military involvement, coups d'etat (where armed resistance or attack is involved), military revolts, wars for independence, etc" (p. 14). Their death estimates included both civilian and military deaths (p. 15).

2. Bouthoul and Carrere (1978) listed 366 major armed conflicts over a period of 234 years from 1740 to 1974. They used six quantitative criteria, at least one of which had to be met for admission to their list, and included "foreign and civil wars, occupations by force, military penetrations, revolutions, uprisings and insurrections, massacres and genocide, and other violent troubles with important consequences" (pp. 83–84). Their death estimates, when available, included both civilians and soldiers, and also deaths from conflict-related massacres, epidemics and famines.

3. Dunnigan and Martel (1987) listed 409 wars over a period of 201 years from 1786 to 1987, defining a war as "organized violence caused by national governments" (p. 11). Their death estimates included military and (where available) civilian losses.

4. Richardson (1960a) listed 315 "deadly quarrels" or "fatal quarrels"

over a period of 132 years from 1820 to 1952, each of which caused more than 317 deaths, including civilian as well as military deaths, and also including deaths from famine and disease resulting from the war. However, only those 106 "fatal quarrels" with more than three thousand deaths were "large enough to be called wars in the popular sense of the word" (p. 257).

5. Small and Singer (1982) listed 224 wars over a period of 164 years from 1816 to 1980, using three quantitative definitions of a war: (1) interstate wars were defined by one thousand military battle deaths among all system members (p. 55); (2) colonial and imperial wars were defined by one thousand military battle deaths per year of system members only (p. 56); and (3) civil wars were defined by one thousand civilian and military battle deaths per year (p. 213). In general, their wars were defined as "recurrent exercises in legitimized homicide" (p. 35).

This chapter will present only a very brief review of these various studies, more details of which will be found in the references to the original studies, and in Eckhardt (1981b) for Richardson. Although they will not be reviewed in this chapter, Westing (1982) listed 45 "high-fatality" wars in the twentieth century with more than 30,000 civilian and military deaths each from 1899 to 1980, totaling about 86 million deaths (50 million of which were attributed to the Second World War), which would be prorated to 92 million for the total century. This prorating was done on the basis of the fatalities which occurred since 1945, so as not to exaggerate the twentieth century by including the world war fatalities in this prorating procedure. Westing's wars will be included in the summary tables at the end of this chapter for comparison with the lists of lower-fatality wars.

There have been many studies of post–World War II wars, none of which will be reviewed in this chapter. Leitenberg (1977) listed and referenced 56 studies of post–World War II wars and conflicts plus 22 studies of military coups during the same time period. Kaye, Grant and Emond (1985) listed and referenced 90 studies of post–World War II major armed conflicts, 29 of which also included conflicts prior to World War II. Both of these sources would be recommended for those wanting more information on wars since 1945.

## Kaye, Grant and Emond, 1720–1985

Kaye et al. (1985) found that "over most of the period covered (1720–1900), the chance of success for the committer [starter] was close to 50%. From 1901 to 1950, it dropped to 33% and after 1950 it seems to be around 25%" (p. 3). This finding was similar to that of Eckhardt (1989c), providing some support for the claim that it hardly pays to start a war nowadays. Kaye et al. "hoped that figures like these will tend to discourage nations (and actors) from initiating new wars" (p. 53).

There were only nine independent nations in 1721, according to Kaye et al., 21 in 1800, 55 in 1900, and approximately 160 in 1985 (p. 20). One of their conclusions was that "the increase in number of conflicts from 1720 to 1985 seems roughly proportional to the increase in world population over the same period" (p. 22). There were 12 conflicts with more than one million deaths each, which accounted for 83 percent of all deaths in the 504 conflicts where death estimates were available (p. 27). The world wars in the twentieth century accounted for 55 percent of all deaths in this time period.

Only one of their wars (World War II) killed more than 1 percent of the world population at the time, but "even World War II did little to slow down the rate of growth in the world's population" (p. 33), suggesting that war was not an effective way of controlling population growth. The average duration of their wars was four years, but only three years from 1851 to 1950, four and one-half years prior to 1850, and five years after 1950 (p. 35).

It is of some interest to note that 15 countries were involved in more than 20 conflicts each (p. 44). It is of even greater interest to note that the top five are the permanent members of the UN Security Council today: Britain (146), France (122), Russia (95), the United States (77) and China (72). It seems that the top warmakers have been put in charge of keeping the peace of the world. The moral of this must be: If you want to rule the world, go to war as often as you can. Since 1950, the United States has moved into top position (41), followed by the USSR (25), Britain (22) and France (16). China (10) has fallen to the level of Iran (10), and to less than that of Egypt (11) and Cuba (14).

So far as location was concerned, China occupied top place with 52 conflicts occurring there, followed by India (28), Turkey (27) and Russia (21). Five geographic regions shared an approximately equal number of conflicts (p. 45): Asia (180), Europe (141), America (123), Africa (113) and the Middle East (108), but Asia was significantly high and the Middle East was significantly low.

Participants per conflict increased over these centuries: 3.2 for the eighteenth century, 3.6 for the nineteenth century, and 4.2 for the twentieth century (p. 62). These participants included parties that provided arms and other supplies, as well as those more directly involved.

According to Kaye et al. there were about 3 million (prorated) war deaths in the eighteenth century, 20 million in the nineteenth century (14 million of which were attributed to the Taiping and Sinkiang revolts in China), and 76 million (prorated as previously for Westing) in the twentieth century (51 million of which were attributed to the two world wars). These war death differences between these three centuries were partly due to increasing frequencies of war (68 in the eighteenth, 277 in the nineteenth, and 380 in the twentieth, when the frequencies were prorated for the eighteenth and twentieth centuries), increasing deaths per war in thousands (115 in the eighteenth, 76 in the nineteenth and 324 in the twentieth) and the increasing number of sovereign nations that could engage in war (20 in 1750, 38 in 1850 and 75 in 1950). However, even when war deaths were controlled for sovereign nations, nineteenth century deaths were three and one-half times as many as those in the eighteenth century, twentieth century deaths were twice as many as those in the nineteenth century and twentieth century deaths were seven times as many as those in the eighteenth century. Since similar results were obtained when war deaths were controlled for world population, these results showed that the increase in war deaths over these three centuries could not be explained by the increase in sovereign nations or world population alone.

## Bouthoul and Carrere, 1740–1974

Bouthoul and Carrere (1978) used six quantitative criteria, at least one of which had to be met in order for any conflict to qualify as one of their "major armed conflicts." The six criteria were: (1) more than one state, (2) more than one province or a capital, (3) more than one year, (4) more than one thousand deaths, (5) important internal results and (6) important international results (p. 83). Most of their conflicts met from two to five of these criteria. Only 20 met only one of them; only 17 met all six of them.

Prorating for the eighteenth and twentieth centuries, 68 of these conflicts occurred in the eighteenth century, 173 in the nineteenth century and 203 in the twentieth century. There were 4.4 (prorated) million deaths in the eighteenth century, 17.7 million in the nineteenth century (11 million of which were attributed to the Taiping Rebellion), and 75.2 million in the twentieth century. When the number of sovereign nations and world population were taken into account, twentieth century deaths were more than twice that in the nineteenth century, which was more than twice that in the eighteenth century (Eckhardt 1987b, p. 64).

Using Bouthoul and Carrere's data for the twentieth century, Eckhardt and Kohler (1980) found that 60 percent of the conflicts involved at least one imperial power, defined as "a state which has full or partial control of colonies, dominions, dependencies and or has full or partial control of nation-states via stationing of military forces, the loyalty of ruling parties, or substantial control of the economy of those nation-states" (Kohler 1975, p. 56). According to this definition, control over others was the essence of imperialism. Kohler identified 15 imperial powers during the years 1816 to 1974, which were imperial powers throughout the twentieth century except for Austria-Hungary and Turkey—which lost their imperial status at the end of World War I—and Germany, Italy and Japan—which lost their imperial status by the end of World War II—and Belgium and the Netherlands which lost their status in the early 1960s. China and India were latecomers, starting after World War II. Those who were still imperial leaders in 1974 included China, England, France, India, Portugal, the USSR, Spain and the United States. According to this definition, 93 percent of twentieth century war-related deaths occurred in imperial conflicts (Eckhardt and Kohler 1980, p. 359). Western imperial powers were involved in 89 percent of the total deaths caused by the 15 most violent imperial conflicts. No simple trend of increasing or decreasing armed violence during the twentieth century was found in Bouthoul and Carrere's death estimates taken decade by decade. The correlation between these estimates and decades was not significant.

## Dunnigan and Martel, 1786–1987

Dunnigan and Martel (1987) listed 409 wars, defined as "organized violence caused by national governments" (p. 11). About half of the deaths in all of the wars were caused by the Napoleonic Wars, the Taiping Rebellion and both world wars. The four direct causes of war were listed as grudges, disorders (which caused about half the deaths), bullies and paranoia (p. 26). For those of us who live in hope that nuclear weapons will never be used because of their horrible nature, Dunnigan and Martel remind us that "unfortunately, history is rife with wars in which horrible weapons were used. Poison gas during WWI is a good example because it was used despite a general understanding that it harms the side using it as much as the intended victim" (p. 57).

Their 409 wars in 201 years resulted in 163 million deaths, according to their estimates (p. 250).

Before 1945, about half of their wars involved major powers (p. 82), but most of the wars since then have involved relatively minor powers in the Third World of Afro-Asia and Latin America.

Like Eckhardt (1989c) and Kaye et al. (1985), Dunnigan and Martel found that "the aggressor in a war will lose most of the time" (p. 151). "Defenders win more wars than attackers" (p. 155). However, colonial wars were an exception to this general rule (p. 151). Altogether, aggressors lost twice as many wars as defenders did, according to their estimates (p. 264).

Looking at those wars during the nineteenth and twentieth centuries only (since there were only 14 years of wars available in the eighteenth century), and prorating the twentieth century data to make them comparable to those of the nineteenth century, there was not much difference between these two centuries in their war frequencies: 203 in the nineteenth century and 215 (prorated) in the twentieth century. Wars in the twentieth century lasted longer than those in the nineteenth century, but this was entirely due to the length of wars since 1945: 7.7 years per war compared to 4.9 years per war prior to this time.

The greatest difference between the nineteenth and twentieth centuries was in their war deaths, which were about 32 million in the nineteenth century and 142 million (prorated as previously) in the twentieth century, so that twentieth century war deaths were about 4.4 times those of the nineteenth century. However, the number of sovereign nations were twice as many in the twentieth century (75/38), and the world population was twice as much (2.5 billion/1.2 billion). Both sets of these figures were estimated at the middle of both centuries. Taking these data into account, deaths per sovereign nation were still more than twice as many in the twentieth century and deaths per world population were still more than twice as many. The twentieth century was clearly and significantly more violent than the nineteenth century, which was consistent with similar findings by Eckhardt (1989c), and Eckhardt (1987b) using Bouthoul and Carrere's data, so that war deaths were increasing more than twice as much as either the increase in sovereign nations or the increase in the world population from the nineteenth to the twentieth centuries.

# Richardson, 1820–1952

Lewis Fry Richardson was among the first of the pioneers of peace research, along with Sorokin and Wright, who appeared during or shortly after the First World War. His first effort, undertaken while he was working with the Friends' Ambulance Unit during the First World War, was multigraphed at his own expense and given away: "It was little noticed. Some of my friends thought it funny. But for me it was quite serious.... It is still difficult, in 1953 [the year of his death], to publish work on that subject" (Eckhardt, 1981b, p. 248).

Richardson (1960a) listed 315 "deadly quarrels," each one of which caused more than 317 deaths in wars ending from 1820 to 1952. Most of these quarrels (209 of them) killed from three hundred to three thousand civilians and soldiers, including military deaths from war-related disease and famine. The other 106 quarrels with more than three thousand deaths were "large enough to be called wars in the popular sense of the word" (p. 257). These 315 quarrels caused more than 47 million deaths, 36 million (76 percent) of which were caused by the two world wars in the twentieth century (p. 153). Nine (3 percent) of the wars caused 90 percent of the war deaths. The deaths from all 315 wars were responsible for about 1.3 percent of all deaths from all causes during this time (p. 153). If we could find out how to prevent the few big wars, we could go a long way toward solving the problem of war.

There were no significant differences between the frequencies of war before and after 1885 (p. 141), but more deadly quarrels were significantly more frequent, and they lasted longer, in the twentieth century. War deaths in the twentieth century were almost eight times as many as those in the nineteenth century, and almost four times as many when population growth (and the increased number of sovereign nations) were taken into account. These findings contradicted Richardson's conclusion: "There is a suggestion, but not a conclusive proof, that mankind has become less warlike since A.D. 1820" (p. 167). They also question his further conclusion: "Although the facts about casualties are very variable and very uncertain [which can hardly be denied], they do plainly show a remarkable independence of the destructiveness of weapons" (p. 160).

Richardson's most general hypothesis concerning the causes of war and peace was that similarities would contribute to peace while differences would contribute to war (p. 28). However, differences in class, language and religion were associated with no more wars than were similarities, according to Richardson. Less than 10 percent of his wars were class-wars (p. 206). Among 13 languages studied by Richardson, only the Chinese language was associated with peace and the Spanish language with war: "For the other chief languages the statistics neither confirm nor refute Zamenhof's belief that a common language, by promoting mutual understanding, would have a pacificatory effect" (p. 230).

As to religious similarities and differences, although Christians and Muslims did not fight *within* themselves any more or less than expected by chance

(p. 239), they did fight *each other* more than expected by chance (p. 245). Confucian-Taoist-Buddhists, on the other hand, fought within themselves *less* than expected by chance (p. 239), which Richardson attributed largely to Confucianism in China (pp. 241–242). Richardson concluded that individualism contributed to more than expected Spanish-speaking wars, while the Confucian "emphasis on social behavior" (p. 229) contributed to less than expected Chinese-speaking wars. Character and temperament, according to Richardson, accounted for war more than could be explained "in terms of individuals, or of doctrines, or of institutions" (p. 228). This conclusion was consistent with Sorokin's emphasis on tribal egoism in the causation of war, as well as with Toynbee's and Wright's analyses of civilization and war presented in Chapter 5.

A small number of Great Powers engaged in most of Richardson's larger wars (p. 173): Britain (30 percent) France (22 percent), Russia (19 percent), Turkey (16 percent), China (15 percent), Spain (12 percent), Germany (11 percent), Italy (11 percent), Austria (10 percent), Japan (10 percent) and the United States (10 percent). In spite of this finding, Richardson refused to find such Great Powers guilty of aggression, but rather explained their aggression away by taking the number of their borders into account, and finding a significant correlation of .77 between the number of borders and the number of external wars (p. 179). Since the number of their borders included the borders of their colonies (p. 191), the nations with the larger number of borders had conquered the larger number of colonies, so that the correlation between borders and wars was clearly a correlation between imperialism and war. Richardson also chose to ignore the fact that, although many nations engaged in wars during his time period, 9 percent of these nations were engaged in 86 percent of these wars (Eckhardt, 1981b, p. 264).

Finally, Richardson excused the Great Powers of war-making by taking into account their numerous contacts which provided more opportunities for making war. Using worldwide sea-powers as an indication of having more contacts and more opportunities for making war, Richardson concluded that *"the worldwide sea-powers made much less pugnacious use of their opportunities for contact than did the local powers"* (p. 280). Consequently, Richardson concluded that imperial powers were "much less pugnacious" than small local powers.

Richardson also minimized economic causes of war by emphasizing the fact that only 29 percent of the causes of his larger wars were economic, while ignoring the fact that 70 percent of these same wars involved economic causes (p. 210).

While Richardson found that similarities in general did not contribute to peace, he did find that common government made for less civil war than foreign war for smaller wars (and conversely for larger wars). Since class, language and religious similarities had been ruled out by previous findings already mentioned, this left the possibility of intermarriage, which he found difficult to distinguish from the effects of common government (pp. 295–296, 313). Consequently, common government might be responsible for fewer small civil wars. However, the same findings could be turned around so as to explain more small foreign wars instead of fewer small civil wars (since Richardson's finding in this case was entirely relative), in which case there is some evidence to show that imperial wars tended to be small (Eckhardt 1981b, p. 268).

Wright found himself in some agreement with Richardson on 16 out of 17 findings, ranging from "entirely consistent" to "not necessarily inconsistent" (Richardson 1960a, pp. ix–xiii).

Taking advantage of computers, which were not available to Richardson, Rummel (1967) factor-analyzed 21 variables for the 779 pairs of combatants engaged in Richardson's 315 wars. The 21 variables measured the intensity of wars, types of war, similarities and differences between the pairs of combatants, etc. Four measures of the intensity of war (number of dyads, duration, deaths and army size) were loaded .45 or more on a factor with date and European involvement (p. 180). This first factor showed that the intensity of Richardson's wars increased as time went on from 1820 to 1952 and as more European nations were involved in them. Five measures of similarity, including language, religion, physique and clothing, were loaded on a second factor unrelated to the first, so that these similarities and differences were not associated with the intensity of war. Whether wars were international, communal, civil or colonial was not associated with intensity, but international wars were associated (.33) with colonial wars at the secondary level of analysis. Rummel concluded that "common causal conditions and attributes are involved for national and subnational groups, but that they may be has not been suggested by the results" (p. 182). However, the results show that nationality (European) and time (later date) were common conditions underlying the intensity of Richardson's wars.

According to Rummel, Denton (1966) factor-analyzed Richardson's wars over time (instead of over dyads), finding a correlation of .33 between size or intensity and time. Denton also found a cultural similarity factor which was, presumably, independent of intensity (Rummel 1967, pp. 180–81).

Although generally approving Richardson's work and most of his results, Wilkinson (1980) suggested some improvements that could be made: (1) revise the original 59 code symbols; (2) search for more wars, using 10 times as many historical sources [Richardson used at least 70 such sources]; (3) update Wright's theories and use them to place Richardson's facts in clearer perspective (pp. 120–21).

While Wright compared his results with those of Richardson by inspection, and while Denton and Rummel factor-analyzed Richardson's data, Wilkinson reduced Richardson's 59 coding symbols to 26 and performed frequency counts, percentages and crosstabulations on 780 pairs of combatants. His results were generally similar to previous results except where similarities and differences were concerned: "The propensity of any two groups to fight increases as the differences between them (in language, religion, race and cultural style) increase. A homogeneous world would probably be a more peaceful one. . . . Similarity, equality, connectedness and cooperation tend toward pacificity" (pp. 119–20). In spite of these differences, Wilkinson's conclusions were generally consistent with those of others: "As to practical conclusions, the key topics for contemporary peace strategy seem to be how to promote great-power detente, and how to accelerate world economic development" (p. 121).

In brief summary, Richardson generally found no significant differences in the frequency, duration and intensity of war due to differences in class, culture, power, race or time. Common government seemed to reduce smaller civil wars, while character, contagion and contiguity contributed to wars in general. Wright generally agreed with Richardson's conclusions on the basis of comparison by inspection. So did Rummel on the basis of his factor analyses of Richardson's data, but he added that war intensity did not differ according to types of war, but did increase over time and with European involvement. Wilkinson also agreed in general on the basis of his recoding of Richardson's symbols, which he analyzed by frequency counts, percentages and crosstabulations. He disagreed in finding that cultural and racial similarities contributed to peace, while Great Powers contributed to war.

## Small and Singer, 1816–1980

Singer and Small (1972) and Small and Singer (1982) have been working on their correlates of war for over a quarter of a century now, but I shall limit myself primarily to reviewing their latest book (1982), which includes a list of 118 international wars from 1816 to 1980 and 106 civil wars over the same period. (All page numbers cited in this section refer to their 1982 book unless otherwise noted.) Singer and Small have been more careful and precise in their conceptual and operational definitions than any other authors in this field.

International wars included interstate, imperial and colonial wars. Following Richardson, they defined wars primarily in terms of their fatalities, limiting these to battle deaths only. Interstate wars between two or more sovereign nations had to generate one thousand battle deaths of military personnel in order to be included in their list. Imperial and colonial wars between a sovereign nation and unrecognized or dependent entitites had to generate one thousand battle deaths per year of the military personnel of the sovereign nation involved. Imperial and colonial wars, taken together, were called extra-systemic wars in order to indicate that at least one of the parties was outside of the system of sovereign nations. Civil wars between governments and anti-governmental groups had to generate one thousand civilian and military battle deaths per year. Using these definitions, there were 67 interstate wars from the beginning of 1816 to the end of 1980 plus 51 extra-systemic wars, making 118 international wars plus 106 civil wars, so that there were 224 wars in all.

## International Wars

When several measures of international war were correlated with one another, they were all mildly correlated with one another, ranging from .03 to .51. Nation months, battle deaths, deaths/capita and deaths/nation months were most highly correlated with one another .39 to .51; population was least correlated with these war measures. International war frequencies did not differ significantly between the nineteenth and twentieth centuries (pp. 129–30), but nation months of war and battle deaths did increase, even when they were controlled for number of nations in the system; but all frequencies went down when controlled for number of nations, and extra-systemic months and deaths also went down. When smaller time periods were taken of 33 and 11 years each, the results showed no significant trends in frequencies, nation months or deaths (p. 141).

Using Poisson distributions and spectral analyses, no cycles were found in nation months of international war begun (p. 149), but there was the suggestion of a weak 28-year cycle for wars under way (p. 150), which became 14–21 years when the two world wars were omitted from the analyses (p. 156). No national cycles were found (p. 157). Seasonally, more international wars began in the spring or fall than in summer or winter (p. 161).

Using the 82 *nations* which had engaged in one or more international wars during this time period, the war measures were much more highly correlated with one another than when they had been correlated over the 118 international *wars* (p. 179). The top-ranked nations were all central to the system of sovereign nations, and most of them were major powers, leading to the conclusion that "most of the war in the system has been accounted for by a small fraction of the nations, most of which would be found near the top of any hierarchy based on diplomatic status, military-industrial capability, or related indicators. . . . [T]he top-ranked nations were compelled to fight often and at length either to maintain their position or to achieve it" (p. 180).

Winners of international wars suffered far fewer deaths than losers on average (p. 186), but 29 percent of them suffered more deaths than losers (p. 185). System members won extra-systemic wars (against non-members) 67 percent of the time (p. 188), but their battle deaths were not much greater when they lost than when they won. Most major powers won more than they lost, except for China (p. 192).

Initiators won 68 percent of the interstate wars they started (p. 195), and suffered fewer deaths than the "target" nations with about the same relative frequency. There seemed to be no relationship between battle deaths and war termination: "In brief, it would seem to take more than the systematic extinction of human lives to bring national governments to the conference table" (p. 201).

## Civil Wars

Following Richardson, Small and Singer considered "the violent taking of human life the primary and dominant characteristic of war" (p. 206). Like

Richardson, they emphasized the unreliability of death estimates, and they also emphasized the fact that these are *nothing but* estimates, and far from precise or exact counts. They required one thousand battle deaths per year on the average for their civil wars, as they did for their extra-systemic wars. But, unlike their international wars, civil war deaths included civilians as well as soldiers (p. 213).

Interveners on the side of the government in civil wars were on the winning side two-thirds of the time (p. 234). The United States, England and France were the top interveners, being engaged in more than one-half of all interventions during this time period, 1816–1980. The governments won two-thirds of all civil wars (p. 235), so that the insurgents of these wars won only one-third of them.

The war measures were correlated with one another across the 103 completed civil wars about the same as they were correlated across the 110 completed international wars: .08 to .48 (p. 243). But population was negatively correlated with these war measures, instead of being positively correlated as in international wars. However, population was least correlated ( −.34) with the war measures in this civil matrix even as it was in the international matrix (.28).

Twentieth century battle deaths were greater than those in the nineteenth century (p. 262), but there was no difference in nation months of war (p. 264), and there were no trends at all when the war measures were controlled for number of nations and pre-war populations (p. 266).

There were no cycles in civil wars begun (p. 269), but there was the suggestion of a 28-year cycle (and perhaps a 42-year cycle) in wars under way (p. 271). There were no seasonal variations in the beginning of civil wars (p. 272), which seemed to be wars for all seasons.

When the war measures were correlated across the 54 *nations* engaged in civil war during this time period, the correlations were again similar to those obtained across the 82 nations engaged in international wars, and much higher than those obtained across the 103 completed civil *wars* (p. 289).

## Conclusion

One hundred-eighteen international wars caused about 31 million combat deaths, or 2 million per decade (p. 293). There was no increasing trend in frequency, battle deaths, or nation months, when these measures were controlled by the number of nations in the system. There was the suggestion of a 15–20 year cycle in the amount of international war under way. Spring and fall were favorite seasons for starting international wars, particularly up to 1871. European nations were the most war-prone (p. 294). Losers suffered more battle deaths than winners in two-thirds of interstate wars. Initiators won almost 70 percent of interstate wars, and suffered fewer battle deaths 60 percent of the time.

One hundred-six civil wars caused nine million civilian and military battle deaths (p. 294). There was no increasing trend in any war measures when they were controlled by number of nations and pre-war populations. There was the suggestion of a 28-year cycle, and a weaker 42-year cycle.

In general, civil war patterns were remarkably similar to those of international wars (p. 295), and these patterns were generally similar to those reported by Richardson, Sorokin, Wright and others. These similarities were all the more remarkable considering the differences in these various lists of wars. When the number of wars present in any two lists was divided by the number in either of them, in order to provide a percentage measure of agreement, Singer and Small's (1972) list of 93 international wars agreed 40 percent with all 133 wars in Wright's list, 31.5 percent with all 97 wars in Sorokin's list, and 22.6 percent with all 289 wars in Richardson's list (1972 p. 79). These percentages might have been up to twice as high if Small and Singer's (1982) civil wars had been available in 1972, since the other three lists included civil as well as international wars.

## Comparison of War Lists

The six lists in Table 11.1 (including Westing) in Appendix B ranged from covering one century (the twentieth) to three centuries (eighteenth to twentieth). Consequently, all six lists are obviously not comparable to one another. However, the first two lists are comparable in this respect, since they covered all three centuries (when prorated). Likewise, the second three lists are comparable in this respect, since they covered the last two centuries (when prorated). Since Westing covered only the high-fatality wars of the twentieth century, his list would not be expected to be comparable to any other list in this table.

In addition to the lack of comparability in century coverage, there is another obvious lack of comparability in the definition of war shown in the last column in the top half of Table 11.1. Kaye et al. and Bouthoul and Carrere required no minimum number of deaths in order for a conflict to get into their lists.

Small and Singer's definition of war was somewhat similar to that of Dunnigan and Martel, but their one thousand deaths had to occur to military personnel only in international wars, and they had to occur in battle only in all wars. This definition of war reduced the number of wars which obtained entry to their list. Only Westing had a fewer number of wars, and that was obviously because of his higher requirement of 30,000 deaths before a war could get into his list.

The average length of a war should not have been influenced by the definition of a war, but these averages varied from 1.9 years for Small and Singer to 5.8 years for Dunnigan and Martel. There seems to be no correlation between definition and duration. What accounts for the variation in duration remains to be determined.

Those three authors, who looked for a relationship between starting and winning a war, generally agreed that starters won the wars that they started no more than about half of the time, as shown in Table 11.1. This reliable finding would suggest that it hardly paid to start a war, unless you could win from one war what it cost you to fight two wars. However, this half-and-half conclusion varied with types of wars. You could win about two-thirds to as much as three-quarters of the international and imperial wars that you started, but you were likely to lose the same proportion of civil and colonial wars that you started. The percentage of starters winning would seem to depend upon how well armed the starters were relative to their targets. The better armed starters were more likely to win, while the less well armed starters were more likely to lose.

European deaths constituted 59 percent of all battle deaths in Small and Singer's data. It would, of course, be possible to obtain rough estimates of the proportion of deaths in various world regions from all of these lists, and this should be done. In the meantime, this percentage suggests that Europe suffered more than other continents from the wars of the last two centuries. In addition, a survey of three lists of battles and one list of wars from about the fifteenth century B.C. to the twentieth century A.D., showed that the European percentage of these battles and wars ranged from 46 percent to 62 percent, but these percentages were much less during the last three centuries, especially those for war frequencies (Eckhardt 1989b).

The last three columns in the bottom half of Table 11.1 show the war deaths and frequencies by centuries, as well as the number of sovereign nations and the size of the world population. In spite of the differences in war frequencies and death estimates in Table 11.1, there is much less variation in the ratios between centuries in Table 11.2.

## Frequency Ratios

The frequency ratios between the nineteenth and twentieth centuries show no great difference between these ratios, ranging from 0.9 to 1.4 for the absolute frequencies. The ratios also show that war frequencies did not change very much from one century to the other, although there was some increase, except for Richardson. When these frequencies were controlled for the number of sovereign nations in the world (as shown in parentheses), assuming that more such nations make more wars possible (both between and within the greater number of sovereign nations), then the frequencies were cut in half, since there were about twice as many sovereign nations in the twentieth century as there were in the nineteenth. The same thing happened when the absolute frequencies were controlled for the size of the world population. While it may make some sense to control for the number of nations in evaluating the frequency of wars, it does not seem to make as much sense to control for the size of world population, since wars are made by nations, not by populations. More nations (or their political equivalents, that is, sovereign political entities) make more wars possible, but more people do not. People don't make war, their governments (or would-be governments) do. Just because governments do make wars, according to all of the definitions of war offered by the authors reviewed in this book, does not mean that they have to do so. They are authorized to do so, but not obligated, and certainly not compelled, to do so. Consequently, the fact that nations can and do make wars tells us nothing as to why they do so more often at some times compared with others, or why they do so at all.

Furthermore, there is a problem with the assumption that more nations make more wars. According to Tilly, there were about 500 independent political units in 1500, compared to about 25 in 1900 (referenced in Goldstein 1988, p. 284 note), but there were far fewer wars in the fifteenth century than there were in the nineteenth century. More generally, there were presumably far more sovereign entities in the Middle Ages under feudalism than in the modern period, but there were far more wars in modern times than there were in medieval times.

The second column of ratios in the top half of Table 11.2 shows the relations between frequencies in the eighteenth and nineteenth centuries. Here, both the absolute and relative frequencies show an increase from the eighteenth to the nineteenth centuries, but the relative increases for Bouthoul and Carrere's frequencies are no more than 1.5, which is not much.

Finally, so far as the war frequencies are concerned, the last column in the top half of Table 11.2 shows the ratios in the absolute and relative frequencies between the eighteenth and twentieth centuries. The absolute ratios range from 3.0 to 5.6, but the relative ratios do not amount to much. There can hardly be any question that war frequencies increased from the eighteenth to the nineteenth and twentieth centuries, but the increases from the nineteenth to the twentieth centuries did not amount to much.

Even though sovereign nations and world population doubled from the nineteenth to the twentieth centuries (the same as they did from the eighteenth to the nineteenth centuries), war frequencies did not double at all but increased by only 1.2 times, taking the average of the five authors' ratios. In short, doubling the nations and the peoples did not affect the number of wars very much at all, suggesting that the assumption that wars are determined by either nations or peoples may be false. It seems to be a reasonable assumption, but it does not work out in practice between the nineteenth and twentieth centuries. And when we look at the ratios between the eighteenth and nineteenth centuries, the war frequencies more than doubled (in the case of two authors out of three) even when they were controlled for both nations and peoples. To be sure, in the third case of Bouthoul and Carrere, the controls did reduce the ratio to no more than 1.5, which is not very impressive, although it is greater than one. It would seem that the negligible increase in war frequencies required no explanation from the nineteenth to the twentieth centuries, and the significant increase from the eighteenth to the nineteenth centuries was only about half accounted for by the increase in nations and peoples. It would not seem to be a very sound procedure to use explanatory variables in one case which were not required in the other.

## Death Ratios

The death ratios in the bottom half of Table 11.2 are much higher than the frequency ratios. On the average, these death ratios show that war-related deaths increased more than two times from century to century, even after controlling for sovereign nations and world population. The question remains whether these controls are necessary. While the number of sovereign nations makes the frequency of war more possible, it seems not to be the case that this number has anything to do with the number of war deaths. For example, during the Middle Ages, when there were many more sovereign political entities in the world than there are today, both war frequencies and war deaths were far less than they are today. Although the number of nations could increase the number of wars, they do not always do so, and there seems to be no reason why they should influence the number of war deaths.

Surely the size of the population can have an influence on the number of war deaths. At the very least, war deaths cannot exceed population. And, the more people there are, the more people there are to kill. But, the number of people hardly obligates, and never compels, anyone to kill them. Unlike the mountain that is climbed just because it is there, the number of people are seldom, if ever, killed just because they are there. The size of the population may set an upper limit on the number of potential war deaths, but it can hardly explain the actual number. And even if it could do so, the average death ratio at the bottom of Table 11.2 shows that it, like the number of sovereign nations, fails to do so, since even the controlled death ratios show that war deaths increased by three times from the eighteenth to the nineteenth centuries and by more than 2.5 times from the nineteenth to the twentieth centuries.

Finally, looking at the deaths per war in Table 11.3 in Appendix B, these figures enable us to evaluate the relative intensity of the average war in each century. The average deaths per war in the last row of this table for the twentieth century excluded Westing, since his high death requirement would naturally make his average death per war very high (close to two million deaths per high-fatality war). The average deaths per war then turned out to be 110,000 in the eighteenth century, 89,000 in the nineteenth century, and 446,000 in the twentieth century. The average war deaths in the twentieth century (highly influenced by the two world wars) was four times higher than that in the eighteenth century and five times that in the nineteenth century.

## Summary

Tables 11.2 and 11.3 show that war frequencies did not increase very much from the nineteenth to the twentieth centuries, but both of these centuries had about four times as many wars as the eighteenth century. Deaths per war did not change very much from the eighteenth to the nineteenth century, but they did go down a bit, only to rise greatly in the twentieth century. Total war deaths per century increased by almost five times from the eighteenth to the nineteenth century, and by 5.6 times from the nineteenth to the twentieth century. War deaths cannot be explained by war frequencies, nor by the number of sovereign nations, nor by the size of the world population during these three centuries.

# Chapter 12
# Civilized Battles
# Throughout History

## Introduction

Recorded battles do not go so far back as wars do, but they seem to be more comparable to one another than wars. For this reason, it seems desirable to look at several lists of battles in order to see whether these confirm or deny the results found in the lists of wars that were previously considered.

While some record of wars went back as far as 2000 B.C. (Kohn 1987) and even 3000 B.C. (Dupuy and Dupuy 1986), the recorded battles reviewed in this chapter went back no further than 1500 B.C., and not many of these took place before 500 B.C. The three sources of battles reviewed and analyzed in this chapter were Harbottle (1904, revised and updated by Bruce, 1981); Eggenberger (1967, revised in 1985); and Dupuy and Dupuy (1986).

## *Harbottle's* Dictionary of Battles *(1981)*

There were 2110 battles in Bruce's (1981) revision of Harbottle (1904), starting with Troy about 1100 B.C. All important battles of all major wars were included in this dictionary, but neither "important" nor "major" was defined. A battle was defined as "combat between larger or relatively large armed forces ... to include — where they are significant — sieges ... raids ... and relatively minor actions" (p. 7), when these latter contributed to main battles. Since World War II, Malaysia, Algeria, Congo, Biafra and others were omitted because they involved "guerrilla warfare without notable battles" (p. 7). Consequently, twentieth century frequencies were reduced by the amount of guerrilla warfare without notable battles, which was considerable after the Second World War.

## *Eggenberger's* Encyclopedia of Battles *(1985)*

First published in 1967, this encyclopedia was revised and updated by the author in 1985. According to the author, "this book attempts to provide the essential details of all the major battles in recorded history. It covers more than 1,560 separate and distinct military engagements, from the first battle of Megiddo in 1479 B.C. to the fighting in Vietnam in the 1960s" (p. iii), updated to Grenada in 1983 in the second edition. "In addition to entries for major battles there are about 150 brief entries that identify parts of larger battles.... Also included within the alphabetical arrangement are more than eighty entries for the major wars of the world, from the Persian-Greek wars to the Vietnam conflict" (p. iv).

The author defined a battle "as a confrontation between opposing armed forces that resulted in casualties or in a change in the military situation" (p. iv). This definition included some raids and sieges, either on account of their casualties (which were not specified) or on account of their military effect (the nature of which was not specified). According to this definition, there could be a battle without any casualties, as long as it had some military effect. "The need to broaden the definition of a battle has been highlighted by warfare in the twentieth century in which entire countries became a single battlefield and the military action was sustained over a period of weeks or even months.... The struggle for the Soviet Union [1941–1944], a contest spread over thousands of miles and lasting three years, has been rightly called history's greatest continuous land battle" (p. iv). Clearly, this definition would reduce the number of battles in the twentieth century.

## *Dupuy and Dupuy's* Encyclopedia of Military History *(1986)*

This monumental work of 1524 pages is a military history from 3500 B.C. to A.D. 1983, and even into early 1984. Although the means and techniques of war have changed through the ages, the purpose of war has remained the same, according to these authors, and that purpose is to force one's will upon others. As military historians, their own purpose was "to provide a reliable, relatively complete, and authoritative reference work covering the entire sweep of world military history" (p. xiii). They have probably succeeded in this purpose more than anyone else has at the present time. At the same time, these authors were well aware of the difficulties of their task: "No work which deals with the activities of men of all nations and all parts of the world since the dawn of history can hope to be either completely accurate or totally comprehensive.... In many instances, we have been forced to choose among amazingly diverse and conflicting accounts of a single event, guided by common sense and the most objective possible evaluation of the sources.... Finally, no historical work can include everything about anything" (pp. xiii–xiv). In spite of these difficulties and problems, the authors "tried to include everything of significance in world military history. Unfortunately, significance is not only subjective; it can change from time to time and from circumstance to circumstance" (p. xiv). As these authors clearly recognized, historical "significance" is far from being a constant, consistent and reliable criterion.

## Analyses of Harbottle's Battles

Table 12.1 in Appendix B shows the distribution of Harbottle's battles over geographical space and historical time. The first battle (the siege of Troy) occurred in the Middle East (Turkey) in the twelfth century B.C. Harbottle and Bruce found only five battles prior to the fifth century B.C., at which time battles increased in frequency, especially in Europe during the five centuries when the Greek city-states and the Roman Republic were most active and most civilized. The last column shows that the majority of battles (62 percent of the total 2110) occurred in Europe.

Only five of the 32 centuries showed less than 50 percent of these battles occurring in Europe: the twelfth B.C., sixth B.C., seventh A.D., twelfth and the nineteenth. The mean frequency of European battles was not significantly higher than that of non–European battles (that is, battles occurring outside of Europe), when both sets of frequencies were logged to correct for the skewness of their distributions. However, the total number of battles occurring in Europe was significantly greater than that of all other geographical regions added together.

The correlation between European and non–European frequencies over these 32 centuries was .79, significant at the .01 level of confidence, which simply means that a correlation as high as this would be expected by chance less than one time out of one hundred. This correlation means that the *relative* frequency of non–European battles over these centuries was quite as reliable as that of European battles. This, in turn, means that the total frequency over these centuries is a generally reliable measure of the *pattern* of battle frequencies, although it may not be a reliable measure of the *level* of these frequencies, which may be much higher than those recorded by Harbottle (1904) and Bruce (1981).

This conclusion was further confirmed by the correlation between the European percentage of battles and these 32 centuries, which was .33. This correlation was not significant at the .05 level of confidence, which means that a correlation as high as this could have occurred by chance more than five times out of one hundred. Even if it had been significant, a correlation of .33 would mean that only 11 percent of the variance was shared in common by these two variables: European percentage of battles and centuries. This finding means that the *percentage* of battles occurring in Europe increased over these centuries but not by a large amount.

Since the *pattern* (or relative frequency) of these 2110 battles over these 32 centuries seems to be fairly reliable, holding outside of Europe as well as inside Europe, the correlation between the total frequencies (logged) and these centuries should be a fairly reliable measure of how much these battle frequencies were increasing or decreasing over these centuries. The correlation was .82 (accounting for 67 percent of their common variance), suggesting that battles worldwide were generally and significantly and exponentially increasing in frequency in the course of these 32 centuries — in spite of the reduced frequency of battles in the twentieth century in this data set, presumed to be caused by the number of guerrilla wars without any "notable battles."

Neither Harbottle (1904) nor Bruce (1981) provided enough death estimates to use these as an estimate of the intensity of these battles during this time period. Battle frequencies themselves might provide such a measure of intensity, since battles are usually of short duration, often a day or two, so that they are more likely to be roughly equivalent to one another than wars are. Consequently, the number of battles in a war or in a century may provide an adequate measure of intensity, if battle frequency and war intensity can be shown to be significantly related to each other.

In order to determine if this was the case, I correlated the number of battles per war with the number of deaths per war. When I did this for Wright's (1965) battles during the last five hundred years and Levy's (1983) death estimates during the same time, I found a correlation of .69 (significant at the .0001 level of confidence) between Wright's battles per war and Levy's deaths per war over 74 wars. When I repeated this operation for Wright's battles per war and Sorokin's (1937) casualties per war, the correlation was .79 over 65 wars. These correlations suggested that battle frequency per war or per century may be taken as a rough measure of war's intensity whenever death estimates are unavailable, which is often the case prior to the last two or three centuries.

Although these correlations are of some help, they are limited to the modern period, and may not apply to previous historical periods. The only systematic estimate of intensity available prior to the modern period is Sorokin's (1937, vol. 3) war casualty estimates for nine major European nations from 500 B.C. to A.D. 500, and then from 900 to 1925. Although these estimates may not be the best, they are the only ones that we have. When I correlated Harbottle's battles per century with Sorokin's casualties per century over these 21 centuries, the correlation was .79 (significant at the .01 level of confidence), suggesting that the battle frequencies since 500 B.C. would provide at least a rough measure of war's intensity over these centuries.

To be sure, I have correlated *European* war casualty estimates with *world* battle frequencies, but we have already noted that Europe was highly correlated with the world in this respect. However, in order to provide a more positive check, I correlated with Harbottle's European battle frequencies, in which case the correlation was still .79, so that this correlation seems to be fairly reliable, holding for Europe as well as for the world over these 21 centuries.

It should be noted that this significant correlation was obtained in spite of the fact that Sorokin's casualty estimates for the twentieth century (when multiplied by four to prorate them for the entire century) were very high, while Harbottle's (Bruce 1981) twentieth century battle frequencies were very low. Consequently, this correlation is a conservative estimate of the relation between battle frequencies and war casualties over this time period, 500 B.C. to A.D. 500 and 900 to 2000.

These correlations would suggest that not only were battles increasing in their frequency from 1200 B.C. to A.D. 2000 (if we assume that the correlation would be similar if casualty estimates had been available back to 1200 B.C.), but that wars were also increasing in their intensity over this period.

## Analyses of Eggenberger's Battles

Although Eggenberger updated his 1967 edition in 1985, this later edition added only seven *wars* and no *battles*, so that the data in this chapter are based on his 1967 data, which included over 1560 battles from 1479 B.C. to A.D. 1966. Table 12.2 in Appendix B shows almost 1900 battles because I included every entry, including about 150 partial battles, more than 80 major wars and dozens of country entries. For the sake of greater accuracy, only the battles should have been included, since these duplications may have increased the European frequencies. However, they have probably not changed the *pattern* of frequencies over the centuries.

Eggenberger found Jerusalem to be the location of nine battles: "the most fought-over place in the world" (p. iv). Next came Adrianople (Turkey), Constantinople, and Rome, with seven battles each; then Warsaw, with six battles; Pavia (Italy), with five; and Alexandria, Baghdad, Paris, Prague, and Ravenna (Italy), with four battles each. These "most fought-over places" were fought over more frequently in Europe than the Middle East.

The first battle in Table 12.2 occurred at Megiddo in Palestine, 1479 B.C. (according to Eggenberger's dating of this battle). The first 12 battles which occurred before the fifth century B.C. all occurred in the Middle East, and none in Europe. From the fifth century B.C. onward, Europe predominated over the rest of the world except in the third, seventh, twelfth and nineteenth centuries, which was somewhat similar to Harbottle's distribution in this respect.

The last column in Table 12.2 shows that 59 percent of all battles occurred in Europe, which was similar to Harbottle's 62 percent, although both of these percentages could have differed from 50 percent simply by chance. Since Eggenberger provided a list of sources which did not include Harbottle, I wrote to inquire about this, in order to determine whether Eggenberger's list was independent of Harbottle's or not. Eggenberger replied that he knew of Harbottle's book and that he had a copy of it in his library, but he did not refer to it because there was some information in it that he could not verify and some that was overturned by research findings since 1904. He was apparently unaware of Bruce's revised and updated versions. It seems reasonable to assume that Eggenberger's list of battles was independent of Harbottle's list.

In spite of getting off to a late start, Europe's mean battle frequency over these 35 centuries was higher than that of non–Europeans, but this difference was not statistically significant, so that the difference could have occurred by chance, as in the case of Harbottle's difference.

The correlaton between European and non–European battles over these 35 centuries was .79, which was the same as Harbottle's correlation over 32 centuries, so that the historical pattern of battle frequencies for these two regions shared 62 percent of their variance in common in both of these data sets. Consequently, any Eurocentric bias in these data did not prevent the non–European pattern from being similar to the European pattern.

In spite of the similarity of *pattern* between Europe and non–Europe, the European *percentage* of battles was significantly increasing over these centuries, the correlation between these percentages and the centuries being .67, which was different from the nonsignificant finding in Harbottle's European percentages. This was probably due to the complete absence of any European battles during the first ten centuries of Eggenberger's time period as shown in Table 12.2.

When Eggenberger's total battle frequencies (logged) were correlated with his 35 centuries, the correlation was .89, which indicated a significant and exponential increase in worldwide battles over these centuries. This correlation was somewhat higher than that found for Harbottle, because Eggenberger's battles did not diminish in the twentieth century as much as Harbottle's did. Consequently, time alone could account for 80 percent of the variance in Eggenberger's battles over these centuries. Of course, "time alone" includes whatever else happened during that time, such as increasing civilization, increasing imperial sizes, increasing population, increased numbers of sovereign nations, improvements in communication, transportation and lethality of weapons, etc. Eventually, all of these variables (and many more besides) have to be taken into account in order to explain the increasing frequency of battles over these centuries.

Finally, the question has to be raised as to whether Eggenberger's battle frequencies may be taken as a measure of war's intensity, whenever war casualties or fatalities are unavailable for this purpose. In order to determine this, Eggenberger's worldwide frequencies and European frequencies (both logged to correct for skewness) were correlated with Sorokin's European casualties of war from 500 B.C. to A.D. 500 and from 900 to 2000 (also logged to correct for skewness). The results were remarkably similar to those obtained for Harbottle's battles. The correlation was .81 between Eggenberger's worldwide battles per century and Sorokin's European war casualties per century, and the correlation was .79 between Eggenberger's European battles per century and Sorokin's European war casualties per century. These results from the analyses of both Harbottle's and Eggenberger's battle frequencies, taken together, suggest a fairly reliable conclusion that, indeed, battle frequencies per century may be used as a measure of war intensity whenever casualty or fatality estimates are unavailable. Whenever such estimates are available, they would, of course, be preferred as a more positive measure of war intensity.

When Eggenberger's battles per war were correlated with Sorokin's casualties per war, the correlation was .63 (significant at the .01 level of confidence) across 83 wars that occurred from 499 B.C. to A.D. 1918. Although this correlation was lower than that found between Wright's battles per war in modern times with both Sorokin's casualties and Levy's deaths per war in modern times, it was significant, showing that battles per war, as well as battles per century, were at least a fair indicator of war's intensity since 500 B.C. as well as in modern times.

## Analyses of the Dupuys' Battle Frequencies

The Dupuys referred to both Eggenberger and Harbottle in their general bibliography. However, the fact that their index of battles contained more than twice as many battles as either of the previous authors would suggest that their survey of military history was more comprehensive than those previous efforts. Like Eggenberger, the Dupuys started with the Battle of Megiddo, which they dated 1469 B.C., and which they claimed to be the "first recorded battle of history" (Dupuy and Dupuy 1986, p. 6). Whatever military encounters occurred before this date were presumably too fuzzy to be called a battle, although none of the authors reviewed in this book defined a battle very precisely. When I requested a definition of "battle" and "war" from Trevor Dupuy, I received no reply, although he had been kind enough to reply to an earlier inquiry.

Out of 4460 battles and sieges that I counted in their index, only 15 (or one-third of 1 percent) occurred before the fifth century B.C., so that even this most comprehensive military history failed to find many battles prior to this time. Although it found more than Harbottle (less than one-fourth of 1 percent), it found less than Eggenberger (six-tenths of 1 percent). The average of these three would indicate that less than four-tenths of 1 percent of all recorded battles occurred prior to the fifth century B.C., suggesting that battles did not amount to much prior to this time. This cannot be a function of Eurocentricity, since all of the battles so recorded occurred in the Middle East prior to the eight century B.C., and only one of them (Troy) involved Europeans. To be sure, Europe was not the only geographical region short of battles prior to the fifth century B.C., since there were none in any region other than the Middle East, the scene of historical action in the archaic and ancient periods of world history. Even so, the few battles recorded prior to the fifth century B.C. would suggest that archaic and ancient history was not characterized by a high level of military intensity.

The last column of Table 12.3 in Appendix B shows that 52 percent of this sample of the Dupuys' battles occurred in Europe, suggesting that their data were less Eurocentric than those of Harbottle (62 percent) and Eggenberger (59 percent). For this reason, in addition to their greater frequency, the Dupuys' battles would be recommended as the most reliable data base for the study of battles.

Although on average battles occurred in Europe more frequently than in the rest of the world during the 35 centuries in this sample (which constituted about one-half the Dupuys' total battles and sieges), this difference was not significant and could have occurred by chance.

The correlation between European and non–European battles in this sample over these 35 centuries was .85, suggesting that the European and non–European patterns were very similar to each other, as was the case with both Harbottle and Eggenberger.

The European percentage of battles increased over these 35 centuries (r = .56\*\*), but so did the non–European percentage (r = .43\*\*), since both had 0 percent in this *sample* during the first eight centuries from 1500 to 700 B.C.

When the *total* battle frequencies (N = 4460) were correlated over these centuries, the correlation was .93, which was higher than either Harbottle (.82) or Eggenberger (.89), but not by much. The adequacy of the sample of the Dupuys' battles used in this section was shown by the fact that the correlation between this sample of battles and these 35 centuries was .92. These three separate data sets, taken together, provide a very reliable measure of the significant and exponential increase in battles over these centuries. They also suggest quite strongly that battles occurred very infrequently, if at all, prior to the fifteenth century B.C., and not much more frequently prior to the fifth century B.C. The relations between these three sets of battle frequencies over the last 35 centuries are shown graphically in Figure 12.1.

Finally, we want to know if the Dupuys' battle frequencies can be used as a measure of war intensity, when more positive measures of casualties or fatalities are not available. In order to determine this, I correlated the Dupuys' total battle frequencies with Sorokin's war casualties over those 21 centuries for which the latter were available. The Dupuys' total frequencies were correlated with Sorokin's casualties .76, and the sample of their European frequencies were correlated with Sorokin's casualties (all of which were European) .78, so that the total frequencies represented the European frequencies adequately enough, and both correlations showed that battle frequencies were highly correlated with war intensities, so that they may be used as a measure of the same in the absence of casualty or fatality estimates.

## Summary

All three sets of battle frequencies, which were relatively independent of one another, showed that recorded battles did not amount to much prior to the fifth century B.C., and did not amount to anything at all prior to the fifteenth century B.C., as shown in Table 12.4 in Appendix B. So far as history has generally been a history of war, these findings would suggest, however tentatively, that history may not have begun very much before 500 B.C. At that time European civilizations developed rapidly and tended to predominate over the rest of the world in the number of battles located in its region. In addition, Europe also took part in some one-third of the battles located in the rest of the world. Consequently, Europe was the warmaker par excellence so far as recorded battles are concerned. It remains to be determined how much this reflected human history in its entirety and how much it reflected the Eurocentricity of human history as we know it.

# Figure 12.1   Battle Frequencies,
# 1500 B.C. to A.D. 2000

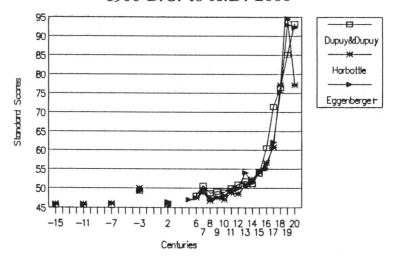

Notes to Figure 12.1: Dupuy and Dupuy = The frequency of battles per century was obtained from the Index of Battles and Sieges in Dupuy and Dupuy (1986, pp. 1500–15). Harbottle = The frequency of battles per century was obtained from Harbottle (Bruce, 1981). Eggenberger = The frequency of battles per century was obtained from Eggenberger (1985). All three sets of frequencies were standardized to a mean of 50 and a standard deviaton of 10, in order to make them comparable to one another.

Two of the most consistent and outstanding findings from the analyses of these three data sets were similar to those that emerged from the analyses of the three lists of wars in Chapter 10: (1) There were no recorded battles before 1500 B.C., and (2) thereafter Europe was the location of at least half of these battles during the time period.

Concerning (1), the burning question is the same as that in Chapter 10: Were there battles prior to this time that were not recorded, nor recorded clearly, or were there simply no battles worth recording? Since historians have tended to record battles whenever there was a shred of evidence of their occurrence, I assume that the battles prior to 1500 B.C. were not worth recording, or else they would have been recorded.

The military historians, Dupuy and Dupuy, had this to say about the virtual equivalence of history and war: "The ancient history which began with Bronze Age cultures is known to us largely in the terms of military history. The record is almost entirely devoted to migrations, wars and conquests. Not until about 1500 B.C., however, are we able to visualize the actual course of any of the constant wars of the Middle East, or dimly to perceive primitive military

# Figure 12.2   Region % Battles, 1500 B.C. to A.D. 2000

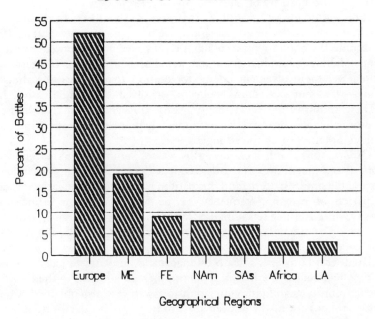

Notes to Figure 12.2: This regional distribution of battles was based on the sample of the Dupuys'
battles, as shown in Table 12.3, whose notes provide some further information on this sample of 2451 battles. Europe = Europe, including the USSR. ME = Middle East, including
North Africa. FE = Far East, including Southeast Asia. NAm = North America, including
Canada and the United States. SAs = South Asia, including India and Pakistan. Africa =
Sub-Saharan Africa, including South Africa. LA = Latin America, including the Caribbean
and Central America.

---

organization and methods of combat. By the sixth century B.C. relatively comprehensive and more or less continuous records of war become available" (1986,
p. 1).

Before leaving this first point of interest, it might be worth reiterating the
suggestion that civilization and war may not have begun as early as conventional chronology would have it. Dayton (1978) found many contradictons in
conventional chronology. Heinsohn (1988) has provided evidence for the up-
dating of the beginning of civilization. And Wescott (1989) has presented
arguments to the effect that civilization may have begun much later than we
think. The statistical evidence presented in this chapter is consistent with the
arguments and evidence put forth by these authors.

Concerning point (2), the burning question is this: Does the relative frequency of battles located in Europe, not to mention those involving Europe but located outside of Europe, reflect the "reality" of events or does it merely reflect the Eurocentricity of European historians?

If our historians were unduly Eurocentric, we should expect them to find more European battles in archaic and ancient times. On the contrary, they found quite the opposite prior to 500 B.C. On average, there were five times as many Middle Eastern battles as there were European battles. This ratio held almost as well for involvement as it did for location: in only one case — the siege of Troy — was a European entity — Greece — involved in a Middle Eastern battle. These findings argue very strongly against Eurocentricity in this set of battles, especially in archaic and ancient times when one might expect the Eurocentric temptation to be the strongest.

Other points worth mentioning by way of summary are the following: European and non–European battle frequencies over these centuries followed a remarkably similar pattern, and this pattern was one of exponential increase. This pattern of increasing frequency may be taken as a pattern of increasing intensity, since all three sets of battle frequencies were significantly correlated with Sorokin's estimates of war casualties from 500 B.C. to A.D. 500 and from 900 to 2000. In addition, Wright's modern battle frequencies were significantly associated with both Levy's death estimates and Sorokin's casualty estimates over nine half-century periods in modern times. In addition to these correlations per century, significant correlations per war were also obtained. Consequently, although it might be premature to try to predict deaths from battles with any precision, a preliminary attempt in this direction will be made in the next chapter.

Europe was the location of at least one-half the battles since 1500 B.C. If these findings are reliable, and if they are not due to Eurocentricity, they raise at least two crucial questions for further research. What is it about Europe and or Europeans that has made Europe the location of so many battles and wars? What is it about Europeans that have made them the most warlike group of people in human history?

The regional distribution of a sample of the Dupuys' battles (N = 2451) is shown graphically in Figure 12.2.

## Chapter 13
# War-Related Deaths Since 3000 B.C.

## Previous Estimates

In order to estimate the number of war-related deaths since 3600 B.C., Beer (1974) extrapolated Singer and Small's (1972) 29 million military battle deaths for international wars, 1816–1965, to 1.1 billion battle deaths for all of history. When Bouthoul and Carrere's (1978) 85 million civilian and military deaths for all wars, 1740–1974, were extrapolated by Beer (1981), this resulted in about two billion deaths for all wars, from 3600 B.C. to A.D. 1974. Both of these estimates were obtained without taking any possible trends into account. In other words, Beer made the simplifying assumption that war-related deaths were of the same intensity throughout historical time.

## Present Effort

In this chapter I have tried to take possible trends into account. I started with my list of wars and related deaths for 1500–1990 (Sivard 1990), where a war was defined as "any armed conflict, involving at least one government, and causing at least one thousand civilian and military deaths per year," as discussed in Chapter 9. These deaths included those from famine and disease where these were war-related. This list provided death estimates for the last five centuries. The twentieth century estimate was prorated by using the death estimates since 1945 to arrive at an estimate for the last decade of the century, which was added to those estimates up to 1990.

The only systematic estimates available for 500 B.C. to A.D. 1500 are those of Sorokin (1937, vol. 3) for nine major European nations only. In order to convert these to worldwide estimates, the following procedure was followed. Sorokin's European casualty estimates for each of these centuries was divided by the number of European battles per century, which were obtained from Dupuy and Dupuy (1986). These European casualties per battle were then multiplied by all of the Dupuys' battles, in order to provide an estimate of worldwide casualties for these centuries. Since Sorokin had no casualty estimates for the Dark Ages, 500–900, I filled these centuries in with a liberal estimate of three thousand casualties per battle, which was higher than the average for the late Middle Ages, 1000–1500.

In order to estimate the casualties before 500 B.C., I should have liked to use the mean casualties per battle in the late Middle Ages, 1000–1500, but there were *no* recorded battles prior to 1500 B.C., and not many prior to 500 B.C., as noted in the previous chapter. Since there were some rough estimates of the number of wars back to 3000 B.C., which I obtained from Dupuy and Dupuy, I multiplied these wars by the number of casualties per war in the late Middle Ages, which was three thousand. It seemed reasonable to assume that archaic and ancient wars were no more violent than late medieval wars on average, and probably less violent than those of the classic period of history, 500 B.C.–A.D. 500.

Finally, I checked these death estimates against those which the Dupuys (1986) and Kohn (1987) provided for some of their battles and wars. I settled for the highest estimate per century so that the earlier centuries would not be underestimated. I also equated the casualties with deaths, so as not to underestimate the earlier centuries.

The result of these procedures is shown in Table 13.1 in Appendix B, where the death estimates are given in thousands. In the column next to them, the percentage of deaths estimated for each century is shown. Population estimates were obtained from McEvedy and Jones (1978) in order to see how much of the increases in deaths could be explained by population growth. The number of wars were obtained from the Dupuys (1986).

According to these procedures the total number of war-related deaths since 3000 B.C. was more than 150 million, as shown in Table 13.1. Since approximately 40 billion people have lived since about 3000 B.C. (Westing 1981), and since about 5 billion of us are still alive, that leaves 35 billion deaths during this time, 150 million (or 0.4 percent) of which were caused by war.

Each of the centuries prior to the sixteenth accounted for less than 1 percent of all war deaths. In fact all of them added together accounted for little more than 4 percent of these deaths, while almost 96 percent of war deaths were estimated to occur in the modern period of history, 1500–2000. Little more than one-tenth of 1 percent occurred during the archaic and ancient periods of history, 3000–500 B.C., 1.6 percent of them occurred during the Middle Ages, and 2.4 percent of them occurred during the classic period of history. Within the modern period, the twentieth century stands out, accounting for 73 percent of total deaths, followed by the nineteenth century accounting for 13 percent.

Judging from these estimates, as crude as they are, and as subject to change as they must be by further research, war-related deaths have been increasing over the last 50 centuries. When death estimates were divided by population estimates, this measure was significantly correlated with centuries, so that population growth alone could not explain the increase in war deaths over these 50 centuries. In other words, war-related deaths were increasing significantly faster than population growth.

When the estimated deaths were divided by the war frequencies, there was a significant correlation between this measure and centuries. According to this correlation, not only was war-related violence increasing over this time period, but the violence *per* war was also increasing. In other words, the increase in war deaths over these centuries could not be explained by the increasing frequency of wars alone, since war deaths were increasing faster than war frequencies.

Looking at modern times, where the estimates were more reliable than they were for earlier times, war deaths rose from the sixteenth to the twentieth century. This finding was consistent with previous findings based on the modern death estimates of seven other authors (Eckhardt 1990a). War frequencies, on the other hand, did not change very much from century to century during the modern period. Deaths per population and deaths per war both increased as a general rule over these five centuries.

## Summary and Tentative Conclusions

This has to be considered a very preliminary study indeed. It is at the most no more than a first approximation of estimates that may be changed considerably by further research. At the least it may provide a motive for others to develop these measures to a greater degree of sophistication than I have done so far.

Until then, these results suggest that 73 percent of all war-related deaths since 3000 B.C. have occurred in the twentieth century A.D., prorating the data up to the end of the century. Another 23 percent occurred from 1500 to 1900, so that the modern period of history accounted for 96 percent of all war-related deaths. The Middle Ages accounted for 1.6 percent, while the classic period accounted for 2.4 percent, so that between them, from 500 B.C. to A.D. 1500 (2000 years), they accounted for 4 percent of all war-related deaths, leaving the archaic and ancient periods of history from 3000 B.C. to 500 B.C. (2500 years) to account for little more than one-tenth of 1 percent of all war-related deaths. Even the sixteenth century accounted for only 1 percent; the seventeenth century, 4 percent; the eighteenth century, 4.6 percent; and nineteenth century, almost 13 percent. War had to wait for the twentieth century to do the overwhelming proportion of its damage in human history, primarily in the two world wars which accounted for more than half of all twentieth century deaths.

Regionally, I found that about one-half of all battles and wars since 3000 B.C. occurred in Europe, suggesting that about one-half of all war-related deaths may have occurred in Europe, since battle and war frequencies over these centuries were highly correlated with Sorokin's war casualties (Eckhardt 1990b). For this chapter, I obtained the European war-related deaths in modern times, and compared them with the total deaths presented by six authors, and obtained the following European percentages for various time periods: 67 percent for Eckhardt's worldwide death estimates for civilians and soldiers, 1700–1987 and 1500–1990 (Sivard 1987, 1990); 56 percent the world-wide estimates (civilians and soldiers) of Kaye et al. (1985) for 1720–1985; 59 percent for Bouthoul and Carrere's (1974) worldwide death estimates for civilians and soldiers, 1740–1974; 79 percent for Richardson's (1960a) world-wide death estimates for civilians and soldiers, 1820–1952; 62 percent for Small and Singer's (1982) worldwide death estimates for civilians and soldiers in the civil wars of sovereign nations and for soldiers only in the international wars of sovereign nations, 1816–1980; and 66 percent for Westing's (1982) world-wide death estimates for civilians and soldiers in high-fatality wars of the twentieth century.

If we take the simple average of these six percentages, then 65 percent of all war-related deaths in modern times were European. This is a very crude estimate indeed. It included the deaths of Turks in Europe, but this was balanced by the omission of European deaths in Africa, Asia and Latin America. Modern estimates are presumably more reliable than previous estimates, so that my estimate of one-half of all war-related deaths occurring in Europe, based on battle and war frequencies, was probably too conservative.

According to these findings, European places and modern times were the most violent places and times in human history. This raises a question about the reliability of these estimates. How much were they biased by the Eurocentricity and moderncentricity of authors who were American, British and French living in the twentieth century? I have argued elsewhere (Eckhardt 1990b) why I believe that they were not unduly biased, because our historians and other scholars have always given the Middle East, *not* Europe, priority in making civilizations, empires and wars in archaic and ancient times. If they had wanted to be biased, or if they could not help themselves from being so, surely their bias would have been expressed in their treatment of archaic and ancient data, but it was not.

How, then, can we explain the violence of Europe and modern times? I have argued elsewhere (Eckhardt 1989b) that civilizations, empires and wars have grown together in a dialectical evolutionary manner, feeding into one another in such a way as to promote one another in a process which tends to obstruct its own progress in the short run at regional levels of analysis (characterized by the rise and fall of particular civilizations), but which has grown exponentially in the long run at the global level of analysis (characterized by world civilization). Modern times, and especially the twentieth century, have built upon past times, and modern space-time has found its focus in modern Europe, which has been the most civilized and imperial society in human history. Hence, modern Europe has been the most violent society in human history.

However, European violence may be in the process of obstructing its own progress since the end of the Second World War. Relatively few war-related deaths have occurred in Europe since that time. There have been 176,000 such deaths, which was less than 1 percent of the total 22 million war-related deaths from 1945 to 1989 (Sivard 1989; Wood 1990). On the basis of data such as

# Figure 13.1 War-Related Deaths, 3000 B.C. to A.D. 2000

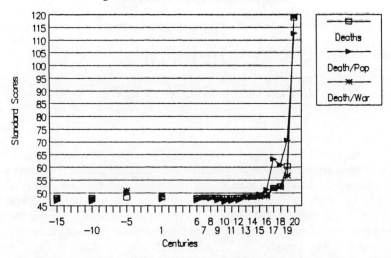

Notes to Figure 13.1: Deaths = Eckhardt's (Sivard, 1990) death estimates from 1500 to 1990. Death estimates prior to 1500 were based on Sorokin's (1937, vol. 3) casualty estimates and the Dupuys' (1986) battle frequencies. Deaths/Pop = Deaths per population = Deaths divided by McEvedy and Jones (1978) population estimates. Deaths/War = Deaths divided by war frequencies (Kohn, 1987).

---

this, Melko (1990) has argued not only for peace in our time (in Europe), but for the possibility of this European peace going on for another century or so. We shall have to wait and see about that.

In the meantime, what does peace in the space-time of late twentieth century Europe do to my dialectical evolutionary theory of civilizations, empires and wars? Surely, Europe has not de-civilized itself, but it has gone a long way toward de-colonizing itself, voluntarily or involuntarily, as the case might be. My dialectical evolutionary theory did include the possibility of civilization without war if civilization could shed itself of imperialism, dominance and exploitation (Eckhardt 1990a). Perhaps Europe is in the process of becoming nonviolent in spite of itself. And if Europe can do it, why not a world civilization without war? We have nothing to lose but our empires, which the Soviet Union is even now in the process of shedding.

*Chapter 14*
# A Dialectical Evolutionary Theory

*A Brief Review*

The general argument of this book has been that civilizations, empires and wars emerged out of the agricultural revolution, prior to which primitive peoples had little or nothing to fight for, nothing much to fight with and no surplus to pay for the fighting. Those tribes that gradually moved out of gathering and hunting into farming and herding about ten thousand years ago developed a vested interest in the land, which gave them something to fight for. Their wars did not amount to much, however, because their weapons were still primitive, and they had little surplus with which to pay for the fighting. Those who made some small gains at the expense of others, including by the making of slaves, began to build up a small surplus that enabled them to spend a little more on soldiers and weapons, which made them more successful in war and more prosperous in peace. The more warlike tribes gradually became bigger through the conquest of others and their territory.

Eventually they acquired enough land, labor and capital so that they had to keep accounts, leading to the development of literacy among some of their rulers, of central headquarters (temples, etc.) where scribes did their clerical and accounting work, and of the beginnings of the military sophistication needed to maintain and expand their war-gotten gains. This stage of development in the dialectical evolutionary process happened about five thousand years ago and came to be called civilization, which led to empires (civilizations seeking to expand), when warfare really started to come into its own. The process was very gradual or evolutionary, as well as dialectical — feeding back and forth from civilization to empire to war.

It was still a long time before there was enough surplus to support permanent standing armies, which did not come into being until the sixteenth century B.C. Even then, the level of military activity remained relatively low for another thousand years, with no more than three or four wars per century being recorded, and seldom more than one or two notable battles per century, often none at all. War made a great leap about 500 B.C., as did civilizations and empires, followed by another great leap in modern times and yet another in the

178

twentieth century, so that today we have never been so civilized nor so warlike. This is a very general theory of the development of war and civilization, which does not deny that some primitive and civilized peoples have been more peaceful than others, but this relative peacefulness may be more effectively studied in the framework of the general theory. Some evidence to support this theory has been presented, but this evidence will be abbreviated and consolidated in this chapter. More research (as always) needs to be done.

## The Theory

A "dialectical evolutionary theory" is a rather high-sounding phrase for a rather simple and straightforward notion, as presented in Eckhardt (1991). The theory tries to relate the concepts of civilization, empire and war to one another in such a way that their interaction results in positive feedback loops leading them upward and onward in a spiraling motion, until the interaction leads them in the opposite direction by way of negative feedback loops. The theory is especially interested in what determines which direction these loops take. This special part of the theory will be discussed later in this chapter in a section on power, after we focus on the more general relatons among civilizations, empires and wars.

In order to establish the relationships among civilizations, empires and wars, we had to find ways of measuring these variables. Then it was simple enough to correlate these measurements with one another, and to find out how they varied together, if at all. We shall review these measurements here and then proceed to their correlations.

## Measuring Civilizations

Both Kroeber (1944) and Sorokin (1941) provided a means of measuring civilization. Their methods were similar in that they both counted the number of (mostly) men who had engaged in civilized or cultural activities sufficiently to get themselves recognized in encyclopedias and textbooks for the quality of their accomplishments. Kroeber was more selective than Sorokin, counting only "geniuses," which he defined as "superior individuals" (pp. 7–8), whose superiority was established by the consensus of encyclopedia and textbook authors (p. 23). Their activities included philosophy, science, grammar (philology), sculpture, painting, drama and literature. These activites were noted for the period from 3000 B.C. to A.D. 1900 in five civilizations: the Middle East (Egypt, Mesopotamia and Islam), the Far East (China and Japan), south Asia (mainly India), Greece and Rome, and the West (Europe).

Kroeber did not actually count these individuals, but he did identify them, making it possible to get a rough count for various regions at various times. I sorted Kroeber's seven cultural activities over the 49 centuries from

3000 B.C. to A.D. 1900, logged them to correct for skewness, and then correlated them with one another. All of the correlations were significant at the .01 level of confidence, ranging from .43 between grammar and drama to .89 between painting and sculpture. They were all significantly correlated with time (as measured by centuries) from .64 (grammar) to .92 (literature), so that the number of "geniuses" in the world (as represented by the geographical regions of Europe, the Far East, India and the Middle East) were increasing exponentially over these 49 centuries. When this correlation matrix was factor-analyzed, a single factor emerged: literature (.95), century (.92), science (.92), sculpture (.89), painting (.86), philosophy (.85), drama (.80) and grammar (.75). Factor scores could be generated to provide a measure of world civilization, but the simple sum of the seven activities (as measured by the number of "geniuses") will be adequate for the time being.

This sum was used to measure the rise and fall of civilizations in the four geographical regions of the world: Europe (including Greece and Rome), India, the Far East (China and Japan) and the Middle East (Egypt, Mesopotamia and Islam). These four (logged) regions were significantly correlated with one another over these 49 centuries, except for Europe with the Middle East. They were all significantly correlated with time, but the Middle Eastern correlation was significant only at the .10 level of confidence. When this correlation matrix was factor-analyzed, two factors were generated, the first of which was: the Far East (.98), century (.96), India (.88), Europe (.84) and the Middle East (.29). The low loading of the Middle East on this factor shows that its pattern of rising and falling civilized activities ("geniuses") was not so correlated with time (centuries) as the other three regions were, as shown in Table 14.1 in Appendix B, where the Middle East provided the overwhelming majority of "geniuses" in the first two millennia from 3000 to 800 B.C., after which Europe led for the most part until A.D. 500, followed by the Far East for a few centuries. Then the Middle East prevailed for a few more centuries, until Europe led again after the twelfth century.

When the three non–European regions were added together, the sum of their "geniuses" was correlated .66 with the European sum, so that both Europe and the rest of the world (Asia) were significantly similar in the historical distribution of their "geniuses." When all four regions were added together (resulting in the same sum as the seven civilized activities), this provided a measure of world civilization, which is shown in the next to the last column of Table 14.1. Although the European and non–European *pattern* of civilized activities were similar, the same cannot be said about the *level* of their activities, where Europe produced more than twice as many "geniuses" as the rest of the civilized world during these 49 centuries: 72 percent of the total, as shown in the last column of the last row in Table 14.1.

Sorokin (1941, pp. 328–29) also provided a measure of cultural values going back to 4000 B.C., but the data were rather sketchy until the eleventh century B.C., and they were more Eurocentric than Kroeber's "geniuses," in that Europeans constituted 85 percent of Sorokin's total. These data represented historical persons who were mentioned in the ninth edition of the *Encyclopaedia Britannica* (published 1875–1889), as having made a notable contribution to one or more fields of culture, including statesmanship, philosophy, religion, literature, fine arts, miscellany, scholarship, science, music and business. John V. Boldyreff gathered these data for his doctor's dissertation, but Sorokin is the most accessible reference for them. Each person was weighted by the number of lines used to describe his (or her) accomplishments. Only one figure was provided for the fourth millennium B.C., another one for the third millennium B.C., and one for the fifteenth century B.C. After that, data were available for every 50 years from 1050 B.C. to A.D. 1849. Sorokin provided arithmetic averages of the ten cultural areas previously listed, noting that "almost all ten series move more or less alike in a similar direction, parallel" (1941, p. 352). In this respect Sorokin's ten cultural activities were similar to Kroeber's seven civilized activities: all tended to rise and fall together.

However, as already noted, the historical persons in the ninth edition of the *Encyclopaedia Britannica* were largely Europeans, so that the use of them to represent *world* civilization may be questionable. To test the validity of this procedure, I correlated the European scores (Sorokin 1937, vol. 3, p. 516) with the non–European scores (total score minus European scores) over the 49 centuries. The correlation, when both scores were logged to correct for skewness, was .90, which showed that, regardless of the difference in *level*, the *pattern* of European scores was quite similar to that of non–European scores over these centuries, and consequently that this measurement of world civilization was quite adequate for the purpose of comparing the relative civilization levels of these 49 centuries, although it might be inadequate for comparing European and non–European civilizations within any century or for all centuries taken together. The correlation between centuries and the total (logged) score was .92, showing a significant and exponential increase in the number of these historical persons over these centuries.

When Sorokin's historical persons were logged and correlated with Kroeber's (logged) "geniuses," the correlation was .93, suggesting that either Kroeber's "geniuses" or Sorokin's historical persons could be used as a measure of world civilization. Sorokin's historical persons were used in earlier chapters of this book, but Kroeber's "geniuses" will be used in this chapter because they are less Eurocentric, and they provide a further breakdown of non–European civilizations which is not available in Sorokin's data.

Sorokin also provided a count of scientific discoveries and technological inventions (1937, vol. 2, ch. 3), which could be used as a measure of European and world civilization, since they were correlated .89 with Sorokin's world civilization and .91 with Sorokin's European civilization. However, they will not be used in this chapter, because no breakdown outside of European civilization is possible with these data.

Naroll et al. (1971), like Kroeber and Sorokin, "concluded that the counting of creative individuals was the most useful measure of the total creativity of the society to which they belonged at the period of time in which they lived"

(p. 182). Naroll et al. used these counts of Kroeber's data to measure a civilization's creativity. I assume that these counts may be used as a measure of civilization itself. This assumption seems to be implied in the work of Kroeber and Sorokin. Kroeber's problem was to study "high cultural developments" (1944, p. 6). Individual "geniuses" were used as an index of these cultural developments. The curves of "different activities of [Egyptian] culture" (p. 240) were taken as rough indicators of "Egyptian civilization as a whole" (p. 241). Likewise, the Assyrian history of sculpture was "also the outline of the history of higher civilization in accentuated form" (p. 311). Sorokin referred to the weighted number of his historical persons as an indicator of the "total creativeness of cultural values" (1941, p. 323), and again as an indicator of "cultural creativeness" (p. 325), so that Naroll's interpretation of Kroeber's data came closer to that of Sorokin than to that of Kroeber. My interpretation of Kroeber's data will follow that of Kroeber to the effect that the number of individual "geniuses" provide a measure of the height of civilization itself. It is quite possible that Naroll et al. and Sorokin assumed implicitly that creativeness and civilization were synonymous terms or, at least, indicative of each other.

## Measuring Empires

Taagepera's (1978) imperial sizes will be used in this chapter as a measure of empires, by which Taagepera meant "any large sovereign political entity whose components are not sovereign" (p. 113). He measured empires in terms of square megameters, each one of which is equivalent to 386,000 square miles. Empires were not sizeable prior to 600 B.C., when the Medes and the Persians introduced a degree of hierarchical bureaucracy (satrapy) unknown before in human history. Even from 500 B.C. to A.D. 1500, the "progress" in imperial sizes was not spectacular. Then there was a great change as the world moved the modern period of history following 1600, one that Taagepera attributed to the European industrial-communication revolution. History, however, clearly shows the rise and fall of civilizations and empires, not only once, but several times.

Although the global picture is an ever upward spiral, so far, the regional pictures are full of falls and rises, as shown in Table 3.4 in Appendix B, which shows the waxing and waning of eight regional empires, whose imperial sizes were summed in the last column, providing a measure of how much of the earth was under imperial control century by century. This sum shows that empires occupied very little of the earth up to and including the eighth century B.C. Imperial areas did not cover 1 percent of the earth's land surface until the sixteenth century B.C. In the fifteenth to twelfth centuries B.C., all the imperial areas together constituted no more than 2 percent of the earth's land — most of that controlled by China and Egypt — after which imperial areas returned to the 1 percent level until the seventh century B.C.

In the sixth century B.C., less than 6 percent of the earth's land surface was held by empires. This grew to 95 percent in the twentieth century A.D. While some 94 percent of the land was roamed by gatherers and hunters, farmers and herders in 600 B.C., there was only 5 percent of the earth so occupied by the twentieth century A.D. Self-sufficient primitive tribes and villages were clearly no match for civilized communities with their civilized ways of conquest, domination and exploitation. Still, it took more than 2500 years to dominate those peoples fully, over which time civilizatons decimated one another from time to time in the process.

## Measuring Wars

The most important measurement of war is the number of deaths caused by it. However, these data were not available much before the modern period. However, I found a significant correlation of .70** between battles per war and deaths per war during the modern period, and I also found a significant correlation of .91** between battles per half-century and war deaths per half-century during the modern period (Eckhardt 1990a), suggesting that battles may be used to measure war's intensity in the absence of more positive data on war deaths. Since then, I have found significant correlations between several sets of battle and war frequencies, on the one hand, and two sets of war casualties and deaths, on the other, over the centuries from 1500 B.C. to A.D. 2000, and over battles per war and casualties/deaths per war. Thus, there is hardly any doubt that battle and war frequencies may be used as indicators of war intensities, when casualties or fatalities are not available for this purpose. These correlations are shown in Table 14.2 in Appendix B.

Although written records have been kept since 3000 B.C., the first recorded battle did not occur until about 1469 B.C. between Egypt and the Palestinians at Megiddo (Dupuy and Dupuy 1986, p. 6). In that century and the seven centuries to follow there was no more than one recorded battle per century until the seventh century B.C., when there were three recorded battles, and the sixth century B.C., six recorded battles (Dupuy and Dupuy 1986). Other authors (Harbottle 1904, revised by Bruce 1981; Eggenberger 1985) found even fewer battles prior to 500 B.C., the earliest being at Troy in the twelfth century B.C. Wars, themselves, averaged only five or six per century from 2000 B.C. to 500 B.C. (Kohn 1987), and the war record prior to 2000 B.C. was rather vague at best, although there is some evidence that some wars occurred prior to that time (Dupuy and Dupuy 1986).

Since records have been kept since about 3000 B.C., and since historians have always been careful to record such events, I assume that no record of these events in historical times means that they either did not occur, or, if they did, were insignificant. In a 1500-page encyclopedia of military history (Dupuy and Dupuy 1986), only 15 pages, or 1 percent of the total, was devoted to the "dawn of military history" from 3500 to 600 B.C. In short, the first half of military history was such as to require very little space, presumably because not much happened, until the emergence of the Medes and the Persians about 600 B.C., when war started to become an art. It was much later that it started to become a science as well.

I have analyzed three sets of battles (Bruce's Harbottle 1981; Eggenberger 1967, 1985; and Dupuy and Dupuy, 1986) and three sets of wars (Dupuy and Dupuy 1986; Kohn 1987; and Sorokin 1937, vol. 3). Since battles are more like one another in their intensity than wars, they would be preferred as an overall measure of a war's intensity. Since the Dupuys' battles are more numerous and less Eurocentric than Harbottle's and Eggenberger's battles, they will be used as the preferred measure of war's intensity in this chapter. Their total distribution is shown in the last column of Table 14.3. About half of this total has been sorted according to regions, and this sample is shown in the rest of this table. The sample was quite adequate, since it was correlated .99 with the total number of battles over the centuries. The Dupuys' battles were significantly correlated with other lists (Sorokin 1937; Wright 1965; Bruce 1981; Eggenberger 1985; Kohn 1987), in addition to which it was the most comprehensive and reliable list available.

## Correlations Between Civilizations, Empires and Wars at the Global Level of Analysis

We now have the measurements that we need for the purpose of correlational analysis: the number of "geniuses" as a measure of civilization or creativity, imperial sizes as a measure of empires, and battle frequencies as a measure of the destructiveness or intensity of war. Correlations, of course, measure only similarities of distribution, *not* causes, which have to be determined by logical argument or empirical evidence outside of the statistical situation.

The dialectical evolutionary theory of civilizations, empires and wars suggests that these three should be significantly correlated with one another and, furthermore, that all three should be correlated with time. The correlation between both the raw and the logged scores of world civilization and empire was .90, accounting for 81 percent of the variance. At the world level, the correlation between civilization and empire was very high indeed. The more civilized we became, the larger was the area of the earth that came under imperial control. Civilizations and empires may not be twins, but they are very close relatives indeed. Civilization seemed to precede empire in time, but empire had the effect of spreading civilization over larger territories, which generally included more people. If civilization was the nurturing parent of empire, empire returned the favor by increasing the territory over which civilization was extended. According to this description, there was a dialectical evolutionary relationship between civilization and empire at the global level of analysis, in the sense that they fed into each other, each contributing to the other's growth.

When the sum of the Dupuy (1986) battles over these centuries was correlated with the sum of imperial sizes, both variables being logged to correct
for skewness, the correlation was .94, which was significant well beyond the
.001 level of confidence. When these battles were correlated with the sum of
Kroeber's seven civilized activities, both variables being logged, the correlation
was .94, which was significant well beyond the .001 level of confidence. The
correlations among these three variables were all more than .90, suggesting a
very close relationship among them, which is more than enough to confirm the
dialectical evolutionary theory. It is worth noting that these three measures
were obtained from three independent sources (Kroeber, Taagepera and the
Dupuys), so that their correlations were not contaminated by any bias that
might have been generated had they been obtained from a single source.

When these three measures were logged and correlated with the 50 centuries from 3000 B.C. to A.D. 2000 (as a measure of historical time), and when
these correlations were factor-analyzed, a single factor emerged from this process: number of battles (.98), imperial sizes (.98), centuries (.97) and number
of "geniuses" (.97). The components of this factor are shown in Figure 14.1,
where the raw scores in Tables 14.1, 3.4 and 12.3 have been converted into standard scores with a mean of 50 and a standard deviation of 10, in order to make
these three sets of scores comparable to one another. Factors, like correlations,
establish structural similarities, but *not* causal direction which has to be
established outside of statistical analysis.

These results clearly show, not only that civilizations, empires and wars
were highly correlated with one another, but also that all of them were highly
correlated with time — that all were increasing significantly and exponentially
over these centuries at the global level of analysis.

## Regional Correlations

This confirmation at the global level was further confirmed at the regional
levels. All four of these variables were significantly correlated with one another
in Europe and non–Europe, and also in the Middle East, India and the Far
East, taken separately. When these correlation matrices were factor-analyzed,
a single factor emerged in all regions, as shown in Table 14.3 in Appendix B.
The factor coefficients were all significant, but the loading of Kroeber's "geniuses" in the Middle East was rather low.

As far as they go, these results confirm the dialectical evolutionary theory
of fairly close relationships among civilizations, empires and wars over the centuries and support this theory at regional levels of analysis as well as at the
global level. It is worth reiterating that the measures of these three variables
were obtained from three independent sources.

These statistical findings were consistent with Kroeber's (1944) findings by
inspection: "A definitely successful [Egyptian] dynasty regularly meant military
expansion, accumulation and diffusion of wealth, notable building operations,

## Figure 14.1  Civilizations, Empires and Wars 3000 B.C. to A.D. 2000

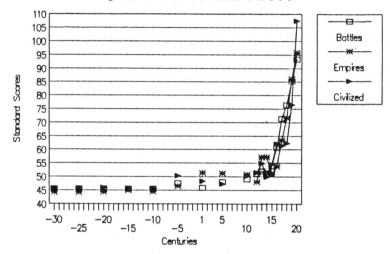

Notes to Figure 14.1: Battles = The frequency of battles per century from Dupuy and Dupuy (1986). Empires = The sum of imperial sizes from Taagepera (1978). Civilized = The sum of civilized activities from Kroeber (1944). All three sets of frequencies were standardized to a mean of 50 and a standard deviation of 10, in order to make them comparable to one another.

high-grade sculpture, painting, and often literature.... So regular, on the whole, is the concordance of the several curves that evidently they are all only functions of one underlying factor or group of related factors" (p. 240). Indeed, only one underlying factor was found by later statistical analysis.

Kroeber stated further that "it is evident that Assyrian sculpture followed the fortunes of empire, as Egyptian sculpture had done earlier.... It is clear that whether the period was one of city-states or of empires, the achievements of sculpture were dependent on military and political successes" (pp. 245, 247). "The books [encyclopedias and textbooks] regularly describe the architecture, sculpture, and painting [in Egypt] as rising and falling in accord with the politico-economic fortunes to a surprising degree" (p. 665). The correlation between national achievement and cultural achievement was only partial in China (p. 670) and low in India (p. 684), but "on the whole, ethnic or national energy and higher cultural energy tend to be related; but ... the relationship is not complete.... To the question whether there may be national fluorescences without accompanying cultural ones, the answer must be yes, although such happenings are rare in history" (pp. 795, 844). The agreement between Kroeber's insights and the results of factor analysis are striking indeed.

Sorokin made similar observations about the relationship of civilizations, empires and wars: "In the life history of nations, the magnitude of war, absolute and relative, tends to grow in the periods of expansion — political, social, cultural, and territorial — of the nation at least as frequently as in the periods of decline. In such periods of blossoming the war activities tend to reach the highest points, probably more frequently than in the periods of decay, and vice versa. Such seems to be one of the relatively valid but limited generalizations" (1957, p. 565). This was true for the glory that was Greece and the grandeur that was Rome: "In the life history of a nation, in its occupied areas, most of the periods of its political, social, economic, moral and mental effervescence, the most brilliant periods in its history, the period of the climax of its grandeur, power, magnificence, and genius are usually also the periods of its high militarism and warfare" (p. 568). Sorokin said the same of the magnitude of revolutions in Greece: "In the history of Greece the most turbulent centuries and periods were, like those periods of the maximum of war activities, not the periods of decline but of resplendence, when Greek culture reached its peak" (p. 583).

Similar conclusions about the relationships between political or military success and artistic creativity can be drawn from Kavolis (1972, ch. 3), who observed that "a correlation between periods of warfare and those of artistic creativity has been noted, mostly in Asian civilizations, by Mukerjee (1951, pp. 27–28) and, in Europe, by Sorokin (1937, vol. 3, p. 365)" (p. 40). Kavolis' historical analysis suggested that "artistic creativity tends to increase in periods following those of intensive goal-oriented action (warfare or political consolidations) in the political sphere" (p. 54).

Kavolis (p. 155) also cited a factor analysis of 40 modern nations, 1837–1937, by Cattell, Breul and Hartman (1952), who found that creative variables, such as high creativity in science and philosophy, high musical creativity, and the winning of many Nobel Prizes for achievements in science, literature and efforts for peace, tended to cluster with aggressive variables, such as a large number of riots and frequent involvement in war (p. 415). Since large gross imperial area was also loaded on this factor, this factor related measurements of modern civilization, empire and war to one another. A similar factor was also reported for an earlier study of 69 modern nations, 1837–1937, and in several other studies (Cattell et al. 1952, p. 416).

However, Naroll et al. (1971) found no significant relationship between their counts of Kroeber's "geniuses" and the *number of years* of external warfare of the most "conspicuous state" or Great Power of the civilization during any century. Since the average lengths of wars tend to increase as we go back in time, even though the actual fighting time decreases, duration may not be as accurate a measure of war's intensity as the *number of battles* used in the present study. Naroll et al. also found no significant relationship between creativity and the size of the civilization's largest city, the growth of the civilization and the degree of centralization: "On the other hand, we found some tentative support for the hypothesis that the more politically fragmented a civilization [the number of independent states within it], the higher its creativity level" (p. 187). This last correlation was .286, which was significant at the .05 level of confidence, but which accounted for only 8 percent of the total variance. The authors recognized the need to re-test this hypothesis on a new sample before it could be credited.

## Some Theories About Regional Rises and Falls

Although civilizations, empires and wars increased significantly and exponentially at the global level, there were falls as well as at the regional levels, which is why the regional factor coefficients in Table 14.4 were lower than the global ones.

Spengler (1926–28) attributed these rises and falls to something like the biological process of birth, development, maturity and decay. This process of growth and decay seemed determined by the nature of the process itself. There was not much in this theory to prevent the decline of the West that Spengler predicted.

Toynbee (1972) was less deterministic, emphasizing that the adequacy of responses to challenges was the determining factor for rises and falls. Adequate or appropriate responses contributed to rising, while inadequate or inappropriate responses contributed to falling. Spengler's emphasis was on moral, religious and spiritual challenges more than on physical or environmental challenges, but he also emphasized that civilizational rising and falling depended very much upon the rising and falling of the economy: "The inability of a pre-scientific agricultural economy to bear this economic load [of providing more and more civilian and military services] is evidently one of the causes of the unwished-for collapses by which so many universal states have been overtaken so many times in succession" (Toynbee and Caplan 1972, p. 63).

Just *who* or *what* challenged particular civilizations was not made entirely clear, nor was just *how* these civilizations responded. But the concept allows for some free play in the study of the rise and fall of civilizations and challenges us to find out what it means operationally, if we can, so that it can be examined more scientifically.

More recently, the economic factor has also been emphasized by Kennedy (1987) to account for the rise and fall of the Great Powers in modern history. Armed force is what makes or breaks a Great Power, according to this theory, and armed forces cost money. Great Powers need money to become great in the first place, and more money to remain great. But there seems to be a strong tendency for Great Powers to overspend. Military expenditures exceed their economic base, exhausting the economy in the process, so that the next war is lost to an upcoming power that has not yet bankrupt its economy with its military expenditures. "The historical record suggests that there is a very clear connection *in the long run* between an individual Great Power's economic rise and fall and its growth and decline as an important military power (or world empire)" (p. xxii). Kennedy emphasized "in the long run," because he is talking about a process that takes time as well as money; even so, his study of just the last five hundred years convinced him that "there is a very strong correlation between the eventual outcome of the *major coalition wars* for European or global mastery, and the amount of productive resources mobilized by each side.... [V]ictory has repeatedly gone to the side with the more flourishing productive base.... [T]he power position of the leading nations has closely paralleled their relative economic position over the past five centuries" (Kennedy 1987, pp. xxiii–xxiv).

In short, wars cost money. To be sure, they can also make money for somebody, and therein lies the gamble: Can you (whoever you are) realize more than the effort costs? If so, war can be profitable for somebody, ignoring the casualties for the moment. Somebody may amass surplus wealth from war. But, if wars cost more than they make, bankruptcy follows and down goes the empire. The trick seems to be to make war profitable by making somebody else pay for it, while ignoring the casualites on both sides, civilians as well as soldiers.

## The Nature of Power

Both Kennedy and Toynbee make sense to me, but I must add to their theories a psychosocial factor that helps me understand why civilizations fall after rising. The key lies in the nature of power itself.

My basic argument is that power tends to be self-defeating. The will to power is a process that obstructs its own progress. I am using the phrase "will to power" at the psychosocial level of analysis, not at the individual level. Somehow, it seems, the immorality of self-righteousness, the myth of superiority, and the divine right of might work very well in helping civilizations to rise, to expand the range of their power over others. But there comes a time when what once succeeded starts to fail and to contribute to the fall of what has risen.

This process that obstructs its own progress seems to be some function of power itself, or some reaction to power, such that the inequality (or lack of balance) of power gives rise to social forces that try to balance or equalize power, thus neutralizing power. We need to find out more about power and how it works against itself in the long run.

Whatever it is, it is expressed by an ideology that works on the way up, but that turns against itself on the way down. On the way up, the ideology (the myth of superiority) is confirmed by its success. As long as you are winning, nothing has to be explained except your superiority, which is simply asserted without explanation. But, on the way down, the ideology has to justify and rationalize its failure. What makes such successes end in failure? Its dependence on power, whose inequalities generate a will to equality that brings down power from its throne of superiority.

## Summary and Conclusions

The dialectical evolutionary theory proposed relationships between civilizations, empires and wars, such that these three would interact as to promote one another's growth up to a point where surplus wealth is depleted. At this point civilizations, empires and wars could no longer be afforded, so empires shrank and wars were lost. These losses, however, were somebody else's gain. The losses took the form either of direct conquest by others with more surplus wealth, or of decentralization which made the smaller units prey to future conquest. Consequently, the way up and the way down were virtually the same way of conquest, either directly and immediately, as in the case of Alexander's conquest of the Persian empire, or indirectly and sequentially, as in the case of the many times that Chinese empires were fragmented into feudal states which were later centralized by another conqueror. In either event civilizations, empires and wars tended to grow together, wars serving as both midwives and undertakers in the rise and fall of civilizations and empires in the course of human history.

This dialectical process of evolution (and devolution) presumably began among primitive peoples, although there are few traces of it until the beginning of civilization some five thousand years ago. Even then evidence is sparse for battles and wars, which did not clearly emerge until about 1500 B.C., and which did not amount to much until about 500 B.C. However, something like this process may be responsible for some of the movement from the primitive bands to the larger tribes of gatherers and hunters to the villages of the farmers and herders who emerged some ten thousand years ago.

The same process was presumably responsible for the movement from the agricultural villages to the civilized cities that emerged some five thousand years ago. Neither anthropological nor archeological evidence suggested much growth in population nor territory among the gatherers and hunters, and not much more among the farmers and the herders. Even the first 2500 years of civilization showed no dramatic increases in population or territory, not in signs of civilization, such as statesmanship, philosophy, religion, literature, fine arts, scholarship, science, music, business, etc.

The great leap forward in all of these areas occurred about 600 B.C., when the Medes and the Persians developed civilization, empire and war into arts based on a hierarchical delegation of power such as the world had not known before. The next great leap came with the Muslims in the seventh century A.D., another with the Mongols in the thirteenth century, and finally with the Europeans in the sixteenth century. The Europeans reached their apex in the nineteenth and twentieth centuries, but they may well be running out of surplus wealth today. However, they have fallen and risen again before, so that even if they may be on their way down now this hardly precludes another rise in the future unless, of course, someone blows up the whole world in the meantime.

While the global development tended to spiral upward during the last five thousand years (judging by Kroeber's "geniuses," Taagepera's imperial sizes, and Dupuy and Dupuy's battles), regional areas had their rises and their falls. Consequently, the general pattern suggested by the analyses in this chapter was that of an evolutionary trend in one direction at the global level, which was composed of somewhat cyclical processes at regional levels. At both the global and regional levels, civilizations, empires and wars were significantly related to one another, tending to rise and fall together. How do we explain this basic finding?

It was only after we became civilized, that is, dependent upon land, labor, capital and trade for making a living, that imperialism and militarism began to make any sense. Then they became necessary in order to gain, maintain and increase the surplus wealth required to make a civilization.

At the regional levels, the rises were associated with the establishment of centralized controls by a strong leader whose income exceeded his expenditures in the process. When his or his followers' expenditures exceeded their incomes, then came the falls, which were characterized by decentralization, feudalization or foreign conquest. In all cases, the way up not only increased the *quantity* of civilization, empire and war, but also changed the social *structure* to one of greater inequality, indicated by slavery, caste, class, social stratification, etc. This inequality characterized the relations *between* civilizations as well as *within* them. It would, of course, be desirable to develop more precise measures of these inequalities in the process of further research. So far, the evidence is largely qualitative, and needs to be strengthened by making it more quantitative.

These inequalities gave rise to a social sense of injustice that generated a will to equality; the will to equality acts to dethrone the will to power from within or from without. These two social forces, between them, would seem to be an essential aspect of the rise and fall of civilizations. The precise relations will have to wait for better measures of social inequalities, which can then be correlated with available measures of civilizations, empires and wars.

What can it be that disguises the true nature of self-destruction, so as to permit us to destroy ourselves without knowing it? At the individual level of analysis, rationalization is what enables us to destroy ourselves without recognizing what we are doing, as the psychoanalysts of the twentieth century have suggested. At the social level of analysis, ideology performs the function of rationalization, as the Marxists have suggested. Like rationalization at the individual level, ideology rationalizes the absurd at the social level. It makes the absurd appear to be rational. In this manner ideology makes social destruction possible by social deception. According to this hypothesis we need to recognize the rationality of the Golden Rule, the categorical imperative, or the will to equality as the keys toward a sustainable civilization.

The terms "rise" and "fall," "up" and "down," etc., follow conventional usage. However, so far as they may connote value judgments of "better" and "worse," they may well be questioned. More civilization and more empire meant more war. More civilization would seem to be "better," at least for those who get it or who get more of it. More empire may be better for the imperial civilizations, but not necessarily for their colonies. More war would definitely seem to be worse but those who win the wars might not agree. A crucial question for further research is: Do the pleasures of civilization justify the horrors of war? A more pressing question is: Can we have civilization without war?

Unless we have an instinct of exploitation (which I doubt very much), that is, a desire to benefit ourselves at the expense of others, it would seem that we have no need for war. Human nature is pretty much determined by human beings and human choices. The dialectical evolutionary theory would suggest that we gradually developed ourselves into a pattern of domination and exploitation which virtually made war inevitable. So far as this is true, it means that we can change the structure of the civilization that we have created by changing our choices, which means changing our values, not human nature, whatever that may be.

What values need to be changed in order to have a civilization without domination and exploitation, and therefore without war? One clue would seem to lie in the basic difference between primitive and civilized societies. Primitive societies seem to be more free and equal in their human relations than the civilized societies that we have created so far (Eckhardt 1975, 1982). If we created more free and equal human relations, we might be able to create a civilization without war. But we have much more to learn before we can achieve that happy ending.

# Chapter 15
# Summary and Conclusions

## Primitive Warfare

The quantitative studies of primitive warfare reviewed in Chapter 1 were generally agreed that warfare was a function of development rather than instinct. Warfare itself was generally defined as a group effort that was sanctioned by the group: "armed, licit, lethal public combat" (Naroll 1964, p. 6). Some minimum number of deaths was presumably required, but this minimum was seldom if ever made explicit. Development was defined socially in terms of the division of labor based on professional and caste lines. Economic development proceeded from gathering and hunting at the lowest level to farming and herding at the highest level. Political development proceeded from the clan to the tribe to the chiefdom to the state. All forms of development in these studies were positively correlated with one another, so that there was a single type of development, any form of which could serve as an indicator of development in general.

Warfare was measured in a variety of ways in these studies: incidence, frequency, prevalence, intensity, preparations, attitudes and goals (warlikeness, expectations, causes, purposes and reasons). These various measures were always significantly correlated with one another, so that there was a single type of primitive militarism, any form of which could serve as an indicator of primitive militarism in general. The positive correlations between war preparations and the frequency and intensity of war convinced most authors that preparations provoked primitive war more than they deterred them, thus confirming the arms race theory of war rather than the deterrence theory at this level of development.

Most forms of development were significantly correlated with most forms of militarism. The more highly developed societies were generally the more militaristic: "The more primitive the people, the less warlike it appears to be" (Wright 1965, p. 68). To be sure, this was a statistical finding which established a general rule, not a universal law. There were exceptions to this general rule, as to any other.

Although development contributed to all forms of primitive warfare, internal as well as external, and defensive as well as offensive, it contributed most of all to offensive external warfare which, in turn, contributed to territorial expansion and, consequently, to cultural survival of the militarily fittest. This sequence has been most succinctly expressed by Otterbein: "political centralization → military sophistication → offensive external war → territorial expansion" (1977 p. 699).

Warfare was also associated with crime and its punishment, games of chance and strategy, full-time entrepreneurs, social stratification and slavery, suggesting that these other activities were also functions of development. Slavery was clearly a result of warfare. The cause-effect relations between warfare and other variables were not quite so clear.

Where personality variables were available, warfare was associated with anxiety, frustrating childhood disciplines, narcissism, and sexual repression at all ages (including the Oedipus complex). Whether warfare was a function of these personality variables, or vice versa, is an open question. Both might be more parsimoniously explained as functions of development. In summary, primitive warfare seemed to be a function of an authoritarian culture and an anxious, frustrated, egoistic personality which, in turn, might simply be a function of an authoritarian culture.

Hunting and warring were primarily male activities in primitive societies, so that these activities have often been ascribed to male aggression. However, there seems to be no significant difference in aggressiveness between the sexes in primitive societies. And primitive warfare seems not to be motivated by aggression, but rather a carefully planned and rationally executed behavior, designed to accomplish certain social purposes such as defense, revenge, prestige, plunder, land and power. While warriors (and hunters) have largely been men, women have cheered on these activities, celebrated their victories, and shared in the spoils. Had they not been biologically chosen for the areas of bearing and nursing children, there would probably have been just as many women warriors and hunters as men. The division of labor between the sexes would seem to be based on practical considerations rather than motivational differences.

For several million years, when humans made their living by gathering and scavenging, there was presumably no warfare at all, since there were no tools, let alone weapons, until about two million years ago when men began to hunt. Humans biologically similar to ourselves emerged about 100,000 years ago and left a large number of cave paintings, some of which depicted hunting, but none of which depicted war. Bands of gathering-hunters, numbering about 25-50 people each, could hardly have made much of a war. There were not enough people to fight, no arms with which to fight, and nothing to fight about. Then, ten thousand years ago, we settled down to farming and herding in villages, we develped a vested interest in land and cattle, and something like a war became possible. This agricultural revolution eventually resulted in food surpluses, making civilization (living in cities) possible, starting about five thousand years ago. Then war began to come into its own.

Before proceeding, it is important to recall the things that were *not* associated with primitive warfare, so far as established by quantitative studies:

race, temperature, cultural exchanges (although these tended toward warfare), hostility, language, region of the world, terrain, feuds, diet, kin type, property inheritance, lineage, cousin marriage, family organization, authority within the family, divorce rate, status of women and fertility level.

The anthropological evidence summarized by Textor (1967) suggested that war started some time after the agricultural revolution some ten thousand years ago, after we had a vested interest in land and cattle, which gave us something to fight for. It was about this time that cave paintings depicted something like human warfare, where a few stick persons were apparently shooting arrows at each other, that is, fighting with weapons — one of the basic criteria for defining a war. Whether a few armed persons constitute an army is questionable.

Although humans may have been aggressive in their primitive societies, the expression of this aggression seemed to be limited to feuds with their personal purposes and did not extend to wars with their social purposes. While humans were little more than scavengers, our territorial instincts, if we had any, hardly served any purpose, since territory had little to do with our surviving. Even after we started to gather and hunt, territory was still not of vital interest to us. It was only after we settled down to farming and herding that the land became of real importance and, therefore, something worth fighting for.

The anthropological evidence suggested that primitive warfare was a function of human development more than human instinct or human nature (Wright 1965; Broch and Galtung 1966; Eckhardt 1975). Personal frustration also played a role, but frustraton itself was probably a function of social development. In any event, social development, personal frustration, war preparation, war glorification and warfare itself, including killing, mutilating and torturing the enemy, all seemed to feed into one another in a vicious spiral, suggesting a dialectical evolutionary theory of development and warfare. In general, more developed societies engaged in more warfare, so far as quantitative studies of primitive warfare suggested. And these more developed societies were more authoritarian, more compulsive and more egoistic in their structure, judging by Textor's (1967) correlations and Eckhardt's (1975) analyses of them.

Consequently, there seems to be some quantitative evidence to support the contention that warfare emerged prior to the urban revolution, but not much before the agricultural revolution. Furthermore, there is some evidence to suggest that the frequency and intensity of primitive warfare increased as primitive development progressed.

## Civilized Warfare

The evidence is overwhelming that warfare did not come into its own until after the emergence of civilization some five thousand years ago. Civilizations, empires and wars tended to grow together, wars serving as both midwives and undertakers in the rise and fall of civilizations in the course of human history.

Civilizations, empires and wars all shared a number of key characteristics. The desire to dominate and exploit others, in order to benefit some at the expense of others, seemed to prevail. In all three cases, there seemed to be an inordinate concern for oneself at the expense of others. All three seemed to be processes which obstructed their own progress. In short, they were all processes of self-destruction, the nature of which was hidden by self-deception in the form of some ideology or other. Regardless of the different forms which these ideologies might take, they all had one thing in common: the belief that they were superior to all other ideologies, the belief that they were right and all others wrong and the belief that compromise was a sign of doubt or lack of faith in one's own ideology. This process of self-destruction, rationalized and justified by self-deception, was a violation of the Golden Rule and the Categorical Imperative, both of which recommended the consideration of others as well as oneself. These self-deceptive ideologies were all characterized by some form of egoism as opposed to some form of altruism.

Why did civilized peoples fight much more than primitive peoples? An answer might be that they had more material things over which to fight, they had metal weapons with which to fight and above all, they had some surplus wealth to pay for it all. The "savage" gatherers and hunters had little to fight over, and not much more than primitive bows and arrows to fight with. Furthermore, they had neither surplus population nor surplus wealth to support anything like professional soldiers. The "barbarian" farmers and herders had more to fight over, but nothing better to fight with, and still no surplus population or wealth to support anything like an army. Civilized people fought over land, labor, capital and trade, all of which contributed to expansion at another's expense, often at the expense of primitive peoples who could not defend themselves against civilized armies and weapons.

However, there is something very unstable about the process of civilization so far, since civilizations which rise or expand eventually fall or contract in area, population, power and wealth. Civilization seems to be a process which obstructs its own progress. Too much of its energy seems to be wasted in power struggles: (1) one civilization against another, (2) civilizations against barbarians (farmers and herders) and savages (gatherers and hunters), (3) peasant and slave rebellions within civilizations and (4) power struggles within the ruling class of any civilization.

These power struggles translated into four types of war which have characterized every civilization that we know: (1) power wars, (2) imperial (and colonial) wars, (3) class wars and (4) civil wars. The essence of civilization itself seems to be exploitation, which benefits some at the expense of others. Exploitation violates the categorical imperative of doing what every one else can do and keep on doing. This seems to be why civilizations have failed so far. Our own civilization will also fail unless we find a way of being civilized without dominating and exploiting one another.

Clearly, exploitation can only be enforced by means of arms, so that civilization and warfare have been inextricably linked to each other throughout human history, to the benefit of some at the expense of others in the short run, but to the detriment of all in the long run. This pattern of domination and exploitation has repeated itself over and over again in the course of human history. Toynbee described it in terms of disunity leading to unity by conquest, which sooner or later led to disunity by rebellion, and so on, over periods ranging from one hundred to one thousand years.

Not only did civilization bring war in its wake, but the more civilized people became, the more warlike they became.

It would seem that war and slavery tended to exhaust a civilization making it fair game for other predators, civilized or barbarian. The desire to dominate others to benefit oneself violates the categorical imperative; it might be hypothesized that this basic violation is responsible for most human violence, in which case our own civilization will be saved only if we can somehow get the categorical imperative back at the center of human motivation, where it presumably was among primitive people.

Toynbee expressed this combination of war and slavery as follows: "War and Class have always been with us ever since the first civilizations emerged.... Of the 20 or so civilizations known to modern Western historians [the number increased by 1972], all except our own appear to be dead or moribund, and ... we invariably find that the cause of death has been either War or Class. To date, these two plagues have been deadly enough, in partnership, to kill off 19 out of 20 representatives of this recently evolved species of human society.... Greco-Roman civilization finally died of the twin diseases of War and Class in the course of the 5th, 6th, and 7th centuries of the Christian era" (1948 pp. 23–24).

## Wright's Study of War

Until recently, Wright (1965) was the only author who attempted a quantitative study of war from ancient times to the present for all regions of the world. He did this with the aid of Toynbee's (1934–39) description of 26 civilizations, and with the aid of some 60 colleagues and students at the University of Chicago for some 16 years from 1926 to 1942. His method was simply to rate these civilizations according to their warlikeness and other military characteristics, military techniques, battle frequencies and general characteristics, including political organization and social hostility (Wright 1965, pp. 571–72).

Although this was a noble effort, its reliability has to be questioned, since these ratings have not been replicated by anyone else, presumably because of the tremendous amount of work and quality of expertise involved in the process. The ratings were made more manageable by limiting them to the universal state of each civilization, which lasted for only about 260 years on the average, and which started as early as 2300 B.C. in Mesopotamia, and which ended as late as A.D. 1854 in Japan, so that Toynbee's 26 civilizations covered about four thousand years of human history. This universal state, which occurred at the height of the civilization, was a time of stability, when records were likely to be more reliable. But the task of rating even these universal states on some 30 variables would seem to be most difficult indeed. Wright and his colleagues deserve very high praise indeed for their efforts, no matter how reliable their ratings turn out to be. In the meantime, until some other brave soul attempts to replicate them, they are all we have, so it seems desirable to make the most of them for the time being.

I correlated 32 of Wright's variables with one another, and factor-analyzed this correlation matrix. The first factor was a general factor which I labeled "General Militarism," since it included all of the military characteristics, all of the military techniques and all of the battle frequencies. In addition to the militarism variables, this factor was also related to larger populations, heterogeneous populations, intercivilization contacts, living civilizations, commerce, hostility, Eastern civilizations and later historical period in time. This militarism factor was more related to later civilizations than to earlier ones, including those with larger and more heterogeneous populations to whom commerce was important. Neither agriculture (grazing versus irrigation) nor geography (plateaus and steppes versus maritime and rivers) was significantly related to this factor of General Militarism. This general factor, as crude as it is, and as far as it goes, supports the notion that later civilizations were more warlike than earlier ones. However, later civilizations were also more populous than earlier ones, so that we have here, as in the case of primitive societies, a contamination of development with size, leaving unanswered questions: What makes societies, primitive or civilized, more warlike? their level of development or simply their size? Which came first, size of development? Did size cause development, or did development cause size? More likely the latter; but even more likely, they may have "caused" each other in a dialectical evolutionary process.

The second general factor was characterized by plateau and steppe geography, imperialistic battle frequency, hostility, grazing versus irrigation, warlikeness, lack of commerce, lack of fortification, political absolutism, offensive battle frequency, archery, western civilizations, less population, later historical period, attack superiority and lack of navy. This factor might well be labeled Offensive Militarism, with its emphasis on attack rather than defense. Compared to the General Militarism factor, this factor was characterized by more hostility, herding versus farming, less commerce, political absolutism, more western than eastern, less population and later historical period. This factor, with its emphasis on herding versus farming and commerce, and on lesser population, would seem to fit more nomadic civilizations, so that this factor might be labeled Nomadic Militarism. In this factor, we find more militarism associated with less population, suggesting that population, as such, was not essential to militarism. Nomadic militarism was also limited to the land (lack of navy), while general militarism was not so limited.

Both of these general factors of militarism supported the notion that later civilizations were more militaristic than earlier civilizations, regardless of population. Nomadic or offensive militarism, like general militarism, was also a function of civilizational development, but it would seem that general militarism was more civilized than nomadic militarism.

When factor scores were generated for the 26 civilizations on the first two general factors, Europe (Western, Classical and Orthodox) and the Middle East (Syria, Babylonia and Persia) obtained the highest scores on General Militarism, while American civilizations (Maya, Yucatan, Andes and Mexico) obtained some of the lowest scores. Nomadic (Tartars and Arabs) and American civilizations (Mexico and Andes) obtained the highest scores on Offensive Militarism, while Asian civilizations (China and India) obtained some of the lowest scores. General Militarism, Offensive Militarism, Total Militarism and Wright's Warlikeness were all significantly correlated with one another (.58 to .85).

The most general and most reliable finding of Wright's studies of civilized war was that war and civilization go together, so that the more civilized people become, the more warlike we might expect them to be. This association between civilization and war replicated Wright's (and others') finding of a similar association between primitive development and primitive war.

As to the causes of civilized war, Wright emphasized political and economic interests, such as dominance and independence, and the conquest of territory, cattle and slaves. He believed that primitive war was less involved with these economic and political goals.

## Sorokin's Social Dynamics

Sorokin's (1937–1941) monumental work was being done during the 1930s at about the same time that Wright's monumental work was in progress. It was as if they were both trying to head off the Second World War. They failed, of course, but not for lack of trying. Their efforts were seldom, if ever, matched before or since.

While Wright covered the whole world and the whole of human history, with the help of Toynbee's 26 civilizations, Sorokin limited himself to the wars and revolutions of 11 major European nations from 600 B.C. to 1925. As in the case of Wright, Sorokin performed no statistical analyses upon his quantitative data, presumably because of the mass of data and the lack of computers.

REVOLUTIONS. Sorokin found neither periodic cycles nor linear trends in his 1622 revolutions but only irregular fluctuations. Revolutions were not associated with wars in general, nor with unsuccessful wars in particular. Nor were revolutions associated with what he termed Ideational or Sensate cultures, but only with the transition from one culture type to the other. However, this transitional theory did not hold up under statistical analyses. Revolutionary magnitudes increased over these 25 centuries, but they did not increase during transitional centuries. Sorokin's geometric averages of revolutionary magnitudes were highly and significantly correlated with both revolutionary frequencies and with revolutionary durations over 25 centuries, but not with the domestic transitional centuries.

WARS.    Sorokin and his colleagues compiled a list of 967 wars, which were reduced to 656 wars when duplicates were removed, with no wars listed during four medieval centuries from 500 to 900, presumably because no wars were mentioned by the historians consulted by Sorokin and his colleagues for these four centuries. Sorokin's list of wars included civil, colonial, imperial and international wars.

As with revolutions, Sorokin was careful to note the difficulties in constructing his list of wars: missing data, unreliable data and the fact that long wars included long inactive periods between battles, so that war duration would not be a very reliable indicator of war intensity.

Granting these difficulties, and assuming that casualties were the best indicator of war intensity, Sorokin estimated military casualties (dead and wounded) by multiplying the typical percent of army casualties by the number of years any war lasted. This procedure overestimated the casualties of those longer wars in earlier periods of time in comparison with shorter wars in later periods. Although Sorokin recognized this problem he did not take it into account in the calculation of his estimates nor in the interpretation of his results.

Sorokin's most general findings were as follows: there were no regular periodicities nor linear trends in war over these 25 centuries, but only irregular fluctuations, as in the case of revolutions. Also like revolutions, wars seemed to occur during the rise of civilizations more often than, or at least as often as, during their fall. This was believed to be a relatively valid generalization. Sorokin found no relationship between war intensities and culture types, but ideational types were more likely to have religious wars, while sensate types were more likely to have economic wars. The most valid hypothesis of all (as in the case of revolutions) was that wars increased in magnitude during the transition from sensate to ideational cultures, or vice versa.

So far as Sorokin's transitional theory of wars was concerned, I found no significant relation between transitional centuries and war casualties per population for Greece, Rome and Europe, neither taken separately nor taken together. Casualties per population (.93) were significantly loaded on a factor with sensation (.73), but transitional centuries were not significantly related to this factor. Analysis of variance also showed that casualties per population did not differ significantly between stable and transitional centuries.

As in the case of revolutions, I found Sorokin's war frequencies, durations and casualties (all logged to normalize their distributions) to be significantly correlated with one another (.64 to .91). However, although the first two were highly correlated with each other (.91), their correlations with casualties were only in the .60s, so that neither one would be a very good measure of war intensity. War casualties (logged) were significantly correlated (.57) with casualties per population, but the latter was not at all correlated with war frequencies nor war durations.

Casualties (logged) and casualties per population were not significantly correlated with the International Sum of transitional centuries either for Rome (N = 9 centuries) or Europe (N = 11 centuries), whether taken separately or taken together. Also, when Greece (N = 4 centuries) was taken alone, the correlations between its transitional centuries, casualties and casualties per population were high but not significant. Finally, when Greek casualties were added to Roman casualties, this addition was not significantly correlated with transitional centuries. These results provided even less support for Sorokin's transitional theory of wars than they did for his transitional theory of revolutions.

On the whole we have to conclude that Sorokin's transitional theory was not valid, so far as it was tested by his own measures. His transitional centuries should, of course, be correlated with other measures of revolution, war and transition over these centuries, as a further test of this theory.

RELIABILITY. Three other measures of war were available for this purpose: when Harbottle's (1904, 1981) battles were divided into two groups — those fought in Europe and those fought elsewhere — 62 percent of his 2110 battles were fought in Europe. When those fought in Europe were correlated with those fought outside during the 25 centuries from 500 B.C. to A.D. 1984, the correlation was significant (.71 when both sets of battles were logged to normalize their distributions). The correlation between Sorokin's European casualties and Harbottle's European battles over these 25 centuries (excluding the sixth to the ninth centuries, for which no Sorokin war data were available) was .83, which was not much higher than the correlation of .81 between Sorokin's total casualties and Harbottle's total battles over these same centuries.

The rationale for using the number of battles as a measure of war intensity, and therefore as comparable to war casualties used for the same purpose, was that I had previously found that Wright's battles per war during the last five hundred years was correlated .70, significant at the .01 level of confidence, when they were correlated with Levy's (1983) deaths per war over the same time period, for 73 wars which both lists had in common and for which both lists had available data. I interpreted this correlation to indicate that battles might be used in place of deaths as a rough measure of war intensity. This finding of a correlation across wars has been reinforced by the present finding of a significant correlation over centuries, from 500 B.C. to the twentieth century. Sorokin's war casualties were also significantly correlated .77 with the Dupuys' (1986) battles (N = 4460) over these same centuries, and .72 with the frequency of Kohn's (1987) war (N = 1826) over the same centuries. Not only do these findings support the use of battle frequency as a measure of war intensity, but also the use of war frequency over this time period.

In addition, these findings show that Sorokin's measures of war frequency, duration and intensity were relatively reliable, so far as they were significantly correlated with several other battle and war measures from 500 B.C. to the twentieth century.

RECAPITULATION. The most general and reliable findings of this study are that both war casualties and casualties per population were highly correlated with sensate cultures on a single factor, but these measures were not significantly correlated with century, revolution, nor transitional centuries. The revolutionary magnitude was highly correlated with centuries on another factor, but not at all with sensate type of culture, wars, nor transitions. Finally, transitional centuries were correlated with each other on a third factor, but not with anything else in this matrix. Nor, might I add, have I found any other measure of anything with which these transitional centuries are significantly correlated. They seem to be as random as anything can get.

However, these results were not so clear-cut when Sorokin's measures were included in a matrix with some other measures of battles and wars. This was because the results of factor analysis are relative to the subjects included in the analysis and to the variables included in the matrix. In this case, the subjects were the same, that is, the centuries from 500 B.C. to the twentieth century, excluding the sixth to the ninth centuries, but the variables included other measures of war in addition to Sorokin's casualty measures.

The most general factor was labeled "War," where most of Sorokin's war measures, except casualties per population, were loaded along with other measures of battle and war frequencies and also with Sorokin's revolutionary measures. All of these measures increased over the centuries. So far as Sorokin's measures of war casualties and war years were loaded on this factor, it should be noted that the increase of these variables over these centuries occurred in spite of the fact that earlier wars were exaggerated in their lengths, and therefore in their casualties, by Sorokin's method of estimating casualties by multiplying their typical percentage of army size by the number of years that the war lasted.

The second factor was labeled "Sense," where Sorokin's casualties, both absolute and relative, were loaded with sensate culture, and negatively loaded with Sorokin's revolutionary measures.

The correlation of war casualties with the sensate type of culture was entirely limited to Sorokin's measures of war casualties, so that this finding was not generalizable to other measures of war so far available and analyzed. This research will continue, of course, but for the time being we have to conclude that the relation of war to sensate cultures is not very reliable outside of Sorokin's casualty measures.

That leaves us with only one reliable conclusion from this study: war and revolution frequencies, durations and intensities have increased over the centuries since 500 B.C. in the case of wars and since 600 B.C. in the case of revolutions. The finding of a significant relation between Sorokin's sensate type of culture and war casualties, both absolute and relative to nations and populations, seems to be reliable enough, but not generalizable to measures of battle and war frequencies other than Sorokin's casualties. In spite of this exception, Sorokin's war measures were in general agreement with the measures of others. It was impossible to check the reliability of his revolutionary measures because of the lack of other similar lists. Nor could I check the reliability of his sensate factor, since no one else has developed any similar measure. Sorokin deserves our greatest admiration and gratitude for quantifying his data as much as he did. Had he not done so, it would have been quite difficult if not impossible to confirm or to deny any of his assertions, hypotheses or theories.

Finally, when I correlated Sorokin's European war casualties per population with time from the tenth century to the twentieth century, the correlation was .90, showing that European war casualties per population have increased from century to century during the last millennium (Eckhardt 1982). All of these findings from my analyses of Sorokin's quantitative data support the theory that war and revolution and civilization grow together, assuming that we have been getting more civilized during the last millennium, which seems like a reasonable assumption.

SOROKIN'S THEORIES OF CIVILIZATION, EMPIRE AND WAR.   Sorokin's later post–World War II theory of war emphasized striving for superiority, lust of power, private property, egoism and governments themselves as the agents of civilized power (1947, 1954, 1959). This was quite a change from his pre-war theory which emphasized power, and especially military power, as a deterrent to revolution, at least, and presumably as a deterrent to war as well. His previous theory was simply an early version of the "peace through strength" notion so popular in the world today. His post-war theory of peace emphasized love, altruism, disarmament and a universal moral order.

It would seem that Sorokin's later theory emphasized the need to change the focus of civilization from egoism to altruism in order to change it from war to peace. The later Sorokin believed that "creative love" was required as an antidote to "egoistic poison. With such a purification the very roots of intergroup warfare are cut off; with the roots destroyed, the warfare itself is bound to die out. Such is the prescription for elimination of the curse of intergroup conflicts from the human universe" (1954 p. 462). This prescription had to overcome the tremendous obstacles thrown up by "ego-centered pride and the sense of one's own superiority" (p. 468). In short, civilization needed to be changed from authoritarianism to egalitarianism, from egoism to altruism, and from compulsion to compassion, in order to change from war to peace. This prescription was very similar to those of Toynbee and Wright, except that the latter two placed more emphasis upon world government (a universal legal order) than Sorokin, who placed more emphasis upon a universal moral order.

## Modern Warfare

A number of authors have provided quantitative data on modern warfare starting about 1500. Sorokin (1937 vol. 3), Wright (1965), Levy (1983) and Eckhardt (Sivard 1991) provided data for all five centuries of modern times. Kaye et al. (1985) and Bouthoul and Carrere (1978) provided data for most of the last three centuries. Richardson (1960a) and Small and Singer (1982) provided data for most of the last two centuries. And Westing (1982) provided data for the major wars of the twentieth century.

Table 15.1 in Appendix B shows the number of deaths (or casualties in the case of Sorokin, and battles in the case of Wright) per century in the modern period since 1500. These estimates are given in millions, except in the case of Wright, where the number of important battles per century are given. These latter have been placed in parentheses to distinguish them from the other estimates in millions of deaths (or casualties, in the case of Sorokin). The first three rows in Table 15.1 were very much Eurocentered. Sorokin provided estimates for nine European nations only. Levy's (1983) estimates were limited to 14 Great Powers, 11 of which were European nations, and the other three of which (the United States, Japan and China) did not become Great Powers until the twentieth century. Wright's battles occurred in Europe 87 percent of the time, and those that occurred outside of Europe involved European nations for the most part. These Eurocentric estimates followed a similar pattern. They tended to increase from the sixteenth to the twentieth century, except for a drop in the nineteenth century.

The rest of the war death estimates were more worldwide, but they did not start until the eighteenth century, except for Eckhardt (1991). In all of these cases, the estimates increased steadily from century to century. These figures show that, assuming that we were becoming more civilized over these centuries, we were simultaneously killing more people throughout the world. They would also suggest that, although Europe may have been suffering less war in the nineteenth century, this was not the case for the world as a whole.

Other measures in the bottom half of Table 15.1 shows that the number of nations in the world was also increasing from the eighteenth to the twentieth century, as were world population, revolutionary magnitudes, scientific discoveries, technological inventions, materialistic culture and imperial sizes during the last five centuries. If scientific discoveries and technological inventions can be taken as a measure of development (materialistic development, to be sure), then we again find warlikeness growing with development during these centuries. The increase in the average imperial size over these same centuries also confirmed the growth of empires with the growth in warlikeness.

Table 15.2 in Appendix B shows these same estimates divided by world population. The results were the same when the estimates were divided by European population. These relative measures still show an increasing trend in deaths per population from century to century as a general rule, the main exceptions to which occur in the first three Eurocentric rows. For the absolute measures in Table 15.1, the twentieth century was always higher than previous centuries. For the relative measures in Table 15.2, the twentieth century was always higher than previous centuries, except for Wright's battles in the eighteenth century. This table shows that population increase alone could not account for all of the increase in war deaths during the last five centuries, since these deaths still increased even after population was statistically controlled.

When the measures of war intensity were divided by the number of nations, the number of scientific discoveries, the number of technological inventions and the imperial sizes — in order to control for these measures of science and size — the controlled war measures were significantly higher in the twentieth century than in any of the previous four centuries, with only a few exceptions which were limited to Levy and Wright.

These estimates for modern warfare, both absolute and relative, generally supported a relationship between the development of modern civilization, the growth of modern imperial sizes and the destructiveness of modern warfare. The precise mechanisms by which increasing civilization led to increased intensity of war remain to be established by further research. The dialectical evolutionary theory proposed in this book suggests that expanding civilization increased inequalities which—having been brought about by armed violence—required more armed violence in order to maintain the status quo. Some evidence to support the relations between conflict, imperialism and inequality has been provided by Eckhardt and Young (1977) and Eckhardt (1984). The opposing forces fed into each other, spiraling alternately up and down with the rise and fall of empires.

According to the dialectical evolutionary theory proposed in this book, all three of these social inventions—civilizations, empires, and wars—started about the same time, that is, about 3000 B.C., although this claim is not hard and fast, but allows for the possibility of civilizations existing without empires (such as the Greek and Sumerian city-states), and even of empires existing without war (such as the possibility of relatively nonviolent conquests, especially in archaic and ancient times).

The theory can hardly deny the possibility of wars without empires (the Greek and Sumerian city-states fought with one another) and even of some wars without civilization (there is anthropological evidence of war among the more developed primitive peoples, especially after the agricultural revolution). Consequently, the theory should be taken as proposing some general rules, not universal laws. In short, the dialectical evolutionary theory is a theory of probability and not one of certainty, although the probabilities are fairly high, as suggested by the correlations among the three variables at both the global and regional levels of analysis, and by the generalization of these correlations by factor analysis.

Extrapolating the linear trends of civilization, empire and war at the global level into the future, it looks as if we are bound to become more civilized and more warlike in the future, even though we have reached a (total) imperial limit, since virtually all of the world today is under various degrees of political control. Consequently, imperial territory is subject to changing rulers in the future, but not to any further overall increase, short of colonizing outer space (which may happen in due time). Obviously, this limit does not prevent existing civilizations from fighting over the possession of existing empires.

Extrapolating these same linear trends into the past brings us to a virtual zero in civilization, empire and war about 3000 B.C., at earliest, according to most estimates available today. Civilized wars probably did not amount to much during the first half of human history from 3000 to 600 B.C. Nor did civilizational activities and imperial sizes. These data, rough as they are, suggest that early civilizations and empires were not very warlike, and that primitive tribes and villages were virtually peaceful, except for some feuding and raiding.

The extrapolations into the future seem to bode ill for the future, but extrapolations never determine anything. Their predictions may be taken into account by human beings and used in such a way as to falsify those predictions.

On the other hand, the extrapolations into the past seem to deny that theory of human nature that holds it to be inherently warlike. Human nature may very well be aggressive at the interpersonal level, and even feudlike and raidlike if we insist (which I do not), but we hardly seem to be innately warlike, judging by the evidence at hand. For several million years, we roamed this earth without leaving any trace of war or a territorial imperative. It was only after we became civilized, that is, dependent upon land, labor, capital and trade for making a living, imperialism and militarism arose.

So far as historical records show, war followed imperialism, even as imperialism followed civilization, at least at their beginnings. How do we break that chain of events?

Unless we have an instinct of exploitation (which I doubt very much), that is, an inherent drive to benefit ourselves at the expense of others, it would seem that we have no basic need for war. If we developed in ourselves a pattern of domination and exploitation — that made war inevitable — then we have the means to change the structure of the civilization we created. We must change our choices and our values.

If we learn from primitive (unwarlike) peoples and create a civilization of more free and equal human relations, we might be able to recreate a world without war.

## Conclusions

In answer to the question, "Did civilizations, empires and wars foster one another?" the answer seems to be an unequivocal "Yes." All three were shown to interrelate among primitive, civilized and modern peoples. These empirical findings confirmed the theories about war and civilization expressed by Toynbee, Sorokin and Wright (among others), according to which war and civilization were motivated by a sense of superiority and self-righteousness, which rationalized and justified the destructiveness of their behavior. What was not always clearly recognized was just how destructive these behaviors were, since the *structural* violence caused by armed violence in the form of imperialism tended to be invisible, from the imperial point of view. Furthermore, the self-destructiveness of these behaviors was completely concealed by the self-deception of self-centeredness and self-righteousness so characteristic of civilized peoples, who tend to believe in their innate superiority to others especially to primitive peoples. Finally, the ultimate destruction possible with nuclear warfare was never foreseen in our worst nightmares. However, even the possibility of total destruction has not yet led us to make an ethical response to its challenge. Without this ethical response, we may be doomed to self-destruct, guided by the will to power.

In answer to the question, "Can we have civilization without war?" the answer again seems to be an unequivocal "Yes." The empirical and statistical evidence presented in this book makes it clear that the *way* we developed civilization so far is the problem, which can be solved by changing the *direction* of civilization or by changing its *structure*. Toynbee, Sorokin and Wright all pointed to the authoritarian, egoistic, and compulsive nature of civilization as its war-making essence. All of them called for an ethical solution to the problem of self-destruction. That is, we can prevent war by restructuring civilization so that our human relations are more equalitarian, altruistic and compassionate. Whether we shall need a world government seems to be problematic. If we can make these structural changes, we may not need a world government, although they will make one more possible. If we cannot make these structural changes, a world government will either be impossible to achieve or, if achieved, may well become another part of the problem instead of a part of its solution.

# Afterword
## by David Wilkinson

In *Civilizations, Empires and Wars*, the late William Eckhardt has located areas in which war research of a scientistic character can progress by giving less attention to some old problems and theses, which can be treated as (at least for now) in eclipse, and more to some others—and to some new problems. In general, attention is needed to developing terms, tools of analysis, and tests for distinguishing between similar yet importantly different functional imputations and associated causal hypotheses. I shall accordingly review Eckhardt's chapters in order to suggest directions in which the scientistic research debate might evolve. My suggestions occasionally reflect a fairly definite, even enthusiastic, agenda in civilizational taxonomics as well as a rather less definite disposition toward caution in polemological systematics.

## Chapter 1. Primitive Warfare

**1.1** We can, I think, properly be fairly inattentive to the proposition "warfare is a function of instinct, independent of development." It might next be in order to formulate tests to distinguish between two other propositions, "warfare is a function of development, independent of instinct," vs. "warfare is a function of (faster-varying) 'development' and (slower-varying) 'instinct'." "Instinct" may no longer be the best name for this variable.

**1.2** We can probably set aside as unlikely the proposition "war preparations deter war more than they provoke war." The next stage in this argument would seem to be to try to differentially test the proposition "war preparations independently increase the probability of war" and "the same factors that provoke wars provoke prior preparations therefor." When war is endemic, will not groups be more likely to prepare for it than when it is uncommon? Are war preparations perhaps consequences of warlikeness?

**1.3** Can we distinguish between the propositions "warfare is a function of an authoritarian culture," "an authoritarian culture is a function of (chronic) warfare," and "(chronic) warfare and authoritarian culture are functions of a third variable?" And of what is an authoritarian culture a function? Of development? If so, is "modern" culture linearly more authoritarian than "medieval," "classical," "archaic" and "primitive?" Freudians might be tempted to think so.

1.4  Setting aside the proposition "primitive warfare was an unplanned and nonrational function of aggression," can we distinguish by some test between the propositions "primitive warfare was a well planned and rationally executed behavior rather than a function of aggression" and "primitive warfare was well planned and rationally executed as well as a function of aggression?"

1.5  Can we totally distinguish between the propositions "warfare came rather late in primitive development" and "individual and collective homicide came rather early in human social evolution, but deadly quarrels scaled up in magnitude with social size?" At a small enough social scale, does not the scaling of war shrink to the point where "war" becomes indistinguishable from "murder" and "army" from "band?" If we fail to study murder rates in small societies do we fall into Rousseauianism more or less inadvertently?

1.6  Is development perhaps a function of warlikeness rather than, or in addition to, the reverse? Some groups have moved from massacring to conquering to ruling, taxing, accumulating, and "developing." To what extent does the causal relationship operate in the direction of this evolution?

1.7  It is interesting, and seems odd, to see warfare associated with both full-time enterprise and slavery. Are two separate associative processes at work? Are the alternative socioeconomic forms well enough defined?

1.8  Is gender bias in warring fully accounted for by women's childbearing and rearing occupations? Do these activities function to satisfy the same motivations as warfare?

1.9  Anthropological models of levels of political development often look like stages of progress. States, systems, and empires however look more like alternative unstable phases of an untrastable system. It is not clear that either reflects "development" with respect to the other. At this stage, then, what becomes of the correlation between development and militarism? The mobbing of dominant powers by their near-peers in general war interrupts Otterbein's sequence; does this imply a "higher" level of political development? If so, then the correlation may hold, for general wars have been particularly sanguinary.

## Chapter 2. Archaic and Ancient Wars, 3000 to 500 B.C.

**2.1** To what extent can the effects of cultural-technological development (providing accumulations of surplus to be looted, to be protected, to be extracted, to fungibly found weaponry and fund warfare) sufficiently explain the major "archaic" resort to warfare? In the language of motive, means and opportunity, do they adequately account for motive, and even for opportunity? Cultural-technological development may have provided to humanity, already equipped with fairly constant motivation, not only the means to express it more effectively and on a larger scale, but also, indirectly, the opportunity to do so, as demographic clustering and crowding round centers removed or reduced the opportunity for those attacked to flee from conquest, enslavement and killing.

## Chapter 3. Classic Wars, 500 B.C. to A.D. 500

**3.1** While agreeing that empires rise and fall, and that cities rise and fall, I have argued elsewhere that civilizations rise and merge but almost never fall.

Accordingly, vis-à-vis Eckhardt's interpretation of the "classical" empire data as showing multiple rises and falls of civilization, I would say the problem is to find out what it was that rose and fell, covarying with imperial size. Urbanization may be part of the answer, but I doubt that that is all there is to it. I am not sure, however, that it is possible to come to grips with this problem until the issue of the cross-civilizational validity of the Archaic-Classical-Medieval periodization is addressed; likewise the issue of the analytical separability of the Middle East, Persia and Greece, all of which I would characterize in the millennium 500 B.C.–A.D. 500 as regions of a single, Central civilization.

## Chapter 4. Medieval Wars, A.D. 500 to 1500

**4.1** The decline in European war casualties and European imperial sizes A.D. 500–1500 and the rise in Middle Eastern empire sizes seem easier to treat as mutually "compensating" if these areas are seen as regions of a single ("Central") civilizational social system, in which there was an eastward core shift from (Mediterranean) Europe to the Middle East between the Classial and Medieval periods.

**4.2** The idea of self-righteousness as a historical force has a strong commonsense appeal. Is it reasonable? Is it constant or does it vary across personalities, cultures, time? Is it a prime mover, or an intervening variable? Of

what might it be a function? Could it be a psychological effect of chronic warfare? A survival trait in a war-prone environment?

## Chapter 5. Modern War: An Overview

**5.1**  Is "Western civilization" a taxonomically sound concept? If so, to
what extent can a civilization be treated as an agent that acts, to what extent
only as a structure within which agents work?

**5.2**  Is "warlikeness" satisfactorily measured by imperial size? A very "warlike" states system might incidentally mob and dismember large empires.

**5.3**  Is "warlikeness" attributable to civilizations, empires *and* imperial
metropoles?

**5.4**  If imperial size does measure warlikeness, does it do so only as a lag-
ging indicator?

**5.5**  Might rate of growth, or rate of size change, of empires better indicate "warlikeness?"

**5.6**  If civilizations don't fall but empires do, then neither war nor class
would seem to cause the fall of civilizations, yet they may still be implicated
in their rise.

**5.7**  Can there be a quantitative measurement of the degree to which
wars vary over time in violating basic rules of ethics? Are these rules themselves
variable in time and space? Do they fluctuate e.g. between sensate and ideational? Do they progress?

## Chapter 6. Wright's List of Modern Wars, 1480–1964

**6.1**  What, if any wars, defined otherwise than by Wright, were systematically overlooked by Wright's definition of war as a legal condition? To what
extent, if any, would the inclusion of the excluded wars force an alteration of
his conclusions; and to what extent should these conclusions then be restricted
to "legal" wars?

## Chapter 7. Levy's List of Great Power Wars, 1495–1975

**7.1**  What sort of subset of the whole war data set (however defined) is
Levy's collection? How do its characteristics differ from or reflect those of the
whole set?

## Chapter 10. Civilized Wars Throughout History

**10.1** The different definitions of Wright, Levy, Sorokin, Kohn, Dupuy and Dupuy, Eckhardt, Kaye et al., Bouthoul and Carrere, Dunnigan and Martel, Richardson, Small and Singer, and Westing forcibly suggest the desirability of a comparative study of the whole set of different definitions of war used to collect data for quantitative analysis. What universe of cases would exist if all studies' lists were combined? What are the peculiarities of each definition's sample of that universe? How far, if at all, do their conclusions follow from the unified definitions?

**10.2** To what extent is it possible, and how is it possible, to find "starters" of wars? "Aggressors?" Is it appropriate to find "starters" for belligerent pairs within wars instead? Would doing so alter the starters' rate of success?

**10.3** Why are starters lately having more trouble? Does the balance-of-power mechanism exist, increasingly working and discriminating against them? Or are attackers becoming increasingly irrational, concerned more with justice than with victory? Would this reflect a swing from sensate to ideational politics?

**10.4** It seems worthwhile to emphasize the predominantly Anglo-American and pacifist associations of scientist war studies. What would be the most desirable directions, and expected results, of diversification in these respects?

**10.5** Given the number of cases with interstate and internal belligerent pairs, is the dichotomy between international and civil wars self-explanatory? Justifiable? Useful?

## Chapter 13. War-Related Deaths Since 3000 B.C.

**13.1** I feel very unsure of the utility of Europe as a transhistorical unit of analysis. I agree that war-data Eurocentricity needs to be disentangled with care from the objective or subjective Eurocentricity of history or historians. Nevertheless I also agree that modern Europe was very probably unusually violent. Better measurements and theory are needed before we strongly affirm that it was the most civilized and imperial of societies, hence the most violent.

## Chapter 14. A Dialectical Evolutionary Theory

**14.1** I feel strong reservations about using creativeness as a measure of civilization, whether synonymously or indicatively. Accordingly I would say that what has been correlated in this chapter is only creativeness and war. I suspect that Nietzsche would, and Toynbee and Quigley would not, readily accept this association as meaningful. It certainly warrants further exploration.

**14.2**   To the extent that conquest-empires destroy provincial culture, loot it, or enslave and enlist its makers in the metropolitan service, their archeological record will show a possibly spurious imperial creativity which only a close scrutiny of their histories (e.g., Rome's parasitization of its eastern provinces) will dispel. It may well be that the net creativity of a civilization decreases in those epochs when cosmopolitan dynasts make their capitals flower with tyrant art; measurements taken only at the center will be completely out of phase with the whole.

**14.3**   The contrast of "global" vs. "regional" is meaningful in one sense for the present century, which is monocivilizational (but polycultural), in another for previous centuries. For multiregional civilizations not of global scope, most notably Central civilization c. 1500 B.C. to c. A.D. 1900, an intermediate level of analysis is needed for mapping rises and falls and correlating them to global and regional data. (The regions themselves will grow and move over millennia, and must be kinematically mapped in order to contextualize war and battle data approximately.)

**14.4**   It does seem very likely that there are transhistorical and transcultural phenomena of rationalization and ideology at work behind the various historical justifications of war. It is not clear whether this reflects a choice (freely reversible) of rationalization as a value, or the (not freely reversible) evolution of a mechanism of rationalization.

## Chapter 15.   Summary and Conclusions

**15.1**   Can one show that the Golden Rule and the Categorical Imperative are transhistorically and transculturally valid rules for all, so that noncompliance is a violation?

**15.2**   To what extent is violation of the ethical teachings of Jesus and Kant freely choosable? I think of Richardson's remark, "The less a type of behavior is subject to free choice, the less also is it subject to moral condemnation. . . . I did not know quite what to condemn, until I had found out what was mechanical." Are there mechanisms of moral determination?

**15.3**   I believe the most enduring findings of Eckhardt's study will be the partly discovered, partly recovered propositions: initiating a war is very risky; most war fatalities are noncombatants; the war death toll and war magnitudes have risen strikingly since A.D. 1500.

**15.4** I remain far less sanguine than Eckhardt about primitive warfare, human nature, civilized arrogance, the historicity of the categorical imperative, free will, the *past* self-destructiveness of warlike civilizations, and the world having reached an imperial limit.

**15.5** I would judge the most fruitful line of research to follow up in this study would be the more detailed measurement of civilizations and of empires.

William Eckhardt has herein undertaken the large-scale meta-analysis of long-term statistical studies of war. It is a worthy enterprise well begun.

## Appendix A
# Statistics

In this appendix various statistical techniques are described as briefly and as clearly as possible. These techniques are basically of two different kinds: (1) correlations, factor analyses and regression analyses, which measure the similarities and differences in the *distribution* of variables; and (2) *t* tests and analyses of variance (F-tests) which measure the similarities and differences in the *mean scores* of various groups (e.g., nations, regions, decades, centuries). (Chi-square tests are also used for the latter purpose when the measures are *frequencies* instead of mean scores.) These basic methods may be applied to two or to more than two variables, as shown in the following table:

## Statistical Methods of Analysis

| *Content of Measurement* | *Number of Variables* | |
|---|---|---|
| | *Two Variables* | *More Than Two* |
| Similarities and Differences of *Patterns* | Correlation Coefficient | Factor Analysis Regression Analysis |
| Similarities and Differences of *Levels* | *Chi-square for frequencies* | *Chi-square for frequencies* |
| | *t* test for mean scores | F-test (analysis of variance) for mean scores |

These statistical methods of analysis are extremely useful in establishing similarities and differences between patterns and levels with a specified degree of probability. However, they tell us nothing about the causal direction of the relations between variables. Causes have to be determined by empirical (preferably experimental) evidence and logical or theoretical argument independent of the statistical situation.

## Probability Levels, or Levels of Confidence

Correlation, factor and regression coefficients range from 0 to 1 (or −1, in case of a negative relationship). Zero indicates *no* relation at all. One (1) indicates a perfect positive relation. Minus one ( −1) indicates a perfect negative relation. The probability of any coefficient (and the probability of any mean difference) being significantly different from zero is indicated as follows:

**** Significant at the .0001 level of confidence, which means that a coefficient, *t*, or F as large as the one being tested, could have occurred by chance less than one in 10,000 times.
 *** Significant at the .001 level of confidence.
  ** Significant at the .01 level of confidence.
   * Significant at the .05 level of confidence.

This latter probability (*) is generally accepted as the minimum level to determine statistical significance (not to be confused with substantial significance). Statistical significance is simply a measure of reliability, indicating that a similarity or difference will probably be found 5/100 times, given a similar sample of items and subjects tested under similar conditions. Substantial significance is determined by the size of the similarity or difference, not by the size of the probability. Correlation and factor coefficients in the text are at least significant at the .05 level of confidence unless otherwise indicated.

 ' Significant at the .10 level of confidence, which can be considered to be statistically significant *if and only if* a hypothesis is being tested, that is, if we have specified a hypothesized similarity or difference prior to an experiment.
ns Not significant at the .05 level of confidence.

## Explained Variance

The percent of the variance explained by any coefficient is expressed by the square of the coefficient. For example, if r = .70, the distribution of one set of scores can explain 49 percent (.70 × .70) of the variance in another set of scores. That is to say that they share 49 percent of their variance in common.

## Factor Analysis

Factors may be unrotated or rotated, and rotated factors may be independent (orthogonal) or correlated with one another (oblique). The first unrotated factor is called a general factor in this book, because it generalizes as many variables as possible into a single factor. A general factor represents as much of the complexity as possible in an set of variables, while rotated factors try to simplify this complexity as much as possible.

Rotated factors are very useful in developing scales to measure a set of very similar variables. General factors are more useful in combining a complicated set of variables. General factors are used more often than not in this book.

Orthogonal rotation results in independent (uncorrelated) factors. Oblique rotation results in correlated factors. Oblique factors can then be correlated with one another, which will bring them back together into a second-order factor similar to the general factor from which they were obtained.

*Appendix B*

# Tables

## Table 2.1 Factor Scores on Militarism

| Civilizations | Universal State | Gen Mil | Off Mil | Tot Mil | War-like | Terr Mm² | War + Terr |
|---|---|---|---|---|---|---|---|
| Syria | 500B.C.–A.D.975 | 66 | 54 | 60 | 11 | 1.0 | 54 |
| Arabia | A.D.1086–1454 | 52 | 67 | 60 | 10 | 1.0 | 52 |
| Persia | A.D.1453–1572 | 60 | 59 | 60 | 11 | 2.3 | 57 |
| Tartar | (A.D.1400–1750) | 50 | 69 | 60 | 12 | 5.5 | 64 |
| Greece/Rome | 31B.C.–A.D.250 | 67 | 47 | 57 | 12 | 4.4 | 63 |
| Japan | A.D.1598–1854 | 59 | 55 | 57 | 12 | 0.4 | 53 |
| Babylonia | 750–538B.C. | 63 | 48 | 56 | 13 | 0.5 | 55 |
| West | A.D.1020–1350 | 69 | 42 | 56 | 8 | 1.0 | 48 |
| Mexico | (A.D.1520–1520) | 46 | 64 | 55 | 11 | 0.2 | 50 |
| Andes | A.D.1430–1530 | 45 | 62 | 54 | 12 | 2.0 | 58 |
| Hittite | 1480–1200B.C. | 50 | 54 | 52 | 10 | 0.5 | 50 |
| Russia | A.D.1192–1350 | 52 | 51 | 52 | 8 | 1.8 | 51 |
| Scandinavia | (A.D.875–1300) | 47 | 56 | 52 | 9 | 0.5 | 48 |
| Orthodox | A.D.1470–1605 | 61 | 41 | 51 | 6 | 1.0 | 45 |
| Yucatan | (A.D.1520–1520) | 42 | 56 | 49 | 8 | 0.1 | 44 |
| Germany | (300B.C.–A.D.400) | 41 | 56 | 49 | 7 | 2.0 | 50 |
| Hindu India | A.D.1525–1707 | 52 | 43 | 48 | 5 | 3.5 | 49 |
| Manchu China | A.D.1380–1830 | 51 | 40 | 46 | 6 | 15.0 | 60 |
| Ireland | (A.D.761–1090) | 41 | 50 | 46 | 5 | 0.1 | 39 |
| Maya | A.D.300–600 | 37 | 50 | 44 | 6 | 0.1 | 40 |
| Classic India | 323B.C.–A.D.475 | 49 | 37 | 43 | 5 | 3.5 | 49 |
| Nestoria | (A.D.569–737) | 30 | 52 | 41 | 3 | 0.8 | 39 |
| Mesopotamia | 2298–1905B.C. | 44 | 37 | 41 | 6 | 0.8 | 44 |
| Minoa | 2000–1700B.C. | 39 | 40 | 40 | 5 | 0.0 | 38 |
| Egypt | 2060–1250B.C. | 39 | 39 | 39 | 6 | 1.0 | 45 |
| Han China | 221B.C.–A.D.170 | 47 | 30 | 39 | 6 | 6.5 | 55 |
| Mean | | 50 | 50 | 50 | 8.2 | 2.1 | 50 |
| Std | | 10 | 10 | 7 | 2.9 | 3.1 | 7 |

*Notes:* Universal state data obtained from Wright (1965, p. 463). Dates in parentheses are estimates based on Wright's data. Gen Mil = 1st factor scores of general militarism. Off Mil = 2nd factor scores of offensive militarism. Tot Mil = Total militarism scores obtained by adding Gen Mil and Off Mil, and then dividing by two. Warlike = Warlikeness ratings from 3 to 13 (Wright, 1965, pp. 571–72). These ratings were the sum of the ratings on political absolutism, bloodthirstiness, imperialistic battle frequency, interstate battle frequency, and popular morale. Terr $(Mm^2)$ = Imperial size in square megameters (Taagepera, 1978a, pp. 116–17). I selected the largest size given by Taagepera during those years given by Wright (1965, p. 463) for the universal state (maturity) of the civilization. For those civilizations not included among Taagepera's three largest empires, their sizes were obtained from Taagepera (1978b, 1979, 1981, 1986, 1987 correspondence) and from Sivard (1991). War + Terr = War ratings and territorial sizes were standardized (after territorial sizes were logged to correct for skewness), and then added together and divided by two. This score is tentatively offered as a combination of both the intensity and extent of militarism: how much it was used and how far it went. Much work remains to be done to establish its reliability and validity. It is presented here for further research. General and offensive militarism scores are presented as *t* scores, whose mean is 50 and whose standard deviation is 10, which means that approximately two-thirds of these scores are within one standard deviation of the mean, that is, from 40 to 60. The Tot Mil and War + Terr scores have a mean of 50, but their standard deviations have been reduced to 7 by the averaging process, so that approximately two-thirds of these scores range from 43 to 57. Std = Standard deviation. The mean +/– the standard deviation includes about two-thirds of all scores.

## Table 2.2    Archaic-Ancient Civilizations, Empires and Wars

| Cent | War | Bat | Imp | Civ | Pop | Pages |
|------|-----|-----|------|------|-----|-------|
| – 30 | 0 | 0 | 0.15 | 0.6 | 14 | 1.4 |
| – 29 | 0 | 0 | 0.20 | 0.0 | 15 | 1.4 |
| – 28 | 0 | 0 | 0.26 | 0.0 | 16 | 1.4 |
| – 27 | 0 | 0 | 0.32 | 0.0 | 17 | 1.4 |
| – 26 | 0 | 0 | 0.37 | 0.0 | 18 | 1.4 |
| – 25 | 0 | 0 | 0.43 | 0.0 | 19 | 1.4 |
| – 24 | 0 | 0 | 0.50 | 0.0 | 20 | 1.4 |
| – 23 | 0 | 0 | 0.90 | 0.0 | 21 | 1.4 |
| – 22 | 0 | 0 | 0.40 | 0.0 | 23 | 1.4 |
| – 21 | 0 | 0 | 0.28 | 0.0 | 25 | 1.4 |
| – 20 | 1 | 0 | 0.50 | 0.0 | 27 | 3.1 |
| – 19 | 0 | 0 | 0.80 | 0.0 | 29 | 3.1 |
| – 18 | 0 | 0 | 1.25 | 0.0 | 31 | 3.1 |
| – 17 | 4 | 0 | 1.10 | 0.0 | 33 | 3.1 |
| – 16 | 8 | 0 | 1.35 | 0.0 | 35 | 3.1 |
| – 15 | 2 | 1 | 2.05 | 1.0 | 38 | 4.8 |
| – 14 | 5 | 0 | 2.25 | 0.0 | 41 | 4.8 |
| – 13 | 7 | 1 | 2.70 | 0.0 | 44 | 4.8 |
| – 12 | 4 | 1 | 2.65 | 0.0 | 47 | 4.8 |
| – 11 | 3 | 1 | 1.60 | 8.7 | 50 | 4.8 |
| – 10 | 3 | 0 | 1.00 | 1.8 | 62 | 4.8 |
| – 9 | 4 | 1 | 1.15 | 9.7 | 74 | 4.8 |
| – 8 | 16 | 1 | 1.15 | 11.3 | 86 | 4.8 |
| – 7 | 18 | 3 | 3.10 | 12.3 | 98 | 4.8 |
| – 6 | 8 | 6 | 7.85 | 48.1 | 110 | 4.8 |
| Sum | 83 | 15 | 34.3 | 93.5 | 993 | 77.5 |
| Mean | 3.3 | 0.6 | 1.4 | 3.7 | 40 | 3.1 |

| Cent | War | Bat | Imp | Civ | Pop | Pages |
|------|-----|-----|-----|-----|-----|-------|
| Std | 4.9 | 1.3 | 1.6 | 10.0 | 27 | 1.6 |
| % Total | 4.6% | 0.3% | 1.2% | 0.7% | 0.8% | 6.8% |

*Notes:* War frequencies were calculated from Kohn (1987). Battle frequencies were calculated from Dupuy and Dupuy (1986). Imperial sizes in square megameters were calculated from Taagepera (1978a). Civilized activities were calculated from Sorokin (1941). Population (in millions) was calculated from McEvedy and Jones (1978). Pages were calculated from Garraty and Gay's (1972) *Columbia History of the World.* This measure was simply a rough count of the number of pages devoted to each century. Std = Standard deviation. Percentage totals were obtained by dividing the sum of each variable in these 25 centuries by its sum for all 50 centuries from 3000 B.C. to A.D. 2000.

## Table 3.1   Comparison of Mean Scores from Archaic to Classic Periods

| Variables | Archaic | | Ancient | | Classic | F | R² |
|-----------|---------|---|---------|---|---------|---|-----|
| Century | − 23 | < | − 10.5 | < | 0 | 110**** | 87% |
| Wars (Kohn) | 0.9 | < | 7 | < | 19 | 64**** | 80% |
| Battles (D & D) | 0 | < | 1.5 | < | 41 | 188**** | 92% |
| Imperial Size | 0.6 | < | 2.6 | < | 13.6 | 122**** | 88% |
| Civilization | 0.0 | < | 9.3 | < | 75 | 93**** | 85% |
| Population | 23 | < | 65 | < | 169 | 163**** | 91% |
| Pages (G & G) | 2 | < | 4.8 | < | 15 | 103**** | 87% |

*Notes:* See the notes following Table 2.2 for a description of the variables and for references to their sources. Signs of "less than" indicate significant differences as determined by analyses of variance (F-test) and Duncan's multiple-range test. **** Significant at the .0001 level of confidence, which means that an F as high as this could occur less than once in ten thousand times by chance. R² indicates how much of the variance in each variable could be explained by the difference between these historical periods. Wherever necessary, variables were logged to correct for their skewed distributions prior to analyses of variance. The archaic period extended from 3000 to 1500 B.C. The ancient period extended from 1500 to 500 B.C. The classic period extended from 500 B.C. to A.D. 500.

## Table 3.2   Comparison in Terms of Percentages

| Variables | Archaic | Ancient | Classic | Subtotal |
|-----------|---------|---------|---------|----------|
| Century (Avg) | − 23 | − 10.5 | 0 | − 12.9 |
| # Centuries | 15 | 10 | 10 | 35 |
| % Centuries | 30% | 20% | 20% | 70% |
| Wars (Kohn) | 0.7% | 3.8% | 10.5% | 15.1% |
| Battles (D & D) | 0.0 | 0.3 | 9.0 | 9.3 |
| Imperial Size | 0.5 | 2.2 | 11.5 | 14.2 |
| Civilization | 0.0 | 0.7 | 5.7 | 6.4 |
| Population | 3.1 | 5.9 | 15.2 | |

| Pages (G & G) | 2.6 | 4.2 | 13.3 | 20.1 |
|---|---|---|---|---|
| Average % Var | 1.1% | 2.9% | 10.9% | 14.9% |
| Average/Century | 0.037 | 0.145 | 0.545 | 0.213 |

*Notes:* See the notes following Table 2.2 for a description of the variables, and for references to their sources. The percentages in all cases are the percentages of the grand totals (not shown in this table) of all 50 centuries. The subtotal in this table is simply the sum of the three historical periods. Average % Var is the average percent of the six variables. Average/Century is Average % Var divided by % Centuries.

## Table 3.3   Classic Civilizations, Empires and Wars

| Cent | War | Bat | Imp | Civ | Pop | Pages |
|---|---|---|---|---|---|---|
| -5 | 23 | 42 | 6.25 | 92.6 | 120 | 11.2 |
| -4 | 29 | 43 | 5.70 | 106.6 | 135 | 11.2 |
| -3 | 25 | 75 | 11.85 | 50.6 | 150 | 11.2 |
| -2 | 21 | 30 | 15.15 | 33.5 | 165 | 11.2 |
| -1 | 20 | 61 | 16.40 | 105.7 | 170 | 11.2 |
| 1 | 11 | 9 | 18.40 | 103.6 | 180 | 19.2 |
| 2 | 9 | 12 | 13.80 | 66.9 | 190 | 19.2 |
| 3 | 15 | 44 | 14.70 | 46.7 | 190 | 19.2 |
| 4 | 19 | 38 | 15.80 | 84.3 | 190 | 19.2 |
| 5 | 20 | 51 | 17.90 | 56.1 | 195 | 19.2 |
| Sum | 192 | 405 | 136 | 747 | 1685 | 152 |
| Mean | 19.2 | 40.5 | 13.6 | 74.7 | 168.5 | 15.2 |
| Std | 6.1 | 20.2 | 4.4 | 27.3 | 25.9 | 4.2 |
| % Total | 10.5% | 9.0% | 11.5% | 5.7% | 15.2% | 13.3% |

*Notes:* See the notes following Table 2.2.

## Table 3.4   Regional and Global Imperial Sizes (3000 B.C. to A.D. 2000)

| Century | Egypt | Meso | India | China | Turkey | Persia | CentAs | Europe | World |
|---|---|---|---|---|---|---|---|---|---|
| -30 | 0.15 | 0.00 | | | | | | | 0.15 |
| -29 | 0.20 | 0.00 | | | | | | | 0.20 |
| -28 | 0.25 | 0.01 | | | | | | | 0.26 |
| -27 | 0.30 | 0.02 | | | | | | | 0.32 |
| -26 | 0.35 | 0.02 | | | | | | | 0.37 |
| -25 | 0.40 | 0.03 | | | | | | | 0.43 |
| -24 | 0.40 | 0.05 | 0.05 | | | | | | 0.50 |
| -23 | 0.20 | 0.60 | 0.10 | | | | | | 0.90 |
| -22 | 0.10 | 0.20 | 0.10 | | | | | | 0.40 |
| -21 | 0.10 | 0.03 | 0.15 | | | | | | 0.28 |
| -20 | 0.20 | 0.10 | 0.20 | | | | | | 0.50 |
| -19 | 0.50 | | 0.20 | 0.10 | | | | | 0.80 |
| -18 | 0.50 | | 0.30 | 0.45 | | | | | 1.25 |
| -17 | 0.25 | 0.45 | | 0.40 | | | | | 1.10 |

| Century | Egypt | Meso | India | China | Turkey | Persia | CentAs | Europe | World |
|---|---|---|---|---|---|---|---|---|---|
| − 16 | 0.65 | 0.20 | | 0.40 | 0.10 | | | | 1.35 |
| − 15 | 1.00 | 0.40 | | 0.50 | 0.15 | | | | 2.05 |
| − 14 | 0.90 | 0.40 | | 0.65 | 0.20 | 0.10 | | | 2.25 |
| − 13 | 1.00 | 0.25 | | 0.90 | 0.45 | 0.10 | | | 2.70 |
| − 12 | 0.75 | 0.20 | | 1.10 | 0.40 | 0.20 | | | 2.65 |
| − 11 | 0.60 | 0.35 | | 0.55 | 0.10 | | | | 1.60 |
| − 10 | 0.40 | 0.15 | | 0.45 | | | | | 1.00 |
| − 9 | 0.20 | 0.60 | | 0.35 | | | | | 1.15 |
| − 8 | | 0.70 | | 0.25 | 0.20 | | | | 1.15 |
| − 7 | 0.50 | 1.30 | | | 0.15 | 1.15 | | | 3.10 |
| − 6 | 0.65 | 0.60 | 0.50 | 0.10 | 0.50 | 5.50 | | | 7.85 |
| − 5 | | 0.15 | 0.30 | 0.30 | | 5.50 | | | 6.25 |
| − 4 | | 0.20 | 1.00 | 0.50 | | 4.00 | | | 5.70 |
| − 3 | | 1.20 | 3.50 | 1.30 | | 5.20 | 0.50 | 0.15 | 11.85 |
| − 2 | | | 3.00 | 2.50 | | 3.30 | 5.70 | 0.65 | 15.15 |
| − 1 | | | 1.50 | 6.20 | | 3.20 | 2.00 | 3.50 | 16.40 |
| 1 | | | 3.50 | 6.50 | | 2.50 | 1.50 | 4.40 | 18.40 |
| 2 | | | 1.20 | 5.70 | | 2.50 | | 4.40 | 13.80 |
| 3 | | | 1.30 | 5.50 | | 3.50 | | 4.40 | 14.70 |
| 4 | | | | 2.80 | | 3.50 | | 9.50 | 15.80 |
| 5 | | | 1.70 | 5.80 | | 3.50 | 1.00 | 5.90 | 17.90 |
| 6 | | | | 6.40 | 1.30 | 3.40 | 7.20 | 2.70 | 21.00 |
| 7 | | 9.00 | | 5.20 | | | 2.80 | 1.00 | 18.00 |
| 8 | | 11.00 | | 5.20 | | | 7.50 | 1.00 | 24.70 |
| 9 | | 4.50 | 1.00 | 3.00 | 1.00 | 2.00 | 4.70 | 2.30 | 18.50 |
| 10 | | 3.10 | | 3.00 | 1.00 | 2.30 | 5.00 | 2.60 | 17.00 |
| 11 | | 2.50 | | 3.00 | 4.00 | | 5.00 | 2.50 | 17.00 |
| 12 | | 3.30 | | 4.30 | | | 2.50 | | 10.10 |
| 13 | | 3.00 | 2.50 | 2.00 | | | 25.20 | | 32.70 |
| 14 | | 2.00 | 2.80 | 15.00 | | 4.00 | 8.00 | 1.00 | 32.80 |
| 15 | | 2.00 | | 6.50 | 1.00 | 2.30 | 2.50 | 2.80 | 17.10 |
| 16 | | | 2.00 | 3.50 | 4.50 | 2.00 | | 12.20 | 24.20 |
| 17 | | | 3.00 | 11.30 | 4.00 | 2.00 | | 28.50 | 48.80 |
| 18 | | | 1.00 | 15.00 | 4.00 | 2.00 | | 47.00 | 69.00 |
| 19 | | | | 13.50 | 5.00 | 2.00 | | 84.50 | 105.00 |
| 20 | | | | 9.70 | 4.00 | 1.65 | | 113.90 | 129.25 |
| Sum | 10.55 | 48.61 | 30.90 | 149.90 | 32.05 | 67.40 | 81.10 | 334.90 | 755.41 |
| Mean | 0.21 | 0.97 | 0.62 | 3.00 | 0.64 | 1.35 | 1.62 | 6.70 | 15.11 |
| Std | 0.29 | 2.12 | 1.03 | 4.00 | 1.37 | 1.70 | 4.02 | 19.61 | 24.01 |

*Notes:* The largest size achieved by any empire in any century was entered in this table. For the few centuries (the twenty-ninth, twenty-seventh, and twenty-sixth B.C.) not included in Taagepera (1978a), his data were interpolated. The imperial regions in this table closely followed Taagepera's "empire cores" (1978a, p. 116). Africa and America are omitted from this table because of the lack of data for these regions: among the (then) three largest empires, those omitted are only Carthage in 500 B.C., Ptolemee in the third century B.C., Mali in A.D. 1300, Inca in A.D. 1500 and Canada in the twentieth century. Carthage and Ptolemee were included in Mesopotamia. Canada and Latin America in the twentieth century and the USA in the nineteenth and twentieth centuries were included in Europe, since they were essentially European colonies that had only recently become independent.

# Table 3.5  Mean Scores of Classic Wars and Internal Disturbances

|  | *Greece* | *Rome* |
|---|---|---|
| **Wars** (Civil, Colonial, Imperial and Interstate) | | |
| Dates | 500–146B.C. | 390B.C.–A.D.476 |
| # Centuries | 4 | 9 |
| Frequency | 9 (4) | 10 (4) |
| Duration (Yrs) | 62 (33) | 47 (19) |
| Casualties/ 1000 Pop | 23 (16) | 19 (19) |
| Casualties/ 1000 Army | 50 (8) | 53 (9) |
| Casualties/ War Year | 1.26 | 2.11 |
| **Disturbances** (Riots, Rebellions, Coups, etc.) | | |
| Dates | 600–146B.C. | 509B.C.–A.D.476 |
| # Centuries | 5 | 10 |
| Frequency | 18 (9) | 17 (12) |
| Duration (Yrs) | 23 (17) | 22 (16) |
| Geometric Average | 254 (154) | 254 (182) |
| **Ideation** (Faith) | 38.8 (5.3) | 45.0 (9.1) |

Based on Sorokin's (1937, vol. 3) data

*Notes:* Figures in the body of the table are mean scores per nation per century. Figures in parentheses are standard deviations from the mean. War casualties included both dead and wounded in the army. The geometric average of the internal disturbances was an average of social area, duration, size of masses involved and intensity. There were no significant differences between Greece and Rome on any of these mean scores. All observed differences could have occurred by chance. The ideation scores were obtained from a factor analysis of eight of Sorokin's (1937, vol. 2) measures of philosophy, religion, and science over 26 centuries. Ideation was a general factor characterized by faith versus sense and reason in epistemology, by idealism versus materialism in ontology, and by love versus happiness and principles in ethics. These mean scores show that the classic centuries were sense-oriented, as a general rule, although Rome changed significantly from sense (37.2) toward faith (52.8) in the Christian era.

# Table 3.6   Correlations of Classic Wars and Disturbances with Time

|  | Greece | Rome |
|---|---|---|

**Wars** (Civil, Colonial, Imperial and Interstate)

| | Greece | Rome |
|---|---|---|
| Dates | 500–146B.C. | 390B.C.–A.D.476 |
| # Centuries | 4 | 9 |
| Frequency | – 18 | – 31 |
| Duration (Yrs) | – 97* | – 53 |
| Casualties/ 1000 Pop | – 78 | – 35 |
| Casualties/ 1000 Army | – 72 | – 42 |
| Casualties/ Year of War | – 27 | – 01 |

*Disturbances* (Riots, Rebellions, Coups, etc.)

| | Greece | Rome |
|---|---|---|
| Dates | 600–146B.C. | 509B.C.–A.D.476 |
| # Centuries | 5 | 10 |
| Frequency | – 42 | 64* |
| Duration (Yrs) | – 37 | 59' |
| Geometric Average | – 37 | 54 |

| | Greece | Rome |
|---|---|---|
| *Ideation* (Faith) | – 57 | 97** |

Based on Sorokin's (1937, vol. 3) data

*Notes:* See notes following Table 3.5. Figures in the body of the table are correlation coefficients with decimal points omitted. Positive correlations indicate an increase in wars or internal disturbances over the centuries shown in parentheses in the columns. Negative correlations indicate a decrease in wars or disturbances over the centuries shown in the columns. Ideation was significantly increasing between the time of the Roman Republic and the Empire.

** Significant at the .01 level of confidence.
 * Significant at the .05 level of confidence.
 ' Significant at the .05 level, *if and only if* a one-tailed test can be justified, which is the case only if a hypothesis is being tested.

# Table 4.1 Mean Scores of Wars and Internal Disturbances

| | *Greece* | | *Rome* | | *Medieval Europe* |
|---|---|---|---|---|---|
| **Wars** (Civil, Colonial, Imperial and Interstate) | | | | | |
| Dates | 500–146B.C. | | 390B.C.–A.D.476 | | A.D.906–1500 |
| # Centuries | 4 | | 9 | | 6 |
| WarFreq | 9 (4) | | 10 (4) | | 13 (6) |
| Duration (Yrs) | 62 (33) | | 47 (19) | | 41 (25) |
| Casualties/ 1000 Pop | 23 (16) | | 18 (19) | > | 5 (4) |
| Casualties/ 1000 Army | 54 (8) | | 55 (9) | > | 33 (10) |
| Casualties/ Year of War | 1214 (380) | < | 2061 (690) | > | 947 (619) |
| Casualties/ War | 9645 (4370) | | 9864 (6800) | > | 2050 (1500) |
| **Internal Disturbances** (Riots, Rebellions, Coups, etc.) | | | | | |
| Dates | 600–146B.C. | | 509B.C.–A.D.476 | | A.D.531–1499 |
| # Centuries | 5 | | 10 | | 10 |
| Frequency | 18 (9) | | 17 (12) | | 13 (4) |
| Duration (Yrs) | 23 (17) | | 22 (16) | | 21 (9) |
| Geometric Average | 254 (154) | | 254 (182) | | 179 (49) |
| **Ideation** (Faith) | 39 (5) | < | 53 (6) | < | 59 (4) |
| Dates | 600–0B.C. | | A.D.1–500 | | A.D.500–1500 |
| # Centuries | 6 | | 5 | | 10 |

Based on Sorokin's (1937, vol. 3) data

*Notes:* Figures in the body of the table are mean scores per nation per century. Medieval means were based on data for Austria-Hungary, England, France and Russia. Figures in parentheses are standard deviations from the means. War casualties include both dead and wounded in the army, excluding losses from disease and epidemics. The geometric average of the internal disturbances was an average of social area, duration, numbers of people involved and intensity. Signs of "greater than" and "less than" indicate significant differences as determined by analysis of variance and *t* tests, at the .05 level of confidence or better. Other differences could have occurred by chance. The ideation scores were obtained from a factor analysis of eight of Sorokin's (1957) measures of philosophy, religion and science over 26 centuries. Ideation was a factor characterized by faith versus sense and reason in epistemology, by idealism versus materialism in ontology, and by love versus happiness and principles in ethics. These mean scores show that the classic centuries B.C. were more sense-oriented, while the medieval centuries were more faith-oriented.

# Table 4.2   Correlations of Wars and Disturbances with Time

|  | *Greece* | *Rome* | *Medieval Europe* |
|---|---|---|---|
| **Wars** (Civil, Colonial, Imperial and Interstate) | | | |
| Dates | 500–146B.C. | 390B.C.–A.D.476 | A.D.906–1500 |
| # Centuries | 4 | 9 | 6 |
| Frequency | – 18 | – 31 | 82* |
| Duration (Yrs) | – 97* | – 53 | 91* |
| Casualties/ | | | |
| 1000 Pop | – 78 | – 35 | 98** |
| Casualties/ | | | |
| 1000 Army | – 53 | – 42 | 93** |
| Casualties/ | | | |
| Year of War | – 28 | + 14 | 92** |
| Casualties/ | | | |
| War | – 94' | – 42 | 84** |
| | | | |
| **Disturbances** (Riots, Rebellions, Coups, etc.) | | | |
| Dates | 600–146B.C. | 509B.C.–A.D.476 | A.D.531–1499 |
| # Centuries | 5 | 10 | 10 |
| Frequency | – 42 | 64* | 58' |
| Duration (Yrs) | – 37 | 59' | 53 |
| Geometric | | | |
| Average | – 37 | 54 | 57' |
| | | | |
| *Ideation* (Faith) | – 57 | 96** | – 75* |

Based on Sorokin's (1937, vol. 3) data

*Notes:* See the notes following Table 4.1. Figures in the body of the table are correlation coefficients with decimal points omitted. Positive correlations indicate an increase in wars or internal disturbances over the centuries shown in parentheses in the columns. Negative correlations indicate a decrease in wars or disturbances over the centuries shown in the columns. Ideation (faith versus sensation) increased during the ten centuries of the classic period, reaching a zenith in the eighth century, since which it has steadily declined.

** Significant at the .01 level of confidence.
 * Significant at the .05 level of confidence.
 ' Significant at the .05 level of confidence, *if and only if* a one-tailed test of significance can be justified, which is the case only if a hypothesis is being tested.

# Table 4.3  Mean Scores by Five-Hundred Year Periods

| | Roman Republic | | Roman Empire | Dark Ages | Middle Ages |
|---|---|---|---|---|---|

*Wars* (Civil, Colonial, Imperial and Interstate)

| | Roman Republic | | Roman Empire | Dark Ages | Middle Ages |
|---|---|---|---|---|---|
| Dates | 390–0B.C. | | A.D.1–476 | A.D.906–1000 | A.D.1000–1500 |
| # Centuries | 4 | | 5 | 1 | 5 |
| Frequency | 13 (5) | | 8 (1) | 5 (<) | 14 (5) |
| Duration (Yrs) | 62 (17) | > | 34 (9) | 10 | 47 (22) |
| Casualties/ 1000 Pop | 33 (22) | > | 11 (4) | 1 (>) | 5 (4) |
| Casualties/ 1000 Army | 57 (13) | | 50 (0) | 22 (>) | 36 (9) |
| Casualites/ Year of War | 2253 (1249) | | 1895 (363) | 320 (>) | 961 (103) |
| Casualties/ War | 11,220 (9300) | | 8079 (3100) | 889 (>) | 2089 (1700) |

*Disturbances* (Riots, Rebellions, Coups, etc.)

| | Roman Republic | | Roman Empire | | Dark Ages | Middle Ages |
|---|---|---|---|---|---|---|
| Dates | 509–0B.C. | | A.D.1–476 | | A.D.531–1000 | A.D.1000–1500 |
| # Centuries | 5 | | 5 | | 5 | 5 |
| Frequency | 10 (11) | < | 24 (7) | > | 11 (3) | 16 (3) |
| Duration (Yrs) | 15 (18) | | 30 (11) | | 16 (4) | 27 (8) |
| Geometric Average | 180 (221) | | 330 (109) | | 146 (45) | 210 (28) |

| | Roman Republic | | Roman Empire | | Dark Ages | | Middle Ages |
|---|---|---|---|---|---|---|---|
| *Ideation* (Faith) | 37 (2) | < | 53 (6) | > | 62 (3) | > | 56 (2) |

Based on Sorokin's (1937, vol. 3) data

*Notes:* See the notes following Table 4.1. The ideation mean scores show that the classic centuries B.C. were more sense-oriented, while the medieval centuries were more faith-oriented, especially the first half of the Middle Ages from A.D. 500–1000. Actually, these scores increased until the eighth century, since which they have declined.

# Table 4.4  Factor Analysis of Internal Disturbances (N = 25 centuries)

| Variable | Factor 1 | Factor 2 | Communalities |
|---|---|---|---|
| Revolutionary Magnitude | 96* | | 94% |
| Century | 88* | | 79% |
| Transitions | | 90* | 85% |
| Ideation | 46 | –53 | 50% |
| Variance % | 49% | 28% | 77% |

*Notes:* The 25 centuries were from 500 B.C. to A.D. 2000, after the twentieth century was prorated. Only factor loadings over 45 were printed in this table (multiplied by one hundred to eliminate decimal points). Transitional centuries were identified by their occurring in three out of four of Sorokin's lists (1937 vol. 3, 1941, 1947, 1957). According to that standard, nine of these 25 centuries were transitional: 5 B.C., 2 B.C., 1 B.C., A.D. 3, A.D. 8, A.D. 13–15, and A.D. 20. The communalities are simply the sums of the factor loadings squared. They tell us how much of the variance in each variable can be explained by both factors or, conversely, they tell us how much of the variance in both factors can be explained by each variable. Revolutionary magnitudes, for example, were well explained by these two factors (94 percent of the variance), while only one-half (50 percent) of the variance in ideation was explained by these two factors. The asterisked factor loadings are greater than the root mean square of all the values in the factor matrix, which is taken here to be an arbitrary mark of significance. This table shows that revolutionary magnitudes were significantly associated with centuries in Factor 1; that is, these magnitudes increased over these centuries, but were not at all related to the transitional centuries in Factor 2. They were also somewhat related to ideation, indicating that "more religious" centuries experienced higher revolutionary magnitudes.

# Table 4.5  Factor Analysis of Wars and Revolutions (N = 20 centuries)

| Variable | Factor 1 | Factor 2 | Factor 3 | $h^2$ |
|---|---|---|---|---|
| Casualties/ Pop | 93* | | | 95% |
| Casualties/ Army | 90* | | | 95% |
| Ideation | – 73* | 55 | | 86% |
| Revolutionary Magnitude | | 91* | | 93% |
| Century | | 75* | – 53 | 92% |
| Transitions (War) | | | 83* | 85% |
| Transitions (Rev) | | | 70* | 85% |
| Variance % | 38% | 29% | 23% | 90% |

*Notes:* See the notes following Table 4.4. The 20 centuries were from 400 B.C. to A.D. 500 and from 900 to 2000. The centuries from 500 to 900 were omitted because Sorokin provided no war data for these four centuries. Eight of these 20 centuries were transitional for revolutions, as identified in the notes of Table 4.4, and 11 of them were transitional for wars: 3–1 B.C., A.D. 3–5, A.D. 13–16, and A.D. 20. Factor 1 shows that war casualties relative to population and to army size were negatively related to ideation; that is, "religious centuries" suffered fewer relative casualties. Factor 2 shows that revolutionary magnitudes increased over the centuries; they were also somewhat related to ideation. Neither wars nor revolutions were significantly related to transitional centuries, which were loaded together on Factor 3.

# Table 4.6 Analysis of Variance Between Stable and Transitional Centuries (N = 25)

| Variable | F | Grand Mean | Stable Mean (N = 16) | | Transitional Mean (N = 9) |
|---|---|---|---|---|---|
| Century | 0 | 7.8 | 8.1 | = | 7.2 |
| Ideation | 0 | 50.0 | 50.8 | = | 48.4 |
| Revolutionary Magnitude | 2.7 | 512.2 | 444.2 | = | 633.1 |

*Notes:* See the notes following Tables 4.4 and 4.5. None of the F-ratios were significant, so that the mean scores between stable and transitional centuries were not significantly different from each other in century, ideation, or revolutionary magnitude. These results confirm those results found by means of chi-square and factor analysis for revolutionary magnitudes.

## (N = 20 Centuries)

| | | | (N = 9) | | (N = 11) |
|---|---|---|---|---|---|
| Century | 0 | 8.5 | 9.6 | = | 7.6 |
| Casualties/ Pop (logged) | 3 | 2.5 | 2.0 | = | 2.9 |
| Casualties/ Army (logged) | 0 | 4.1 | 4.0 | = | 4.1 |
| Ideation | 0 | 48.2 | 48.0 | = | 48.4 |
| Revolutionary Magnitude | 0 | 514.8 | 491.4 | = | 533.9 |

*Notes:* Relative casualties were logged to normalize the skewness in the raw scores. None of the F-ratios were significant, so that none of the variables in this table differed significantly between stable and transitional centuries, thus confirming the results obtained by chi-square and factor analysis for war casualties as well as revolutionary magnitudes. These various statistical tests, used on Sorokin's various identifications of transitional centuries, whether taken separately or together, leave little doubt that Sorokin's transitional theory of wars and revolutions was *not* confirmed by his own data.

# Table 4.7 Medieval Civilizations, Empires and Wars

| Cent | War | Bat | Imp | Civ | Pop | Pages |
|---|---|---|---|---|---|---|
| 6 | 18 | 53 | 21.0 | 44.6 | 200 | 17.2 |
| 7 | 33 | 102 | 18.0 | 40.2 | 210 | 17.2 |
| 8 | 36 | 66 | 24.7 | 21.0 | 220 | 17.2 |
| 9 | 35 | 73 | 18.5 | 45.0 | 242 | 17.2 |
| 10 | 37 | 70 | 17.0 | 40.7 | 265 | 17.2 |
| 11 | 48 | 91 | 17.0 | 77.7 | 320 | 29.4 |
| 12 | 50 | 108 | 10.1 | 103.2 | 360 | 29.4 |
| 13 | 73 | 125 | 32.7 | 101.7 | 360 | 29.4 |
| 14 | 97 | 112 | 32.8 | 123.8 | 350 | 29.4 |
| 15 | 114 | 164 | 17.1 | 234.4 | 425 | 29.4 |

| | | | | | | |
|---|---|---|---|---|---|---|
| Sum | 541 | 964 | 209 | 832 | 2952 | 233 |
| Mean | 54.1 | 96.4 | 20.9 | 83.2 | 295.2 | 23.3 |
| Std | 30.9 | 33.1 | 7.1 | 63.0 | 77.9 | 6.4 |
| % Total | 29.6% | 21.4% | 15.8% | 6.3% | 5.9% | 20.4% |

*Notes:* See the notes following Table 2.2.

## Table 4.8   Comparison of Mean Scores from Archaic to Medieval Periods

| Variables | Archaic | | Ancient | | Classic | | Medieval | F | $R^2$ |
|---|---|---|---|---|---|---|---|---|---|
| Wars (Kohn) | 0.9 | < | 7 | < | 19 | < | 54 | 185**** | 93% |
| Battles (D & D) | 0 | < | 1.5 | < | 41 | < | 96 | 88**** | 87% |
| Imperial Size | 0.6 | < | 2.6 | < | 13.6 | < | 20.9 | 154**** | 92% |
| Civilization | 0.04 | < | 9.3 | < | 75 | = | 83 | 94**** | 87% |
| Population | 23 | < | 65 | < | 169 | < | 295 | 102**** | 88% |
| Pages (G & G) | 2 | = | 4.8 | < | 15 | < | 23 | 83**** | 86% |
| Century | − 23 | < | − 10.5 | < | 0 | < | 10.5 | 287**** | 95% |

*Notes:* See the notes following Table 2.2 for a description of the variables, and for references to their sources. Signs of "less than" indicate significant differences as determined by analyses of variance (F-test) and Duncan's multiple-range test. "Equal" signs indicate no significant differences. **** Significant at the .0001 level of confidence, which means that an F as high as this could occur less than once in ten thousand times by chance. $R^2$ indicates how much of the variance in each variable can be explained by the difference between these historical periods, or how much of the difference between these historical periods can be explained by the variance in each variable. The first four variables were logged prior to analyses of variance to correct for their skewed distributions.

## Table 4.9   Comparison in Terms of Percentages

| Variables | Archaic | Ancient | Classic | Medieval |
|---|---|---|---|---|
| Wars (Kohn) | 0.7% | 3.8% | 10.5% | 29.6% |
| Battles (D & D) | 0.0 | 0.3 | 9.0 | 21.4 |
| Imperial Size | 0.5 | 2.2 | 11.5 | 15.8 |
| Civilization | 0.0 | 0.7 | 5.7 | 6.3 |
| Population | 3.1 | 5.9 | 15.2 | 26.6 |
| Pages (G & G) | 2.6 | 4.2 | 13.3 | 20.4 |
| Century (Avg) | − 23 | − 10.5 | 0 | 10.5 |
| # Centuries | 15 | 10 | 10 | 10 |
| % Centuries | 30% | 20% | 20% | 20% |
| Average % Var | 1.1% | 2.2% | 10.9% | 20.0% |
| Average/Cent. | 0.037 | 0.145 | 0.545 | 1.00 |

*Notes:* See the notes following Table 2.2 for a description of the variables, and for references to their sources. The percentages in all cases are the percentages of the grand totals (not shown in this table) of all 50 centuries. Average % Var is the average percent of the six variables at the top of the table. Average/Century is Average % Var divided by % Centuries.

## Table 5.1 Average Imperial Sizes Per Century

| Empire | Archaic | Ancient | Classic B.C. | Classic A.D. | Early Middle | Late Middle | Modern | Average (N = 50) | No. |
|---|---|---|---|---|---|---|---|---|---|
| Egypt | .30 | .60 | .31 | | | | | 0.21 | 24 |
| Meso | .11 | .49 | 1.86 | | | | | 0.97 | 35 |
| India | .07 | .05 | 2.16 | 1.54 | 5.52 | 6.16 | | 0.62 | 23 |
| China | .09 | .48 | | 5.26 | 4.56 | 2.56 | 10.60 | 3.00 | 38 |
| Turkey | .01 | .22 | | | .20 | 1.06 | 4.30 | 0.64 | 19 |
| Persia | | .70 | 4.24 | 3.10 | .66 | 1.00 | 1.93 | 1.35 | 25 |
| Rome | | | .90 | 3.52 | | | | 0.44 | 5 |
| Huns (Eu) | | | | 1.40 | | | | 0.14 | 2 |
| Byzant | | | | .38 | .46 | | | 0.08 | 2 |
| CentAsia | | | 1.64 | .50 | 5.44 | 8.64 | | 1.62 | 10 |
| Russia | | | | | .30 | .36 | 15.90 | 1.66 | 7 |
| Spain | | | | | | | 6.34 | 0.63 | 3 |
| England | | | | | | | 14.80 | 1.48 | 2 |
| France | | | | | | | 6.80 | 0.68 | 2 |
| Canada | | | | | | | 2.00 | 0.20 | 1 |
| Sum | .59 | 2.55 | 11.07 | 16.12 | 19.84 | 21.94 | 80.05 | 15.11 | |
| # Cents | 15 | 10 | 5 | 5 | 5 | 5 | 5 | 50 | |
| Date | -2250 | -975 | -225 | 275 | 775 | 1275 | 1786 | -174 | |
| MidEast | .42 | 2.02 | 4.55 | 3.10 | 7.72 | 4.82 | 4.32 | 2.98 | |
| Asia | .09 | .49 | 3.80 | 5.76 | 10.00 | 14.80 | 10.91 | 4.65 | |
| Europe | | | .86 | 5.72 | 1.92 | 1.26 | 63.42 | 6.70 | |

Notes: Archaic = 3000–1500 B.C.; Ancient = 1500–500 B.C.; Classic B.C. = 500–0 B.C.; Classic A.D. = A.D. 1–500. Early Med = 500–1000; Late Med = 1000–1500. Modern = 1500–1975. Average imperial sizes are based on Taagepera (1978a). See the notes following Table 3.4. No. = Number of centuries when an empire was among the top three in imperial size.

# Table 5.2 Modern Civilizations, Empires and Wars

| Cent | War | Bat | Imp | Civ | Pop | Pages |
|------|------|------|--------|---------|------|-------|
| 16 | 139 | 292 | 24.20 | 644.9 | 500 | 91.0 |
| 17 | 148 | 500 | 48.80 | 905.2 | 545 | 85.0 |
| 18 | 152 | 597 | 69.00 | 1294.7 | 720 | 90.0 |
| 19 | 288 | 765 | 105.00 | 2890.2 | 1200 | 153.0 |
| 20 | 283 | 973 | 129.25 | 5780.4 | 2500 | 262.8 |
| Sum | 1010 | 3127 | 376 | 11,515 | 5465 | 682 |
| Mean | 202 | 625 | 75 | 2303 | 1093 | 136 |
| Std | 76 | 259 | 40 | 2131 | 834 | 76 |
| % Total | 55.3% | 69.3% | 56.4% | 87.3% | 49.3% | 59.6% |

Notes: See the notes following Table 2.2 for a description of the variables, and for references to their sources.

## Table 5.3   Civilization, Empire and War Percentages

### Historical Periods

| Variables | Archaic | | Ancient | | Classic | | Medieval | | Modern | Total |
|---|---|---|---|---|---|---|---|---|---|---|
| Years | 15 | | 10 | | 10 | | 10 | | 5 | 50 |
| Century | −23 | | −10.5 | | 0 | | 10.5 | | 18 | −5.1 |
| Wars (Kohn) | 0.7% | V | 3.8% | V | 10.5% | V | 29.6% | V | 55.3% | 99.9% |
| Battles (D & D) | 0% | V | 0.3% | V | 9.0% | V | 21.4% | V | 69.3% | 100% |
| Imperial Size | 0.5% | V | 2.2% | V | 11.5% | V | 17.7% | V | 67.8% | 99.7% |
| Civilization | 0% | V | 0.7% | V | 5.7% | = | 6.3% | V | 87.3% | 100% |
| Population | 3.1% | V | 5.9% | V | 15.2% | V | 26.6% | V | 49.3% | 100.1% |
| Pages (G & G) | 2.6% | V | 4.2% | V | 13.3% | V | 20.4% | V | 59.6% | 100.1% |
| Average % | 1.15% | V | 2.85% | V | 10.87% | V | 20.3% | | 64.77% | 100.1% |

*Notes:* See the notes following Table 2.2 for a description of the variables, and for references to their sources. Average % is simply the average of the six percentages. Signs of "less than" indicate significant differences as determined by analyses of variance (F-tests) and Duncan's multiple-range test.

# Table 5.4 Modern/Other Activity Ratios
## Historical Periods

| Variables | Archaic | Ancient | Classic | Medieval | All Others |
|---|---|---|---|---|---|
| # Centuries | 15 | 10 | 10 | 10 | 45 |
| Avg Century | − 23 | − 10.5 | 0 | 10.5 | − 7.7 |
| Wars (Kohn) | 233 | 29 | 11 | 4 | 2.5 |
| Battles (D & D) | 625 | 417 | 15 | 7 | 4.5 |
| Imperial Size | 136 | 31 | 6 | 4 | 2.1 |
| Civilization | 999 | 248 | 31 | 28 | 13.8 |
| Population | 48 | 17 | 7 | 4 | 2.0 |
| Pages (G & G) | 69 | 28 | 9 | 6 | 3.0 |
| Average Ratio | 352 | 162 | 13 | 9 | 4.7 |

*Notes:* See the notes following Table 2.2 for a description of the variables, and for references to their sources. Average Ratio is simply the average of the six ratios. All Others = Modern/ Sum of Archaic, Ancient, Classic and Medieval.

# Table 5.5 Percentage Comparison of Modern Centuries
## Modern Centuries

| Variables | 16th | 17th | 18th | 19th | 20th | Modern |
|---|---|---|---|---|---|---|
| Wars (Kohn) | 14% | 15% | 15% | 29% | 28% | 101% |
| Battles (D & D) | 9% | 16% | 19% | 24% | 31% | 99% |
| Imperial Size | 6% | 13% | 18% | 28% | 34% | 99% |
| Civilization | 6% | 8% | 11% | 25% | 50% | 100% |
| Population | 9% | 10% | 13% | 22% | 46% | 100% |
| Pages (G & G) | 13% | 12% | 13% | 22% | 38% | 98% |
| Average % | 9.5% | 12.3% | 14.7% | 25.2% | 37.8% | 99.5% |
| 20th/Other | 4.0 | 3.1 | 2.6 | 1.5 | | |

*Notes:* See the notes following Table 2.2 for a description of the variables, and for references to their sources. Average % is simply the average of the six percentages. 20th/Other is the activity ratio between the twentieth century and the other centuries in the modern period.

# Table 6.1 Chi-Square Analyses of Wright's Frequencies

| Century | Wars | Battles | Participants |
|---------|------|---------|--------------|
| 16th | 60 | 87 – | 47 – |
| 17th | 64 | 235 – | 56 – |
| 18th | 38 – | 785 | 52 – |
| 19th | 89 + | 651 – | 106 |
| 20th (prorated) | 84 + | 2420 + | 228 + |
| Total Frequency | 335 | 4178 | 489 |
| Chi-Square | 25** | 4151** | 239** |

(Based on Wright, 1965, p. 651)

*Notes:* ** Significant at the .01 level of confidence, at least. Plus and minus signs in the body of the table indicate significant deviations from the average frequency per century. Almost two-thirds of the wars were fought mainly in Europe, and two-thirds of the participants were European states, but 93 percent of the important battles were fought in Europe. According to Wright's list the majority of wars, battles and participants were European. This was especially true in the sixteenth to the eighteenth centuries, when 89 percent of the wars were fought mainly in Europe, 85 percent of the participants were European states, and 98 percent of the important battles were fought in Europe. This was less true in the nineteenth and twentieth centuries, when 31 percent of the wars were fought mainly in Europe, 52 percent of the participants were European states, and 86 percent of the important battles were fought in Europe.

# Table 6.2 Factor Analysis of Wright's Modern Wars by Time (N = 24, 20-year time periods, 1480–1960)

| Variables | Intensity | Frequency | Start/Win | Communalities |
|-----------|-----------|-----------|-----------|---------------|
| Participants/War | 90* | – 19 | 21 | 89% |
| Battles/War | 86* | 23 | 19 | 84% |
| Great Powers/War | 71* | – 50 | – 31 | 86% |
| War Frequency | – 25 | 85* | – 01 | 78% |
| Century | 56* | 73* | 17 | 88% |
| Years/Win | – 19 | – 69* | 45 | 71% |
| Start/Win | – 15 | 03 | 92* | 87% |
| Explained Variance | 36% | 30% | 18% | 83% |

*Notes:* Factor coefficients greater than the root mean square of all the values in the matrix have been asterisked to indicate an estimate of their statistical significance. Lower values could have been different from zero by chance. Factor coefficients have been multiplied by one hundred in order to remove decimal points for easier reading of the table. Communalities are the sum of the factor coefficients squared; they indicate the percent of variance in each variable explained by all three factors taken together. The figure in the last row and last column indicates the average percent of variance in all variables explained by all three factors taken together. The names given to the three factors were simply generalizations of the variables significantly loaded on the factors.

## Table 6.3   Factor Analysis of
## Wright's Modern Wars by Region
## (N = 8 geographical regions)

| Variables | Intensity | Duration | Participants | $h^2$ |
|---|---|---|---|---|
| Battles | 91* | − 22 | − 02 | 88% |
| Great Powers | 79* | − 17 | − 06 | 66% |
| War Frequency | 72* | 52 | 20 | 83% |
| Start/Win | − 67* | 53 | − 46 | 95% |
| Century | − 84* | − 03 | 37 | 85% |
| Third World | − 86* | 34 | 19 | 90% |
| War Years | 50 | 76* | − 37 | 96% |
| Participants | 40 | 53 | 67* | 89% |
| Explained Variance | 54% | 20% | 13% | 86% |

*Notes:* See notes following Table 6.2. Third World = Afro-Asia and Latin America as the location of these wars. The eight geographical regions were Europe, the Far East, Latin America, the Middle East, North America, northern and South Africa, south Asia and sub–Saharan Africa.

## Table 6.4   Analyses of Variance of
## Wright's Modern Wars (N = 308)

| Variables | F | Mean | Centuries | | | | |
|---|---|---|---|---|---|---|---|
| | | | 16th | 17th | 18th | 19th | 20th |
| (Frequencies) | | (308) | (62) | (65) | (38 − ) | (88 + ) | (55) |
| Years/War | 3* | 4.12 | 4 + | 6 + | 4 + | 3 − | 3 − |
| Start/Win | 1 | 49% | 47% | 39% | 42% | 58% | 50% |
| Participants | 4** | 3.25 | 2.5 − | 2.7 − | 3.9 + | 3.2 + | 4.4 + |
| Great Powers | 6*** | 1.2 | 1.2 − | 1.3 − | 1.9 + | 0.9 − | 1.1 − |
| Battles/War | 14*** | 29 | 2 − | 10 − | 41 − | 22 − | 117 + |

*Notes:* *** Significant at the .001 level of confidence. ** Significant at the .01 level of confidence. * Significant at the .05 level of confidence. If the F-ratio is not significant, as in the case of Start/Win percentage, then the observed differences could have occurred by chance. Plus and minus signs in the body of the table indicate significant differences among these five centuries. Participants and Great Powers were averages per war, the same as Years and Battles. Mean scores in the body of the table were based on raw scores, but the scores were logged for the analysis of variance if their distribution was skewed. Start/Win percentage was based on 211 wars for which these data were available. Battles/War were based on 125 wars for which these data were available. The significance of the differences among the frequencies was determined by a chi-square test, where chi-square = 21, which was significant at the .01 level of confidence.

## Table 6.5 Analyses of Variance of Wright's Modern Wars (N = 308)

| Variables | F-Ratio | Grand Mean | Regions Non-European Mean | European Mean |
|---|---|---|---|---|
| (Frequencies) | 24** (Chi$^2$) | (308) | (118 – ) | (190 + ) |
| Years/War | 8.5** | 4.12 | 3.3 – | 4.6 + |
| Start/Win | 2.9' | 49% | 56% | 44% |
| Participants/War | 0.1 | 3.25 | 2.8 | 3.5 |
| Great Powers/War | 29**** | 1.2 | 0.7 – | 1.5 + |
| Battles/War | 0.3 | 29 | 9 | 32 |
| Century | 133**** | 18.0 | 19.1 + | 17.4 – |

Notes: **** Significant at the .0001 level of confidence. ** Significant at the .01 level of confidence. ' Significant at the .05 level of confidence if a one-tailed test of significance is warranted, that is, if there is reason to believe that the difference should be in one direction rather than the other. See the notes at the bottom of Table 6.4. Plus and minus signs in the body of the table indicate significant differences between these two geographical regions. Where the F-ratio is not significant, then the difference between regions could have occurred by chance. The significance of the difference in frequencies was determined by a chi-square test rather than an F-ratio. The non–European region included 34 Latin American wars, 28 in the Middle East (including North Africa and Central Asia), 23 wars in the Far East, 15 in South Asia, 12 in sub–Saharan Africa, and 6 in North America.

## Table 6.6 Analyses of Variance of Wright's Modern Wars (N = 308)

| Variables | F | Grand Mean | Types of War Balance Mean | Civil Mean | Defensive Mean | Imperial Mean |
|---|---|---|---|---|---|---|
| (Frequency) | 100** | (308) | (140 + ) | (90) | (21 – ) | (57 – ) |
| Years/War | 8**** | 4.12 | 4.3 | 4.1 | 7.5 + | 2.5 – |
| Start/Win | 4** | 49% | 50% – | 40% – | 80% + | 60% |
| Participant | 24**** | 3.25 | 4.3 + | 2.1 – | 2.8 | 2.6 – |
| Great Power | 4** | 1.2 | 1.5 + | 0.8 – | 1.5 + | 0.9 – |
| Battle/War | 2.3' | 29 | 42 | 10 | 5 | 4 |
| Century | 13**** | 18.0 | 18.0 | 18.0 | 16.6 – | 18.8 + |

Notes: See the notes at the bottom of Tables 6.4 and 6.5. The F frequency of 100 was not an F-ratio, but rather a chi-square. Wright (1965, p. 638) defined his types of war as follows: Balance-of-Power = wars between the states of modern civilization. Civil = wars against encroachment or aggression by peoples of a different civilization (mainly the Ottoman Empire during this time period). Imperial = wars of expanding modern civilization at the expense of another culture. (Wright's definitions made it clear that his term "modern civilization" meant Western civilization.)

## Table 7.1   Factor Analysis of
## Levy's Great Power Wars, 1495–1975
## (N = 119)

### (Using Logged scores for skewed distributions)

| Variables | Deaths | Time | Years | Communalities |
|---|---|---|---|---|
| Deaths/Pop (log) | .97 * | | | 94% |
| Total Deaths (log) | .97 * | | | 96% |
| Nation-Years (log) | .86 * | – .32 | .38 | 98% |
| # Great Powers (log) | .79 * | | | 65% |
| Deaths/Year (log) | .77 * | .47 | – .35 | 94% |
| Great Powers Both Sides | .69 * | – .30 | – .30 | 65% |
| Years (log) | .66 * | – .40 | .62 * | 97% |
| Beginning Date | | .96 * | | 97% |
| Century | | .96 * | | 96% |
| Ending Date | | .96 * | | 97% |
| Death/Nation-Year (log) | .61 * | .61 * | – .32 | 84% |
| Explained Variance | 46% | 34% | 9% | 89% |

Notes: Asterisked values are greater than the root mean square of all of the factor loadings, to provide a rough estimate of the relative significance of the loadings. Factor loadings less than
.30 were omitted from this table for the sake of readability. Explained Variance = the sum
of squared factor loadings divided by the number of variables, and shows how much of the
variance in all the variables is explained by each factor, on average. Communalities = the
sum of squared factor loadings, and shows how much of the variance in each variable is explained by all of the factors added together. Levy (1983) used the term "Great Power Wars"
to indicate those wars with at least one Great Power on each side, while the phrase "wars
involving great powers" was used to indicate those wars with one or more Great Power on
one side only. I have used the term "Great Power Wars" (with or without capitals) to indicate
those wars with at least one Great Power on either one or both sides of any war.

## Table 7.2  Factor Analysis of Levy's
## Great Power Wars, 1495–1975
## (N = 119)

(Using the raw scores of all variables)

| Variables | Factor 1 | Factor 2 | Communalities |
|---|---|---|---|
| Deaths/Nation-Years | .84* | | 71% |
| Deaths/Population | .83* | | 75% |
| Total Deaths | .82* | | 72% |
| Deaths/Year | .77* | | 61% |
| # Great Powers | .65* | | 74% |
| Great Powers Both Sides | | .70* | 54% |
| Nation-Years | .45 | .68* | 66% |
| Years | | .57 | 34% |
| Ending Date | .62* | – .71* | 89% |
| Century | .62* | – .71* | 89% |
| Beginning Date | .62* | – .72* | 90% |
| Explained Variance | 41% | 29% | 70% |

*Notes:* See the notes following Table 7.1. Three factors were generated by the criterion of eigen-values exceeding unity, but only the first two have been presented here, since the third factor contained no significant loadings, although it explained another 13 percent of the total variance.

## Table 7.3  Analyses of Variance Among Centuries

| Variables | F | Mean (N = 119) | 16th (N = 34) | 17th (N = 29) | 18th (N = 17) | 19th (N = 20) | 20th (N = 15) |
|---|---|---|---|---|---|---|---|
| Begin | 721*** | 1697 | 1547 < | 1646 < | 1748 < | 1843 < | 1937 |
| End | 678*** | 1701 | 1552 < | 1652 < | 1754 < | 1845 < | 1939 |
| | | | | | | | |
| Years | 3** | 4.35 | 5 | 6+ | 6+ | 2 – | 2 |
| Nation-Years | 3* | 10.2 | 9 | 13 | 18 | 5 – | 7 |
| # GP | 1 | 2.21 | 2 | 2 | 3 | 2 | 2 |
| GP Both Sides | 4** | 0.54 | 0.8 + | 0.6 | 0.3 – | 0.3 – | 0.3 – |
| | | | | | | | |
| Total Deaths | 3* | 281 | 28 | 139 | 222 | 128 | 1472 + |
| Deaths/Pop | 3* | 2310 | 364 | 1517 | 2089 | 1085 | 10,737 + |
| Deaths/Nat-Yr | 6*** | 18,667 | 3304 | 5722 | 7400 | 31,395 | 78,803 + |
| Deaths/Year | 4** | 21 | 6 – | 18 | 25 | 33 + | 42 + |
| | | | | | | | |
| Raw Factors | | | | | | | |
| Death + Time | 15*** | 0.0 | – 0.6 | – 0.2 | 0.3 | 0.4 | 1.3 + |
| GP-Time | 28*** | 0.0 | 0.7 + | 0.4 | 0.04 | – 1.0 – | – 1.2 – |
| | | | | | | | |
| Log Factors | | | | | | | |
| Death + GP Time + | 2' | 0.0 | 0.1 | 0.2 + | 0.4 + | – 0.5 | – 0.0 |
| Death/Yr | 263*** | 0.0 | – 1.0 < | – 0.4 < | 0.2 < | 1.0 < | 1.7 |
| Years | 3** | 0.0 | – 0.4 | 0.2 | 0.6 + | – 0.1 | 0.2 |

*Notes:* *** Significant at the .001 level of confidence. ** Significant at the .01 level of confidence. * Significant at the .05 level of confidence. ' Significant at the .10 level of confidence. GP = Great Powers. Plus, minus, and signs of "less than" indicate significant differences between mean scores as determined by Duncan's multiple-range test. The four wars in the fifteenth century were omitted from the body of this table, but they were included in the grand mean. Log factors were those factor scores obtained from the factor analysis of logged variables (Table 7.1). Raw factors were those factor scores obtained from the factor analysis of raw variables (Table 7.2). When skewed variables were logged, the results were similar, except for Total Deaths and Deaths/Pop, whose F-ratios were not significant.

# Table 7.4   Analyses of Variance Between Regions

| | | | Regions | | |
|---|---|---|---|---|---|
| *Variables* | *F* | *Mean* (N = 119) | *Europe* (N = 105) | | *Others* (N = 14) |
| Century | 43*** | 17.5 | 17.2 | < | 19.6 |
| Begin | 47*** | 1697 | 1669 | < | 1905 |
| End | 46*** | 1701 | 1674 | < | 1908 |
| Years | 3 | 4.35 | 4.6 | = | 2.5 |
| Nation-Years | 4' | 10.2 | 11.1 | = | 3.7 |
| # GP | 4' | 2.21 | 2.3 | = | 1.5 |
| GP Both Sides | 7** | 0.54 | 0.58 | > | 0.21 |
| Total Deaths | 0 | 281 | 305 | = | 99 |
| Deaths/Pop | 0 | 2310 | 2526 | = | 693 |
| Deaths/Nat-Yr | 0 | 18,667 | 18,991 | = | 16,236 |
| Deaths/Year | 0 | 21 | 21 | = | 19 |
| Raw Factors | | | | | |
| Death + Time | 2 | 0.0 | − 0.1 | = | 0.4 |
| GP-Time | 39*** | 0.0 | 0.2 | > | − 1.4 |
| Log Factors | | | | | |
| Death + GP | 5* | 0.0 | 0.1 | > | − 0.5 |
| Time + | | | | | |
| Death/Yr | 32*** | 0.0 | − 0.2 | < | 1.3 |
| Years | 6* | 0.0 | − 0.1 | < | 0.6 |

*Notes:* See the notes following Table 7.3 Other (regions) included the Far East (N = 7), South Asia (N = 2), North America (N = 2), and Africa, Latin America and the Middle East (N = 1 each). When skewed variables were logged, the results were similar except that Europe was significantly higher than Other in #GP (number of Great Powers involved), Nation-Years, and Deaths/Pop[ulation].

# Table 7.5    Analyses of Variance Between Great Powers

| Variables | F | Mean (N = 119) | One Side (N = 55) | | Both Sides (N = 64) |
|---|---|---|---|---|---|
| | | | *Great Powers* | | |
| Century | 11*** | 17.5 | 18.0 | > | 17.1 |
| Begin | 11*** | 1697 | 1743 | > | 1658 |
| End | 11** | 1701 | 1746 | > | 1663 |
| Years | 9** | 4.35 | 3.0 | < | 5.5 |
| Nation-Years | 35*** | 10.2 | 3.2 | < | 16.2 |
| # GP | 77*** | 2.21 | 1.2 | < | 3.1 |
| Total Deaths | 3.6' | 281 | 22 | = | 503 |
| Deaths/Pop | 4.5* | 2310 | 192 | < | 4130 |
| Deaths/Nat-Yr | 1.2 | 18667 | 12657 | = | 23831 |
| Deaths/Year | 11*** | 21 | 11 | < | 29 |
| Raw Factors | | | | | |
| Death + Time | 5* | 0.0 | – 0.2 | < | 0.2 |
| GP-Time | 115*** | 0.0 | – 0.8 | < | 0.7 |
| Log Factors | | | | | |
| Death + GP | 104*** | 0.0 | – 0.7 | < | 0.6 |
| Time + Death/Yr | 11*** | 0.0 | 0.3 | > | – 0.3 |
| Years | 12*** | 0.0 | 0.3 | > | – 0.3 |

*Notes:* See the notes following Tables 7.3 and 7.4. When skewed variables were logged, the results were similar, with one exception: Total Deaths were significantly lower when Great Powers were on one side only than when they were on both sides.

# Table 7.6    Mean Factor Scores of Top Twelve Wars

| Variables | Factor 1 Death and Time | Factor 2 One-Sided and Time | t |
|---|---|---|---|
| Both-Sided GP | 83% (39%) > | 0% (0%) | 7.5** |
| Beginning Date | 1837 (101) < | 1928 (33) | 3.0** |
| Duration in Years | 5.84 (5.0) > | 1.59 (2.34) | 2.67* |
| Average Deaths in Thousands | 2329 (3944) > | 36 (71) | 2.0* (2.8**log) |
| Total Deaths in Thousands | 27,947 | 431 | |
| Total Deaths % Grand Total | 83.6% | 1.3% | |

(Based on Factor Analysis of Raw Scores in Table 7.2)

*Notes:* ** Significant at the .01 level of confidence. * Significant at the .05 level of confidence. Figures in parentheses are standard deviations. All of the death measures in this table were 65 times greater for the top 12 wars on Factor 1 compared with the top 12 wars on Factor 2.

# Table 7.7   Comparison of Levy's and Wright's Wars

| Variables | Levy (N = 119) | | Wright (N = 308) |
|---|---|---|---|
| Dates | 1495–1975 | | 1480–1964 |
| Years | 480 | | 484 |
| Average Century | 17.5 (1.46) | < | 18.0 (1.43) |
| #GP/War | 2.21 (1.52) | > | 1.19 (1.37) |
| Years/War | 4.35 (4.66) | = | 4.12 (5.30) |
| GP Wars | 100% | | 68% |
| Cycles | None | | 50-years |

*Europe Compared with Other Regions of the World*

| | | | |
|---|---|---|---|
| Location of Wars | 88% | > | 62% |
| Deaths or Battles | 96% | | 93% |
| Years/War | 4.6 = 2.5 | | 4.6 > 3.3 |
| #GP/War | 2.3 = 1.5 | | 1.5 > 0.7 |
| Death(Battle)/War | 305 = 99 | | 32 = 9 |
| Average Century | 17.2 < 19.6 | | 17.4 < 19.1 |

*Notes:* Signs of "greater than," "less than," and "equal to," as well as plus and minus signs, indicate significant differences and similarities as determined by *t* tests.

*Correlations over Five Centuries* (Historical trends)

| | | |
|---|---|---|
| Frequencies of War | – .82' | .55ns |
| Years | – .93* | – .18ns |
| Total Deaths (Battles) | .81' | .95* |
| Death(Battle)/War | .87' | .66ns |
| Years/War | – .77ns | – .65ns |
| GP/War | .00ns | .00ns |

*Correlations over 45 Decades* (Historical Trends)

| | | |
|---|---|---|
| Deaths (Battles) | .31* | .39** |
| Years of War | – .41** | – .11ns |
| War Frequencies | – .34* | .28' |
| Deaths/War | .30* | .41** |
| Years/War | – .29* | – .29* |
| GP/War | .06ns | .18ns |

*Notes:* ** Significant at the .01 level of confidence, at least. * Significant at the .05 level of confidence. ' Significant at the .10 level of confidence. ns *Not* significant at the .10 level of confidence. Positive correlations with time indicate variables increasing over time. Negative correlations with time indicate variables decreasing over time.

*General Wars*

| Frequency | 10 | 15 |
|---|---|---|
| Death (Battle) % Total | 87% deaths | 75% battles |

Levy, Wright Correlations of
  General War Deaths (Battles)                .90** (N = 10)
                                             .92** (N = 15)

*Correlations Between Levy and Wright*

|  | *Over Five Centuries* | *Over 45 Decades* |
|---|---|---|
| Frequency of War | − .05ns | .28* |
| Years | .37ns | .54** |
| Total Deaths (Battles) | .89** | .94** |
| Deaths (Battles)/War | .77ns | .74** |
| Years/War | .80ns | .69** |
| GP/War | .99** | .43** |

*Correlations Between Levy and Wright over 13 Great Powers*

Frequencies of War          .91**

*Definitions*

| War | 1,000 deaths | 50,000 troops |
|---|---|---|
| General War | 2/3 GP and >1000 deaths/ million European population | GP each side and >2 Years |

*Factor Analyses*

| Century and Death 3, 4 Variables | Single Factor (1) Death + GP (2) Century − Years | Single Factor (1) Battle + GP (2) Century − Years |
|---|---|---|
| 5–10 Variables | (1) Death + GP + Cent (2) Cent − GP − Years | (1) Battle + GP (2) Century − Years |
| Time Analyses | (1) Death + Half- Cent (2) GP + Years (3) Frequency | (1) Battle + GP + Century (2) Freq + Cent − Years (3) Years |

# Table 8.1 Analyses of Variance Between Mean Scores for Wars

N = 656 Wars by Five-hundred-year periods, 500 B.C. to A.D. 1925

| Variables | F-Ratios | Grand Mean | Pentacossy B.C. | A.D. | (500-year) Med | Mod | Means $R^2$ |
|---|---|---|---|---|---|---|---|
| # Centuries | | (21) | 5 | 5 | 6 | 5 | NA |
| # Wars | 496** (Chi) | 175 (pro) | 66 – | 30 – | 181 | 385 + | 42% |
| Years/War | 5.7 *** | 3.73 | 6.5 + | 4.2 | 3.1 | 3.5 | < 3% |
| Log | 7.2 **** | 1.1 | 1.5 + + | 1.3 + | 0.9 – – | 1.1 – | 3% |
| Start/Win | 3.5 * | 45% | 47% | 57% + | 51% | 39 – | < 2% |
| Log | 3.5 * | 0.3 | 0.3 | 0.4 + | 0.4 | 0.3 – | < 2% |
| Army Size | 1.4 | 296 | 232 | 200 | 68 | 461 | < 1% |
| Log | 42 **** | 4.1 | 4.9 + | 4.9 + | 3.3 – | 4.5 + | 16% |
| Casualties | 0.7 | 59 | 13 | 10 | 3 | 107 | < 1% |
| Log | 47 **** | 1.0 | 1.9 + | 1.9 + | – 0.1 – | 1.5 + | 18% |
| Cas/Year | 0.8 | 12.4 | 2 | 2 | 0.6 | 23 | < 1% |
| Log | 54 **** | – .07 | 0.4 + | 0.6 + | – 1.0 – | 0.4 + | 20% |
| Participants | 12 **** | 2.46 | 2.1 – | 2.0 – | 2.1 – | 2.8 + | 5% |
| Great Powers | 26 **** | 1.1 | 0.6 – | 1.2 + | 0.7 – | 1.4 + | 11% |

*Notes:* The figures in the body of this table are mean scores, except for centuries and wars, which are simply frequencies. The pentacossies are labeled "B.C." for the five hundred years beginning 500 B.C., "A.D." for the five hundred years ending A.D. 500, "Med" for the six hundred years ending 1500 and "Mod" for the five hundred years that will end in 2000. (But note that since Sorokin's data ended about 1925, it covers only the first quarter of the twentieth century.) If the frequency of wars in the twentieth century were prorated accordingly, it would be increased from 14 to 56 wars, making the twentieth century pentacossy = 385 wars. By the same token, since there were six centuries in the medieval pentacossy, the war frequency of 217 has to be divided by six and multiplied by five to give a prorated frequency of 181 for the medieval period. With or without prorating, the frequencies for the first two pentacossies constituting the classic period were signficantly lower than average, while the frequency for the last pentacossy constituting the modern period was significantly higher than average, according to a chi-square test of the difference between these frequencies. These significant differences between war frequencies were canceled out in the mean scores (obtained by dividing the total scores by the war frequencies). That is, Army Size = Army Size/War, etc. Army Size, Casualties, and Cas/Year are all stated in thousands. Plus and minus signs in the body of the table indicate mean scores significantly higher and lower in relation to other mean scores in the same row, as determined by Duncan's multiple range test. The absence of any plus or minus sign indicates that the mean score for that pentacossy was not significantly different from the grand mean of all 656 scores. Because of extreme skewness, Army Size, Casualties, and Cas/Year were logged to obtain a more normal distribution. The $R^2$ in the last column is the percent of variance in any variable that was explained by these pentacossies. Percents less than 5 are substantially negligible even where they are statistically significant, as indicated by the asterisks attached to the F-ratios. * Significant at the .05 level of confidence. ** Significant at the .01 level of confidence. *** Significant at the .001 level of confidence. **** Significant at the .0001 level of confidence. Most of these variables were obtained from Sorokin (1937, vol. 3), except that Start/Win, Participants and Great Powers were supplied by the present author, based on information provided by encyclopedias and other sources, including the *Encyclopedia of Military History* (Dupuy and Dupuy 1986), Wright (1965), *Dictionary of Wars* (Kohn 1987), Levy (1983), Small and Singer (1983), etc.

# Table 8.2  Analyses of Variance Between Mean Scores for 21 Centuries

| Variables | F-Ratios | Grand Mean | B.C. | A.D. | Med | Mod | R² |
|---|---|---|---|---|---|---|---|
| # Centuries | | 21 | | | | | |
| | | (Total) 5 | 5 | 6 | 5 | | NA |
| *Sorokin's Data* | | | | | | | |
| War Freq/ | | | | | | | |
| Cent | 21**** | 33 | 13 – | 6 – | 36 | 77 + | 79% |
| WarYrs/Cent | 10*** | 120 | 86 – | 25 – | 113 – | 260 + | 64% |
| Starters Win | 10*** | 15 | 6 – | 3 – | 19 + | 30 + | 63% |
| Army Size | 2.4' | 17,898 | 3065 | 1202 | 2465 | 67,947 | 30% |
| Log | 14**** | 8 | 8 – | 7 – | 7 – | 11 + | 71% |
| Casualties | 1.5 | 5276 | 176 | 60 | 107 | 21,794 | 21% |
| Log | 16**** | 5 | 5 – | 4 – | 4 – | 11 + | 73% |
| Cas/Year | 1.5 | 1097 | 25 | 12 | 20 | 4544 | 21% |
| Log | 15**** | 4 | 3.0 – | 2.5 – | 2.5 – | 6.9 + | 73% |
| Participants | 34**** | 85 | 28 | 12 – | 75 + | 228 + + | 86% |
| Log | 27**** | 4 | 3.2 – | 2.6 – | 4.1 + | 5.4 + + | 83% |
| Great Powers | 40**** | 37 | 8 – | 7 – | 24 – | 112 + | 88% |
| Log | 17**** | 3 | 2.0 – | 2.1 – | 2.9 – | 4.7 + | 75% |
| *Other Data* | | | | | | | |
| BatSum (D & D) | 36**** | 200 | 50 – | 31 – | 112 | 624 + | 82%(87%) |
| HarBruce | 17**** | 98.4 | 40.4 | 13.4 – | 44.3 | 306 + | 65%(75%) |
| Bat/Pop (D & D) | 14**** | 0.37 | 0.34 | 0.16 – | 0.32 | 0.67 + | 72% |
| HarBruce/Pop | 8** | 0.19 | 0.28 + | 0.07 – | 0.12 – | 0.32 + | 58% |
| Imperial Size | 10*** | 5.5 | 2.6 | 3.6 | 4.2 | 11.8 + | 61%(63%) |
| Europe Pop | 25**** | 82 | 24 – | 33 | 55 + | 223 + + | 51%(81%) |
| World Pop | 28**** | 440 | 148 – | 189 – | 347 | 1093 + | 51%(83%) |

*Notes:* See the notes following Table 8.1. But note that while the mean scores in Table 8.1 are the means per war, the mean scores in this table are the means per century. B.C. = 500–0 B.C. A.D. = A.D. 1–500. Med = 900–1500. Mod = 1500–2000. Bat/Pop (D & D) = Dupuy and Dupuy's (1986) Index of Battles and Sieges (pp. 1500–15). N = 4460 battles and sieges from 1469 B.C. to A.D. 1984, most of which were included in these 21 centuries (N = 4151 = 93 percent total). HarBruce/Pop = Harbottle's *Dictionary of Battles* as edited by Bruce (1981). N = 2110 Battles, most of which were included in these 21 centuries. Imperial Size = based on Taagepera (1978a). Europe Pop and World Pop = population estimates obtained from McEvedy and Jones (1978). Europe Pop was used in my count of Sorokin's casualties divided by population. World Pop was used in my count of Harbottle's and the Dupuys' battles divided by population. The percentages in parentheses under R² were those obtained when log scores were used to correct the raw scores for extreme skewness. The logged scores were always used to determine significant differences among mean scores, althugh raw scores are always shown in the body of the table. These percentages indicate the percent of variance in the mean scores that can be explained by the differences among the pentacossies. The relationship may be either linear or nonlinear. Where the F-ratio is not significant, the percentages are not reliable and should be ignored.

## Table 8.3 Analyses of Variance Between Mean Scores for Modern Wars (N = 343)

| Variables | F-Ratios | Grand Mean | Centuries of War 16th | 17th | 18th | 19th | 20th | $R^2$ |
|---|---|---|---|---|---|---|---|---|
| War Frequency | 26** (Chi) | 77 | 91 | 72 | 58 – | 108 + | 56 – | 6% |
| Years/War | <1 | 3.5 | 3.7 | 4.4 | 3.3 | 3.2 | 2.0 | <1% |
| Start/Win | <2 | 39% | 35% | 31% | 38% | 48% | 36% | 2% |
| Participants | 4** | 2.8 | 2.3 – | 2.5 – | 3.3 | 3.1 | 4.1 + | 5% |
| Great Powers | 8**** | 1.4 | 1.0 – | 1.2 – | 2.0 + | 1.4 – | 2.1 + | 9% |
| Army Size | 6**** | 461 | 150 | 306 | 620 | 241 | 4324 | 7% |
| Casualties | 6**** | 107 | 8.2 | 41.3 | 87.0 | 37.5 | 1717 + | 7% |
| Casu/Year | 7**** | 23 | 2 | 4 | 11 | 17 | 354 + | 7% |
| Army Log | 6**** | 4.5 | 4.2 – | 4.6 | 5.1 + | 4.1 – | 5.2 + | 6% |
| Casu Log | 5*** | 1.5 | 1.2 – | 1.8 | 2.3 + | 1.0 – | 2.2 + | 6% |
| Cas/Yr Log | 5*** | 0.4 | 0.1 – | 0.6 | 1.1 + | 0.07 – | 1.3 + | 6% |

*Notes:* See the notes following Table 8.1. Since the war frequency of 14 in the twentieth century covered only 1900–25, it was multiplied by four to extend to the whole century. The significant differences between war frequencies were obtained by means of chi-squares. The percentage figure in the $R^2$ column was the square of the contingency coefficient for this row only.

## Table 8.4 Analyses of Variance Between Mean Scores for Modern Wars (N = 343)

| Variables | F-Ratios | Grand Mean | Regions of War Europe | Afro-Asia | $R^2$ |
|---|---|---|---|---|---|
| War Frequency | 78** (Chi) | 171.5 | 253 + | 90 – | 19% |
| Century | 129**** | 17.66 | 17.26 – | 18.78 + | 27% |
| Years/War | 2 | 3.5 | 3.8 | 2.8 | < 1% |
| Start/Win | 15**** | 39% | 33% – | 56% + | 4% |
| Participants | 0 | 2.8 | 2.8 | 2.8 | 0% |
| Great Powers | 6* | 1.4 | 1.5 + | 1.1 – | < 2% |
| Army Size | 2 | 461 | 597 | 78 | < 1% |
| Casualties | <1 | 107 | 144 | 4 | < 1% |
| Casu/Year | <1 | 23 | 31 | 1 | < 1% |
| Army Log | 42**** | 4.5 | 4.8 + | 3.6 – | 11% |
| Casu Log | 49**** | 1.5 | 1.9 + | 0.3 – | 13% |
| Cas/Yr Log | 68**** | 0.4 | 0.8 + | – 0.8 – | 17% |

*Notes:* See the notes following Table 8.1.

## Table 8.5   Analyses of Variance Between Mean Scores for Modern Wars (N = 343)

| Variables | F-Ratios | Grand Mean | Types of War Civ | Col | Imp | Intl | $R^2$ |
|---|---|---|---|---|---|---|---|
| War Frequency | 215** (Chi) | 86 | 65 – | 71 | 196 + | 11 – | 39% |
| Century | 15**** | 17.66 | 16.9 – | 18.3 + | 17.7 | 17.8 | 11% |
| Years/War | 2 | 3.5 | 2.3 | 3.9 | 3.9 | 1.7 | < 2% |
| Start/Win | 17**** | 39% | 14% – | 21% – | 54% + | 36% | 13% |
| Participants | 2 | 2.8 | 2.3 | 3.1 | 2.9 | 3.3 | < 2% |
| Great Powers | 9**** | 1.4 | 0.7 – | 1.4 | 1.5 | 2.4 + | 8% |
| Army | < 1 | 461 | 146 | 236 | 645 | 498 | < 1% |
| Casualties | < 1 | 107 | 19 | 33 | 165 | 96 | < 1% |
| Cas/Year | < 1 | 23 | 6 | 3 | 34 | 53 | < 1% |
| Army Log | 2 | 4.5 | 4.2 | 4.2 | 4.6 | 4.7 | < 2% |
| Cas Log | 2' | 1.5 | 1.2 | 1.1 | 1.7 | 2.1 | 2% |
| Cas/Yr Log | 3* | 0.4 | 0.3 | 0.05 | 0.5 | 1.4 + | 2% |

*Notes:* Civ = civil. Col = colonial. Imp = imperial. Intl = international. See the notes following
   Table 8.1.

## Table 8.6  Analyses of Variance Between Mean Scores for Modern Wars (N = 343)

| Variables | F-Ratios | Grand Mean | Eth | Ind | Left | Pow | Right | Terr | | $R^2$ |
|---|---|---|---|---|---|---|---|---|---|---|
| | | | | | | *Causes of War* | | | | |
| War Frequency | 518** (Chi) | 57 | 26 – | 70 | 9 – | 25 – | 6 – | 207 + | | 60% |
| Century | 12**** | 17.66 | 16.7 – | 18.3 + | 16.4 – | 17.4 – | 19.2 + | 17.6 + | | 15% |
| Years/War | <1 | 3.5 | 3.6 | 3.5 | 1.7 | 1.8 | 4.8 | 3.8 | | 1% |
| Start/Win | 8**** | 39% | 19% | 20% | 22% | 24% | 0% – | 51% + | | 10% |
| Participants | <1 | 2.8 | 2.6 | 3.0 | 2.0 | 3.0 | 2.7 | 2.8 | ∨ | 1% |
| Great Powers | 2' | 1.4 | 1.2 | 1.3 | 0.7 | 0.9 | 1.0 | 1.5 | | 3% |
| Army Size | 0 | 461 | 341 | 145 | 109 | 156 | 607 | 631 | ∨ | 1% |
| Casualties | 0 | 107 | 66 | 10 | 8 | 20 | 138 | 160 | ∨ | 1% |
| Cas/Year | 0 | 23 | 3 | 2 | 2 | 10 | 44 | 34 | ∨ | 1% |
| Army Log | 3* | 4.5 | 4.1 | 4.1 | 3.8 | 4.5 | 6.1 + | 4.6 + | | 4% |
| Cas Log | 4** | 1.5 | 0.8 | 1.0 | 0.8 | 1.6 | 3.7 + | 1.7 | | 5% |
| Cas/Yr Log | 3** | 0.4 | –0.17 | –0.00 | 0.2 | 0.8 | 2.0 + | 0.5 | | 4% |

*Notes:* Eth = ethnic (including religious) differences. Ind = independence. Left = leftist ideology. Pow = political with no apparent ideological differences. Right = rightist ideology. Terr = territory (including land, labor, capital and trade). See the notes following Table 8.1.

# Table 8.7   Comparison of Levy's, Wrights and Sorokin's Modern Wars

| Variables | Levy (N = 119) | Wright (N = 308) | Sorokin (N = 343) |
|---|---|---|---|
| Dates | 1495–1975 | 1480–1964 | 1500–1925 |
| Years | 480 | 484 | 425 |
| Average Century | 17.5 (1.46) | 18.0 (1.43) | 17.66 (1.28) |
| #GP/War | 2.21 (1.52) | 1.19 (1.37)   =   | 1.37 (1.26) |
| Years/War | 4.35 (4.66)   = | 4.12 (5.30)   =   | 3.54 (5.78) |
| GP Wars | 100% | 68% | 83% |
| Cycles | None | 50-year | Fluctuations |

*Europe Compared with Other Regions of the World*

| | | | | | | |
|---|---|---|---|---|---|---|
| Location of Wars | 88% | | 62% | | 74% | |
| Deaths or Battles | 96% | | 93% | | 99% | |
| Years/War | 4.6 = 2.5 | | 4.6 | 3.3 | 3.8 = 2.8 | |
| #GP/War | 2.3 = 1.5 | | 1.5 | 0.7 | 1.5 | 1.1 |
| Death(Battle)/War | 305 = 99 | | 32 = 9 | | 144 = 4 ( Log) | |
| Average Century | 17.2 | 19.6 | 17.4 | 19.1 | 17.3 | 18.8 |

*Notes:* Signs of "greater than," "less than," and "equal to," as well as plus and minus signs, indicate significant differences and similarities as determined by *t* tests.

*Correlations over Five Centuries* (Historical Trends)

| | | | |
|---|---|---|---|
| Frequencies of War | − .82' | .55ns | − .36ns |
| Years | − .93* | − .18ns | − .74ns |
| Deaths (Battles) | .81' | .95** | .86' |
| Death(Battle)/War | .87* | .66ns | .83' |
| Years/War | − .77ns | − .65ns | − .88* |
| GP/War | .00ns | .00ns | .58ns |

*Correlations over 45 Decades* (Historical Trends)

| | | | |
|---|---|---|---|
| Deaths (Battles) | .31* | .39** | .26' |
| Years of War | − .41** | − .11ns | − .22ns |
| War Frequencies | − .34* | .28' | − .17ns |
| Deaths/War | .30* | .41** | .29* |
| Years/War | − .29* | − .29* | − .19ns |
| GP/War | .06ns | .18ns | − .08ns |

*Notes:* ** Significant at the .01 level of confidence, at least. * Significant at the .05 level of confidence. ' Significant at the .10 level of confidence. ns *Not* significant at the .10 level of confidence. Positive correlations with time indicate variables increasing over time. Negative correlations with time indicate variables decreasing over time. Levy's, Wright's and Sorokin's measures of deaths, durations and frequencies of war were generally significantly correlated with one another, so that there was significant agreement among them concerning the relative distribution of these three variables over the 45 decades from 1500 to 1950. The actual number of decades varied from 43 to 47. This agreement is rather remarkable, considering their different definitions of war (see p. 253, top of page), their different samples of nations, and their different purposes.

| Definitions | Levy | Wright | Sorokin |
|---|---|---|---|
| War | 1,000 Deaths | 50,000 Troops | History Mention |

*Correlations over Five Centuries* (N = 5)

| | Levy, Wright | Levy, Sorokin | Sorokin, Wright |
|---|---|---|---|
| Frequency of War | − .05ns | .60ns | .43ns |
| Years | .37ns | .58ns | .46ns |
| Deaths (Battles) | .89* | .99** | .88* |
| Deaths (Battles)/War | .77ns | .99** | .75ns |
| Years/War | .80' | .90* | .68ns |
| GP/War | .99** | .61ns | .61ns |

*Correlations over 45 Decades* (N = 45)

| | Levy, Wright | Levy, Sorokin | Sorokin, Wright |
|---|---|---|---|
| Wars | .28* | .37* | .58** |
| Years | .54** | .51** | .48** |
| Deaths(Battles) | .94** | .96** | .81** |
| Deaths(Battles)/War | .74** | .82** | .85** |
| Years/War | .69** | .67** | .65** |
| GP/War | .43** | .64** | .13ns |

*Factor Analyses*

| Century and Death | Single Factor | Single Factor | Single Factor |
|---|---|---|---|
| 3, 4 Variables | 1.Death + GP | 1.Battle + GP | 1.Cas + GP + Cent |
| | 2.Cent − Years | 2.Cent − Years | 2.Cent − Years |
| 5–10 Variables | 1.Death + GP + Cen | 1.Battle + GP | 1.Cas + GP + Cent |
| | 2.Cent − GP − Yrs | 2.Cent − Years | 2.Years + StWin |
| Time Analyses | 1.Death + HalfCen | 1.Bat + GP + Cent | 1.Cas + GP − Freq |
| | 2.GP + Years | 2.Freq + Cent − Yrs | 2.Decade − Yrs |
| | 3.Frequency | 3.Years | |

*Analyses of Variance Among Modern Centuries*

| | | | | | Centuries | | | |
|---|---|---|---|---|---|---|---|---|
| Variable | F | Mean | 16 | 17 | 18 | 19 | 20 | $R^2$ |
| **Deaths** | | | | | | | | |
| Levy | 3* | 711 | 94 − | 403 − | 377 − | 257 − | 3155 + | 23% |
| Sorokin | 4** | 202 | 9 − | 55 − | 167 − | 39 − | 2000 + | 30% |
| Wright | 4** | 80 | 9 − | 23 − | 79 − | 63 − | 376 + | 35% |
| **Years** | | | | | | | | |
| Levy | 3* | 11 | 17 + | 17 + | 10 | 4 − | 5 − | 21% |
| Sorokin | 1 | 3.6 | 3.8 | 4.4 | 3.6 | 3.0 | 2.3 | 9% |
| Wright | 2' | 27 | 24 | 40 + | 17 − | 28 | 24 | 18% |

| Variable | F | Mean | 16 | 17 | 18 | 19 | 20 | $R^2$ |
|----------|---|------|----|----|----|----|----|----|
| | | | | | *Centuries* | | | |

| Variable | F | Mean | 16 | 17 | 18 | 19 | 20 | $R^2$ |
|----------|------|------|-------|-----|-------|-----------|--------|-------|
| **Freqs** | | | | | | | | |
| Levy | 2' | 2.5 | 3.5 + | 2.9 | 1.7 − | 2.0  2.1 | | 17% |
| Sorokin | 14**** | 8.0 | 10.2 + | 7.7 | 4.5 − | 10.5 + 5.3 − | | 59% |
| Wright | 5** | 6.5 | 6.0 | 6.5 | 3.8 − | 8.8 + 7.9 + | | 32% |

*Notes:* These century means were based on decades. When century means were based upon wars, then Levy's deaths and Sorokin's casualties were still significantly higher in the twentieth century. Although Wright's battles were also higher, they were not significantly higher than the eighteenth century.

## Table 9.1   Wars and Related Deaths, 1500–2000

| Century | Wars | Deaths | Civilian% | Start/Win | Great Powers |
|---------|------|--------|-----------|-----------|--------------|
| 16th. | 60 − | 1613 − | 45 | 47 | 1.4 + |
| 17th. | 36 − | 6108 − | 50 | 47 | 1.4 + |
| 18th. | 55 − | 7001 − | 43 | 47 | 1.2 + |
| 19th. | 211 + | 19,423 − | 50 | 48 | 0.7 − |
| 20th(pro) | 251 + | 110,929 + | 58 | 38 | 0.6 − |
| Total | 613 | 145,074 | 56% | 44% | 0.8 |

*Twentieth Century by Decades:*

| | | | | | |
|------|-------|-----------|----|--------|-------|
| 1900 | 22 | 824 − | 78 | 36 | 0.9 + |
| 1910 | 28 | 28,456 + | 50 | 50 + | 1.0 + |
| 1920 | 18 | 530 − | 50 | 56 + | 0.6 |
| 1930 | 20 | 4029 − | 57 | 50 + | 0.9 + |
| 1940 | 21 | 52,637 + | 60 | 29 | 0.9 + |
| 1950 | 24 | 4658 − | 55 | 46 | 0.8 + |
| 1960 | 23 | 6424 − | 56 | 39 | 0.5 |
| 1970 | 20 | 2868 − | 67 | 45 | 0.2 − |
| 1980 | 50 + | 5578 − | 74 | 17 − | 0.2 − |

*Notes:* War = any armed conflict, involving at least one government, and killing at least one thousand people per year. Deaths are given in thousands. Great Powers were obtained from Levy (1983): France, United Kingdom, Austria-Hungary until 1918, Spain until 1808, Turkey until 1699, Netherlands 1609–1713, Sweden 1617–1721, Russia since 1721, Germany since 1740, Italy 1861–1943, USA since 1898, Japan 1905–1945, China since 1949. This column presents Great Powers per war on the average. Plus and minus signs indicate frequencies and mean scores significantly higher and lower than average. Frequencies were evaluated by the chi-square technique. Mean scores were evaluated by Analysis of Variance (F test) and Duncan's multiple range test.

# Table 9.2 Comparison of Wars
## 1700-1987 and 1500-1990

| Variables | 1700-1987 | 1500-1990 |
|---|---|---|
| Wars | 471 | 588 |
| Start/Win | 44% | 44% |
| 20th SW% | 39% | 38% |
| Europe SW% | 45% | 42% |
| Deaths | 101,552 | 140,149 |
| Deaths/War | 216 | 238 |
| Civilian % Deaths | 50% | 56% |
| 20th Civilian % | 50% | 58% |
| Europe Civilian % | 49% | 55% |
| Years | 1,145 | 1,583 |
| Years/War | 2.4 | 2.7 |
| 20th % Wars | 49% | 41% |
| 20th % Years | 52% | 42% |
| 20th % Deaths | 86% | 76% |
| Europe % Wars | 24% | 34% |
| Europe % Years | 22% | 39% |
| Europe % Deaths | 65% | 67% |
| Intl. % Deaths | 74% | 73% |
| Territory % Deaths | 67% | 77% |

| Factor Analyses | N = 29 Decades | N = 49 Decades |
|---|---|---|
| Centuries | .96 | .89 |
| Wars | .95 | .94 |
| Decades | .91 | .91 |
| Parties | .90 | .95 |
| Years | .81 | .86 |
| Deaths | .68 | .75 |
| Civilian % Deaths | .65 | .75 |
| Great Powers/War | -.65 | -.52 |
| Start/Win | -.62 | -.13ns |

*Notes:* Start/Win and SW% = the percentage of starters who won wars they started. Intl. % Deaths = percentage of deaths occurring in international wars. Territory % Deaths = percentage of deaths occurring in wars caused by territorial disputes, including disputes over land, labor, capital and trade. All of the factor loadings were significant ($>.50$), except for Start/Win in 1500-1990.

# Table 9.3   Comparison of Levy, Wright, Sorokin and Eckhardt

| Variables | Levy (N = 119) | Wright (N = 308) | Sorokin (N = 343) | Eckhardt (N = 588) |
|---|---|---|---|---|
| Dates | 1495–1975 | 1480–1964 | 1500–1925 | 1500–1990 |
| Years | 480 | 484 | 425 | 490 |
| Avg Century | 17.5 (1.46) < | 18.0 (1.43) > | 17.66 (1.28) < | 18.86 (1.27) |
| #GP/War | 2.21 (1.52) > | 1.19 (1.37) = | 1.37 (1.26) > | 0.82 (1.06) |
| Years/War | 43.5 (4.66) = | 4.12 (5.30) = | 3.54 (5.78) > | 2.69 (4.02) |
| GP % Wars | 100% + | 68% | 83% | 55% – |
| Cycles | None | 50-years | Fluctuations | NA |

*Europe Compared with Other Regions of the World*

| | | | | |
|---|---|---|---|---|
| War Location | 88% + | 62% | 74% | 34% – |
| Deaths(Bats) | 96% | (93%) | 99% | 67% – |
| Years/War | 4.6 > 3.3 | 4.6 > 3.3 | 3.8 = 2.8 | 3.1 = 2.5 |
| #GP/War | 2.3 = 1.5 | 1.5 > 0.7 | 1.5 > 1.1 | 1.4 > 0.5 |
| Death/War | 305 = 99 | (32 = 9) | 144 > 4 | 475 > 119 |
| Avg Century | 17.2 < 19.6 | 17.4 < 19.1 | 17.3 < 18.8 | 18.0 < 19.3 |

Notes: Signs of "greater than," "less than," and "equal to," as well as plus and minus signs, indicate significant differences and similarities as determined by chi-square or *t* tests.

*Correlations over Five Centuries* (Historical Trends)

| | | | | |
|---|---|---|---|---|
| Death/War | .87* | (.66ns) | .83' | .74ns** |
| Years/War | – .77ns | – .65ns | – .88* | – .50ns |
| GP/War | .00ns | .00ns | .58ns | – .94* |
| Wars | – .82' | .55ns | – .36ns | .88* |
| Years | – .93* | – .18ns | – .74ns | .87* |
| Deaths | .81' | (.95*) | .86' | .97** |

*Correlations over 45 Decades* (Historical Trends)

| | | | | |
|---|---|---|---|---|
| Deaths | .31* | (.39**) | .26' | .38** |
| Years | – .41** | – .11ns | – .22ns | .49** |
| Wars | – .34* | .28' | – .17ns | .76** |
| Deaths/War | .30* | .41** | .29* | .37** |
| Years/War | – .29* | – .29* | – .19ns | – .23ns |
| GP/War | .06ns | .18ns | – .08ns | – .60** |

Notes: Levy's, Wright's, Sorokin's and Eckhardt's measures of deaths, durations and frequencies of war were generally significantly correlated with one another, so that there was significant agreement among them concerning the relative distribution of these three variables over the 45 decades from 1500 to 1950. The actual number of decades varied from 43 to 48. This agreement is rather remarkable, considering their different definitions of war (see next page), their different samples of nations, and their different purposes. Positive correlations with time indicate that variables were increasing over time. Negative correlations with time indicate that variables were decreasing over time.

| Definitions | Levy | Wright | Sorokin | Eckhardt |
|---|---|---|---|---|
| War | 1,000 Deaths | 50,000 Troops | History Mention | 1t Deaths per Year |

*Correlations over Five Centuries* (N = 5)

| | Levy, Wright | Levy, Sorokin | Sorokin, Wright |
|---|---|---|---|
| Wars | − .05ns | .60ns | .43ns |
| Years | .37ns | .58ns | .46ns |
| Deaths(Battles) | .89* | .99** | .88* |
| Deaths(Battles)/War | .77ns | .99** | .75ns |
| GP/War | .99** | .61ns | .61ns |
| Years/War | .80ns | .90* | .68ns |

| | Eckhardt, Wright | Eckhardt, Levy | Eckhardt, Sorokin |
|---|---|---|---|
| Wars | .82' | − .50ns | .03ns |
| Years | − .02ns | − .78ns | − .60ns |
| Deaths(Battles) | .89* | .91* | .94* |
| Deaths(Battles)/War | .57ns | .94* | .97** |
| GP/War | .19ns | .19ns | − .38ns |
| Years/War | .97** | .71ns | .50ns |

*Correlations over 45 Decades* (N = 45)

| | Levy, Wright | Levy, Sorokin | Sorokin, Wright |
|---|---|---|---|
| Wars | .28* | .37* | .58** |
| Years | .54** | .51** | .48** |
| Deaths(Battles) | .94** | .96** | .81** |
| Deaths(Battles)/War | .74** | .82** | .85** |
| GP/War | .43** | .64** | .13ns |
| Years/War | .69** | .67** | .65** |

| | Eckhardt, Wright | Eckhardt, Levy | Eckhardt, Sorokin |
|---|---|---|---|
| Wars | .59** | − .06ns | .34* |
| Years | .27' | .22ns | .34* |
| Deaths(Battles) | .91** | .96** | .90** |
| Deaths(Battles)/War | .67** | .78** | .53** |
| GP/War | .07ns | .34* | .58** |
| Years/War | .51** | .42** | .23ns |

*Notes:* ** Significant at the .01 level of confidence, at least. * Significant at the .05 level of confidence. ' Significant at the .10 level of confidence. ns *Not* significant at the .10 level of confidence.

*Analyses of Variance Among Modern Centuries*

| | | | | | Centuries | | | |
|---|---|---|---|---|---|---|---|---|
| *Variable* | *F-Ratio* | *Grand Mean* | *16* | *17* | *18* | *19* | *20* | *R²* |
| **Deaths** | | | | | | | | |
| Levy | 3* | 711 | 94 – | 403 – | 377 – | 257 – | 3155 + | 23% |
| Sorokin | 4** | 202 | 9 – | 55 – | 167 – | 39 – | 2000 + | 30% |
| Wright | 4** | 80 | 9 – | 23 – | 79 – | 63 – | 376 + | 35% |
| Eckhardt | 4** | 196 | 26 – | 270 – | 133 – | 89 – | 502 + | 26% |
| **Years** | | | | | | | | |
| Levy | 3* | 11 | 17 + | 17 + | 10 | 4 – | 5 – | 21% |
| Sorokin | 1 | 3.6 | 3.8 | 4.4 | 3.6 | 3.0 | 2.3 | 9% |
| Wright | 2' | 27 | 24 | 40 + | 17 – | 28 | 24 | 18% |
| Eckhardt | 2 | 3.1 | 3.2 | 4.9 | 3.1 | 2.2 | 2.4 | 13% |
| **Wars** | | | | | | | | |
| Levy | 2' | 2.5 | 3.5 + | 2.9 | 1.7 – | 2.0 | 2.1 | 17% |
| Sorokin | 14**** | 8.0 | 10.2 + | 7.7 | 4.5 – | 10.5 + | 5.3 – | 59% |
| Wright | 5** | 6.5 | 6.0 | 6.5 | 3.8 – | 8.8 + | 7.9 + | 32% |
| Eckhardt | 27**** | 12.3 | 6 – | 4 – | 5.5 – | 21 + | 25 + | 71% |

*Notes:* These century means were based on decades. When century means were based on wars, Levy's deaths and Sorokin's casualties were still significantly higher in the twentieth century. Although Wright's battles were also higher, they were not significantly higher than for the eighteenth century. Although Eckhardt's pattern was the same for deaths and years, the differences were not significant, because of the greater variability around the mean scores. In this table (as in others) Wright's data under "Deaths" contain his battle frequencies, *not* casualties or deaths.

# Table 10.1  Kohn's Wars by Century and by Region, 2000 B.C. to A.D. 2000

| Century | Europe | Mid-East | Far East | South Asia | Latin Amer. | North Amer. | Sub-Sahara | Total | Non-Europe | Europe % |
|---|---|---|---|---|---|---|---|---|---|---|
| -20 | 1 | | | | | | | 1 | 0 | 100% |
| -19 | | | | | | | | 0 | 0 | NA |
| -18 | | | | | | | | 0 | 0 | NA |
| -17 | | 4 | | | | | | 4 | 4 | 0% |
| -16 | | 8 | | | | | | 8 | 8 | 0% |
| -15 | 1 | 1 | | | | | | 2 | 1 | 50% |
| -14 | 1 | 4 | | | | | | 5 | 4 | 20% |
| -13 | | 7 | | | | | | 7 | 7 | 0% |
| -12 | 1 | 3 | | | | | | 4 | 3 | 25% |
| -11 | 1 | 2 | | | | | | 3 | 2 | 33% |
| -10 | | 3 | | | | | | 3 | 3 | 0% |
| -9 | | 4 | | | | | | 4 | 4 | 0% |
| -8 | 1 | 15 | | | | | | 16 | 15 | 6% |
| -7 | 2 | 16 | | | | | | 18 | 16 | 11% |
| -6 | 1 | 7 | | | | | | 8 | 7 | 13% |
| -5 | 19 | 4 | | | | | | 23 | 4 | 83% |
| -4 | 17 | 8 | | 4 | | | | 29 | 12 | 59% |
| -3 | 14 | 8 | | 3 | | | | 25 | 11 | 56% |
| -2 | 13 | 6 | 1 | 1 | | | | 21 | 8 | 62% |
| -1 | 13 | 7 | | | | | | 20 | 7 | 65% |
| 1 | 5 | 4 | 2 | | | | | 11 | 6 | 45% |
| 2 | 3 | 5 | 1 | | | | | 9 | 6 | 33% |
| 3 | 8 | 6 | 1 | | | | | 15 | 7 | 53% |
| 4 | 17 | 1 | | 1 | | | | 19 | 2 | 89% |
| 5 | 16 | 3 | 1 | | | | | 20 | 4 | 80% |
| 6 | 9 | 7 | 1 | 1 | | | | 18 | 9 | 50% |

# Table 10.1 Cont.

| Century | Europe | Mid-East | Far East | South Asia | Latin Amer. | North Amer. | Sub-Sahara | Total | Non-Europe | Europe% |
|---|---|---|---|---|---|---|---|---|---|---|
| 7 | 11 | 5 | 8 | 9 | | | | 33 | 22 | 33% |
| 8 | 25 | 5 | 4 | 2 | | | | 36 | 11 | 69% |
| 9 | 25 | 8 | | 2 | | | | 35 | 10 | 71% |
| 10 | 24 | 5 | 4 | 4 | | | | 37 | 13 | 65% |
| 11 | 34 | 1 | 8 | 5 | | | | 48 | 14 | 71% |
| 12 | 28 | 5 | 13 | 4 | | | | 50 | 22 | 56% |
| 13 | 42 | 10 | 16 | 5 | | | | 73 | 31 | 58% |
| 14 | 70 | 2 | 15 | 10 | | | | 97 | 27 | 72% |
| 15 | 94 | 6 | 12 | 2 | | | | 114 | 20 | 82% |
| 16 | 78 | 12 | 21 | 18 | 9 | 1 | | 139 | 61 | 56% |
| 17 | 74 | 7 | 24 | 18 | 3 | 17 | | 148 | 74 | 50% |
| 18 | 50 | 11 | 26 | 24 | 9 | 27 | 5 | 152 | 102 | 33% |
| 19 | 59 | 17 | 48 | 17 | 53 | 54 | 40 | 288 | 229 | 20% |
| 20 | 81 | 41 | 45 | 14 | 70 | 1 | 31 | 283 | 202 | 29% |
| | | | | | | | | | | |
| Sum | 838 | 268 | 251 | 144 | 144 | 100 | 81 | 1826 | 988 | 46% |
| Mean | 21 | 7 | 6 | 4 | 4 | 3 | 2 | 46 | 25 | 43% |
| StdDev | 26 | 7 | 12 | 6 | 14 | 10 | 8 | 68 | 48 | 29% |

Notes: The twentieth century was prorated by dividing Kohn's frequencies by 83 (since his data ended in 1983) and multiplying by 100, so as to make the twentieth century comparable to the previous centuries.

# Table 10.2   Statistical Summary of Wars

|  | *Sorokin* (1937) | *Dupuys* (1986) | *Kohn* (1987) |
|---|---|---|---|
| First Event | Greco-Persia | Egypt | Greece |
| Starting Year | 500 BC | 3000 BC | 2000 BC |
| Centuries | 21 | 50 | 40 |
| Frequency | 698 | 1266 | 1826 |
| Euro% Freq | 84% | 43% | 46% |
| # < 5th BC | 0 | 64 | 83 |
| % < 5th BC | 0% | 5.06% | 4.55% |
| Europe < 50% | 0 Cs. | 34 Cs. | 19 Cs. |
| Years/War | 3.6 | 10.9 | 5.4 |
| Start/Win | 45% | 45% | 53% |
| % Same Region | 67% | 70% | 69% |
| # Participant | 2.6 | NA | 2.45 |
| # Great Power | 1.1 | NA | 0.7 |
| Eur%,Cent $r$ | NA | .71**** | .45** |
| Non%,Cent $r$ | NA | −.68**** | .18nsr |
| Eur > Non | NA | $t = 1.8$nsd | $t < 1$nsd |
| Eur,Non $r$ | NA | .85**** | .74**** |
| Total,Cent $r$ | .79**** | .95**** | .93**** |
| Total,Cas $r$ | .68*** | .75**** | .71**** |
| Eur,Cas $r$ | NA | .54** | .54** |
| Mod%Total | 55% | 50% | 55% |
| *Modern* (N = 5) | | | |
| Total,Cent $r$ | −.24nsr | .34nsr | .89* |

*Notes:* Cs. = centuries. $r$ = correlation coefficient. $t$ = $t$ test of significant difference. nsd = no significant difference at the .05 level of confidence. nsr = no significant correlation at the .05 level of confidence. Cas = Sorokin's war casualties limited to 21 centuries, 500 B.C. to A.D. 500 and 900 to 2000. Mod%Total = percentage of all wars occurring in the modern period, 1500–2000. The *Modern* Total, Century $r$ in the last row is based on only the sixteenth to the twentieth centuries of the modern period.

# Table 10.3 Dupuys' Pages Assigned
## to Various Time Periods

| Time Period | Years | Pages | Years/Page |
|---|---|---|---|
| 3500–600B.C. | 2900 | 15 | 193.33 |
| 600–1B.C. | 600 | 106 | 5.66 |
| A.D.1–600 | 600 | 77 | 7.79 |
| 600–1000 | 400 | 79 | 5.06 |
| 1000–1500 | 500 | 170 | 2.94 |
| 500–1600 | 100 | 74 | 1.35 |
| 1600–1700 | 100 | 86 | 1.16 |
| 1700–1800 | 100 | 122 | 0.82 |
| 1800–1900 | 100 | 185 | 0.54 |
| 1900–1925 | 25 | 99 | 0.25 |
| 1925–1945 | 20 | 185 | 0.11 |
| 1945–1974 | 29 | 147 | 0.20 |
| 1974–1984 | 10 | 55 | 0.18 |
| (1975–2000) | (25) | (138) | (.18) |
| | | | |
| 3500B.C.–A.D.2000 | 5500 | 1400 | 3.93 |
| | | | |
| Arc-Ancient (3500–600B.C.) | 2900 | 15 | 193.33 |
| Classic (600B.C.–A.D.600) | 1200 | 183 | 6.56 |
| Medieval (A.D.600–1500) | 900 | 249 | 3.61 |
| Modern (A.D.1500–2000) | 500 | 1036 | 0.48 |

Notes: As rough as these figures may be, they clearly show what Taagepera (1988) has called "the fading rate of history." Going back in history, according to my interpretation, means going back to fewer newsworthy events, such as battles and wars, as well as other civilized activities, such as those measured by Taagepera from the data provided by Grun (1979): history and politics, literature and theatre, religion and philosophy, visual arts, music, science and technology, and daily life. Taagepera (1988) also analyzed four other sources providing data on art, history and creativity, with similar (exponential) results.

# Table 11.1 Comparison of Six Lists of Wars Since 1700

| Authors | Dates | Deaths (m) | Years | Deaths(t)/ Year | Wars | Deaths Required |
|---------|-------|------------|-------|-----------------|------|-----------------|
| Kaye et al. | 1720–1985 | 94 | 265 | 355 | 654 | None |
| Bouthoul | 1740–1974 | 88 | 234 | 376 | 366 | None |
| Dunnigan | 1786–1987 | 163 | 201 | 811 | 409 | 1000/War |
| Richardson | 1820–1952 | 48 | 132 | 364 | 315 | 317/War |
| Small | 1816–1980 | 40 | 165 | 242 | 224 | 1000/Year |
| Westing | 1900–1980 | 86 | 80 | 1075 | 45 | 32,000/War |

| Authors | Avg. War Duration | Start/Win | European % Deaths | Deaths (Frequencies) 18th | 19th | 20th |
|---------|-------------------|-----------|-------------------|---------------------------|------|------|
| Kaye et al. | 3.7 | 51% | NA | 3(68) | 20(277) | 76(380) |
| Bouthoul et al. | 4.1 | NA | NA | 4(68) | 18(173) | 75(203) |
| Dunnigan et al. | 5.8 | 33% | NA | NA | 32(203) | 142(215) |
| Richardson | 2.6 | NA | NA | NA | 7(250) | 55(230) |
| Small et al. | 1.9 | 48% | 59% | NA | 6(116) | 40(156) |
| Westing | 4.2 | NA | NA | NA | NA | 92(56) |
| Average | 4.1 | 44% | 59% | 4(62) | 19(222) | 87(254) |

| | | | | | | |
|---|---|---|---|---|---|---|
| Number of Sovereign Nations | | | | 20 | 38 | 75 |
| World Population (millions) | | | | 720 | 1200 | 2500 |

*Notes:* Authors have been identified and referenced in the text. Deaths by century for the first two authors have been prorated for the eighteenth to the twentieth centuries. Deaths for the next three authors have been prorated for the nineteenth and twentieth centuries. Westing's deaths have been prorated for the twentieth century. The "Wars" in the top half of this table have not been prorated, but their frequencies by centuries have been prorated in the bottom half of the table. The "Deaths Required" column indicates the minimum number of deaths required for a war to be included in any list. Dunnigan and Martel did not explicitly require one thousand deaths per war, but all of their wars (except one) met this requirement, and 93 percent of their wars met the requirement of one thousand deaths per war year. Deaths(m) = deaths in millions. Deaths(t)/Year = deaths in thousands per year. The average war deaths and frequencies by century were based on the first four authors only, whose war definitions were more like one another than they were to the last two authors: Small and Singer with battle deaths only, and Westing with 30,000 deaths required. The number of sovereign nations was obtained from Singer and Small (1972) for 1850 and 1950; the number used for 1750 was obtained from Taylor and Hudson (1972) for 1775. World populations for 1750, 1850 and 1950 were obtained from McEvedy and Jones (1978). These figures will be used in Table 11.2 in order to control deaths and frequencies for number of sovereign nations and size of world population.

# Table 11.2   War Frequency and
# Death Ratios Between Centuries

| Authors | Frequency Ratios Between Centuries | | |
|---------|-----------|-----------|-----------|
| | *20th/19th* | *19th/18th* | *20th/18th* |
| Kaye et al. | 1.4(0.7)0.7 | 4.1(2.2)2.4 | 5.6(1.5)1.6 |
| Bouthoul and Carrere | 1.2(0.6)0.6 | 2.5(1.3)1.5 | 3.0(0.8)0.9 |
| Dunnigan and Martel | 1.1(0.55)0.5 | | |
| Richardson | 0.9(0.45)0.4 | | |
| Small and Singer | 1.3(0.65)0.6 | | |
| Average | 1.2(0.59)0.56 | 3.3(1.8)2.0 | 4.3(1.2)1.3 |

| | *Death Ratios Between Centuries* | | |
|---------|-----------|-----------|-----------|
| Kaye et al. | 3.8(1.9)1.8 | 6.7(3.5)3.7 | 25.3(6.7)7.3 |
| Bouthoul et al. | 4.2(2.1)2.0 | 4.5(2.4)2.6 | 18.8(5.0)5.4 |
| Dunnigan et al. | 4.4(2.2)2.1 | | |
| Richardson | 7.9(4.0)3.8 | | |
| Small et al. | 6.7(3.4)3.2 | | |
| Average | 4.8(2.7)2.6 | 5.6(3.0)3.2 | 22.0(5.9)6.4 |

*Notes:* There are three ratios under each comparison between centuries. The first ratio is the absolute ratio between war frequencies and war deaths between centuries. The second ratio (in parentheses) is the first ratio divided by (controlled for) the ratio between the number of sovereign nations between centuries. The third ratio is the first ratio divided by (controlled for) the ratio between the size of world population between centuries. All of these ratios are based on the data in Table 11.1.

# Table 11.3   Deaths in Thousands Per War by Centuries

| Authors | 18th | 19th | 20th | Total |
|---------|------|------|------|-------|
| Kaye et al. | 115 | 76 | 324 | 195 |
| Bouthoul | 105 | 125 | 564 | 325 |
| Dunnigan | | 158 | 684 | 428 |
| Richardson | | 36 | 374 | 198 |
| Small | | 52 | 282 | 184 |
| Westing | | | 1929 | 1929 |
| Average | 110 | 89 | 446 | |

*Notes:* Kaye et al.'s figures were obtained by dividing their death estimates by the number of conflicts for which they had estimates, which were 504 in all, since there were 150 conflicts for which they had no death estimates. The same was done with Bouthoul and Carrere's figures, since there were 86 conflicts for which they had no death estimates. Westing's deaths per war were excluded from the twentieth century average.

# Table 12.1 Harbottle's Battles, 1200 B.C. to A.D. 2000

| Century | Europe | Mid-East | Far East | South Asia | Latin Amer. | North Amer. | Sub-Sahara | Total | Non-Europe | Europe% |
|---|---|---|---|---|---|---|---|---|---|---|
| -12 | | 1 | | | | | | 1 | 1 | 0% |
| -11 | | | | | | | | | | NA |
| -10 | | | | | | | | | | NA |
| -9 | | | | | | | | | | NA |
| -8 | 2 | | | | | | | 2 | | 100% |
| -7 | 1 | | | | | | | 1 | | 100% |
| -6 | | 1 | | | | | | 1 | 1 | 0% |
| -5 | 43 | 1 | | | | | | 44 | 1 | 98% |
| -4 | 34 | 12 | | 1 | | | | 47 | 13 | 72% |
| -3 | 32 | 11 | | | | | | 43 | 11 | 74% |
| -2 | 17 | 4 | | | | | | 21 | 4 | 81% |
| -1 | 44 | 4 | | | | | | 48 | 4 | 92% |
| 1 | 10 | 3 | | | | | 1 | 14 | 4 | 71% |
| 2 | 2 | | | | | | | 2 | | 100% |
| 3 | 9 | 2 | | | | | | 11 | 2 | 82% |
| 4 | 14 | 13 | | | | | | 27 | 13 | 52% |
| 5 | 11 | | | | | | | 11 | | 100% |
| 6 | 12 | 5 | | | | | | 17 | 5 | 71% |
| 7 | 8 | 21 | | | | | | 29 | 21 | 28% |
| 8 | 6 | 0 | 2 | | | | | 8 | 2 | 75% |
| 9 | 14 | 2 | | | | | | 16 | 2 | 88% |
| 10 | 12 | 0 | | | | | | 12 | | 100% |
| 11 | 20 | 5 | 1 | 3 | | | | 29 | 9 | 69% |
| 12 | 12 | 5 | 8 | 2 | | | | 27 | 15 | 44% |
| 13 | 34 | 4 | 5 | 4 | | | | 48 | 14 | 71% |
| 14 | 55 | 4 | 5 | 2 | | | | 66 | 11 | 83% |
| 15 | 81 | 4 | 1 | 0 | | | | 86 | 5 | 94% |

# Table 12.1  Cont.

| Century | Europe | Mid-East | Far East | South Asia | Latin Amer. | North Amer. | Sub-Sahara | Total | Non-Europe | Europe% |
|---|---|---|---|---|---|---|---|---|---|---|
| 16 | 82 | 5 | 7 | 9 | 8 | | | 111 | 29 | 74% |
| 17 | 142 | | 2 | 3 | 6 | | | 153 | 11 | 93% |
| 18 | 190 | 12 | 1 | 66 | 9 | 43 | 1 | 322 | 132 | 59% |
| 19 | 262 | 15 | 24 | 80 | 73 | 78 | 59 | 591 | 329 | 44% |
| 20 | 159 | 64 | 88 | 5 | 5 | 1 | | 322 | 163 | 50% |
| | | | | | | | | | | |
| Sum | 1308 | 199 | 144 | 175 | 101 | 122 | 61 | 2110 | 802 | 62% |
| Mean | 41 | 6 | 5 | 5 | 3 | 4 | 2 | 66 | 25 | |
| Std | 62 | 12 | 16 | 18 | 13 | 15 | 10 | 123 | 65 | |

*Notes:* Harbottle's battles were originally published in 1904, but these data were obtained from Bruce's (1981) revision. The twentieth century was prorated by dividing Bruce's frequency from 1950 to 1980 by 30 and multiplying this by 20 in order to get an estimated number of battles for the last two decades. The estimate for these last two decades was then added to Bruce's frequency from 1900 to 1980, so as to make the twentieth century comparable to the previous centuries. In spite of this prorating, the twentieth century frequency was much lower than that of the nineteenth century, because Bruce was unable to find any "notable battles" in the guerrilla warfare of the latter half of the twentieth century. Bruce also arrived at a rather low estimate of world war battles. As a result, the twentieth century frequencies are probably underestimates. Means and standard deviations have been rounded off to whole numbers.

## Table 12.2 Eggenberger's Battles, 1500 B.C. to A.D. 2000

| Century | Europe | Mid-East | Far East | South Asia | Latin Amer. | North Amer. | Sub-Sahara | Total | Non-Europe | Europe% |
|---|---|---|---|---|---|---|---|---|---|---|
| -15 |  | 1 |  |  |  |  |  | 1 | 1 | 0% |
| -14 |  |  |  |  |  |  |  |  |  | NA |
| -13 |  | 1 |  |  |  |  |  | 1 | 1 | 0% |
| -12 |  | 1 |  |  |  |  |  | 1 | 1 | 0% |
| -11 |  |  |  |  |  |  |  |  |  | NA |
| -10 |  |  |  |  |  |  |  |  |  | NA |
| -9 |  |  |  |  |  |  |  |  |  | NA |
| -8 |  | 1 |  |  |  |  |  | 1 | 1 | 0% |
| -7 |  | 3 |  |  |  |  |  | 3 | 3 | 0% |
| -6 |  | 5 |  |  |  |  |  | 5 | 5 | 0% |
| -5 | 28 | 3 |  |  |  |  |  | 31 | 3 | 90% |
| -4 | 19 | 8 |  |  |  |  |  | 27 | 8 | 70% |
| -3 | 26 | 6 |  |  |  |  |  | 32 | 6 | 81% |
| -2 | 8 | 4 |  |  |  |  |  | 12 | 4 | 67% |
| -1 | 35 | 7 |  |  |  |  | 1 | 43 | 8 | 81% |
| 1 | 10 | 6 |  |  |  |  |  | 16 | 6 | 63% |
| 2 | 4 | 3 |  |  |  |  |  | 7 | 3 | 57% |
| 3 | 5 | 5 |  |  |  |  |  | 10 | 5 | 50% |
| 4 | 11 | 3 |  |  |  |  |  | 14 | 3 | 79% |
| 5 | 12 |  |  |  |  |  |  | 12 |  | 100% |
| 6 | 9 | 6 |  |  |  |  |  | 15 | 6 | 60% |
| 7 | 10 | 24 |  |  |  |  |  | 34 | 24 | 29% |
| 8 | 11 | 2 | 1 | 1 |  |  |  | 15 | 4 | 73% |
| 9 | 13 | 3 |  |  |  |  |  | 16 | 3 | 81% |
| 10 | 16 | 5 |  |  |  |  |  | 21 | 5 | 76% |
| 11 | 23 | 8 |  | 2 |  |  |  | 33 | 10 | 70% |
| 12 | 18 | 17 | 1 | 1 |  |  |  | 37 | 19 | 49% |

# Table 12.2 Cont.

| Century | Europe | Mid-East | Far East | South Asia | Latin Amer. | North Amer. | Sub-Sahara | Total | Non-Europe | Europe% |
|---|---|---|---|---|---|---|---|---|---|---|
| 13 | 54 | 14 | 3 | 2 | | | | 73 | 19 | 74% |
| 14 | 44 | 3 | 1 | 2 | | | | 50 | 6 | 88% |
| 15 | 70 | 3 | | | | | 1 | 74 | 4 | 95% |
| 16 | 66 | 6 | 1 | 5 | 3 | 1 | | 82 | 16 | 80% |
| 17 | 129 | 1 | 4 | | 1 | 7 | 1 | 143 | 14 | 90% |
| 18 | 140 | 4 | 1 | 15 | 4 | 92 | 1 | 257 | 117 | 54% |
| 19 | 138 | 9 | 12 | 27 | 38 | 155 | 34 | 413 | 275 | 33% |
| 20 | 207 | 52 | 123 | 3 | 12 | 2 | 7 | 406 | 199 | 51% |
| Sum | 1106 | 214 | 147 | 58 | 58 | 257 | 45 | 1885 | 779 | 59% |
| Mean | 32 | 6 | 4 | 2 | 2 | 7 | 1 | 54 | 22 | |
| Std | 49 | 9 | 20 | 5 | 7 | 30 | 3 | 100 | 57 | |

*Notes:* Eggenberger's battles were updated to 1984, but there were only seven additions made, and these were all wars, not battles, so that this table includes only those battles and other entries in his 1967 edition. The twentieth century was prorated by subtracting his world war battles from his total frequency, dividing this by 56, multiplying by 34, and adding this to the total frequency. Means and standard deviations have been rounded off to whole numbers.

# Table 12.3 Sample of Dupuys' Battles, 1500 B.C. to A.D. 2000

| Century | Europe | Mid-East | Far East | South Asia | Latin Amer. | North Amer. | Sub-Sahara | Total | Non-Europe | Europe% |
|---|---|---|---|---|---|---|---|---|---|---|
| -15 | | | | | | | | 0 | 0 | NA |
| -14 | | | | | | | | 0 | 0 | NA |
| -13 | | 1 | | | | | | 1 | 1 | 0% |
| -12 | | | | | | | | 0 | 0 | NA |
| -11 | | | | | | | | 0 | 0 | NA |
| -10 | | | | | | | | 0 | 0 | NA |
| -9 | | | | | | | | 0 | 0 | NA |
| -8 | | | | | | | | 0 | 0 | NA |
| -7 | | 3 | | | | | | 3 | 3 | 0% |
| -6 | | 2 | | | | | | 2 | 2 | 0% |
| -5 | 14 | 5 | | | | | | 19 | 5 | 74% |
| -4 | 19 | 9 | | 1 | | | | 29 | 10 | 66% |
| -3 | 37 | 6 | | | | | | 43 | 6 | 86% |
| -2 | 10 | 12 | | | | | | 22 | 12 | 45% |
| -1 | 23 | 10 | | 1 | | | | 34 | 11 | 68% |
| 1 | 3 | 2 | | | | | | 5 | 2 | 60% |
| 2 | 3 | 5 | | | | | | 8 | 5 | 38% |
| 3 | 10 | 15 | | | | | | 25 | 15 | 40% |
| 4 | 11 | 5 | 1 | | | | | 17 | 6 | 65% |
| 5 | 18 | 3 | | | | | | 21 | 3 | 86% |
| 6 | 4 | 12 | 1 | | | | | 17 | 13 | 24% |
| 7 | 14 | 50 | 1 | 2 | | | | 67 | 53 | 21% |
| 8 | 19 | 13 | 3 | 3 | | | | 38 | 19 | 50% |
| 9 | 29 | 15 | 5 | 1 | | | | 50 | 21 | 58% |
| 10 | 22 | 19 | | | | | | 41 | 19 | 54% |
| 11 | 25 | 26 | | 3 | | | | 54 | 29 | 46% |
| 12 | 26 | 32 | 2 | 9 | | | | 69 | 43 | 38% |

# Table 12.3  Cont.

| Century | Europe | Mid-East | Far East | South Asia | Latin Amer. | North Amer. | Sub-Sahara | Total | Non-Europe | Europe% |
|---|---|---|---|---|---|---|---|---|---|---|
| 13 | 45 | 18 | 11 | 5 | | | 1 | 80 | 35 | 56% |
| 14 | 38 | 5 | 4 | 6 | | | | 53 | 15 | 72% |
| 15 | 68 | 8 | 9 | | | | | 85 | 17 | 80% |
| 16 | 99 | 18 | 7 | 20 | 1 | 2 | 1 | 148 | 49 | 67% |
| 17 | 203 | 18 | 14 | 22 | 6 | 18 | 9 | 290 | 87 | 70% |
| 18 | 207 | 28 | 5 | 32 | 13 | 52 | 1 | 338 | 131 | 61% |
| 19 | 134 | 31 | 19 | 44 | 42 | 115 | 34 | 419 | 285 | 32% |
| 20 | 202 | 88 | 140 | 12 | 5 | 2 | 24 | 473 | 271 | 40% |
| Sum | 1283 | 459 | 222 | 161 | 67 | 189 | 70 | 2451 | 1168 | 52% |
| Mean | 51 | 16 | 16 | 12 | 13 | 38 | 12 | 70 | 33 | |
| Std | 64 | 18 | 35 | 13 | 15 | 43 | 13 | 118 | 66 | |

*Notes:* This sample of the Dupuys' battles was obtained from all of their battles and sieges listed on pages 1500–8 (1986). This sample included all of those battles starting with the letters A through L, plus some of those starting with the letter M. The twentieth century was prorated by the same method used for Harbottle as described in the notes to Table 12.1. The means and standard deviations were rounded off to whole numbers.

# Table 12.4  Statistical Summary of Battles

|  | *Harbottle* (1981) | *Eggenberger* (1985) | *Dupuys* (1986) |
|---|---|---|---|
| Starting Year | 1100 BC | 1479 BC | 1469 BC |
| First Event | Troy | Megiddo | Megiddo |
| Centuries | 32 | 35 | 35 |
| Frequency | 2140 | 2011 | 4511 |
| # < 5th C. | 5 | 12 | 15 |
| % < 5th C. | 0.23% | 0.6% | 0.33% |
| Europe  50% | 6 Cs. | 4 Cs. | 12 Cs. |
| Eur%,Cent $r$ | .33nsr | .67** | .56** |
| Non%,Cent $r$ | .10nsr | .26nsr | .43** |
| Eur > Non | $t = 1.8$nsd | $t = 1.0$nsd | $t = 0.2$nsd |
| Eur,Non $r$ | .79** | .79** | .85** |
| Total,Cent $r$ | .82** | .89** | .93** |
| Total,Cas $r$ | .79** | .81** | .76** |
| Eur,Cas $r$ | .79** | .79** | .78** |
| | | | |
| *Modern* | | | |
| Total,Cent $r$ | .99*** | .99*** | .98** |

*Notes:* Cs. = centuries. $r$ = correlation coefficient. $t = t$ test of significant difference. nsd = no significant difference at the .05 level of confidence. nsr = no significant correlation at the .05 level of confidence. Cas = Sorokin's war casualties limited to 21 centuries, 500 B.C. to A.D. 500 and 900 to 2000. The *Modern* Total, Century $r$ in the last row is based on only the sixteenth to the twentieth centuries of the modern period. In spite of the low N = 5, these results show that battle frequencies were significantly and exponentially increasing during the last five centuries as well as over the whole of history.

# Table 13.1   War-Related Deaths Since 3000 B.C.

| Cent | Deaths | Cent% | Pop | Wars | Death/ Pop | Death/ War |
|------|--------|-------|-----|------|------------|------------|
| − 30 | 3 | 0.002% | 14 | 1 | 0.21 | 3 |
| − 29 | 3 | 0.002% | 15 | 1 | 0.20 | 3 |
| − 28 | 3 | 0.002% | 16 | 1 | 0.19 | 3 |
| − 27 | 3 | 0.002% | 17 | 1 | 0.18 | 3 |
| − 26 | 3 | 0.002% | 18 | 1 | 0.17 | 3 |
| − 25 | 5 | 0.003% | 19 | 1 | 0.26 | 5 |
| − 24 | 3 | 0.002% | 20 | 1 | 0.15 | 3 |
| − 23 | 3 | 0.002% | 21 | 1 | 0.14 | 3 |
| − 22 | 3 | 0.002% | 23 | 1 | 0.13 | 3 |
| − 21 | 6 | 0.004% | 25 | 2 | 0.24 | 3 |
| − 20 | 3 | 0.002% | 27 | 1 | 0.11 | 3 |
| − 19 | 3 | 0.002% | 29 | 1 | 0.10 | 3 |
| − 18 | 3 | 0.002% | 31 | 1 | 0.10 | 3 |
| − 17 | 3 | 0.002% | 33 | 1 | 0.09 | 3 |
| − 16 | 9 | 0.006% | 35 | 3 | 0.26 | 3 |
| − 15 | 9 | 0.006% | 38 | 3 | 0.24 | 3 |
| − 14 | 15 | 0.010% | 41 | 5 | 0.37 | 3 |
| − 13 | 15 | 0.010% | 44 | 5 | 0.34 | 3 |
| − 12 | 12 | 0.008% | 47 | 4 | 0.26 | 3 |
| − 11 | 9 | 0.006% | 50 | 3 | 0.18 | 3 |
| − 10 | 6 | 0.004% | 62 | 2 | 0.10 | 3 |
| − 9 | 6 | 0.004% | 74 | 2 | 0.08 | 3 |
| − 8 | 18 | 0.012% | 86 | 6 | 0.21 | 3 |
| − 7 | 33 | 0.022% | 98 | 11 | 0.34 | 3 |
| − 6 | 15 | 0.010% | 110 | 5 | 0.14 | 3 |
| − 5 | 264 | 0.174% | 120 | 6 | 2.20 | 44 |
| − 4 | 428 | 0.283% | 135 | 18 | 3.17 | 24 |
| − 3 | 630 | 0.416% | 150 | 20 | 4.20 | 32 |
| − 2 | 371 | 0.245% | 165 | 24 | 2.25 | 15 |
| − 1 | 762 | 0.503% | 170 | 16 | 4.48 | 48 |
| 1 | 117 | 0.077% | 180 | 6 | 0.65 | 20 |
| 2 | 224 | 0.148% | 190 | 8 | 1.18 | 28 |
| 3 | 356 | 0.235% | 190 | 12 | 1.88 | 30 |
| 4 | 300 | 0.198% | 190 | 14 | 1.58 | 21 |
| 5 | 198 | 0.131% | 195 | 12 | 1.02 | 17 |
| 6 | 53 | 0.035% | 200 | 13 | 0.27 | 4 |
| 7 | 200 | 0.132% | 210 | 30 | 0.95 | 7 |
| 8 | 170 | 0.112% | 220 | 27 | 0.77 | 6 |
| 9 | 73 | 0.048% | 242 | 24 | 0.30 | 3 |
| 10 | 3 | 0.002% | 265 | 30 | 0.01 | 0 |
| 11 | 57 | 0.038% | 320 | 47 | 0.18 | 1 |
| 12 | 129 | 0.085% | 360 | 39 | 0.36 | 3 |
| 13 | 410 | 0.271% | 360 | 67 | 1.14 | 6 |
| 14 | 501 | 0.331% | 350 | 62 | 1.43 | 8 |
| 15 | 878 | 0.580% | 425 | 92 | 2.07 | 10 |
| 16 | 1613 | 1.065% | 500 | 123 | 3.23 | 13 |

| Cent | Deaths | Cent% | Pop | Wars | Death/ Pop | Death/ War |
|------|--------|-------|-----|------|-----------|-----------|
| 17 | 6108 | 4.035% | 545 | 113 | 11.21 | 54 |
| 18 | 7001 | 4.624% | 720 | 115 | 9.72 | 61 |
| 19 | 19,423 | 12.830% | 1200 | 164 | 16.19 | 118 |
| 20 | 110,929 | 73.273% | 2500 | 120 | 44.37 | 924 |

| Period | Deaths | Period% |
|--------|--------|---------|
| Archaic | 56 | 0.037% |
| Ancient | 138 | 0.091% |
| Classic | 3650 | 2.411% |
| Medieval | 2474 | 1.634% |
| Modern | 145,074 | 95.827% |
| Total | 151,392 | 100.00% |

| | Deaths | % |
|--------|--------|---|
| − 30 to − 25 | 15 | 0.01% |
| − 25 to − 20 | 20 | 0.01% |
| − 20 to − 15 | 21 | 0.01% |
| − 15 to − 10 | 60 | 0.04% |
| − 10 to − 5 | 78 | 0.05% |
| − 5 to 0 | 2455 | 1.62% |
| 0 to 5 | 1196 | 0.79% |
| 5 to 10 | 499 | 0.33% |
| 10 to 15 | 1975 | 1.30% |
| 15 to 20 | 145,074 | 95.83% |

*Notes:* Deaths are given in thousands. Archaic = 3000–1500 B.C. Ancient = 1500–500 B.C. Classic = 500 B.C.–A.D. 500. Medieval = 500–1500. Modern = 1500–2000. Correlations with centuries: Death .85**, Pop .98**, War .96**, Death/Pop. 63**, Death/War .48**. These five variables were all logged. **Significant at the .01 level of confidence. N = 1266 wars.

# Table 14.1   Kroeber's (1944) Geniuses

| Century | Europe | Far East | India | Mid-East | Non Euro | Total | Euro% |
|---|---|---|---|---|---|---|---|
| − 30 | 0 | 0 | 0 | 4 | 4 | 4 | 0% |
| − 29 | 0 | 0 | 0 | 0 | 0 | 0 | NA |
| − 28 | 0 | 0 | 0 | 3 | 3 | 3 | 0% |
| − 27 | 0 | 0 | 0 | 4 | 4 | 4 | 0% |
| − 26 | 0 | 0 | 0 | 2 | 2 | 2 | 0% |
| − 25 | 0 | 0 | 0 | 4 | 4 | 4 | 0% |
| − 24 | 0 | 0 | 0 | 0 | 0 | 0 | NA |
| − 23 | 0 | 0 | 0 | 0 | 0 | 0 | NA |
| − 22 | 0 | 0 | 0 | 0 | 0 | 0 | NA |
| − 21 | 0 | 0 | 0 | 0 | 0 | 0 | NA |
| − 20 | 0 | 0 | 0 | 9 | 9 | 9 | 0% |
| − 19 | 0 | 0 | 0 | 6 | 6 | 6 | 0% |
| − 18 | 0 | 0 | 0 | 6 | 6 | 6 | 0% |
| − 17 | 1 | 0 | 0 | 2 | 2 | 3 | 33% |
| − 16 | 1 | 0 | 0 | 2 | 2 | 3 | 33% |
| − 15 | 1 | 0 | 0 | 2 | 2 | 3 | 33% |
| − 14 | 1 | 0 | 0 | 2 | 2 | 3 | 33% |
| − 13 | 0 | 0 | 0 | 9 | 9 | 9 | 0% |
| − 12 | 0 | 0 | 0 | 1 | 1 | 1 | 0% |
| − 11 | 0 | 0 | 0 | 0 | 0 | 0 | NA |
| − 10 | 0 | 0 | 0 | 2 | 2 | 2 | 0% |
| − 9 | 2 | 0 | 0 | 3 | 3 | 5 | 40% |
| − 8 | 7 | 0 | 0 | 2 | 2 | 9 | 78% |
| − 7 | 14 | 1 | 0 | 6 | 7 | 21 | 67% |
| − 6 | 39 | 3 | 5 | 3 | 11 | 50 | 78% |
| − 5 | 108 | 9 | 1 | 2 | 12 | 120 | 90% |
| − 4 | 100 | 11 | 3 | 0 | 14 | 114 | 88% |
| − 3 | 35 | 10 | 4 | 0 | 14 | 49 | 71% |
| − 2 | 45 | 15 | 5 | 0 | 20 | 65 | 69% |
| − 1 | 52 | 6 | 3 | 0 | 9 | 61 | 85% |
| 1 | 59 | 9 | 2 | 0 | 11 | 70 | 84% |
| 2 | 49 | 21 | 13 | 0 | 34 | 83 | 59% |
| 3 | 15 | 18 | 5 | 0 | 23 | 38 | 39% |
| 4 | 25 | 15 | 11 | 0 | 26 | 51 | 49% |
| 5 | 15 | 12 | 19 | 0 | 31 | 46 | 33% |
| 6 | 5 | 19 | 10 | 15 | 44 | 49 | 10% |
| 7 | 1 | 48 | 19 | 8 | 75 | 76 | 1% |
| 8 | 2 | 43 | 11 | 32 | 86 | 88 | 2% |
| 9 | 6 | 27 | 14 | 52 | 93 | 99 | 6% |
| 10 | 9 | 24 | 7 | 77 | 108 | 117 | 8% |
| 11 | 21 | 50 | 6 | 61 | 117 | 138 | 15% |
| 12 | 65 | 34 | 12 | 42 | 88 | 153 | 42% |
| 13 | 121 | 33 | 4 | 29 | 66 | 187 | 65% |
| 14 | 80 | 14 | 3 | 12 | 29 | 109 | 73% |
| 15 | 194 | 18 | 8 | 5 | 31 | 225 | 86% |
| 16 | 391 | 23 | 4 | 6 | 33 | 424 | 92% |
| 17 | 360 | 47 | 5 | 0 | 52 | 412 | 87% |
| 18 | 377 | 56 | 1 | 0 | 57 | 434 | 87% |
| 19 | 767 | 27 | 1 | 0 | 28 | 795 | 96% |
| Sum | 2968 | 593 | 176 | 413 | 1182 | 4150 | 72% |

# Table 14.2 Correlations Between Frequencies and Intensities

| Battle Frequencies | War Casualties | Dates | N | Correlations |
|---|---|---|---|---|
| *Per Century* | | | | |
| Harbottle | Sorokin | 500 B.C.–A.D. 500 A.D. 900–2000 | 21 Cs. | .79** |
| Eggenberger | Sorokin | A.D. 900–2000 | 21 Cs. | .79** |
| Dupuys | Sorokin | A.D. 900–2000 | 21 Cs. | .78** |
| Kohn Wars | Sorokin | A.D. 900–2000 | 21 Cs. | .71** |
| Sorokin Wars | Sorokin | A.D. 900–2000 | 21 Cs. | .67** |
| *Per War* | | | | |
| Eggenberger | Sorokin | A.D. 900–2000 | 83 Wars | .63** |
| Wright | Sorokin | A.D. 1500–1925 | 97 Wars | .79** |
| Wright | Levy | 1500–1940 | 88 Wars | .95** |

*Notes:* Battles were obtained from all authors in Column 1, unless otherwise indicated, such as by "Kohn Wars." Casualties were obtained from Sorokin in Column 2, but deaths were obtained from Levy. ** Correlation was significant at the .01 level of confidence, which means that a correlation as high as this could have been obtained by chance less than one time in a hundred. The authors are located in the reference as follows: Dupuy and Dupuy, 1986; Eggenberger, 1967, 1985; Harbottle, 1904 (Bruce, 1981); Kohn, 1987; Levy, 1983; Sorokin, 1937, vol. 3; Wright, 1965.

# Table 14.3 Factor Analyses of Civilizations, Empires and Wars

| Regions | Century | Geniuses | Empires | Battles | Explained Variance |
|---|---|---|---|---|---|
| World | .97 | .97 | .98 | .98 | 95% |
| Europe | .94 | .93 | .86 | .96 | 85% |
| Non-Europe | .97 | .93 | .96 | .95 | 91% |
| Middle East | .95 | .38 | .94 | .95 | 71% |
| India | .95 | .78 | .69 | .75 | 64% |
| Far East | .97 | .95 | .94 | .80 | 84% |

*Notes:* The figures in the body of the table are factor coefficients, which are a rough measure of the correlation of each variable with the single factor that emerged from the analysis of the correlation matrix in each region. The last column indicates how much of the variance in these variables over the 50 centuries from 3000 B.C. to A.D. 2000 was explained by the single general factor. Non-Europe was simply the sum of the Middle East, India and Far East. Africa and the Americas were left out of these analyses because they became a part of the historical world too late for such analyses to be meaningful in their cases. All of the factor coefficients were significant, according to Harman's (1967) table of standard errors of factor coefficients (p. 435), but the loading of Kroeber's geniuses in the Middle East was rather low.

# Table 15.1    War Deaths in Millions and Other Measures

| Author | 16th C. | 17th C. | 18th C. | 19th C. | 20th C. |
|---|---|---|---|---|---|
| Sorokin (Eu) | 1 – | 4 – | 4 – | 4 – | 96 + |
| Levy (GP) | 1 – | 4 – | 4 – | 3 – | 23 + |
| Wright (Bat) | (89) – | (230) – | (785) – | (629) – | (2439) + |
| Eckhardt (1990) | 2 – | 6 – | 7 – | 19 – | 111 + |
| Kaye (1985) | | | 3 – | 20 – | 76 + |
| Bouthoul (1978) | | | 4 – | 18 – | 75 + |
| Dunnigan (1987) | | | | 32 – | 142 + |
| Richardson (1960) | | | | 7 – | 55 + |
| Small (1982) | | | | 6 – | 40 + |
| Westing (1982) | | | | | 92 |
| Average Death | 1.3 – | 4.7 – | 4.4 – | 13.6 – | 78.9 + |
| *Other Measures* | | | | | |
| Nations (#) | | | 23 – | 38 | 82 – |
| Population(m) | 500 – | 545 – | 720 – | 1200 + | 2500 – |
| Revolutions | 510 – | 606 – | 416 – | 767 | 1380 – |
| Science (#) | 245 – | 492 – | 1034 – | 4937 + | 6624 – |
| Technology(#) | 121 – | 169 – | 519 – | 3477 + | 3708 – |
| Sensate Type | 54 | 55 | 61 | 61 | 64 |
| Imperial Size | 24 | 50 | 69 | 105 | 133 |

*Notes:* Sorokin's (1937, vol. 3) figures included wounded as well as deaths, and they were limited to nine major European nations. Since Sorokin's list of wars ended in 1925, his twentieth century estimate of 24 million casualties was multiplied by four in order to arrive at a pro-rated estimate for the whole century. Levy's (1983) deaths were limited to the Great Powers of each century, which were all European nations, until the United States, Japan and China were added in the twentieth century. Levy's deaths since 1816 were obtained from Singer and Small (1972), but he used primarily Sorokin's (1937, vol. 3) casualties prior to that time. His twentieth century estimate was prorated by taking the sum of his estimates for 1950–75 to be the same as those for 1975–2000. Wright's (1965) figures (in parentheses) are the number of important battles, 93 percent of which were fought in Europe. Wright's battles were correlated .70** with Levy's deaths for 73 wars, so that the number of battles may be taken as a rough measure of a war's intensity. Wright's battles were also correlated .91** over nine half-century periods, and his battles per war were correlated .82** over these same nine time periods. Not only was war intensity increasing over these centuries, but the intensity per war was also increasing. Eckhardt's (Sivard, 1990) war-related deaths included civilians as well as soldiers, and deaths caused by war-related disease and famine as well as by battle. His twentieth century estimate was prorated by using his estimates for 1945–90 to estimate the war deaths for 1990–2000. A similar procedure was used for the rest of the authors in this table, in order not to exaggerate twentieth century deaths by the undue influence of the two world wars. Kaye, Grant and Emond's (1985) deaths included civilians as well as soldiers. Since their list of wars began in 1720, their eighteenth century estimates were prorated in order to obtain an estimate for the whole century. The same was done for the following lists which began after the beginning of any century. Bouthoul and Carrere's (1978) deaths in-cluded civilians as well as soldiers, and deaths caused by war-related famine as well as in bat-tle. Dunnigan and Martel's (1987) deaths included civilians as well as soldiers. Richardson's (1960a) deaths included civilians as well as soldiers, and deaths caused by war-related famine and disease as well as battle. Small and Singer's (1982) deaths included only battle deaths of sovereign states. Although these battle deaths included civilians in civil wars, they included only combat personnel in international wars. Westing's (1982) deaths included only those

civilian and military deaths that occurred in high-fatality wars with at least 32,000 deaths
in the twentieth century. Average Deaths is based on all of the estimates in the top half of
this table except for Wright's battles (in parentheses). Nations = number of independent
nations in the world at the half-century mark. Population = world population in millions
at the half-century mark. Revolutions = European revolutionary magnitudes per nation
from Sorokin (1937, vol. 3). These magnitudes were geometrical averages of area percent,
population percent, duration and violence. Science = number of scientific discoveries from
Sorokin (1957). Technology = number of technological inventions from Sorokin (1957).
Sensate Type = factor scores derived from Sorokin's (1957) culture types as measured by
eight variables: materialism, nominalism, utilitarianism, determinism, empiricism, temporalism, sensate historical persons and singularism. In general, sensate types were
materialistic or scientific as opposed to religious or spiritual in nature, as measured by the
ideational factor. Imperial Size = average size of the six largest empires per century (nine
in the twentieth century) in square megameters from Taagepera (1978a). Plus and minus
signs in the body of the table indicate frequencies significantly higher and lower than
average, as determined by chi-square tests.

# Table 15.2  Measures as a Percent of Twentieth Century Measures

| Author | 16th C. | | 17th C. | | 18th C. | | 19th C. | | 20th C. |
|---|---|---|---|---|---|---|---|---|---|
| Sorokin (Eu) | 1 | (5) | 4 | (18) | 5 | (16) | 4 | (8) | 100 |
| Levy (GP) | 4 | (20) | 17 | (77) | 16 | (55) | 13 | (27) | 100 |
| Wright (Bat) | 4 | (20) | 9 | (43) | 32 | (112) | 26 | (54) | 100 |
| Eckhardt | 2 | (10) | 5 | (23) | 6 | (21) | 17 | (35) | 100 |
| Kaye et al. | | | | | 4 | (14) | 26 | (54) | 100 |
| Bouthoul | | | | | 5 | (17) | 24 | (50) | 100 |
| Dunnigan | | | | | | | 23 | (48) | 100 |
| Richardson | | | | | | | 13 | (27) | 100 |
| Small | | | | | | | 15 | (31) | 100 |
| Avg. Percent | 2.8 | (14) | 8.75 | (40) | 11.3 | (39) | 17.9 | (37) | 100 |

*Other Measures*

| | | | | | | | | | |
|---|---|---|---|---|---|---|---|---|---|
| Nations | | | | | 28 | | 46 | | 100 |
| Population | 20 | | 22 | | 29 | | 48 | | 100 |
| Revolutions | 9 | | 58 | | 40 | | 65 | | 100 |
| Science | 4 | | 7 | | 16 | | 75 | | 100 |
| Technology | 3 | | 5 | | 14 | | 94 | | 100 |
| Sensate Type | 84 | | 86 | | 95 | | 95 | | 100 |
| Imperial Size | 18 | | 37 | | 52 | | 79 | | 100 |

*Notes:* See the notes following Table 15.1. Figures in the body of this table are percentages of the
100 percent in the twentieth century. Figures in parentheses are the same for battles, casualties and deaths divided by world population. The results were almost identical when these
war measures were divided by European population. The Average Percent was based on all
of the data in the top half of this table.

## Appendix C
# Sources of Battles and Wars Reviewed Herein

### Primitive Wars

Hobhouse, Wheeler, and Ginsberg, 1915. N = 630 tribes. War = "an operation conducted in the name of the community as a whole."

Wright, 1942, 1965. N = 650 tribes, many of which were obtained from Hobhouse et al., supplemented by some later sources. War = "group-sanctioned violence against other human beings." Broch and Galtung, 1966, performed some further analyses on Wright's data.

Naroll, 1964, 1966. N = 50 tribes. War = "armed, licit, lethal public combat. A fight between groups of men, using weapons, trying to kill their opponents, a fight sanctioned as right and proper by the mores of the community to which the group belongs and a fight whose occurrence is publicly announced afterwards by the participants."

Textor, 1967. N = 45–87 tribes. War was operationally defined by its prevalence, by the attitude toward military glory, by war preparations, and by the emphasis upon killing, torturing, or mutilating the enemy. Stewart (1971), Russell (1972) and Eckhardt (1975) performed further analyses upon Textor's data.

Otterbein, 1970. N = 50 tribes. War = "a vital activity performed for a political community by its military organization.... Warfare is defined as armed combat between political communities."

### Civilized Battles and Wars

Wright, 1942, 1965. N = Toynbee's 26 civilizations, 2300 B.C. to A.D. 1600. War = "the *legal condition* which *equally* permits two or more *hostile groups* to carry on a *conflict* by *armed* force." Warlike ratings were assigned to these civilizations by summing their ranks on the following five variables: (1) absolutism, (2) bloodthirstiness, (3) imperialistic wars, (4) interstate wars and (5) public morale.

Kohn, 1987. N = 1826 wars, 2000 B.C. to A.D. 2000 (prorated). War = "an overt, armed conflict carried on between nations or states (international war) or between parties, factions, or people in the same state (civil war)." No deaths were required to be included on this list.

Sorokin, 1937. N = 698 wars and 1627 internal disturbances in 11 European nations, 600 B.C. to A.D. 2000 (prorated). War = "a breakdown of the organized relationship between states," but any war mentioned by historians was considered to be important enough to be included in these lists. There were 111 million (prorated) military casualties (dead and wounded) in these wars. Casualty data were not available for internal disturbances.

Harbottle, 1904 (updated and revised by Bruce, 1971 and 1981). N = 2110 battles, 110 B.C. to A.D. 2000 (prorated). Battle = "combat between large or relatively large armed forces." This included "all important battles of all the major wars," but it also included sieges, raids, and relatively minor actions leading to the main battles, while it excluded "guerrilla warfare without notable battles."

Eggenberger, 1967 (updated and revised in 1985). N = 1885 battles, 1479 B.C. to A.D. 2000 (prorated). Battle = "a general fight or encounter between hostile military forces.... A battle may be further defined by distinguishing it from a skirmish, a raid, or a siege ... a confrontation between opposing armed forces that resulted in casualties or in a change in the military situation."

Dupuy and Dupuy, 1986 (2nd revised edition). N = 4460 battles and sieges, 1469 B.C. to A.D. 2000 (prorated), and N = 1266 wars, 3000 B.C. to A.D. 2000 (prorated). No definition of battle nor of war was provided, suggesting that the authors relied upon the historical identification of events as battles and wars.

## Modern Battles and Wars

Wright, 1942, 1965. N = 308 wars, 1480–1964. War was defined as above. Operationally, a war was defined by its legal recognition, or by the involvement of more than 50,000 troops, or by its important legal results. The number of battles identified with some of these wars came to 2659, a battle being defined by at least one thousand casualties on land and at least five hundred casualties at sea.

Levy, 1983. N = 119 wars involving at least one great power, 1495–1975. War = "a substantial armed conflict between the organized military forces of independent political units." There were 33 million Great Power military deaths in these wars.

Eckhardt, 1987. N = 471 wars, 1700–1987. War = "any armed conflict, which includes one or more governments, and which causes deaths of one thousand or more people per year." There were 102 million civilian and military deaths resulting from these wars.

Eckhardt (Sivard, 1990). N = 588 wars, 1500–1990. War was defined as above. There were 140 million civilian and military deaths resulting from these wars.

Kaye, Grant and Emond, 1985. N = 654 major armed conflicts, 504 of which caused 94 million civilian and military deaths, 1720–1985. A major armed conflict = "an armed conflict in which at least one nation must be involved. The violent actions must result in significant casualties, or they must have had a significant effect on the history of the nation or nations involved."

Bouthoul and Carrere, 1976, 1979. N = 368 major armed conflicts, 1740–1978. Major armed conflicts had to involve more than one state, or more than one province, or more than one year, or more than one thousand deaths, or they had to have important results, internal or international. There were 86 million civilian and military deaths in these major armed conflicts.

Dunnigan and Martel, 1987. N = 409 wars, 1786–1986, causing 163 million civilian and military deaths. War = "organized violence by national governments."

Richardson, 1960. N = 315 wars ending in 1820–1952, causing 47 million civilian and military deaths. War = "deadly quarrel," causing at least 317 deaths.

Small and Singer, 1972, 1982. N = 224 wars, 1816–1980, which caused 40 million battle deaths. War = "deadly quarrel," causing at least one thousand military deaths in interstate wars, one thousand military deaths per year of imperial powers in imperial and colonial wars, and one thousand civilian and military deaths per year in civil wars.

Westing, 1982. N = 45 wars, 1899–1980, causing more than 30,000 deaths each. War = "an armed conflict between nations or between groups within a nation." These "high-fatality wars of the twentieth century" caused 86 million deaths, 50 million of which were attributed to the Second World War.

# References

Adams, David B. 1983. "Why There Are So Few Women Warriors." *Behavior Science Research*, vol. 18, 3: 1–13.

_____. 1984. "There Is No Instinct for War." *Psychological Journal*, 5: 140–44.

_____. 1985. "On the Role of Anger in War and Peace." In Juan Jose Sanchez-Sosa, ed., *Proceedings of the XXIII International Congress of Psychology*, 203–10. Acapulco, Mexico: International Union of Psychological Science.

Beer, Francis A. 1974. "How Much War in History: Definitions, Estimates, Extrapolations, and Trends." *SANE Professional Papers in International Studies*, 3: 5–37.

_____. 1981. *Peace Against War*. San Francisco: Freeman.

Bodart, Gaston. 1916. *Losses of Life in Modern Wars*. Oxford: Clarendon.

Bouthoul, Gaston, and Rene Carrere. 1976. *Le defi de la guerre (1740–1974)*. Paris: Presses universitaires de France.

_____, and _____. 1978. "A List of the 366 Armed Conflicts of the Period 1740–1974." *Peace Research*, vol. 10, 3: 83–108. Compiled and translated by Gernot Kohler.

_____. 1979. "Major Armed Conflicts, 1965–1 July, 1978." *Peace Research*, 11: 183–86. Compiled and translated by Gernot Kohler.

Bram, Marvin. 1979. "On the Origins and Purposes of Thinking." In Leon L. Bram, ed., *Funk & Wagnalls New Encyclopedia* 1:49–64. New York: Funk & Wagnalls.

Broch, Tom, and Johan Galtung. 1966. "Belligerence Among the Primitives." *Journal of Peace Research*, 3: 33–45.

Bruce, George. 1981. *Harbottle's Dictionary of Battles from the Earliest Date to the Present Time* (2d rev. ed.) New York: Van Nostrand Reinhold.

Butterworth, Robert Lyle, with Margaret E. Scranton. 1976. *Managing Interstate Conflict, 1945–74: Data with Synopses*. Pittsburgh: University Center for International Studies.

Butterworth, Robert Lyle, 1979. "Interstate Security Disputes, 1965–74: Frequency and Severity." *Peace Research*, 11: 187–95.

Cattell, Raymond B., H. Breul and H. Parker Hartman. 1952. "An Attempt at More Refined Definition of the Cultural Dimensions of Syntality in Modern Nations." *American Sociological Review*, 17: 408–21.

Cioffi-Revilla, Claudio. 1990. *The Scientific Measurement of International Conflict: Handbook of Datasets on Crises and Wars, 1495–1988*. Boulder, Colo.: Lynne Rienner.

Dayton, John. 1978. *Minerals, Metals, Glazing, and Man*. London: Harrap.

Denton, Frank H. 1966. "Some Regularities in International Conflict." *Background*, 9: 283–96.

Dumas, Samuel, and K.O. Vedel-Petersen. 1923. *Losses of Life Caused by War*. Oxford: Clarendon.

Dunnigan, James F., and Willian Martel. 1987. *How to Stop a War: The Lessons of 200 Years of War and Peace*. New York: Doubleday.

Dupuy, R. Ernest, and Trevor N. Dupuy. 1986. *The Encyclopedia of Military History from 3500 B.C. to the Present* (2d rev. ed.). New York: Harper & Row.

Eban, Abba. 1984. *Heritage: Civilization and the Jews*. New York: Summit.

Eckhardt, William. 1972. *Compassion: Toward a Science of Value*. Oakville, Ontario: Canadian Peace Research Institute (Available from the Lentz Peace Research Laboratory of St. Louis).

———. 1975. "Primitive Militarism." *Journal of Peace Research*, 12: 55–62.

———. 1978. "Philosophies of Science: Humanism vs. Positivism." *Peace Research*, 10: 159–63.

———. 1980. *A Manual on the Development of the Concept of Compassion and Its Measurement, 1962–1980* (3d ed.). St. Louis: Lentz Peace Research Laboratory.

———. 1980–1991. "Wars and Related Deaths." In Ruth Leger Sivard. 1980–1991. *World Military and Social Expenditures*. Washington, D.C.: World Priorities.

———. 1981a. "Limits to Knowledge." *Knowledge: Creation, Diffusion, Utilization*, 3: 61–81.

———. 1981b. "Pioneers of Peace Research, I—Lewis Fry Richardson: Apostle of Math." *International Interactions*, 8: 247–73.

———. 1981c. "Pioneers of Peace Research, II—Quincy Wright: Apostle of Law." *International Interactions*, 8: 297–317.

———. 1982. "Atrocities, Civilizations, and Savages." *Bulletin of Peace Proposals*, 13: 343–49.

———. 1983a. "Pioneers of Peace Research, III—Pitirim A. Sorokin: Apostle of Love." *International Interactions*, 10: 147–77.

———. 1983b. "Structural Violence." *Washington University Review of Politics and the Arts*, vol. 10, 1: 23–26.

———. 1984. "Global Imperialism and Global Inequality." *International Interactions*, 11: 299–332.

———. 1987a. "Wars and War-Related Deaths, 1700–1987." In Ruth Leger Sivard, 1987, *World Military and Social Expenditures, 1987–88*, pp. 29–31. Washington, D.C.: World Priorities.

———. 1987b. "The Task of Peace Education: A Value Theory of Peace Education." *Bulletin of Peace Proposals*, 18: 63–71.

———. 1988. "Sorokin's Theories of War and Peace." Paper presented at the annual meeting of the International Society for the Comparative Study of Civilizations, Hampton University, Hampton, Va., May 26–29.

———. 1989a. "Sorokin: Cultures, Transitions, Revolutions, and Wars." Paper presented at the annual meeting of the International Society for the Comparative Study of Civilizations, University of California at Berkeley, June 1–4.

———. 1989b. "A Dialectical Evolutionary Theory of Civilizations, Empires, and Wars." Paper presented at the annual meeting of the International Society for the Comparative Study of Civilizations, University of California at Berkeley, June 1–4. *Comparative Civilizations Review*, 1991, in press.

———. 1989c. "Civilian Deaths in Wartime." *Bulletin of Peace Proposals*, vol. 20, 1: 89–98.

———. 1990a. "Civilizations, Empires, and Wars." *Journal of Peace Research*, vol. 27, 1: 9–24.

———. 1990b. "Battles and Wars Around the World and over the Centuries." Paper presented at the annual meeting of the International Studies Association, Washington, D.C., April 10–14, and at the annual meeting of the International Society for the Comparative Study of Civilizations, University of Illinois at Urbana-Champaign, May 24–27.

_____, and Edward E. Azar. 1978. "Major World Conflicts and Interventions, 1945 to 1975." *International Interactions*, 5: 75–110.

_____, and _____. 1979. "Major Military Conflicts and Interventions, 1965–79." *Peace Research*, 11: 201–7.

_____, and Gernot Kohler. 1980. "Structural and Armed Violence in the 20th Century: Magnitudes and Trends." *International Interactions*, 6: 347–75.

_____, and Christopher Young. 1977. *Governments Under Fire: Civil Conflict and Imperialism.* New Haven: Human Relations Area Files Press.

Eggenberger, David. [1967], 1985. *An Encyclopedia of Battles.* (rev. ed.) New York: Dover.

Ember, Carol R. 1978. "Men's Fear of Sex with Woman." *Sex Roles*, 4: 657–78.

Freud, Sigmund. 1920. *Introductory Lectures on Psychoanalysis.* New York: Boni & Liveright.

_____. 1922. *Beyond the Pleasure Principle.* London: International Psychoanalytic Press.

Funk & Wagnalls. 1979. *New Encyclopedia.* New York: Funk & Wagnalls.

Garraty, John A., and Peter Gay, eds. 1972. *The Columbia History of the World.* New York: Harper & Row.

Glossop, Ronald J. [1983], 1987. *Confronting War: An Examination of Humanity's Most Pressing Problem.* Jefferson, N.C.: McFarland.

Goldstein, Joshua S. 1988. *Long Cycles: Prosperity and War in the Modern Age.* New Haven: Yale University Press.

Grun, Bernard. 1979. *The Timetables of History.* New York: Simon & Schuster.

Harbottle, Thomas B. 1904. *Dictionary of Battles from the Earliest Date to the Present Time.* London: Sonnenschein. (3d ed. revised by George Bruce.) New York: Van Nostrand Reinhold, 1981).

Harman, Harry H. 1967. *Modern Factor Analysis.* Chicago: University of Chicago Press.

Heinsohn, Gunnar. 1988. *Die Sumerer gab es nicht.* Frankfurt am Main: Scarabaus bei Eichborn.

Hobhouse, Leonard T., G.C. Wheeler and Morris Ginsberg. [1915], 1930. *The Material Culture and Social Institutions of the Simpler Peoples: An Essay in Correlation.* London: Chapman & Hall.

Kavolis, Vytautas. 1972. *History on Art's Side.* Ithaca: Cornell University Press.

Kaye, G.D., D.A. Grant and E.J. Emond. 1985. *Major Armed Conflict: A Compendium of Interstate and Intrastate Conflict, 1720 to 1985.* Ottawa: Canadian Department of National Defence.

Kende, Istvan. 1971. "Twenty-five Years of Local Wars." *Journal of Peace Research*, 8: 5–22.

_____. 1979. "Wars from 1965 to 1978." *Peace Research*, 11: 197–99.

Kennedy, Paul. 1987. *The Rise and Fall of the Great Powers: Economic Change and Military Conflict from 1500 to 2000.* New York: Random House.

Kohler, Gernot. 1975. "Imperialism as a Level of Analysis in Correlates-of-War Research." *Journal of Conflict Resolution*, 19: 48–62.

_____. 1986. "Computer Printout of Correlation Matrix of Variables Obtained from Ruth Leger Sivard's *World Military and Social Expenditures, 1983.*" Oakville, Ontario: Sheridan College.

Kohn, George C. 1987. *Dictionary of Wars.* Garden City, N.Y.: Anchor.

Kroeber, Alfred L. 1944. *Configurations of Culture Growth.* Berkeley and Los Angeles: University of California Press.

Krzywicki, Ludwik. 1934. *Primitive Society and Its Vital Statistics*. Warsaw: Mianowski Institute.

Leitenberg, Milton, with the aid of Robert Kalish and Dolores Lombardi. 1977. "A Survey of Studies of Post WWII Wars, Conflicts, and Military Coups." Presentation. Hanaholmen, Finland, September 26–28.

Levy, Jack S. 1983. *War in the Modern Great Power System, 1495–1975*. Lexington: University of Kentucky Press.

Levy, Jack S., and T. Clifton Morgan. 1984. "The Frequency and Seriousness of War." *Journal of Conflict Resolution*, 28: 731–49.

_____, and _____. 1986. "The War-Weariness Hypothesis: An Empirical Test." *American Journal of Political Science*, 30: 26–49.

Lindquist, E.F. 1953. *Design and Analysis of Experiments in Psychology and Education*. Boston: Houghton Mifflin.

McEvedy, Colin, and Richard Jones. 1978. *Atlas of World Population History*. New York: Facts on File.

McNeill, William, 1982. "Civilization." In *Encyclopedia Americana*, 7: 1–6.

Melko, Matthew. 1990. *Peace in Our Time*. New York: Paragon.

Midlarsky, Manus I. 1988. "Major-Minor Powers." *Data Development for International Research*, vol. 3, 1: 2–3.

Mukerjee, Radhakamal. 1951. *The Social Functions of Art*. Bombay: Hind Kittabs.

Naroll, Raoul. 1964. "Warfare, Peaceful Intercourse and Territorial Change: A Cross-Cultural Survey." Mimeo. Buffalo: State University of New York.

_____. 1966. "Does Military Deterrence Deter?" *Trans-Action*, vol. 3, 2: 14–20.

_____. 1967. "Imperial Cycles and World Order." *Peace Research Society Papers*, 7: 83–101.

_____. 1983a. Personal correspondence from the State University of New York, Buffalo, May 31.

_____. 1983b. *The Moral Order: An Introduction to the Human Situation*. Beverly Hills: Sage.

Naroll, Raoul, E.C. Benjamin, F.K. Fohl, M.J. Fried, R.E. Hildreth and J.M. Schaefer. 1971. "Creativity: A Cross-Historical Pilot Survey." *Journal of Cross-Cultural Psychology*, vol. 2, 2: 181–88.

Nietzsche, Friedrich. [1886], 1956. *Beyond Good and Evil*. Chicago: Great Seal Books.

Otterbein, Keith F. 1970. *The Evolution of War: A Cross-Cultural Study*. New Haven: Human Relations Area Files Press.

_____. 1977. "Warfare: A Hitherto Unrecognized Critical Variable." *American Behavioral Scientist*, vol. 20, 5: 693–710.

Rand, Ayn. 1964. *The Virtue of Selfishness*. New York: Signet.

Richardson, Lewis Fry. 1960a. *Statistics of Deadly Quarrels*. Pittsburgh: Boxwood Press.

_____, 1960b. *Arms and Insecurity*. Pittsburgh: Boxwood Press.

Rummel, Rudolph J. 1967. "Dimensions of Dyadic War, 1850–1952." *Journal of Conflict Resolution*, 11: 176–83.

Russell, Elbert W. 1972. "Factors of Human Aggression." *Behavior Science Notes*, 7: 275–312.

Service, Elman R. 1962. *Primitive Social Organization: An Evolutionary Perspective*. New York: Random House.

_____. 1968. "War and Our Contemporary Ancestors." In Morton H. Fried, Marvin Harris, and Robert Murphy, eds., *War: The Anthropology of Armed Conflict and Aggression*, 160–67. Garden City, N.Y.: Natural History Press.

Singer, J. David, and Melvin Small. 1972. *The Wages of War, 1916–1965: A Statistical Handbook*. New York: Wiley.

SIPRI. 1969. *Yearbook of World Armaments and Disarmament.* Stockholm: Almqvist & Wiksell.

Sivard, Ruth Leger. 1980–91. *World Military and Social Expenditures.* Washington, D.C.: World Priorities.

Small, Melvin, and J. David Singer. 1982. *Resort to Arms: International and Civil Wars, 1816–1980.* Beverly Hills, Sage.

Sorokin, Pitirim A. 1937. *Social and Cultural Dynamics, Vol. 2.* New York: American Book.

———. 1937. *Social and Cultural Dynamics, Vol. 3.* New York: American Book.

———. 1941. *Social and Cultural Dynamics, Vol. 4.* New York: American Book.

———. 1947. *Society, Culture and Personality: Their Structure and Dynamics.* New York: Harper. (Reprinted by Cooper Square in New York, 1962).

———. 1954. *The Ways and Power of Love: Types, Factors, and Techniques of Moral Transformation.* Boston: Beacon.

———. 1957. *Social and Cultural Dynamics.* Boston: Porter Sargent. (Originally published in four volumes, 1937–1941).

Sorokin, Pitirim A., and Walter A. Lunden. 1959. *Power and Morality: Who Shall Guard the Guardians?* Boston: Porter Sargent.

Spengler, Oswald, 1926–28. *The Decline of the West.* New York: Knopf.

Stewart, Robert A.C., 1971. "Cross-Cultural Personality Research and Basic Cultural Dimensions Through Factor Analysis." *Personality*, vol. 2, 1: 45–72.

Taagepera, Rein, 1978a. "Size and Duration of Empires: Systematics of Size." *Social Science Research*, 7: 108–27.

———. 1978b. "Size and Duration of Empires: Growth-Decline Curves, 3000 to 600 B.C." *Social Science Research*, 7: 180–96.

———. 1979. "Size and Duration of Empires: Growth-Decline Curves, 600 B.C. to 600 A.D." *Social Science History*, vol. 3, 3 & 4: 115–38.

———. 1981. "Growth-Decline Curves of Empires: Some Regularities." Paper presented at the annual convention of the Internatonal Studies Association, Philadelphia, March 18–21.

———. 1986. "Growth and Decline of Empires Since 600 A.D." Paper presented at the annual convention of the International Studies Association, Anaheim, March 26–29.

———. 1987. Personal correspondence from University of California at Irvine, January 16, 1987.

———. 1988. "The Fading Rate of History." Paper presented at the annual meeting of the International Society for the Comparative Study of Civilizations, Hampton University, Hampton, Va., May 26–29.

Tatje, Terence A., Raoul Naroll and Robert B. Textor. 1970. "The Methodological Findings of the Cross-Cultural Summary." In Raoul Naroll and Ronald Cohen, eds., *A Handbook of Method in Cultural Anthropology.* Garden City, N.Y.: Natural History Press, pp. 649–75.

Textor, Robert B. 1967. *A Cross-Cultural Summary.* New Haven: Human Relations Area Files Press.

Time-Life. 1988a. *The Age of God-Kings: Time Frame 3000–1500 B.C.* Alexandria, Va.: Time-Life Books.

———. 1988b. *Barbarian Tides: Time Frame 1500–600 B.C.* Alexandria, Va.: Time-Life Books.

Toynbee, Arnold J. 1948. *Civilization on Trial.* New York: Oxford University Press.

———. 1950. *War and Civilization.* New York: Oxford University Press.

———, and Jane Caplan. 1972. *A Study of History.* New York: Oxford University Press.

(Revised and abridged one-volume edition of original twelve volumes published 1934–61).

———, and Daisaku Ikeda. 1976. *The Toynbee-Ikeda Dialogue: Man Himself Must Choose.* New York: Kodansha.

Turney-High, Harry H. [1949], 1971. *Primitive War: Its Practice and Concepts.* Columbia: University of South Carolina Press.

Wescott, Roger. 1989. "History, Proto-History, and the Search for Synchronisms." Paper presented at the annual meeting of the International Society for the Comparative Study of Civilizations, University of California at Berkeley, June 1–4.

Westing, Arthur H. 1981. "A Note on How Many Humans That Have Ever Lived." *BioScience*, 31: 523–24.

———. 1982. "War as a Human Endeavor: The High-Fatality Wars of the Twentieth Century." *Journal of Peace Research*, 19: 261–70.

Wilkinson, David. 1980. *Deadly Quarrels.* Los Angeles: University of California Press.

Wood, Bernard. 1990. *Peace in Our Time?* Ottawa: Canadian Institute for International Peace and Security.

Woods, Frederick Adams, and Alexander Baltzly. 1915. *Is War Diminishing? A Study of the Prevalence of War in Europe from 1450 to the Present Day.* Boston: Houghton Mifflin.

Wright, Quincy. [1942] 1965. *A Study of War.* (2d ed.) Chicago: University of Chicago Press.

Zook, David H., Jr., and Robin Higham. 1966. *A Short History of Warfare.* New York: Twayne.

# Index